Research and Development in Intelligent Systems XVIII

T0205361

Springer
London
Berlin
Heidelberg
New York
Barcelona
Hong Kong
Milan
Paris
Singapore
Tokyo

Max Bramer, Frans Coenen and Alun Preece (Eds)

Research and Development in Intelligent Systems XVIII

Proceedings of ES2001, the Twenty-first SGES International Conference on Knowledge Based Systems and Applied Artificial Intelligence, Cambridge, December 2001

 Springer

Max Bramer, BSc, PhD, CEng
Faculty of Technology, University of Portsmouth, Portsmouth, UK

Frans Coenen, PhD
Department of Computer Science, University of Liverpool, Liverpool, UK

Alun Preece, BSc, PhD
Department of Computer Science, University of Aberdeen, Aberdeen, UK

British Library Cataloguing in Publication Data
Research and development in intelligent systems XVIII :
    proceedings of ES2001, the twenty-first SGES International
    Conference on Knowledge Based Systems and Applied
    Artificial Intelligence, Cambridge, December 2001
    1.Expert systems (Computer science) - Congresses
    2.Intelligent control systems - Congresses
    I.Bramer, M.A. (Max A.), 1948- II.Coenen, Frans
    III.Preece, Alun, 1968- IV.British Computer Society.
    Specialist Group on Expert Systems V.SGES International
    Conference on Knowledge Based Systems and Applied
    Artificial Intelligence (21st : 2001 : Cambridge, England)
    006.3'3
    ISBN 1852335351

Library of Congress Cataloging-in-Publication Data
A catalog record for this book is available from the Library of Congress.

ISBN 1-85233-535-1 Springer-Verlag London Berlin Heidelberg
a member of BertelsmannSpringer Science+Business Media GmbH
http://www.springer.co.uk

Typesetting: Camera ready by contributors
Printed and bound at the Athenæum Press Ltd., Gateshead, Tyne and Wear
34/3830-543210 Printed on acid-free paper SPIN 10843939

TECHNICAL PROGRAMME CHAIRMAN'S INTRODUCTION

M.A. BRAMER
University of Portsmouth, UK

This volume comprises the refereed technical papers presented at ES2001, the Twenty-first SGES International Conference on Knowledge Based Systems and Applied Artificial Intelligence, held in Cambridge in December 2001, together with an invited keynote paper by Professor Derek Sleeman. The conference was organised by SGES, the British Computer Society Specialist Group on Knowledge Based Systems and Applied Artificial Intelligence.

The papers in this volume present new and innovative developments in the field, divided into sections on Machine Learning, Constraint Satisfaction, Agents, Knowledge Representation, Knowledge Engineering, and Intelligent Systems.

The refereed papers begin with a paper entitled 'Detecting Mismatches Among Experts' Ontologies Acquired Through Knowledge Elicitation', which describes a systematic approach to the analysis of discrepancies within and among experts' ontologies. This paper was judged to be the best refereed technical paper submitted to the conference.

The remaining papers are devoted to topics in important areas such as agents, knowledge engineering, knowledge representation, planning and constraint satisfaction, with machine learning again the largest topic covered in terms of the number of papers accepted for publication.

This is the eighteenth volume in the *Research and Development* series. The Application Stream papers are published as a companion volume under the title *Applications and Innovations in Intelligent Systems IX*.

On behalf of the conference organising committee I should like to thank all those who contributed to the organisation of this year's technical programme, in particular the programme committee members, the referees and our administrators Linsay Turbert and Lynn Harrison.

Max Bramer
Technical Programme Chairman, ES2001

ACKNOWLEDGEMENTS

ES2001 CONFERENCE COMMITTEE

Dr. Alun Preece, University of Aberdeen *(Conference Chairman)*
Dr Robert Milne, Intelligent Applications Ltd *(Deputy Conference Chairman, Finance and Publicity)*
Richard Ellis, Stratum Management Ltd *(Deputy Conference Chairman, Exhibition)*
Prof. Adrian Hopgood, Nottingham Trent University *(Tutorial Organiser)*
Ann Macintosh, Napier University *(Application Programme Chair)*
Mike Moulton, University of Portsmouth *(Deputy Application Programme Chair)*
Professor Max Bramer, University of Portsmouth *(Technical Programme Chair)*
Dr Frans Coenen, University of Liverpool *(Deputy Technical Programme Chair)*

TECHNICAL PROGRAMME COMMITTEE

Prof. Max Bramer, University of Portsmouth *(Chair)*
Dr. Frans Coenen, University of Liverpool *(Vice-Chair)*
Prof. Adrian Hopgood, Nottingham Trent University
Mr. John Kingston, University of Edinburgh
Dr. Alun Preece, University of Aberdeen

TECHNICAL PROGRAMME REFEREES

Belen Diaz Agudo (Complutense University of Madrid)
Samir Aknine (University of Paris 6)
Andreas Albrecht (University of Hertfordshire)
Rosy Barruffi (University of Bologna)
Yaxin Bi (University of Edinburgh)
Arkady Borisov (Riga Technical University)
Robin Boswell (Robert Gordon University, Aberdeen)
Max Bramer (University of Portsmouth)
Frans Coenen (University of Liverpool)
Susan Craw (Robert Gordon University, Aberdeen)
Bruno Cremilleux (University of Caen)
John Debenham (University of Technology, Sydney)
David Camacho Fernandez (University Carlos III, Madrid)
Mark Hall (University of Waikato)
Ray Hickey (University of Ulster)
Adrian Hopgood (Nottingham Trent University)
Hermann Kaindl (Siemens Austria, Vienna)
Kamran Karimi (University of Regina)
John Kingston (University of Edinburgh)

Peter Lane (University of Nottingham)
Brian Lees (University of Paisley)
Hui Liu (Brunel University)
Peter Lucas (University of Aberdeen)
David McSherry (University of Ulster)
Robert Milne (Intelligent Applications Ltd, Scotland)
Tim Norman (University of Aberdeen)
Stephen Potter (University of Edinburgh)
Alun Preece (University of Aberdeen)
Paul Roach (University of Glamorgan)
Barry Smyth (University College, Dublin)
Kilian Stoffel (University of Neuchatel)
Jonathan Timmis (University of Kent)
Kai Ming Ting (Monash University, Australia)
Ian Watson (University of Auckland, New Zealand)
Nirmalie Wiratunga (Robert Gordon University, Aberdeen)
John Yearwood (University of Ballarat)

CONTENTS

SESSION 4: KNOWLEDGE REPRESENTATION

SESSION 5: KNOWLEDGE ENGINEERING

SESSION 6: INTELLIGENT SYSTEMS

TECHNICAL KEYNOTE ADDRESS

Knowledge Technologies: A ReUse Perspective

(Extended Abstract)

Derek Sleeman

Computing Science Department
The University ABERDEEN AB24 3UE UK
sleeman@csd.abdn.ac.uk
www.csd.abdn.ac.uk

1. Context

In 2000 the EPSRC funded an Interdisciplinary Research Collaboration (IRC) in *Advanced Knowledge Technologies* for the period 2000-2006, which involves 5 UK Universities: Aberdeen, Edinburgh, OU, Sheffield & Southampton. The project seeks to provide an intellectual underpinning for much of eCommerce, and at the same time it is contributing to the definition & realization of the Semantic Web. Six grand challenges have been identified, namely: Knowledge Acquisition, Modelling, Use/ReUse, Retrieval, Knowledge Publishing, & Maintenance. Considerable effort is being expended to ensure that the different knowledge sources can inter-operate. Additionally, several industrial test beds should ensure that the group's earlier & new technologies are integrated; these test beds are in the service & manufacturing sectors, and AKT is also applying these techniques to the Consortium's own information management. In the talk I plan to review each of the above activities, but will focus on ReUse (a holy grail for KBS Research). I will give an overview of what has been achieved to date, & will discuss several current projects in this sub-area.

2. Reuse in Knowledge Engineering

In a sense this theme has had a fairly long history. Shortliffe [1] clearly saw the possibility of reusing the Problem-solving component of MYCIN; in fact he redeveloped MYCIN so that it was completely independent of the domain knowledge, and produced EMYCIN (Empty/Essential) MYCIN which was subsequently used in many other domains. Several others including Kalfaglou et al [2] have identified different components which have been reused in both knowledge engineering and software engineering. These components include PSMs (Problem Solving Methods), ontologies, objects, and sets/repositories of cases. In my presentation I will review each of these sub-fields and indicate some of the successes & residual problems to date.

A substantial focus of our research activity at Aberdeen is whether or not it is possible to (partially) reuse existing Knowledge Bases (KBs). After all, if a company has spent a great deal of time and effort in building a KB to, say, *design* a particular car, it seems sensible to try to reuse parts of that KB when the company builds a KBS to *diagnose* faults with the same car. Before I outline how this has been tackled let me say that various of the challenges identified in the AKT project – namely Knowledge Modelling & Maintenance (which includes Knowledge Refinement) are highly relevant here. Various authors have noticed that if you wish to produce an object-orientated method for a library (ie for reuse), considerable effort has to be expended to "clean up" & generalize a method which is quite effective in a particular program. This I argue is essentially a knowledge Modelling activity, and is certainly a highly significant stage which *precedes* reuse. Similarly, reuse often involves detecting & then extracting relevant chunks of knowledge from a variety of sources, transforming them to conform to some pre-specified goal, and then finally merging them into a coherent entity. We believe that the experience we have built up in the Co-operative Knowledge Acquisition & Knowledge Refinement group at Aberdeen, in implementing systems to refine rule bases, sets/repositories of cases, taxonomies, qualitative models, and constraints will be helpful in addressing the transformation stages inherent in the reuse process, [3, 4, 5, & 6]. Similarly, in the AKT project we are able to draw upon techniques for the transformation of constraints developed in the KRAFT project, [7].

3. Current systems which address KB reuse

Frank Puppe [8] has a very ingenious approach to reusing Knowledge Bases with a number of different Classification algorithms; namely, each of the algorithms must use the identical KB. The Protégé approach to allowing M KBs to intercommunicate with N problem-solvers (PSMs in fact) is to produce a mapping function between each of the entities (so M*N mapping functions are required), [9]. On the other hand the MUSKRAT approach [10] attempts to distinguish between the following 3 situations:

Case 1: The problem-solver can be applied with the KBs already available, ie no acquisition or modification is necessary.

Case 2: The problem-solver needs KB(s) not currently available; therefore these KB(s) must be first acquired.

Case 3: The problem-solver needs KB(s), not currently available, but the requirements can be met by modifying existing KB(s).

Essentially, MUSKRAT addresses the first case by producing a computationally less expensive problem-solver (currently referred to as a meta-problem-solver) which is able to (cheaply) distinguish between possible/plausible solutions and implausible ones. It is then feasible to look in more detail at the resulting set of plausible solutions. Case 2, has been addressed by the COCKATOO system which when given domain knowledge expressed as an EBNF grammar plus constraints, drives the interaction with the domain expert to acquire a set of cases, [11]. Case 3 is essentially between the 2 cases described above and is still being investigated.

Below I outline a number of issues/challenges which form part of our current Research activities; I pose these as a series of questions:

- Can we be sure that the meta-problem-solvers produced currently by MUSKRAT, return all the TP (True Positive) solutions? (This essential assumption & the underlying algorithm will be discussed in the talk.)

- How effective are Knowledge Engineers in reusing (parts of) existing domain KBs when they build a further knowledge-based system in the same domain? We plan to study this empirically by giving knowledge engineers a KB which is capable of *designing* lifts, a specification of the required *diagnostic* system, a specification for the diagnostic inference engine, and we will observe how they proceed with this task.

- Do description logics have a role to play in determining equivalence & spotting inconsistencies in Domain knowledge and between rules? What range of representation schema & inference mechanisms are required for the above tasks?

- Is it viable to represent a KB as a formal grammar (say as an EBNF grammar), and then to formulate the transformation of KB_1 to KB_2 as the transformation of the corresponding grammars, namely $EBNF_1$ to $EBNF_2$?

ADDITIONAL NOTE

- The search for an appropriate KB in the MUSKRAT approach can be seen as the search for knowledge source(s) with particular competences/ characteristics. Could this approach be the basis for an Intelligent Web-based Brokering service?

ACKNOWLEDGEMENTS

This work has been supported in part by the EPSRC through the *Advanced Knowledge Technologies* IRC. Additionally, I acknowledge an EPSRC studentship which supported Simon White. Further, I acknowledge numerous discussions with members of the AKT consortium & in particular with Aberdeen colleagues: Simon White, Alan Preece, Peter Gray & Ernesto Compatangelo.

References

1. Shortliffe, EH (1976). Computer-based Medical Consultation: MYCIN. New York: American Elsevier.

2. Kalfoglou, Y, Menzies, T, Althoff, K-D, & Motta, E. (2000). Meta-Knowledge in systems design: Panacea or undelivered promise. Knowledge Engineering Review, Vol 15, 4, pp381 – 404.

3. Winter, M & Sleeman, D (1995). REFINER+: An Efficient System for Detecting and Removing Inconsistencies in Example Sets. In Research & Development in Expert Systems XII (eds MA Bramer, JL Nealon & R Milne). Oxford: Information Press Ltd. pp 115-132.

4. Alberdi, E & Sleeman, D. (1997). ReTAX: a step in the automation of taxonomic revision. Artificial Intelligence, p 257-279.

5. Winter, M, Sleeman, D & Parsons, T (1997). Inventory Management using Constraint Satisfaction and Knowledge Refinement Techniques. In Proceedings of ES97 (J Hunt & R Miles (eds)) Publ: Oxford: SGES press (ISBN 1 899621 20 2), pp 277-293.

6. Carbonara, L & Sleeman, D. (1999). Effective and Efficient Knowledge Base Refinement. Machine Learning, Vol 37, pp143-181.

7. Preece, A, Hui, K, Gray, A, Marti, P, Bench-Capon, T, Jones, D & Cui, Z. The KRAFT Architecture for Knowledge Fusion and Transformation, In M Bramer, A Macintosh & F Coenen (eds) Research and Development in Intelligent Systems XVI (Proc ES99), Springer, pages 23-38, 1999.

8. Puppe, F., (1998), "Knowledge Reuse among Diagnostic Problem-Solving Methods in the Shell-Kit D3", International Journal of Human-Computer Studies, Academic Press, Vol. 49, No. 4, pp. 627-649.

9. Gennari, J. H., Cheng, H., Altman, R. B., Musen, M. A., (1998), "Reuse, CORBA, and Knowledge-based Systems", International Journal of Human-Computer Studies, Vol. 49, No. 4, pp. 523-546.

10. White, S & Sleeman, D. (1999). A Constraint-based Approach to the Description of Competence. Knowledge Acquisition, Modeling & Management eds D. Fensel and R. Studer. Publ: Springer, p291-308.

11. White, S & Sleeman, D. (to appear). A Grammar-Driven Knowledge Acquisition Tool that incorporates Constraint Propagation. Proceedings of the 1st International Conference on Knowledge Capture (K-Cap'01).

BEST REFEREED TECHNICAL PAPER

Detecting Mismatches among Experts' Ontologies acquired through Knowledge Elicitation

Adil Hameed, Derek Sleeman, Alun Preece
Department of Computing Science
University of Aberdeen
Aberdeen, Scotland, UK
{ahameed, dsleeman, apreece}@csd.abdn.ac.uk
www.csd.abdn.ac.uk

Abstract: We have constructed a set of ontologies modelled on conceptual structures elicited from several domain experts. Protocols were collected from various experts who advise on the selection/ specification and purchase of PCs. These protocols were analysed from the perspective of both the processes and the domain knowledge to reflect each expert's inherent conceptualisation of the domain. We are particularly interested in analysing discrepancies within and among such *experts' ontologies*, and have identified a range of ontology mismatches. A systematic approach to the analysis has been developed; subsequently we shall develop software tools to support this process.

1. Introduction

An *ontology* is an explicit specification of a conceptualisation and is described as a set of definitions of content-specific knowledge representation primitives: classes, relations, functions, and object constants [6]. A collection of such conceptual models, when rich with domain-oriented content, can enable interoperability between systems, facilitate communication amongst people and organisations, and make existing knowledge shareable and reusable. Ontologies are also becoming increasingly important in internet applications as they can enhance the functioning of the World Wide Web in many ways: from providing 'meaning' for annotations in Web pages to empowering innovative services over the emerging Semantic Web [2]. Due to the distributed nature of ontology development, multiple ontologies covering overlapping domains is now the norm, and reconciliation is a vital issue.

Hitherto, most ontologies have been constructed as abstractions over existing software artefacts (viz., knowledge bases, databases, etc.) or built from published/documented reference sources. There is little evidence in the literature with regard to building and managing *experts'* ontologies – inherent conceptualisations elicited directly from human experts. We believe management of experts' ontologies is an important and as yet overlooked issue. The paper describes an approach we have evolved to construct such ontologies. We commence at the very beginning of the knowledge acquisition (KA) cycle and elicit domain knowledge from several human experts. A systematic analysis leads to the formalisation of distinct ontologies that essentially are effective models of each expert's intrinsic conceptual structures. These abstractions then arguably are ideal for enabling the sharing and reuse of the experts' domain and task knowledge in a heterogeneous environment.

1.1 Ontology Mismatches

Utilisation of multiple ontologies with an objective to share/reuse knowledge, even within a common domain, could be hampered by the fact that they may not conform to one another. Inconsistencies might be present at a conceptual level, as well as at the terminological and definition level. It is necessary to detect and resolve such discrepancies, especially among the shared semantics. Correspondences may have to be established among the source ontologies, and overlapping concepts would need to be identified: concepts that are similar in meaning but have different names or structures, concepts that are unique to each of the sources [10]. AI and database researchers have been working on converging ways to identify and resolve inconsistencies that occur in data/knowledge. There is general agreement that formal representations such as ontologies and schemas are necessary to tackle this problem. We carried out a comparative study of three distinct approaches:

Visser *et al.* [15] have proposed a classification of ontology mismatches to explain semantic heterogeneity in systems. They distinguish *conceptualisation mismatches* and *explication mismatches* as the two main categories, described as follows:

Conceptualisation mismatches may arise between two (or more) conceptualisations of a domain. The conceptualisations could differ in the ontological concepts distinguished or in the way these concepts are related as shown below.

- *Class mismatches* are concerned with classes and their subclasses distinguished in the conceptualisation:
    - A *Categorisation mismatch* occurs when two conceptualisations distinguish the same class but divide this class into different subclasses;
    - An *Aggregation-level mismatch* occurs if both conceptualisations recognise the existence of a class, but define classes at different levels of abstraction.

- *Relation mismatches* are associated with the relations distinguished in the conceptualisation. They concern, for instance, the hierarchical relations between two classes or, the assignment of attributes to classes:
    - A *Structure mismatch* occurs when two conceptualisations perceive the same set of classes but differ in the way these classes are structured via relations;
    - An *Attribute-assignment mismatch* occurs when two conceptualisations differ in the way they assign an attribute (class) to other classes;
    - An *Attribute-type mismatch* occurs when two conceptualisations distinguish the same (attribute) class but differ in their assumed instantiations.

Explication mismatches are not defined on the conceptualisation of the domain but on the way the conceptualisation is specified. They occur when two ontologies have different definitions where their terms (T), their definiens (D), or their ontological concepts (C) are identical. Six different types have been specified:

- *Concept & Term* (CT) *mismatch* (same definiens, but differ in concepts & terms)
- *Concept & Definiens* (CD) *mismatch* (same term, different concept & definiens)
- *Concept* (C) *mismatch* (same terms & definiens, but differ conceptually)
- *Term & Definiens* (TD) *mismatch* (same concept, dissimilar terms & definiens)
- *Term* (T) *mismatch* (same concept, same definiens, but different terms)
- *Definiens* (D) *mismatch* (same concept, same term, but different definiens)

Wiederhold [16] contends that "data obtained from remote and autonomous sources will often not match in terms of naming, scope, granularity of abstractions, temporal bases, and domain definitions." He has therefore proposed the following types of data resource mismatches:

- *Key difference* (different naming for the same concept, e.g. synonyms)
- *Scope difference* (distinct domains: coverage of domain members)
- *Abstraction grain* (varied granularity of detail among the definitions)
- *Temporal basis* (concerning 'time', e.g., monthly budget versus family income)
- *Domain semantics* (distinct domains, and the way they are modelled)
- *Value semantics* (differences in the encoding of values)

He states that in order to 'compose' large-scale software there has to be agreement about the terms, since the underlying models depend on the symbolic linkages among the components [17].

Shaw & Gaines [12] have identified four distinct dimensions to map knowledge elicitation problems that are likely to occur when several experts are involved during the evolution of a knowledge-based system. Because experts 'work' with knowledge entities that comprise concepts and terms, ambiguities can arise among the way concepts are agreed upon. For instance, experts may use:

- the same term for different concepts (*Conflict*),
- different terms for the same concept (*Correspondence*),
- different terms and have different concepts (*Contrast*).

Only when they use the same term for the same concept (Consensus) would there be no discrepancy. The authors have also developed a methodology and tools based on the Repertory Grid technique for eliciting, recognising and resolving such differences.

In order to detect factual instances of such mismatches, we have hand-crafted a set of domain ontologies that represent five distinct conceptualisations – the first four were modelled on experts, and the fifth was built from industry-standard sources of reference [4] and [13]. The area of personal computer (PC) configuration/ specification was chosen as an approachable domain. In the following section, we describe how knowledge was acquired from the several domain experts; the third section gives some examples of the kinds of ontological mismatches we have detected. These mismatches have been related to the three approaches cited above. In the last section, we conclude with an overview of our ongoing and further work.

2. Knowledge Acquisition

Knowledge elicitation was carried out in two phases: semi-structured interviews in phase 1 provided protocols, and structured tasks in the second phase enabled us to build glossaries of domain concepts. After each phase, analysis was done to refine the elicited artefact [5]. A preliminary analysis of the protocols also gave us an insight into the problem-solving strategies employed by each expert. Further analyses were carried out to confirm the outcomes prior to the formulation of ontologies. Conceptual graphs were used to model the relationships among domain concepts. A coding scheme was developed for this purpose, and the knowledge engineer was able to apply it consistently, after an independent coder verified the procedure.

2.1 Phase 1: Interviews

We interviewed experts whose technical proficiency is in personal computer systems and who regularly specify and configure PCs for a variety of users. The specification for a PC configuration usually consists of a list of standard components or parts, each of which can have certain specifiable attributes. Standardisation of configurations is an important objective not just for vendors or suppliers who are forced to compete in a demanding market; but also for large corporate buyers who want to keep the cost of new acquisitions and periodic upgrades down.

The questions posed were designed to elicit terms and concepts that the experts use on a regular basis to describe the various domain entities. These, along with the context in which they are used could be said to represent the expert's conceptual model of the domain. We got the experts to discuss several cases where they have advised users about purchasing a suitable PC. Typically, the expert would determine from the prospective user/customer the kind of applications they would be working on and/or ascertain the type of software they would want to run. S/he would then evolve a suitable hardware configuration to meet those requirements.

2.2 Preliminary Analysis

We have interviewed four domain experts in detail, over two sessions, and we were able to obtain an understanding of the inferencing processes 'applied' by the expert, and the distinctive approach taken by each of them for arriving at a suitable PC configuration. The initial analysis provided us with:

- A description of the process (or processes) that each expert follows in order to specify suitable PC configurations. These have been interpreted by the knowledge engineer and presented in the form of flow-charts and schematic diagrams to retain the accuracy of the expert's inferencing.

- The domain vocabularies used by the experts, which consist of terms and definitions that describe their inherent concepts. These have been organised as glossaries.

A technical report has been published [7] with a complete record of the knowledge elicitation sessions in the form of experts' protocols which were transcribed verbatim from audiotapes. Also included are the results of the analyses and a comprehensive set of glossaries extracted from the protocols.

2.2.1 Expert A

Expert A follows a pre-determined procedure to resolve queries from prospective customers. She helps customers select a suitable machine, from a current 'standard specifications' list of one of the approved suppliers. If additional upgrades or add-ons are required, then the buyer can select appropriate items from the set of standard options for the particular machine chosen. The expert ensures that the supplementary items are available with the supplier, viz., extra memory, peripheral devices, or add-ons such as modems, high-resolution monitors, Zip drives. She also makes certain that the total price is within the customer's budget. In case this expert cannot facilitate the selection of an acceptable configuration, or if there are any technical or application-related issues that cannot be resolved easily, she refers these 'non-regular' cases to Expert B, who is her line manager. The problem solving strategy used by Expert A can be described as a 'selection' algorithm [11].

2.2.2 Expert B

Most of the users (prospective customers) that approach Expert B for advice are the so-called 'non-regular' cases. Expert B's decision-making is based around a set of 'standard' system specs that he has devised. These are a starting point of reference. An evaluation of his protocols revealed that the expert follows a process-oriented approach, which consists of a series of distinct tasks/sub-tasks. According to the expert, his reasoning process is not strictly procedural. Instead, he adopts a holistic approach to determine the most suitable PC configuration that will meet the prospective customer's needs. After analysing several protocol segments, it became evident that the expert is following a 'hybrid' inferencing strategy. His inferences lead him on a goal-directed and forward-chaining path, but at times he backtracks when any of the user requirements, budgetary or technical constraints are not satisfied. The following steps model his decision-making process:

a). Begin with the user given requirements (natural language semi-technical phrases);

b). Identify 'key' terms, like processor, memory, graphics…;

c). If terms are imprecise or vague, resolve ambiguities by eliciting more information from the user until requirements are clearer;

d). Also, determine 'functional requirements', viz., understand what kind of tasks the user plans to perform with the PC, which applications would be run, etc.;

e). Ascertain user's budgetary constraints;

f). Select from the set of standard specs, a suitable system (a product/'model' from the supplier's list) that matches most closely the user's requirements and budget;

g). If additional enhancements or upgrades are necessary, then make suitable changes to the relevant components in the specs, keeping track of the budgetary constraint as well as any technical limitations;

h). Repeat step (g) until user and constraints are satisfied.

We believe that this expert's reasoning strategy essentially corresponds to the 'selection' and 'classification' PSM (problem-solving method) as described in [11].

2.2.3 Expert C

Unlike Experts A and B, this expert does not have a pre-determined set of 'standard' system 'specs'. He usually begins specifying a new configuration by starting with the current 'mid-range' system available, and working his way up (or down, as the case maybe), to arrive at a suitable specification. He constantly reassesses the mid-range system by keeping in touch with the state-of-the-art developments in the PC hardware market. The key constraint he bears in mind is the buyer's budget. Depending on how much money the buyer has to spare the expert either enhances or downgrades the 'mid' specification until all the user's requirements are met. The overall procedure employed is a form of the 'classification' algorithm [3] (selection & refinement) [11].

2.2.4 Expert D

Expert D believes that the 'right' way to configure a PC is to begin with a clear understanding of the actual application needs of the prospective user(s). He determines what 'tasks' the user wants to perform. After ascertaining this, he identifies suitable software applications (or packages) that will enable the user to perform these tasks. The expert believes it is necessary to agree on all requisite software before a hardware configuration can be specified. This is carried out in an iterative manner as follows:

a). The minimum system requirements for each software package are obtained from the software publisher;

b). The hardware requirements are then evaluated to determine which application is most greedy, i.e., most demanding, in terms of each specific component. Viz., CPU speed, minimum requirement for main memory, amount of disk space that is necessary, and any specific input/output pre-requisites;

c). Each component, along with its highest measure of requirement, is included on a specification list.

The final iteration would result in the configuration of a machine that would safely run all necessary software packages, thereby ensuring the user can perform all essential tasks. Some leeway may also be provided by enhancing the final configuration in order to 'future-proof' the machine against obsolescence of technology and also to accommodate newer or more advanced versions of software. An algorithm based on the 'classification' [3] and 'selection' methods [11] can best describe the inferencing strategy employed by Expert D with emphasis being placed on the acquisition of the *requirements*, which the machine must meet.

2.3 Phase 2: Structured Elicitation

Although interview is by no means the sole technique in determining conceptual structures, it was deemed an appropriate initial approach towards eliciting domain knowledge from the experts. As such, it is significant that in the first phase of knowledge elicitation, we were able to gain a clear understanding of the strategies/PSMs employed by each expert. Based on these initial results, we administered the following task-based experiments in phase 2 to unambiguously elicit the experts' domain terminology:

2.3.1 Step 1: Eliciting Terms, Definitions & Relations

A collage consisting of several graphic images of the PC (external & internal views) was shown to the experts and they were asked to 'identify' and 'name' the various constituents of the picture(s). After obtaining a list of 'terms', the experts were asked to 'define' each of them in their own words (natural language definition). Sometimes, by way of explanation, the experts provided a specific 'context' in which they discussed certain terms/concepts. The expert was then asked to group/categorise the terms in any way s/he felt pertinent to the task. 'Relations' (and thereby 'constraints') were often explicated, by asking the expert to explain the rationale or criteria behind each categorisation.

2.3.2 Step 2: Eliciting Instances

Next, stimuli, sets of visuals with screen-shots of typical applications that run on the PC, were shown to each expert. Upon identification of each application/ software, s/he was asked to provide a detailed specification of a suitable configuration for a PC that would run such applications. Typical applications considered were word processing, spreadsheets, database, e-mail, network access, Microsoft Windows 95, Windows NT, Linux, financial analysis, CAD/CAM, multimedia, demanding database applications, generic 32-bit applications, various programming environments, graphic-intensive applications, desktop publishing, and video conferencing. As a consequence of this exercise, we obtained several instances of expert-specific PC specifications.

2.3.3 Step 3: Validating the Conceptual Structures

Finally, the expert was shown several examples of specifications on a set of 'cards'; with one specification per card; and asked to 'sort' the cards in various groups/categories until all cards were sorted (Ch. 8: "Knowledge-Elicitation Techniques" in [11]). The expert was then asked to specify the feature/attribute, which had been used to determine the sort and the corresponding values for each of the piles. The expert was then invited to repeat, the sorting as many times as they wished – at each cycle they were asked to specify the feature and the corresponding values. After s/he had provided the features and their definitions, as discussed above, the expert was asked to organise them in any order s/he considered relevant. One of the experts, for instance, decided to give a 'level number' to each set of terms that he thought can be grouped together. For example, level '1' indicates entities that are external and visible, while level '2' designates all the components or devices that are inside the machine. The experts also assigned a 'context', to help clarify the perspective taken by them while defining a certain term.

2.4 Preliminary Analysis

We have been able to elicit the experts' conceptualisations of their domain (terms, definitions, concepts, relations). The experts also grouped the items in various categories and explained the rationale behind the ordering thereby validating their distinctive conceptualisation of the domain. This enabled us to create a hierarchy of levels, while evolving the ontology.

2.4.1 Glossary Building

A list of the domain terms and phrases used by each expert was compiled from her or his protocols and incorporated into a collective glossary. For each concept, suitable definitions and citations were extracted, and a cross-reference to the relevant protocols was made. Finally, standard definitions of essential terms taken from industry-recognised references [4] and [13] were incorporated alongside the experts' descriptions to aid comparisons. We were able to obtain a rich data set of around 600 domain concepts/terms.

2.5 Confirmatory Analysis and Construction of Ontologies

A detailed analysis of the artefacts produced in KA phases 1 & 2 was carried out in order to compare domain concepts and relations and look for discrepancies. First, we extracted an 'interesting' set of terms/concepts from the glossary, which were semantically rich, and modelled each concept in a semi-formal representation.

We decided to employ conceptual graphs (CGs) [14] as they can be used to illustrate unambiguously domain concepts and the associations between them. CGs are formally defined in an abstract syntax and this formalism can be represented in several different concrete notations, viz., in a graphical display form (DF), the formally defined conceptual graph interchange form (CGIF), and the compact, but readable linear form (LF). Each expert's terminology was classified into clusters of similar terms, and categorised as groups of key concepts and their variants. We then extracted, from the expert's protocols, chunks of text that contained a key concept or at least one of the variants. The chunks of text were then marked-up by underlining all domain concepts of interest.

Based on a protocol analysis procedure described in [1], we developed a protocol-coding scheme that enabled us to identify concepts and relationships. Two coders working independently were involved in the analysis to avoid bias and to provide verification. (See [7] for details of the procedure). We present below an instance of protocol coding. Extracts from the experts' protocols (P1 and P2) were marked-up to identify key concepts (and/or their variants):

P1: "The other user who comes along and has a specific requirement – maybe they will need a machine with a very large screen, maybe they will need a machine with more than the normal amount of disk-space or they are looking to have a different machine which is: very large screen, lots of disk space, the fastest processor out there, and in that case I then advise them what their options are, what their limitations are..."

P2: "The area where somebody wanted a machine that is out of the ordinary, was, a department who need machines to install large number of images and process the images and communicate with other people there doing the editing of the journal and processing of images that are involved in that. And so therefore they wanted the fastest processor that they could get, they wanted the largest graphics card that they could get, and they wanted sometimes, something like thirty-six (36) Giga Bytes of disk space, and would have preferred more."

Figure 1 shows the CG that was drawn to denote the relationships between key concepts inherent in P1 and P2.

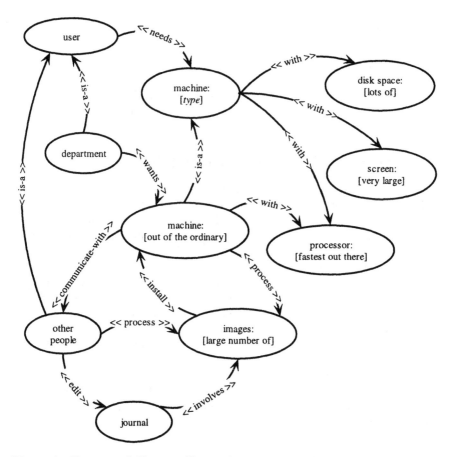

Figure 1. Conceptual diagram illustrating a user requirement for an "out-of-the-ordinary machine" (refer protocol extracts P1 & P2)

Following are examples of graphs written in linear form, representing fragments of conceptual relations in P2:

"The area where somebody wanted a machine that is out of the ordinary, was, a department who need machines to install large number of images and process the images and communicate with other people..."

a). [USER: Department] → (requires)
    → [MACHINE: out of the ordinary] –
        →1 – (install) –
        →2 – (process) –
            → [IMAGES: large number of]
        →3 – (communicate-with)
            → [USER: other people].

"...other people there doing the editing of the journal and processing of images that are involved in that."

b). [USER: other people] -
     →1 - (*edit*) → [JOURNAL]
     →2 - (*process*) → [IMAGES].

c). [JOURNAL] → (*involves*) → [IMAGES].

An organisation (hierarchical or otherwise) of terms, and their relationships is in essence an ontology that models the expert's distinctive conceptual structures.

3. Detecting Ontological Mismatches

Researchers in various areas of computing science are interested in automatic or tool-supported merging of ontologies (or class hierarchies, or object-oriented schemas, or database schemas – the specific terminology varies depending on the field). This has to be done regardless of whether the ultimate goal is to create a single coherent ontology that includes the information from all the sources (*merging*) or if the sources must be made consistent and coherent with one another but kept separately (*alignment*). Presently, the work of mapping, merging, or aligning ontologies is performed mostly by hand, but some tools are now being developed to automate the process, at least partially. However, both automatic merging of ontologies and creation of tools that would guide the user through the process and focus their attention on the likely points of action are in the early stages. Noy & Musen [10] provide a succinct overview of some of the existing approaches to merging and alignment in the field of ontology design, object-oriented programming, and heterogeneous databases. Klein [8] has analysed several problems that hinder the combined use of ontologies. Another recent work [9] uses articulation of ontologies to enable interoperation between knowledge sources.

3.1 Mismatches *among* Experts' Ontologies

While modelling the conceptual structures of each expert, we perceived that there were distinct differences among their individual ontologies. This was due to the fact that when knowledge was being elicited, it was not necessarily provided at the same level of abstraction or with the same measure of detail. Moreover, each expert has her/his own unique conceptualisation of the domain. In order to bring out these distinctions, we looked for discrepancies within and among their ontologies. Presented below are some examples of ontology mismatches in our domain of interest. We identified these by manual inspection, and related them to the three approaches introduced earlier in §1.1. It is interesting to note that discrepancies have been detected at an intra-ontology level as well as at the inter-ontology level. For reasons of space, we include only a few representative examples. Terms/concepts in each expert's ontology are prefixed by the code 'e?-', where '?' denotes a letter 'A'..'D' to identify the expert who provided that particular term. For instance, 'eC-staff' designates the concept 'staff' in expert C's ontology.

Examples are represented here in a semi-formal notation only, as such descriptions allow easy comparison of definitions and conceptual relations.

3.1.1 Examples based on Visser *et al.'s* Classification [15]:

At the conceptualisation stage:

- Class mismatches
  - *Categorisation mismatch:*

    The following conceptualisations differ because the experts have partitioned the same class; as distinguished in their individual ontologies; into a distinct set of subclasses. The symbol '∪' signifies *union,* comprising the specified classes/concepts.

    ```
    expert-C advises eC-staff ∪ eC-students
    expert-B advises eB-users ∪ eB-members-of-staff ∪
                     eB-departments ∪ eB-suppliers ∪ expert-A

    eC-PC is-made-of eC-parts ∪ eC-components
    eB-PC is-based-on eB-std-specs ∪ eB-std-options
    ```

  - *Aggregation-level mismatch:*

    Here, the experts have identified the same (or similar) classes but defined them at dissimilar levels of abstraction. The symbol '→' denotes the relation '*is defined by*'.

    ```
    eB-PC → eB-desktops ∪ eB-laptops
    eC-PC → eC-desktop ∪ eC-tower ∪ eC-portable ∪ eC-server

    eB-space → eB-disk ∪ eB-memory
    eC-memory → eC-RAM ∪ eC-VRAM
    ```

- Relation mismatches
  - *Structure mismatch:*

    Experts B and C have distinguished the same set of classes but differ in the way these classes are structured by means of the relations that associate their concepts. The following descriptions also reveal a difference in granularity of the domain semantics.

    ```
    eC-PC is-made-of eC-parts ∪ eC-components
    eB-PC has-component eB-processor
    ```

  - *Attribute-assignment mismatch:*

    The ontologies differ here in the way they assign an attribute (class) to other classes. While expert B has assigned two disjoint attributes 'disk' and 'space' to the concept 'PC', expert D defined a hierarchical relationship between similar concepts.

    ```
    eB-PC has eB-disk  ⎫  versus   eD-PC has eD-disk has eD-space
    eB-PC has eB-space ⎭
    ```

At the explication stage:

- *Concept & Term mismatch:*

  In Expert B's ontology, the concept 'advice' refers to the provision of a 'spec' (specification) to both 'users' and 'suppliers', albeit in different contexts.

  ```
  eB-advice-to-users    ⇒ eB advises eB-users about eB-spec
  eB-advice-to-supplier ⇒ eB advises eB-supplier about eB-spec
  ```

  This is an instance of a discrepancy *within* the expert's ontology. It is imperative that such intra-ontology mismatches are resolved before any reconciliation with other ontologies is envisaged.

- *Concept & Definiens mismatch:*

  The symbol '←' denotes that the *definiens* which follow the arrow 'define' the term on the left-hand side of the description. The 'AND' operator is used here to concatenate multiple definiens. An incidence of multiple descriptions for the same term implies that the expert gave distinct definitions in different contexts.

  ```
  eA-spec ← eA-supplier AND eA-standard-specs-list

  eB-spec ← eB-specifies AND eB-standard-specs-list
  eB-spec ← eB-specifies AND eB-machine
  eB-spec ← eB-description AND eB-machine AND eB-user

  eC-spec ← eC-requirement AND eC-user
  eC-spec ← eC-requirement AND eC-application
  eC-spec ← eC-specification AND eC-hardware-device
  ```

- *Concept mismatch:*

  Identical terms and definiens, but each expert is referring to a quite different concept.

  ```
  eB-min-spec ← eB-requirement AND eB-PC AND eB-user
  ```
  (referring to user's hardware requirement)
  ```
  eD-min-spec ← eD-requirement AND eD-PC AND eD-user
  ```
  (referring to system specification of software needed by user)

- *Term & Definiens mismatch:*

  ```
  eB-min-spec ← eB-processor-P3 AND eB-memory-128-MB
  eC-basic-PC ← eC-CPU-Pentium AND eC-RAM-64-MegaBytes
  ```

  Although they use different terms and definiens, both experts are referring here to the same concept: a specification for an entry-level PC. This interpretation might be construed as subjective, but more domain-specific knowledge would be required to explicate the subtleties in such concepts.

- *Definiens mismatch:*

  Identical terms denoting same concept, but described by a varied set of definiens.

  ```
  eB-fast-PC ← eB-processor-speed AND eB-memory-amount
  eC-fast-PC ← eC-CPU-Pentium3 AND eC-RAM-128-MegaBytes
  ```

3.1.2 Types of Mismatch according to Wiederhold [16]:

Key difference:
```
eB-RM-Mid-Range-System-Accelerator-Spec2  (reference for customer)
eB-GCAT-03234  (reference for supplier & experts)
```

Scope difference:
```
eB-advice  (advice given by eB to users, etc.)
eA-advice  (technical advice sought by eA from eB)

eA-memory, eD-memory  (referring to RAM)
eB-memory, eC-memory  (referring to RAM and VRAM)
```

Abstraction grain:
```
eC-faster-machine   (referring to speed of computer)
eB-fastest-machine  (referring to speed of CPU)
```

Domain semantics:
```
eB-budget  (funds/financial outlay available to user)
eB-cost    (price of machine quoted by the supplier)
```

3.1.3 Examples to illustrate Shaw & Gaines' [12] four dimensions:

Conflict:

eB-minimum-specification: the given configuration of a standard specification
eC-minimum-specification: requirements of a certain hardware device
eD-minimum-specification: minimum system requirements for satisfactorily running a software

eB-mid-range: referring to the models of machines from one of the approved suppliers
eC-mid-range: the starting point from where he would evolve a customised configuration, given no cost constraints

eA-requests: "Unusual requests: e.g., for non-standard Ethernet card."
eC-requests: "...requests within the hard-disk."

eA-specifications: referring to suppliers' specification lists
eB-specifications: referring to (i) his role in specifying the machines; (ii) the standard specifications; (iii) a user's description of their old machine
eC-specifications: referring to (i) requirements of certain applications; (ii) user requirements; (iii) certain hardware devices (video cards & monitors)

Correspondence:

eB-memory versus eC-RAM
eB-processor versus eC-CPU

Contrast:

eC-staff versus eB-approved-suppliers

Consensus:

eA-monitor, eB-monitor, eC-monitor – all refer to video display unit/screen

4.   Conclusion and Further Work

In this paper, we presented an approach to acquire knowledge and construct multiple experts' ontologies in a uniform way. We have shown how traditional knowledge elicitation and modelling techniques can be applied to the area of ontological engineering. Our work also highlights the need to reconcile mismatches among such ontologies, as a precursor to any distributed development, usage or management of multiple ontologies. A range of ontology mismatches was detected by human inspection, from simple syntactic inconsistencies to a rich array of semantic discrepancies, both at the conceptual and at a taxonomic level. We then compared our findings with relevant work in the areas of database interoperability, knowledge base reuse, and cognitive science.

We now aim to examine if these diverse approaches can be correlated and perhaps unified under a common framework. Subsequently, we intend to build KA/ontology revision tools that would automate some of this process.

5.   Acknowledgements

We would like to express our gratitude to the domain experts. Thanks are also due to Ms. Caroline Green at the Department of Psychology for her assistance in the analysis and verification of protocols.

References

[1]   Alberdi, E., Sleeman, D., & Korpi, M. (2000). Accommodating Surprise and Taxonomic Tasks: The Role of Expertise. *Cognitive Science*, 24 (1), 53-91.

[2]   Berners-Lee, T., Hendler, J, & Lassila, O. (2001). The Semantic Web. *Scientific American*, May 2001, 284 (5), 28-37.

[3]   Clancey, W.J. (1985). Heuristic Classification. *Artificial Intelligence*, 27(3), 289-350.

[4]   CMP Media, Inc. (2000). TechEncyclopedia. (source: *The Computer Desktop Encyclopedia*). http://www.techweb.com/encyclopedia/

[5]   Ericsson, K.A., & Simon, H.A. (1984). *Protocol Analysis*, Cambridge, Massachusetts: MIT Press.

[6]   Gruber, T.R. (1993). A Translational Approach to Portable Ontology Specifications. *Knowledge Acquisition*, 5, 199-220.

[7]   Hameed, A., & Sleeman, D. (2000). Knowledge Elicitation to construct Ontologies in the domain of PC Specification. *AUCS/Technical Report TR0001*. Department of Computing Science, University of Aberdeen.

[8]   Klein, M. (2001). Combining and relating ontologies: an analysis of problems and solutions. *Workshop on Ontologies and Information Sharing*, IJCAI'01, Seattle, USA, August 2001.

[9]   Mitra, P., Kersten, M., & Wiederhold, G. (2000). Graph-Oriented Model for Articulation of Ontology Interdependencies. *Proc. of the 7th International Conf. on Extending Database Technology*, March 2000. Springer-Verlag.

[10]   Noy, N.F. & Musen, M.A. (2000). PROMPT: Algorithm and Tool for Automated Ontology Merging and Alignment. *Proc. of the 17th National Conf. on Artificial Intelligence* (AAAI-2000), Austin, USA.

[11]   Schreiber, G., Akkermans, H., Anjewierden, A., de Hoog, R., Shadbolt, N., Van de Velde, W., & Wielinga, B. (2000). Ch. 6: "Template Knowledge Models" and Ch. 8: "Knowledge-Elicitation Techniques" in *Knowledge Engineering and Management: The CommonKADS Methodology*. Cambridge, Massachusetts: MIT Press.

[12]   Shaw, M.L.G., & Gaines, B.R. (1989). Comparing Conceptual Structures: Consensus, Conflict, Correspondence and Contrast. *Knowledge Acquisition*, 1(4), 341-363.

[13]   Shnier, M. (1996). *Dictionary of PC Hardware and Data Communications Terms*, (1st Ed). O'Reilly & Associates. www.ora.com/reference/dictionary/

[14]   Sowa, J.F., ed. (1998) Conceptual Graphs, *draft proposed American National Standard*, NCITS.T2/98-003.

[15]   Visser, P.R.S., Jones, D.M., Bench-Capon, T.J.M., & Shave, M.J.R. (1997). An Analysis of Ontology Mismatches; Heterogeneity vs. Interoperability. *AAAI 1997 Spring Symposium on Ontological Engineering*, Stanford, USA.

[16]   Wiederhold, G. (1992). Mediators in the Architecture of Future Information Systems. *IEEE Computer*, March 1992.

[17]   Wiederhold, G. (1994). An Algebra for Ontology Composition. *Proc. of 1994 Monterey Workshop on Formal Methods*, September 1994.

SESSION 1:

MACHINE LEARNING I

Using J-Pruning to Reduce Overfitting in Classification Trees

Max Bramer

Faculty of Technology, University of Portsmouth, Portsmouth, UK

max.bramer@port.ac.uk

www.dis.port.ac.uk/~bramerma

Abstract The automatic induction of classification rules from examples in the form of a decision tree is an important technique used in data mining. One of the problems encountered is the overfitting of rules to training data. In some cases this can lead to an excessively large number of rules, many of which have very little predictive value for unseen data. This paper is concerned with the reduction of overfitting during decision tree generation. It introduces a technique known as *J-pruning*, based on the *J-measure*, an information theoretic means of quantifying the information content of a rule.

1. Introduction

The growing commercial importance of knowledge discovery and data mining techniques has stimulated new interest in the automatic induction of classification rules from examples, a field in which research can be traced back at least as far as the mid-1960s [1].

Most work in this field has concentrated on generating classification rules in the intermediate form of a decision tree using variants of the TDIDT (Top-Down Induction of Decision Trees) algorithm [2], [3]. The TDIDT algorithm will be described briefly in Section 2. It is well known, widely cited in the research literature and an important component of commercial packages such as *Clementine*. However, like many other methods, it suffers from the problem of *overfitting* of the rules to the training data, resulting in some cases in excessively large rule sets and/or rules with very low predictive power for previously unseen data.

This paper is concerned with the reduction of overfitting in classification trees. Following a discussion of a number of alternative approaches in Section 3, a new technique known as *J-Pruning* is introduced in Section 4. The method is a refinement of the TDIDT algorithm, which enables a classification tree to be pruned while it is being generated, by making use of the value of the *J-measure*, an information theoretic means of quantifying the information content of a rule. Results are presented for a variety of datasets.

All but two of the datasets used (*wake_vortex* and *wake_vortex2*) were either created by the author or downloaded from the on-line repository of machine learning datasets maintained at the University of California at Irvine [4].

2.   Automatic Induction of Classification Rules

2.1 Example and Basic Terminology

The following example is taken from [2]. Table 1 records a golf player's decisions on whether or not to play each day based on that day's weather conditions.

Outlook	Temp (°F)	Humidity (%)	Windy	Class
sunny	75	70	true	play
sunny	80	90	true	don't play
sunny	85	85	false	don't play
sunny	72	95	false	don't play
sunny	69	70	false	play
overcast	72	90	true	play
overcast	83	78	false	play
overcast	64	65	true	play
overcast	81	75	false	play
rain	71	80	true	don't play
rain	65	70	true	don't play
rain	75	80	false	play
rain	68	80	false	play
rain	70	96	false	play

Table 1. The *golf* Training Set. What combination of weather conditions determines whether the decision is to play or not to play?

The standard terminology is to call Table 1 a *training set* and each of its rows an *instance*. Each instance comprises the values of a number of *attributes* (variables) and the value of a corresponding *classification*. Attributes can be either *categorical* (such as outlook) or *continuous* such as humidity.

One possible set of classification rules that can be derived from Table 1 is as follows:

1. IF outlook = sunny AND humidity <= 75 THEN Class = play
2. IF outlook = sunny AND humidity > 75 THEN Class = don't play
3. IF outlook = overcast THEN Class = play
4. IF outlook = rain AND windy = true THEN Class = don't play
5. IF outlook = rain AND windy = false THEN Class = play

2.2 Inducing Decision Trees: The TDIDT Algorithm

The TDIDT algorithm constructs a set of classification rules via the intermediate representation of a decision tree. At each leaf node of the tree all the corresponding instances have the same classification.

A possible decision tree, corresponding to the classification rules given in Section 2.1, is shown in Figure 1.

To Play or Not to Play?

Figure 1. Decision Tree Corresponding to Table 1

The most commonly used criterion for selecting attributes to split on is probably *Information Gain* [3], which uses the information theoretic measure *entropy* at each stage to split on the attribute which maximises the expected gain of information from applying the additional test. Further details about automatic induction of classification trees are given in [5].

2.3 Using Classification Trees for Prediction

Using Information Gain to select the attribute to split on at each stage of the tree generation process generally produces very compact decision trees, which is highly desirable if the training set contains all possible instances in a given domain. However, in practice the training set generally contains only a sample (often a very small sample) of all possible instances in a domain, and there is no guarantee that using Information Gain (or any other attribute selection criterion) will produce classification trees that correctly predict all previously unseen instances.

A method of estimating the classification accuracy of rules, which will be used throughout this paper, is *ten-fold cross-validation*. First, the original dataset is divided into 10 approximately equal parts. Ten runs of the TDIDT algorithm are then performed, with each of the ten parts used as a test set in turn, and the other nine used as the training set each time. The results of these 10 runs are then combined to give an average number of rules and an average percentage level of predictive accuracy.

Dataset	Instances	Rules	Classification Accuracy
diabetes	768	121.9	70.3
genetics	3190	357.4	89.2
hypo	2514	14.2	99.5
lens24	24	8.4	70.0
wake_vortex*	1714	298.4	71.8

Table 2. TDIDT with Information Gain. 10-fold Cross Validation
* The wake_vortex and wake_vortex2 datasets were obtained from National Air Traffic Services Ltd. (NATS) for use in connection with a practical classification task. The former dataset is a restricted version with only four attributes. The latter is the full version with 51 attributes, 32 of them continuous.

The results in Table 2 and elsewhere have been generated using *Inducer*, one of a suite of packages developed by the author to facilitate experiments with different techniques for generating classification rules. *Inducer* is implemented in Java in the interests of portability and is available both as a standalone application and as an applet. Further information is given in [6] and [7]. All the experiments use the TDIDT algorithm with the Information Gain attribute selection criterion and give the average results from 10-fold cross-validation.

The results in Table 2 show that for some datasets (such as *hypo*) TDIDT with Information Gain can produce compact rulesets with high predictive accuracy. For other datasets the method can produce a large ruleset (*genetics*) or one with relatively low predictive accuracy (*lens24*) or both (*diabetes* and *wake_vortex*).

Despite its limitations, the method is widely used in practice as a benchmark against which other algorithms are evaluated and has proved its worth as a robust method on which it is difficult to improve across a wide range of datasets.

2.4 Overfitting of Rules to Data

The principal problem with TDIDT and other algorithms for generating classification rules is that of *overfitting*. Beyond a certain point, specialising a rule by adding further terms can become counter-productive. The generated rules give a perfect fit for the instances from which they were generated but in some cases are too specific to have a high level of predictive accuracy for other instances. Another consequence of excessive specificity is that there are often an unnecessarily large number of rules. A smaller number of more general rules may have greater predictive accuracy on unseen data, at the expense of no longer correctly classifying some of the instances in the original training set. Even if the level of accuracy is not improved, deriving a smaller number of rules has obvious potential benefits.

3. Using Pruning to Improve Decision Trees

3.1 Post-pruning of Decision Trees

One approach to reducing overfitting, known as *post-pruning*, is to generate the set of classification rules using TDIDT as before and then remove a (possibly substantial) number of branches and terms, by the use of statistical tests or otherwise. Quinlan [2] describes a pruning technique based on predicted error rates, which is used in his well-known system C4.5. A variety of other methods have also been tried, with varying degrees of success. An empirical comparison of a number of methods is given in [8].

An important practical objection to post-pruning methods of this kind is that there is a large computational overhead involved in generating rules only then to delete a high proportion of them. This may not matter with small experimental datasets, but 'real-world' datasets may contain millions of instances and issues of computational feasibility and scaling up of methods will inevitably become important.

Holte [9] reports an empirical investigation of the accuracy of rules that classify on the basis of just a single attribute. These very simple rules perform surprisingly well compared with those produced by much more sophisticated methods. This too strongly suggests that a great deal of the effort involved in generating decision trees is either unnecessary or counterproductive and points to the potential value of a pre-pruning approach, as described in the next section, to avoid generating trees with an excessively large number of branches.

3.2 Pre-pruning of Decision Trees

Pre-pruning a decision tree involves terminating some of the branches prematurely as it is generated.

Each branch of the evolving tree corresponds to an incomplete rule such as

IF x = 1 AND z = yes AND q > 63.5 .... THEN ...

and also to a subset of instances currently 'under investigation'.

If all the instances have the same classification, say $c1$, the end node of the branch is treated by the TDIDT algorithm as a leaf node labelled by $c1$. Each such completed branch corresponds to a (completed) rule, such as

IF x = 1 AND z = yes AND q > 63.5 THEN class = $c1$

If not all the instances have the same classification the node would normally be expanded to a subtree by splitting on an attribute, as described previously. When following a pre-pruning strategy the node (i.e. the subset) is first tested to determine whether or not a termination condition applies. If it does not, the node is expanded as usual. If it does, the branch is *pruned*, i.e. the node is treated as a leaf node labelled with (usually) the most frequently occurring classification for the instances in the subset (the 'majority class').

The set of pre-pruned rules will classify all the instances in the training set, albeit wrongly in some cases. If the proportion of such misclassifications is relatively small, the classification accuracy for the test set may be greater than for the unpruned set of rules.

There are several criteria that can be applied to a node to determine whether or not pre-pruning should take place. Two of these are

- **Size Cutoff**. Prune if the subset contains fewer than say 5 or 10 instances

- **Maximum Depth Cutoff**. Prune if the length of the branch is say 3 or 4

Table 3 shows the results obtained from 10-fold cross-validation with a size cutoff of 5 instances, 10 instances or no cutoff (i.e. unpruned). Table 4 shows the results with a maximum depth cutoff of 3, 4 or unlimited.

Dataset	No Cutoff		5 Instances		10 Instances	
	Rules	% Acc.	Rules	% Acc.	Rules	% Acc.
breast-cancer	93.2	89.8	78.7	90.6	63.4	91.6
contact_lenses	16.0	92.5	10.6	92.5	8.0	90.7
diabetes	121.9	70.3	97.3	69.4	75.4	70.3
glass	38.3	69.6	30.7	71.0	23.8	71.0
hypo	14.2	99.5	11.6	99.4	11.5	99.4
monk1	37.8	83.9	26.0	75.8	16.8	72.6
monk3	26.5	86.9	19.5	89.3	16.2	90.1
sick-euthyroid	72.8	96.7	59.8	96.7	48.4	96.8
vote	29.2	91.7	19.4	91.0	14.9	92.3
wake_vortex	298.4	71.8	244.6	73.3	190.2	74.3
wake_vortex2	227.1	71.3	191.2	71.4	155.7	72.2

Table 3. Pre-pruning With Varying Size Cutoffs

Dataset	No Cutoff		Length 3		Length 4	
	Rules	% Acc.	Rules	% Acc.	Rules	% Acc.
breast-cancer	93.2	89.8	92.6	89.7	93.2	89.8
contact_lenses	16.0	92.5	8.1	90.7	12.7	94.4
diabetes	121.9	70.3	12.2	74.6	30.3	74.3
glass	38.3	69.6	8.8	66.8	17.7	68.7
hypo	14.2	99.5	6.7	99.2	9.3	99.2
monk1	37.8	83.9	22.1	77.4	31.0	82.2

monk3	26.5	86.9	19.1	87.7	25.6	86.9
sick-euthyroid	72.8	96.7	8.3	97.8	21.7	97.7
vote	29.2	91.7	15.0	91.0	19.1	90.3
wake_vortex	298.4	71.8	74.8	76.8	206.1	74.5
wake_vortex2	227.1	71.3	37.6	76.3	76.2	73.8

Table 4. Pre-pruning With Varying Maximum Depth Cutoffs

The results obtained clearly show that the choice of pre-pruning method is important. However, it is essentially *ad hoc*. No choice of size or depth cutoff consistently produces good results across all the datasets.

This result reinforces the comment by Quinlan [2] that the problem with pre-pruning is that the 'stopping threshold' is "not easy to get right - too high a threshold can terminate division before the benefits of subsequent splits become evident, while too low a value results in little simplification". There is therefore a need to find a more principled choice of cutoff criterion to use with pre-pruning than the size and maximum depth approaches used previously, and if possible one which can be applied completely automatically without the need for the user to select any cutoff threshold value. The *J-measure* described in the next section provides the basis for a more principled approach to pre-pruning of this kind.

4. Using the J-measure in Classification Tree Generation

4.1 Measuring the Information Content of a Rule

The *J-measure* was introduced into the rule induction literature by Smyth and Goodman [10], who give a strong justification of its use as an information theoretic means of quantifying the information content of a rule that is soundly based on theory.

Given a rule of the form **If Y=y, then X=x**, using the notation of [10], the (average) information content of the rule, measured in bits of information, is denoted by J(X;Y=y). The value of this quantity is given by the equation

$$J(X;Y = y) = p(y).j(X;Y = y)$$

Thus the J-measure is the product of two terms:

- p(y) The probability that the hypothesis (antecedent of the rule) will occur - a measure of *hypothesis simplicity*
- j(X;Y=y) The *j-measure* (note the small letter 'j') or *cross-entropy* - a measure of the *goodness-of-fit* of a given rule.

The cross-entropy term is defined by the equation:

$$j(X;Y=y) = p(x \mid y).\log_2(\frac{p(x \mid y)}{p(x)}) + (1 - p(x \mid y)).\log_2(\frac{(1 - p(x \mid y))}{(1 - p(x))})$$

Smyth and Goodman state that the j-measure is the only non-negative measure of information satisfying the requirement that "the average information from all rules should be consistent with [Shannon's] standard definition for average mutual information between two [events]".

A plot of the j-measure for various values of p(x), the *a priori* probability of the rule consequent, is given in Figure 2.

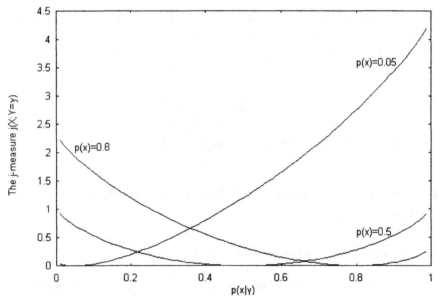

Figure 2. Plot of j-Measure for Various Values of p(x)

The J-measure has two helpful properties concerning upper bounds. First, it can be shown that the value of J(X;Y=y) is less than or equal to $p(y).\log_2(\frac{1}{p(y)})$.

The maximum value of this expression, given when p(y) = 1/e, is $\frac{\log_2 e}{e}$, which is approximately 0.5307 bits.

Second (and more important), it can be proved that the J value of any rule obtained by *specialising* the given rule by adding further terms is bounded by the value

$$J\max = p(y).\max\{p(x \mid y).\log_2(\frac{1}{p(x)}), (1 - p(x \mid y)).\log_2(\frac{1}{1 - p(x)})\}$$

Thus if a given rule is known to have a J value of, say, 0.352 bits and the value of Jmax is also 0.352, there is no benefit to be gained (and possibly harm to be done) by adding further terms to the left-hand side, as far as information content is concerned.

Further information on the J-measure and its uses is given in [11] and [12].

4.2 Using the J-measure for Rule Generation

In what follows, it will be taken as a working hypothesis that rules with high information content are also likely to have a high level of predictive accuracy for previously unseen instances.

In their system ITRULE [10] Smyth and Goodman make use of the availability of an upper bound Jmax on the J values of any possible further specialisations of a rule to generate the best *N* association rules from a given dataset, i.e. those with the highest J values. However, classification problems are normally concerned with finding all the rules necessary to make good classifications rather than, say, the best 50 rules.

The values of J for a set of rules generated from a given training set do not have any consistent range of values (apart from being between 0 and 0.5307). As an example, applying TDIDT with Information Gain to the *diabetes* and *lens24* datasets gives rulesets of 140 and 9 rules, respectively. (Note that these are obtained using the entire dataset as a single training set in each case, not from cross-validation.) The J values for the rules in the *diabetes* ruleset vary from 0.0008 to 0.1056, whereas those for the *lens24* dataset vary from 0.0283 to 0.3390. It is difficult to give any physical interpretation to these values. It would be possible to post-prune a set of rules by discarding all rules except those with the highest *N* values of the J-measure or all those with J values below a certain threshold, but in general this could lead to a large number of instances in the training set left unclassified by the remaining rules and a corresponding loss of predictive accuracy for previously unseen instances. The analysis given in the next section points towards an alternative approach, using pre-pruning.

4.3 A J-measure Interpretation of Overfitting

The results given in Section 3.2 strongly suggest that, beyond a certain point, adding further terms to rules (by splitting on additional attributes) can become counter-productive because of overfitting. Analysing successive forms of a rule using the J-measure clarifies why this happens.

Taking the *lens24* dataset for illustration, one of the rules generated is
    IF tears=2 AND astig=1 AND age=3 AND specRx=1 THEN class=3

This has a J-value of 0.028 and seems a reasonable rule. However, by looking at the way the rule develops term by term a different picture emerges.

After just one term, the rule and corresponding J and Jmax values were
    IF tears=2 THEN class=3   (J=0.210, Jmax=0.531)

In general, specialising a rule by adding further terms may either increase or decrease the value of J (i.e. the information content). However the value of Jmax gives the maximum J value that any possible specialisation of the rule may achieve. In this case Jmax = 0.531, so it seems appropriate to continue developing the rule.

Adding the second term gives
    IF tears=2 AND astig=1 THEN class=3   (J= 0.161, Jmax=0.295)

The J value has gone down from 0.210 to 0.161, but has the potential to increase again, possibly up to 0.295 by further specialisation.

Adding the third and fourth terms completes the picture.

    IF tears=2 AND astig=1 AND age=3 THEN class=3   (J= 0.004, Jmax=0.059)

    IF tears=2 AND astig=1 AND age=3 AND specRx=1 THEN class=3
    (J= 0.028, Jmax=0.028)

It can be seen that adding additional terms to rules can either increase or decrease the value of J. However, the combined effect of adding the three final terms has been to lower the J value (information content) of the rule by almost a factor of 10. If we assume that the J measure is a reliable indicator of the information content and thus the predictive accuracy of a rule, it would have been better to truncate the rule after a single term (classifying all the instances in the majority class). This would have led to more misclassified instances for the training data, but might have led to better predictive accuracy on unseen data.

4.4 J-Pruning

There are several ways in which J values can be used to aid classification tree generation. One method, which will be called *J-pruning*, is to prune a branch as soon as a node is generated at which the J value is less than that at its parent.

Looking at this in terms of partially completed rules, say there is an incomplete rule for the *lens24* dataset

(1) IF tears=2 AND astig=2 ....

Splitting on attribute specRx (which has two values) would add an additional term, making the incomplete rule

(2) IF tears=2 AND astig=2 AND specRx=1 ....
    or
(3) IF tears=2 AND astig=2 AND specRx=2 ....

All the instances corresponding to branch (2) have the same classification, so the rule is completed with that classification in the usual way. However the instances corresponding to branch (3) have more than one classification.

The J-pruning technique now involves a comparison between the J-value of (3) and the J-value of (1). If the former is smaller, the rule is truncated and the instances are all classified as belonging to the majority class, i.e. the class to which the largest number of instances belong. If not, the TDIDT algorithm continues by splitting on an attribute as usual.

The difficulty in implementing the above method is that the value of J depends partly on the class specified in the rule consequent, but when the partial rules (incomplete branches) are generated there is no way of knowing which class that will eventually be. A branch may of course be extended by TDIDT to have a large descendent subtree, obtained by subsequent splittings on attributes, with many leaf nodes each of which has its own classification.

If the rules had been truncated at (1) there are 3 possible ways in which all the instances could have been assigned to a single class. These are listed below with the corresponding values of J and Jmax

    IF tears=2 AND astig=2 THEN class=1 (J = 0.223, Jmax = 0.431)
    IF tears=2 AND astig=2 THEN class=2 (J = 0.084, Jmax = 0.084)
    IF tears=2 AND astig=2 THEN class=3 (J = 0.063, Jmax = 0.236)

There are 3 possible ways in which the instances corresponding to (3) could be assigned to a single class:

    IF tears=2 AND astig=2 AND specRx=2 THEN class=1 (J=0.015, Jmax=0.108)
    IF tears=2 AND astig=2 AND specRx=2 THEN class=2 (J=0.042, Jmax=0.042)
    IF tears=2 AND astig=2 AND specRx=2 THEN class=3 (J=0.001, Jmax=0.059)

If there are only two classes the value of J is the same whichever is taken. When there are more than two classes the J values will generally not all be the same. One possibility would be always to use the J value of the majority class, but in practice it has been found to be more effective to use the largest of the possible J values in each case. Thus the J values for branches (1) and (3) are taken to be 0.223 and 0.042 respectively. Since the value for (3) is lower than for (1), J-pruning takes place and branch (3) is truncated.

Table 5 shows the results obtained using J-pruning with a variety of datasets and the comparative figures for unpruned rules.

Dataset	No J-Pruning		With J-Pruning	
	Rules	% Accuracy	Rules	% Accuracy
breast-cancer	93.2	89.8	66.5	91.3
contact_lenses	16.0	92.5	8.3	92.6
crx	127.5	79.4	20.4	85.4
diabetes	121.9	70.3	6.4	75.1
genetics	357.4	89.2	25.9	78.2
glass	38.3	69.6	9.4	63.5
hepatitis	18.8	82.0	4.5	81.2
hypo	14.2	99.5	7.6	99.3
iris	8.5	95.3	5.7	94.7
lens24	8.4	70.0	6.2	70.0
monk1	37.8	83.9	14.4	67.8
monk2	88.4	43.8	21.3	55.7
monk3	26.5	86.9	12.5	90.9
sick-euthyroid	72.8	96.7	6.8	97.8
vote	29.2	91.7	11.1	94.0
wake_vortex	298.4	71.8	12.0	73.5
wake_vortex2	227.1	71.3	12.4	72.5

Table 5. Comparison of Unpruned and J-pruned Rules

The reduction in the number of rules is clearly considerable for many of the datasets (e.g. from 121.9 to 6.4 for *diabetes* and from 298.4 to 12.0 for *wake_vortex*). This again confirms that the basic (unpruned) form of TDIDT leads to substantial overfitting of rules to the instances in the training set. The predictive accuracy is higher with J-pruning for 10 of the datasets, lower for 6 and unchanged for one (the smallest dataset, *lens24*). There are large increases in accuracy for *crx* and *monk2* and large decreases in accuracy for *genetics* and *monk1*.

The predictive accuracy obtainable from a dataset depends on many factors, including the appropriateness of the choice of attributes, so large improvements should not necessarily be expected from J-pruning (or any other form of pruning). However there are obvious benefits from a large reduction in the number of rules even when there is no gain in accuracy.

4.5 Limitations of the Decision Tree Representation

The method of using the J-measure for pre-pruning adopted here has limitations that relate directly to the use of the decision tree representation imposed by TDIDT.

Suppose that the branch shown as a solid line in Figure 3 has been developed by TDIDT as far as node N_0. (Other irrelevant branches are shown as dotted lines.)

The decision needed is whether or not to develop the branch further by splitting on an additional attribute, giving nodes N_1, N_2 and N_3.

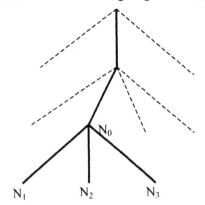

Figure 3. A Partially Generated Decision Tree

Suppose that the J values of nodes N_0, N_1 and N_2 are 0.25, 0.4 and 0.005 respectively, so that the left-hand branch is developed by further splitting and the middle branch is J-pruned. Suppose also that all the instances corresponding to node N_3 have the same classification, so that TDIDT treats it as a leaf node in the usual way. As far as the middle branch, which is J-pruned, is concerned it would have been better if the branch had been terminated a level earlier, i.e. at N_0 (with a higher value of J). However doing so would also have eliminated the left-hand and right-hand branches, which would clearly have been disadvantageous.

One possibility in this case would be to try combining the middle branch with either the left-hand or the right-hand branch. However there are many other possible situations that can arise and it is difficult to deal with all of them satisfactorily within the decision tree framework.

The use of a decision tree representation for rules has previously been identified as a major cause of overfitting ([7], [13]). An example is given in [13] of two rules with no attribute in common which lead to a complex decision tree almost all branches and terms of which are redundant. Further reductions in overfitting are likely to come from incorporating J-pruning or other pre-pruning techniques into algorithms such as Prism [13] that generate classification rules directly rather than through the intermediate representation of decision trees.

5. Conclusions

This paper has demonstrated the potential value of using the information-theoretic J-measure as the basis for reducing overfitting by pre-pruning branches during classification tree generation. The J-pruning technique illustrated works well in practice for a range of datasets. Unlike many other possible measures, the J-measure has a sound theoretical foundation as a measure of the information content of rules.

The decision tree representation of TDIDT is widely used and it is therefore desirable to find methods of pre-pruning that work well with this representation. However, the decision tree representation is itself a source of overfitting. For substantial further improvements techniques that work with algorithms that directly generate classification rules not classification trees will probably be necessary and the J-pruning method would appear to be well suited to this.

References

[1] Hunt, E.B., Marin J. and Stone, P.J. (1966). Experiments in Induction. Academic Press

[2] Quinlan, J.R. (1993). C4.5: Programs for Machine Learning. Morgan Kaufmann

[3] Quinlan, R. (1986). Induction of Decision Trees. Machine Learning, 1, pp. 81-106

[4] Blake, C.L. and Merz, C.J. (1998). UCI Repository of Machine Learning Databases [http://www.ics.uci.edu/~mlearn/MLRepository.html]. Irvine, CA: University of California, Department of Information and Computer Science

[5] Bramer, M.A. (1997). Rule Induction in Data Mining: Concepts and Pitfalls Data Warehouse Report, No. 10, pp. 11-17 and No. 11, pp. 22-27

[6] Bramer, M.A. (2000). Inducer: a Rule Induction Workbench for Data Mining. In Proceedings of the 16th IFIP World Computer Congress Conference on Intelligent Information Processing (eds. Z.Shi, B.Faltings and M.Musen) Publishing House of Electronics Industry (Beijing), pp. 499-506

[7] Bramer, M.A. (2000). Automatic Induction of Classification Rules from Examples Using N-Prism. In: Research and Development in Intelligent Systems XVI. Springer-Verlag, pp. 99-121

[8] Mingers, J. (1989). An Empirical Comparison of Pruning Methods for Decision Tree Induction. Machine Learning, 4, pp. 227-243

[9] Holte, R.C. (1993). Very Simple Classification Rules Perform Well on Most Commonly Used Datasets. Machine Learning, 11, pp. 63-90

[10] Smyth, P. and Goodman, R.M. (1991). Rule Induction Using Information Theory. In: Piatetsky-Shapiro, G. and Frawley, W.J. (eds.), Knowledge Discovery in Databases. AAAI Press, pp. 159-176

[11] Nazar, K. and Bramer, M.A. (1997). Concept Dispersion, Feature Interaction and Their Effect on Particular Sources of Bias in Machine Learning. In Hunt, J. and Miles, R. (eds.), Research and Development in Expert Systems XIV, SGES Publications.

[12] Nazar, K. and Bramer, M.A. (1999). Estimating Concept Difficulty With Cross-Entropy. In Bramer, M.A. (ed.), Knowledge Discovery and Data Mining, Institution of Electrical Engineers, London.

[13] Cendrowska, J. (1987). PRISM: an Algorithm for Inducing Modular Rules. International Journal of Man-Machine Studies, 27, pp. 349-370

Explanation of Attribute Relevance in Decision-Tree Induction

David McSherry

School of Information and Software Engineering, University of Ulster, Coleraine BT52 1SA, Northern Ireland

Abstract

Strategist is an algorithm for strategic induction of decision trees in which attribute selection is based on the reasoning strategies used by doctors. The advantage is that in problem-solving applications of the induced decision tree, the relevance of an attribute or test can be explained in terms of the strategy it was selected to support, such as confirming a target outcome class or eliminating a competing outcome class. However, it is possible that an alternative approach to attribute selection may produce a decision tree with greater predictive accuracy from a given set of training data. The structure of the decision trees that an algorithm produces may also be an important factor in terms of problem-solving efficiency. We present a new algorithm for strategic induction of decision trees in which Strategist's multiple-strategy approach to attribute selection is replaced by the single strategy of increasing the probability of a target outcome class. While sharing Strategist's ability to explain the relevance of attributes in strategic terms, the new algorithm often produces more efficient decision trees than Strategist and matches the accuracy of ID3 on some data sets.

1 Introduction

The importance of intelligent systems having the ability to explain their reasoning is widely recognised [1,2,3]. With test selection in intelligent systems for classification and diagnosis increasingly based on decision trees induced by algorithms like ID3 [4] the question arises of how the system should respond when the user queries the relevance of a selected attribute or test. While a rule-based expert system can show the rule it is trying to fire, it is less obvious how to explain the relevance of tests selected by the methods used in ID3 and other decision-tree algorithms [5,6,7,8,9]. In previous work, we have argued that for the relevance of attributes in an induced decision tree to be explained in terms that are meaningful to users, the induction process should ideally reflect the problem-solving strategies of a human expert [10].

This was the aim that motivated the development of Strategist, an algorithm for *strategic* induction of decision trees [10,11,12] in which attribute selection is based on the evidence-gathering strategies used by doctors, such as confirming a target diagnosis, increasing its probability, or eliminating a competing diagnosis [13,14,15]. Instead of a single measure of attribute usefulness like *information gain* in ID3 (or *gain ratio* in later versions), attribute selection in Strategist is based on a multiple-strategy approach. The algorithm is *goal driven* in that the attribute it selects at a given node depends on the target outcome class it is currently pursuing as its goal. In order of priority, its main attribute-selection strategies are CONFIRM (confirm the target outcome class in a single step), ELIMINATE (eliminate the likeliest alternative outcome class), and VALIDATE (increase the probability of the target outcome class). If more than one attribute is available to support the CONFIRM or ELIMINATE strategies, the attribute selected is the one whose *expected eliminating power* is greatest. A different measure of attribute usefulness is used in the VALIDATE strategy.

Strategist's main advantage is that in problem-solving applications of the induced decision tree, the relevance of a selected attribute can be explained in terms of the strategy it was selected to support, such as confirming the target outcome class or eliminating the likeliest alternative outcome class. However, it is possible that another algorithm may produce a decision tree with greater predictive accuracy from a given set of training data. In applications such as medical diagnosis, even a slight increase in accuracy may outweigh the benefits of explanation. The structure of the decision trees that an algorithm produces may also be an important factor in terms of problem-solving efficiency, for example as measured by the number of questions required on average to reach a conclusion. ID3, for example, is known for its tendency to produce smaller decision trees than most algorithms [16].

In this paper, we investigate the hypothesis that a simplified approach to attribute selection in strategic induction may be beneficial in terms of accuracy and efficiency of the induced decision trees. We present a new algorithm for strategic induction of decision trees called PURSUE in which Strategist's multiple-strategy approach to attribute selection is replaced by the single strategy of increasing the probability of a target outcome class. In Section 2, we describe PURSUE's goal-driven approach to attribute selection and examine its behaviour in comparison with ID3 and Strategist on a well-known data set. In Section 3, we present a lazy version of PURSUE that provides integrated support for incremental learning, problem solving, and explanation. In Section 4, we present the results of an empirical evaluation of PURSUE in comparison with ID3 and Strategist. Related work is discussed in Section 5 and our conclusions are presented in Section 6.

2 Strategic Induction in PURSUE

Like any algorithm for top-down induction of decision trees, PURSUE partitions the data set into subsets corresponding to the values of a selected attribute and recursively applies the same process to each subset. A feature it shares with

Strategist is that the attribute it selects at any stage of the induction process depends on the target outcome class it is currently pursuing as its goal. The target outcome class is the one that is most likely in the current subset of the data set. As in Strategist, the target outcome class is continually revised as the data set is partitioned.

2.1 Measure of Attribute Usefulness

The measure of attribute usefulness used by PURSUE to select the attribute that most strongly supports its strategy of increasing the probability of the target outcome class is called *evidential power*.

Definition 1. *In any subset of a given data set, the evidential power of an attribute A in favour of a target outcome class C_t is*

$$\lambda(A, C_t) = \sum_{i=1}^{n} p(A=v_i \mid C_t) \, p(C_t \mid A=v_i)$$

where $v_1, v_2, ..., v_n$ are the values of A.

At each stage of the induction process, the attribute selected by PURSUE is the one whose evidential power in favour of the target outcome class is greatest. It can be seen from the above definition that an attribute's evidential power is the expected posterior probability of the target outcome class when the attribute's value is known. However, an important point to note is that evidential power is based on the *conditional* probabilities, in the current subset, of an attribute's values in the target outcome class. In contrast, expected entropies in ID3 are based on the *unconditional* probabilities of an attribute's values in the current subset [4]. As the following proposition shows, conditional probabilities are essential in PURSUE. If they were replaced by unconditional probabilities, then all attributes would have the same evidential power.

Proposition 1. *For any attribute A and target outcome class C_t,*

$$\sum_{i=1}^{n} p(A=v_i) \, p(C_t \mid A=v_i) = p(C_t)$$

where $v_1, v_2, ..., v_n$ are the values of A.

PURSUE differs from most decision-tree algorithms, including ID3 and Strategist, in ignoring the effects an attribute may have on other outcome classes. While increasing the probability of the target outcome class is one of the attribute-selection strategies in Strategist, the latter uses a different measure of attribute usefulness. PURSUE also differs from Strategist in not give priority to attributes that can confirm the target outcome class in a single step, instead taking account of the impact of all values of an attribute on the probability of the target outcome class.

It is worth noting that evidential power bears some resemblance to the category utility measure used in COBWEB [17], though the latter involves a product of *three* probabilities and summation over attributes and classes as well as attribute values.

Table 1. Attributes in the contact lenses data set and frequencies of their values

Contact lens type:	None	Soft	Hard	Totals
Age of patient				
young	4	2	2	8
pre-presbyopic	5	2	1	8
presbyopic	6	1	1	8
Tear production rate				
reduced	12	0	0	12
normal	3	5	4	12
Astigmatism				
present	8	0	4	12
absent	7	5	0	12
Spectacle prescription				
hypermetrope	8	3	1	12
myope	7	2	3	12
Totals	15	5	4	24

2.2 The Contact Lenses Data Set

The contact lenses data set is based on a simplified version of the optician's real-world problem of selecting a suitable type of contact lenses, if any, for an adult spectacle wearer [18]. Outcome classes in the data set are no contact lenses, soft contact lenses, and hard contact lenses. Attributes in the data set and frequencies of their values are shown in Table 1. When PURSUE is applied to the contact lenses data set, the target outcome class, with a probability of 0.63, is initially no contact lenses. From Table 1, the probabilities required to compute the evidential power of age in favour of no contact lenses are:

$$p(\text{age} = \text{young} \mid \text{no contact lenses}) = \frac{4}{15}$$

$$p(\text{age} = \text{pre-presbyopic} \mid \text{no contact lenses}) = \frac{5}{15}$$

$$p(\text{age} = \text{presbyopic} \mid \text{no contact lenses}) = \frac{6}{15}$$

$$p(\text{no contact lenses} \mid \text{age} = \text{young}) = \frac{4}{8}$$

$$p(\text{no contact lenses} \mid \text{age} = \text{pre-presbyopic}) = \frac{5}{8}$$

$$p(\text{no contact lenses} \mid \text{age} = \text{presbyopic}) = \frac{6}{8}$$

Table 2. Remaining attributes and frequencies of their values in the subset of the data set with tear production rate = normal

Contact lens type:	None	Soft	Hard	Totals
Age of patient				
young	0	2	2	4
pre-presbyopic	1	2	1	4
presbyopic	2	1	1	4
Astigmatism				
present	2	0	4	6
absent	1	5	0	6
Spectacle prescription				
hypermetrope	2	3	1	6
myope	1	2	3	6
Totals	3	5	4	12

The evidential power of age in favour of the target outcome class is therefore:

$$\lambda(\text{age, no contact lenses}) = \frac{4}{15} \times \frac{4}{8} + \frac{5}{15} \times \frac{5}{8} + \frac{6}{15} \times \frac{6}{8} = 0.64$$

Similarly, the evidential power of tear production rate in favour of no contact lenses is:

$$\lambda(\text{tear production rate, no contact lenses}) = \frac{12}{15} \times \frac{12}{12} + \frac{3}{15} \times \frac{3}{12} = 0.85$$

Finally, the evidential power of both astigmatism and spectacle prescription in favour of no contact lenses is 0.63.

The attribute selected by PURSUE to partition the data set is therefore tear production rate. As the expected entropies in the data set partitions produced by age, tear production rate, astigmatism, and spectacle prescription are 1.29, 0.78, 0.95, and 1.29, tear production rate is also the most useful attribute according to ID3. On the other hand, the second most useful attribute according to ID3 is astigmatism, whereas the second most useful attribute according to PURSUE is age. As the only attribute with a value (reduced) that will confirm the target outcome class in a single step, tear production rate is given priority in Strategist. Similarly, as the only attribute with a value (present) that will eliminate the likeliest alternative outcome class (soft contact lenses), astigmatism is the next most useful attribute according to Strategist.

Table 2 shows the frequencies of values of the remaining attributes in the subset of the data set with tear production rate = normal. The target outcome class now changes to soft contact lenses, the probability of which is currently 0.42. In this subset of the data set, the evidential power of age in favour of soft contact lenses is:

$$\lambda(\text{age, soft contact lenses}) = \frac{2}{5} \times \frac{2}{4} + \frac{2}{5} \times \frac{2}{4} + \frac{1}{5} \times \frac{1}{4} = 0.45$$

---

tear production rate = reduced : no contact lenses
tear production rate = normal
  astigmatism = present
    spectacle prescription = myope : hard contact lenses
    spectacle prescription = hypermetrope
      age of the patient = young : hard contact lenses
      age of the patient = pre-presbyopic : no contact lenses
      age of the patient = presbyopic : no contact lenses
  astigmatism = absent
    age of the patient = young : soft contact lenses
    age of the patient = pre-presbyopic : soft contact lenses
    age of the patient = presbyopic
      spectacle prescription = myope : no contact lenses
      spectacle prescription = hypermetrope : soft contact lenses

---

Figure 1. Decision tree induced by ID3, PURSUE and Strategist
from the contact lenses data set

Similarly, the evidential powers of astigmatism and spectacle prescription are 0.83 and 0.43. Astigmatism is therefore the attribute selected by PURSUE to partition this subset. Once again, this is also the attribute selected by ID3 and Strategist, in the latter case because one of its values (absent) eliminates hard contact lenses, currently the likeliest alternative outcome class.

The complete decision tree induced by PURSUE from the contact lenses data set is shown in Figure 1. As noted in [10], the decision trees induced by ID3 and Strategist from this data set are identical. In fact, the decision trees induced by all three algorithms are identical. Given the size of the data set, this is perhaps not very surprising. More remarkable, though, is the fact that the decision trees induced by ID3 and PURSUE from the Voting Records data set [19] are also identical. With 16 attributes, two outcome classes, and 435 instances, this is a considerably larger data set. The decision tree induced by ID3 and PURSUE has 70 nodes, 15 fewer than the corresponding Strategist tree. PURSUE also produces the same decision tree as ID3 when applied to the complete set of 399 instances in the Roman Numerals data set [11]. This is a data set on which Strategist is known to perform badly in terms of the size of the induced decision tree. The Strategist tree has 39 nodes compared with only 19 nodes for the tree induced by ID3 and PURSUE.

3 Explanation in PURSUE

As we show in this section, PURSUE shares with Strategist the advantage that the relevance of any attribute in the induced decision tree can be explained in strategic terms. As in Strategist, explanations of attribute relevance are delivered on request by a lazy version of PURSUE that provides integrated support for incremental learning, problem solving and explanation.

3.1 Eager and Lazy Learning

Algorithms like ID3 that construct a complete decision tree from a set of training instances for use by an independent problem solver are said to use an *eager* approach to learning. Lazy learning is an alternative approach in which the learning effort is delayed until required for problem solving. Its advantages include low training costs and freedom from commitment to a single hypothesis that covers the entire instance space [16,20,21]. Though usually associated with nearest-neighbour or instance-based algorithms [22], a lazy approach to learning is increasingly being used in algorithms for decision-tree learning [10,11,23,24,25].

As in the eager version of PURSUE, attribute selection in the lazy version is based on the single strategy of increasing the probability of the target outcome class, with evidential power as the measure of attribute usefulness. However, instead of partitioning the data set into subsets corresponding to the values of a selected attribute, PURSUE now asks the user for the value of the selected attribute in the target problem and creates a single subset of the data set consisting of all instances for which the attribute's value is the same as the reported value. This process is recursively applied to the subset until a subset containing a single outcome class is reached. In this way, a single decision *path* is constructed for the target problem. At the end of the consultation, PURSUE reports the classification it has reached as the solution to the problem presented by the user.

PURSUE: The target outcome class is no contact lenses.
          What is the tear production rate?
User: why
PURSUE: *Because if the tear production rate is reduced this will confirm*
          no contact lenses
          What is the tear production rate?
User: normal
PURSUE: The target outcome class is soft contact lenses
          Is astigmatism present?
User: why
PURSUE: *The absence of astigmatism will eliminate hard contact lenses*
          Is astigmatism present?
User: no
PURSUE: What is the age of the patient?
User: why
PURSUE: *Because if the age of the patient is young or pre-presbyopic, this*
          will confirm soft contact lenses
          What is the age of the patient?
User: young
PURSUE: Have confirmed soft contact lenses

Figure 2. Example consultation based on the lazy version of PURSUE

PURSUE:	The target outcome class is no contact lenses
	What is the tear production rate?
User:	unknown
PURSUE:	What is the age of the patient?
User:	why
PURSUE:	*Because if the age of the patient is presbyopic, this will increase the probability of no contact lenses*
	What is the age of the patient?
User:	presbyopic
PURSUE:	What is the spectacle prescription?
User:	why
PURSUE:	*Because if the spectacle prescription is hypermetrope, this will eliminate hard contact lenses*
	What is the spectacle prescription?
User:	hypermetrope
PURSUE:	Is astigmatism present?
User:	why
PURSUE:	*The presence of astigmatism will confirm no contact lenses*
	Is astigmatism present?
User:	yes
PURSUE:	Have confirmed no contact lenses

Figure 3. Example consultation showing PURSUE's ability to tolerate incomplete data

3.2 Explaining the Relevance of a Question

Before answering any question asked by PURSUE, the user can ask why it is relevant. PURSUE differs from Strategist in the way it responds to such requests for explanation. Strategist's explanation depends on the strategy it used to select the attribute. In the CONFIRM, ELIMINATE and VALIDATE strategies, it shows the user the value(s) of the attribute that will confirm the target outcome class, eliminate the likeliest alternative outcome class, or increase the probability of the target outcome class [10]. Though goal driven like Strategist, PURSUE has only the single strategy of increasing the probability of the target outcome class on which to base its explanation of attribute relevance in strategic terms. To compensate for this, it explains the relevance of certain attributes in terms of their *effects*. Thus if the selected attribute has a value that confirms the target outcome class or eliminates the likeliest alternative outcome class, the user is shown this value. If not, the user is shown the value(s) of the attribute that will increase the probability of the target outcome class.

Figure 2 shows PURSUE's ability to explain the reasoning process in a problem-solving consultation based on the contact lenses data set. The decision path lazily constructed by PURSUE from the problem data presented by the user is a fragment of the complete decision tree in Figure 1. In this example, the attributes selected by PURSUE are the same as those that Strategist would choose and its explanations of their relevance are indistinguishable from those that Strategist would provide.

Figure 3 shows a second example consultation in which PURSUE's behaviour differs from that produced by Strategist's multiple-strategy approach to attribute selection. It also illustrates how PURSUE, like other decision-tree algorithms that run in lazy-learning mode, can often tolerate incomplete data in the target problem by selecting the next most useful attribute when the value of the most useful attribute is unknown.

A similar strategy is not possible in eager decision-tree algorithms as there is no record of the attribute that was second best at a given node [24]. When the user reports that the tear production rate is unknown, PURSUE selects age as the next most useful attribute and ultimately succeeds in reaching a unique classification in spite of the missing data. As noted in Section 2.2, astigmatism is the next most useful attribute after tear production rate according to Strategist because it has a value that will eliminate the likeliest alternative outcome class. However, age is slightly preferred by PURSUE because of its greater evidential power in favour of the target outcome class. As this attribute does not have a value that confirms the target outcome class or eliminates the likeliest alternative outcome class, its relevance is explained by PURSUE in purely strategic terms.

4 Experimental Results

We now present the results of experiments in which we compare the performance of ID3, PURSUE, and Strategist on the Roman Numerals data set [11] and five data sets from the UCI Machine Learning Repository [19]. We share the view expressed by Bramer [26] that comparison with an algorithm with equally basic features like ID3 is more appropriate in the evaluation of new algorithms than comparison with a state-of-the-art algorithm like C4.5 [9]. We include in the evaluation a revised version of Strategist that was developed to address a potential problem associated with the algorithm's multiple-strategy approach to attribute selection [11]. Very briefly, the original algorithm's policy of always giving priority to confirming the likeliest outcome class means that it is sometimes forced to select from attributes that only weakly support this strategy, while strategies of lower priority may be more strongly supported by the available attributes. A tactical approach to the selection of a target outcome class has been shown to reduce the algorithm's susceptibility to this problem. We will refer to the original and revised versions of Strategist as Strategist-1 and Strategist-2.

The performance criteria of interest in the evaluation are the accuracy and efficiency of the induced decision trees. An admittedly simplistic measure of a decision tree's efficiency is its *average path length*, or equivalently the average number of questions required to reach a conclusion when the tree is used for problem solving [27]. As all paths in a decision tree are unlikely to be used with equal frequency in practice, its average path length should be regarded as an approximate measure of its problem-solving efficiency. Nevertheless, we consider the average path length of a decision tree to be more important than its overall size, not only in terms of efficiency but also the comprehensibility of explanations of how a conclusion was reached. The number of paths in a decision tree has no bearing on its problem-solving efficiency, though may of course be an important issue in the context of rule discovery [26].

Of the six data sets used in our experiments, Roman Numerals, Voting Records, Tic-Tac-Toe, Chess, and Mushrooms all have two outcome classes with majority class probabilities of 67%, 61%, 65%, 52% and 52% respectively. Car Evaluation has 4 outcome classes. The six data sets range in size from 399 to 8124 instances. None has any continuous attributes and none except Mushrooms has missing values. Only one of the 22 attributes in Mushrooms has missing values and this attribute was excluded from the data set in our experiments. Two versions of the Voting Records data set were used in our experiments. Voting Records (1) is the standard data set with all sixteen attributes. Voting Records (2) differs only in that the attribute that is most useful according to ID3 (physician fee freeze) is excluded.

Our results are based on 10-fold cross validation. In this technique, the data set is randomly divided into ten testing sets of equal size. The algorithms to be evaluated are then applied to each testing set in turn, with the other nine testing sets combined to provide the training set.

Average predictive accuracy of the induced decision trees is shown in Table 3. In this respect, PURSUE matched or exceeded the performance of ID3 on all but two of the data sets. Both algorithms tended to give better results than the two versions of Strategist most notably on Voting Records (1) and Tic-Tac-Toe. Strategist-2 slightly outperformed its predecessor on two of the data sets.

Table 4 shows the average path length of the induced decision trees. In this respect, PURSUE was narrowly outperformed by ID3 on two data sets but gave slightly better results than ID3 on two data sets. Though giving better results on the whole than its predecessor, Strategist-2 was noticeably outperformed by ID3 and PURSUE on Roman Numerals, Voting Records (2), and Chess.

Table 3. Average accuracy of decision trees induced by ID3, PURSUE, and Strategist

Data Set	Size	ID3	PURSUE	Strategist-1	Strategist-2
Roman Numerals	399	100	100	99	100
Voting Records (1)	435	96	95	93	93
Voting Records (2)	435	85	87	85	85
Tic-Tac-Toe	958	87	87	84	84
Car Evaluation	1728	90	89	88	88
Chess KRKPA7	3196	100	100	99	100
Mushrooms	8124	100	100	100	100

5 Related Work

Our review of related work is necessarily brief. However, an extensive bibliography of research on decision-tree learning can be found in Breslow and Aha's survey of techniques for simplifying decision trees [1].

Table 4. Average path length of decision trees induced by ID3, PURSUE, and Strategist

Data Set	ID3	PURSUE	Strategist-1	Strategist-2
Roman Numerals	4.7	4.7	5.8	5.4
Voting Records (1)	4.3	4.4	5.3	4.4
Voting Records (2)	5.6	5.5	6.9	7.0
Tic-Tac-Toe	5.6	5.6	5.8	5.7
Car Evaluation	5.5	5.5	5.5	5.5
Chess KRKPA7	9.0	8.9	12.0	13.1
Mushrooms	2.3	2.4	2.7	2.3

5.1 Rule Discovery in PRISM

PURSUE bears some resemblance to PRISM, an algorithm for *rule* induction that was designed to avoid the problems associated with decision trees, such as their insistence on data that may be unnecessary in the solution of a given problem [18]. PRISM is goal driven in the sense that it induces a set of rules for each outcome class in turn, though there is no revision of the target outcome class as in PURSUE. Given a target outcome class, it selects the attribute *value* that maximises the probability of the target outcome class and forms a subset of the training set consisting of all instances with the selected attribute value. It recursively applies the same process to the subset until a subset containing only the target outcome class is reached. The attribute values used to generate this subset provide the conditions of a discovered rule with the target outcome class on the right-hand side. An overall measure of attribute usefulness is not required in PRISM as its focus is on the selection of attribute values to serve as rule conditions rather than attributes for building a decision tree.

It is worth noting that some of the limitations of decision trees that motivated the development of PRISM can be overcome by a lazy approach to decision-tree induction [24]. The greater flexibility of the lazy approach is illustrated by PURSUE's ability to sometimes reach a unique classification even when the most useful attribute is unknown. However, there has recently been renewed research interest in PRISM as a practical tool for the discovery of classification rules in real-world data sets. A revised version of the algorithm has been shown to be capable of discovering rules that are at least as accurate, and more tolerant to noise, than rules derived from decision trees constructed with information gain as the splitting criterion [26].

5.2 Explaining an Attribute's Relevance in Terms of its Effects

As noted in the introduction, the main advantage of strategic induction is the ability to explain the relevance of an attribute or test in terms of the strategy it was selected to support. An alternative approach is to explain the relevance of an attribute in terms of its effects, or more precisely the effects of its values, such as confirming the likeliest outcome class or eliminating the likeliest alternative outcome class [28]. The latter approach has the advantage that it can be used with any decision-tree algorithm, thus avoiding any trade-off between accuracy and explanation.

For example, the most useful attribute in the contact lenses data set according to both ID3 and Strategist is tear production rate. One value of this attribute (reduced) occurs only in no contact lenses, initially the likeliest outcome class in the data set. Regardless of how it was selected, a reasonable explanation of its relevance is therefore that one of its values confirms no contact lenses. Although this happens to be the explanation that Strategist provides, the difference is that Strategist's explanation is the actual reason for the attribute's selection. A point we would like to emphasise is that explanation of an attribute's relevance in terms of its effects does not amount to an explanation of a decision-tree algorithm's *behaviour*. For example, while such explanations may give the impression of a goal-driven approach to attribute selection, this may not be a true reflection of the algorithm's behaviour, for example in the case of ID3.

Though capable of explaining attribute relevance purely in strategic terms, PURSUE explains the relevance of certain attributes in terms of their effects. Nevertheless, the explanations it provides are reasonably consistent with its attribute-selection behaviour. Confirming the target outcome class in a single step is certainly consistent with PURSUE's strategy of increasing the probability of the target outcome class, and an attribute's ability to eliminate the likeliest alternative outcome class is offered as an explanation of its relevance only if the value that has this effect does not decrease the probability of the target outcome class.

5.3 Explaining How a Conclusion Was Reached

It is useful to distinguish the explanation of attribute relevance in decision trees from the relatively standard technique of using the attribute values on a decision path to explain how a conclusion was reached [23]. This is comparable to the use of a reasoning trace to explain a conclusion reached by a rule-based expert system [3]. Increasing the comprehensibility of such *retrospective* explanations is one of the factors motivating the development of techniques for simplifying decision trees [1,29,30]. For similar reasons, the average path length of a decision tree before simplification may be an important factor in terms of the comprehensibility of explanations of how a conclusion was reached.

LazyDT's *instance-specific* approach to test selection recognises that while the test selected at a given node by most algorithms is best on average, there may be better tests for classifying a specific instance [23]. An advantage of the approach is that decision paths built for specific instances may be shorter and hence provide more concise explanations of how conclusions were reached. On the other hand, LazyDT's requirement for attribute values in the unseen instance to be known in advance of attribute selection, rather than sequentially elicited as in PURSUE, means that the relevance of an attribute cannot be explained when the user is asked for its value.

6 Conclusions

The research presented in this paper attempts to address the complex trade-offs between accuracy, efficiency, and explanation of attribute relevance in decision-tree induction. We have investigated the hypothesis that a simplified approach to strategic induction may improve the accuracy and efficiency of the induced decision trees while retaining the ability to explain attribute relevance in strategic terms. Strategist's multiple-strategy approach to attribute selection [10] is replaced in PURSUE by the single strategy of increasing the probability of the target outcome class. Though capable of explaining attribute relevance in purely strategic terms, PURSUE explains the relevance of certain attributes in terms of their effects, thus providing explanations that closely resemble those that Strategist provides.

Our experimental results generally support the hypothesis that improvements in decision-tree quality are possible with a simplified approach to strategic induction. As well as achieving slight gains in predictive accuracy in comparison with Strategist on some data sets, PURSUE tended on the whole to produce more efficient decision trees. Though differing markedly from ID3 in its goal-driven approach to attribute selection, PURSUE often produces decision trees that closely resemble those produced by ID3, at least when applied to data sets with two outcome classes. This is an encouraging finding, and may account for PURSUE's better overall performance in comparison with Strategist and ability to match the accuracy of ID3 on some data sets.

References

1. Breslow, L.A., Aha, D.W.: Simplifying Decision Trees: a Survey. Knowledge Engineering Review **12** (1997) 1-40
2. Leake, D.B.: CBR in Context: the Present and Future. In Leake, D.B. (ed): Case-Based Reasoning: Experiences, Lessons & Future Directions. AAAI Press/MIT Press (1996) 3-30
3. Southwick, R.W.: Explaining Reasoning: an Overview of Explanation in Knowledge-Based Systems. Knowledge Engineering Review **6** (1991) 1-19
4. Quinlan, J.R.: Induction of Decision Trees. Machine Learning **1** (1986) 81-106
5. Breiman, L., Friedman, J.H., Olshen, R.A., Stone, C.J.: Classification and Regression Trees. Pacific Grove, California (1984)
6. Buntine, W., Niblett, T.: A Further Comparison of Splitting Rules for Decision Tree Induction. Machine Learning **8** (1992) 75-85
7. López de Mántaras, R.: A Distance-Based Attribute Selection Measure for Decision Tree Induction. Machine Learning **6** (1991) 81-92.
8. Mingers, J.: An Empirical Comparison of Selection Measures for Decision-Tree Induction. Machine Learning **3** (1989) 319-342
9. Quinlan, J.R.: C4.5: Programs for Machine Learning. Morgan Kaufmann, San Mateo, California (1993)
10. McSherry, D.: Strategic Induction of Decision Trees. Knowledge-Based Systems **12** (1999) 269-275

11. McSherry, D.: A Case Study of Strategic Induction: the Roman Numerals Data Set. In: Bramer, M., Preece, A., Coenen, F. (eds): Research and Development in Intelligent Systems XVII. Springer-Verlag, London (2000) 48-61

12. McSherry, D.: Interactive Case-Based Reasoning in Sequential Diagnosis. Applied Intelligence **14** (2001) 65-76

13. Elstein, A.S., Schulman, L.A., Sprafka, S.A.: Medical Problem Solving: an Analysis of Clinical Reasoning. Harvard University Press, Cambridge, Massachusetts (1978)

14. McSherry, D.: Dynamic and Static Approaches to Clinical Data Mining. Artificial Intelligence in Medicine **16** (1999) 97-115

15. Shortliffe, E.H. and Barnett, G.O.: Medical Data: Their Acquisition, Storage and Use. In Shortliffe, E.H. and Perreault, L.E. (eds): Medical Informatics: Computer Applications in Health Care. Addison-Wesley, Reading, Massachusetts (1990) 37-69

16. Mitchell, T.M.: Machine Learning. McGraw-Hill (1997)

17. Fisher, D.H.: Knowledge Acquisition Via Incremental Conceptual Clustering. Machine Learning **2** (1987) 139-172

18. Cendrowska, J.: PRISM: an Algorithm for Inducing Modular Rules. International Journal of Man-Machine Studies **27** (1987) 349-370

19. Blake, C., Merz, C.: UCI Repository of Machine Learning Databases. Department of Information and Computer Science, University of California, Irvine, California (1998)

20. Aha, D.W.: Editorial: Lazy Learning. Artificial Intelligence Review **11** (1997) 7-10

21. Aha, D.W.: The Omnipresence of Case-Based Reasoning in Science and Application. Knowledge-Based Systems **11** (1998) 261-273

22. Aha, D.W., Kibler, D., Albert, M.K.: Instance-Based Learning Algorithms. Machine Learning **6** (1991) 37-66

23. Friedman, J.H., Kohavi, R., Yun, Y.: Lazy Decision Trees. Proceedings of the Thirteenth National Conference on Artificial Intelligence, 717-724. AAAI Press, Menlo Park, California (1996) 717-724

24. McSherry D.: Integrating Machine Learning, Problem Solving and Explanation. In: Bramer, M., Nealon, J., Milne, R. (eds): Research and Development in Expert Systems XII. SGES Publications, UK (1995) 145-157

25. Smyth, B., Cunningham, P.: A Comparison of Incremental Case-based Reasoning and Inductive Learning. In: Haton, J-P., Keane, M., Manago, M. (eds): Advances in Case-Based Reasoning. LNAI, Vol. 984. Springer-Verlag, Berlin Heidelberg (1994) 151-164

26. Bramer, M.: Automatic Induction of Classification Rules from Examples using N-Prism. In: Bramer, M., Macintosh, A., Coenen, F. (eds): Research and Development in Intelligent Systems XVI. Springer-Verlag, London (2000) 99-121

27. McSherry, D.: Minimizing Dialog Length in Interactive Case-Based Reasoning. Proceedings of the Seventeenth International Joint Conference on Artificial Intelligence. International Joint Conferences on Artificial Intelligence (2001) 993-998

28. McSherry, D.: Automated Explanation of Attribute Relevance in Decision-Tree Induction. Technology and Health Care **9** (2001) 34-36

29. Bohanec, M., Bratko, I.: Trading Accuracy for Simplicity in Decision Trees. Machine Learning **15** (1994) 223-250

30. Quinlan, J.R.: Simplifying Decision Trees. International Journal of Man-Machine Studies **27** (1987) 221-234

OPTIMISING ASSOCIATION RULE ALGORITHMS USING ITEMSET ORDERING

Frans Coenen and Paul Leng
Department of Computer Science,
University of Liverpool, UK
{frans,phl}@csc.liv.ac.uk

Abstract

Association-rule mining is a well-known method of Knowledge Discovery in Databases, aimed at identifying observable relationships in datasets the records of which can be represented as sets of items. The problem of extracting all possible association rules, however, is computationally intractable, so methods of reducing its complexity are of continuing interest. We here describe some results obtained from a method we have developed, which reduces the task by means of an efficient restructuring of the data accompanied by a partial computation of the totals required. The method is sensitive to the ordering of items in the data, and our experiments show how this property can be used as an implementation heuristic. The results we show demonstrate the performance gain for our method in comparison with a benchmark alternative, and the further gain from using the ordering heuristic.

KEYWORDS: KDD, Data Mining, Association Rules, Partial Support

1 Introduction

Knowledge Discovery in Databases (KDD) is concerned with the extraction of hitherto unrecognised and "interesting" information from within (usually large) datasets. Generally, this information takes the form of some relationship, or association, which can be observed between other categories of information in the data. These relationships can often be expressed in the form of *association rules* [2] which relate database attributes. Methods for identifying such rules have become an important area of research in KDD.

Association-rule mining has been developed, especially, to deal with problems such as supermarket shopping-basket analysis. The key characteristic here is that each database record (e.g. a shopping transaction) takes the form of a list of *items* occurring in the record (a set of items purchased). Many other kinds of data, such as census returns, also have a similar nature or can easily be converted into an equivalent form. The task then is to discover which sets of items typically occur together in records. From this we can infer relationships of the form $A{\rightarrow}B$, where A and B are disjoint sets of items. We interpret an association rule of this kind to mean "when the set of items A occurs in a record, it is likely that B will occur also".

To determine which of all such possible rules are of interest, a number of possible measures can be applied, of which the two most significant are the *support* and the *confidence*. The support for a rule describes the number of instances of the association in the dataset: that is, the number of records that include the set $A \cup B$. Almost all methods for determining association rules begin by excluding from consideration those sets the support for which is below some threshold value, expressed as a proportion of the total number of records. The confidence in a rule, then, is the ratio of the support for the association to the support for its antecedent: i.e. the confidence in the rule $A{\rightarrow}B$ expresses what proportion of records that include the set A also include B. Again, a rule is usually considered "interesting" only if its confidence exceeds some suitably-chosen threshold value.

Because the confidence in any rule can be determined immediately once the relevant support values have been calculated, association-rule mining invariably begins by seeking to establish the support for all those sets which may be involved in interesting rules, These so-called "frequent" sets are those which exceed the prescribed support threshold. The problem here is that the scale of this task is inherently exponential. If there are n possible items that may be included in a record, then an exhaustive computation requires the counting of the support for all 2^n possible sets of items. For most of the applications in which we are interested, n is likely to be 500 or more, making this computationally infeasible. All methods for determining association rules essentially focus on ways of addressing this problem.

We have developed a method for identifying frequent sets and efficiently computing their support totals, by starting with a pass of the database which performs a *partial* summation of the relevant totals, storing these in a set-enumeration tree structure (the *P-tree*). From this the final relevant support totals are computed, using a second tree structure (the *T-tree*) to store these. In this paper we present some experimental results that demonstrate the performance advantage gained from our approach. In particular, we focus on a characteristic of the method which makes its performance sensitive to the order in which the items in a set are considered. We describe the results of experiments with various data sets that show how this characteristic can be used to improve performance.

2 Background

Almost all algorithms for identifying frequent sets attempt to reduce the search space by computing support-counts only for those sets of items which are identified as potentially interesting. The best-known algorithm, "Apriori" [3], does this by repeated passes of the database, successively computing support-counts for single items, pairs, triples, and so on. Since any set of items can be "frequent" only if all its subsets also reach the required support threshold, the *candidate set* of sets of items is pruned on each pass to eliminate those that do not satisfy this requirement.

Apriori and related methods work well for cases for which the candidate sets being considered are relatively small and the algorithm terminates after a small number of database passes. For data in which individual records are densely-populated with items, however, candidate sets may become very large: if all the n single items reach the required threshold of support, for example, then all the $n(n-1)/2$ pairs will be candidates in the second pass, and so on. Large candidate-set sizes create a problem both in their storage requirement and in the computation required as each database record is examined. The implementation described for the Apriori algorithm stores the candidate set in a hash-tree, storing each candidate (a set of items) in a leaf node reached by hashing successively on each item. Then, as each database record is examined, it is necessary to increment the support for each candidate that is a subset of the record. These are located in the hash-tree by hashing successively on each item in the record, and examining all candidates thus found. Clearly, the time for this procedure will depend both on the number of items in a record and the size of the hash-tree.

Many subsequent methods have been developed to address the performance limitations of Apriori. These include strategies which begin by examining subsets of the database [10], or by sampling the database to estimate the likely candidate set [11]. These have the advantage that, in most cases, only one full pass of the database is needed, but the drawback that the candidate set derived is necessarily a superset of the actual set of frequent sets, so again may be very large. Other methods [13] [4] [5] aim to identify *maximal* frequent sets without first examining all their subsets. These algorithms cope better with densely-populated datasets than the other algorithms described, but again require multiple database passes. When the database is contained wholly in main memory, methods of this kind become more attractive [1]. However, it is fair to say that no known method provides a solution which scales satisfactorily to deal with very large and densely-populated databases, so this problem remains of active interest.

The fundamental performance problem of Apriori and related methods is the cost of dealing with all the subsets of densely-populated records, and of locating relevant candidates when the candidate-set becomes very large. In the next section we describe a method we have developed which addresses this problem by performing an initial, very efficient, *partial* computation of support totals, while at the same time reorganising the data to facilitate completion of the calculations needed.

3 Computing support via Partial totals

In the databases we are considering, each record takes the form of a set of individually different items, i.e. a subset of the total set of possible items. The restructuring we perform stores all *distinct* database records in the form of a set-enumeration tree [9]. A complete tree, for a set of items $\{A, B, C, D\}$, is illustrated in Figure 1. What is actually constructed, however, is a partial tree, including only those nodes that represent records actually occurring in the database, plus additional nodes that are created when two or more nodes share a leading subset. The scale of tree thus constructed is linear to the size of the database rather than exponential to the number of items.

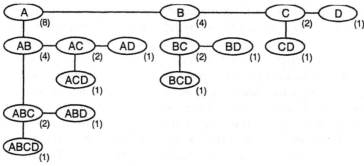

Figure 1: *Tree storage of subsets of* $\{A, B, C, D\}$

A detailed description of the algorithm for building this structure, which we call the *P-tree*, in a single database pass is given in [7]. One significant point to note, with respect to this paper, is that the itemset labels stored at each node (other than in the case of the top level nodes) exclude that part of the label represented by the node's parent. This reduces the overall storage requirements for the P-tree and consequently also contributes to gains in processing efficiency (this is discussed further in Section 5). The structure of the tree makes it easy and efficient to carry out, during its construction, a partial support-count of sets occurring within database records. It is easy to see from Figure 1 that the traversal of the tree necessary to locate any particular node will pass through, en route, all those subsets of the node-set that precede it in the tree ordering. Our tree-construction algorithm takes advantage of this to accumulate (incomplete) *interim* support-counts for all sets placed in the tree, incorporating the counts for all the successor-supersets of the set that are encountered. Figure 1 shows the counts that would arise from a database including exactly one instance of each of the 16 possible sets of items.

The advantage gained by this restructuring is that, by an efficient process in a single database pass, we have carried out a significant portion of the computation that would otherwise be performed repeatedly in each subsequent database pass. To illustrate this, consider the node BC in Figure 1, which has an interim support-count of 2, derived from one instance of BC and one of its successor-superset BCD. To complete the calculation of support for BC, we require to add also the counts for its predecessor-supersets, ABC and $ABCD$. But the contribution from $ABCD$ has already been included in the interim total for ABC, so the latter is the only addition needed to complete the summation of support for the set BC.

The set-enumeration tree structure has been used in a number of other methods, for storing candidates [4] [5], or frequent sets identified [1] rather than as a database surrogate. A rather similar concept to our *P-tree* has been described independently by [8]. Their *FP-tree*, has a more complex structure but quite similar properties to the P-tree, and is built in two database passes. The additional structure facilitates the implementation of an effective algorithm, "FP-growth", which successively generates subtrees from the FP-tree corresponding to each frequent item, to represent all sets in which the item is associated with its predecessors in the tree ordering. Recursive application of the algorithm generates all frequent sets. The drawback of this method is that the structural linkages of the FP-tree cause problems when dealing with data that cannot be wholly contained in main memory. The much simpler P-tree structure, conversely, is easily adaptable to non-memory- resident forms. Unlike the FP-tree method, which is the basis of a specific algorithm, the P-tree is essentially generic in that it is possible, in principle, to apply variants of almost any existing algorithm, using the P-tree as a replacement for the original database.

In order to illustrate and explore the performance gain from this, we have implemented a method based closely on the original Apriori algorithm, applying the Apriori procedure to the nodes in the P-tree rather than to the records in the original database. The principal advantage gained is that for any node of the P-tree, fewer subsets need be considered than would have been the case for the equivalent database record in the original Apriori. This is because support associated with predecessor-subsets of the node will already have been counted when considering the parent of the node in the tree. As an example, consider a record comprising the set of items $ABCD$. In the second pass of Apriori, its subsets to be considered are the pairs AB, AC, AD, BC, BD, and CD. However, within the P-tree, the count associated with $ABCD$ has already been included in the interim total for its parent ABC, and this will be added into the support totals for the subsets of ABC when the latter node is processed. Thus, when processing the node $ABCD$, we need only consider those of its subsets not covered by its parent, i.e. AD, BD and CD (AB, AC and BC having been considered when the node ABC was processed).

The structure of the P-tree also helps us to efficiently locate candidates whose support must be updated. For this purpose, we define a second structure, the *T-tree*, illustrated in Figure 2, to store the candidate set being considered. Again, the figure illustrates a complete tree, whereas in practice the actual tree constructed will include only those nodes that remain under consideration.

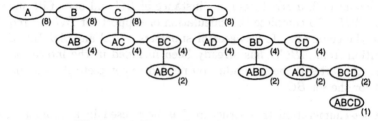

Figure 2: *Tree with predecessor-subtrees*

Each subtree of the T-tree stores predecessor-supersets of its root node. The significance of this is that it localises those sets which need to be considered when we examine the subsets of a P-tree node. Using the example above, when processing the P-tree node $ABCD$, we need to update the support total for AD, BD and CD, all of which are predecessor-supersets of the attribute D which is not included in the parent node. These sets are all located in the T-tree subtree rooted at node D. This allows us to define an efficient algorithm for counting the support of candidates stored in the T- tree. In this algorithm, which we call Apriori-TFP ("Total From Partial"), each node in the P-tree is examined, and its difference from its parent node is used to produce a "search set" S with an associated partial support total. The search set defines the branches of the T-tree which must be traversed. In the Apriori-TFP implementation, each pass of the algorithm builds a new level of the T-tree and uses this procedure to accumulate the support totals for its leaf nodes. At the end of the pass, those nodes that fail to reach the support threshold are removed, and the next level is built, adding only those nodes all of whose subsets remain in the tree. The process reproduces the Apriori methodology, terminating with a T-tree containing just the frequent sets. Note that the method requires each P-tree node to be visited just once on each pass, in any order, so dealing with non-memory-resident data poses no problems.

4   Itemset Ordering

The method we have described for computing support counts uses as a starting point an initial, incomplete computation stored as a set-enumeration tree. Although the actual algorithm described here to compute the final totals is based on the Apriori algorithm, the method itself is generic, in that, once the P-tree has been created, a variety of methods may be applied to complete the summation. Many of these methods, like the one we have illustrated, will be able to take advantage of the partial computation already carried out in the initial database pass to reduce the cost of further multiple passes.

Note, however, that the advantage gained from this partial computation is not equally distributed throughout the set of candidates. For candidates early in the lexicographic order, most of the support calculation is completed during the construction of the P-tree; for example, for the items of Figure 1, support for the sets A, AB, ABC and $ABCD$ will be counted totally in this first stage of the summation. This observation allows us to consider methods which maximise the benefit from this by a suitable ordering of the item set (a heuristic also used, in various ways, by [4], [6], [1] and [8]).

If we know, at least approximately, the expected frequency of each item, then an ordering which places more frequent items earlier in the set ordering would lead to a greater proportion of the summation being completed during construction of the P-tree (an efficient single database pass). The effect to be observed will be a P-tree which is more densely-populated at the left-hand side of the layout of Figure 1. This maximises the number of sets which have near-subsets as parents in the structure, hence reducing the number of subsets that need be considered.

To examine the effects of this, we have carried out a series of experiments. Our aim is, firstly, to investigate the performance gain achieved by using the P-tree and T-tree structures in place of the original database and Apriori hash-tree, i.e. to compare Apriori-TFP with the original Apriori. For this purpose, we have implemented a version of Apriori, as described in [3]. Both this, and our implementation of Apriori-TFP are straightforward, non-optimised Java programs. Secondly, we wish to investigate the effect on performance of ordering items in the way we have indicated.

For these experiments, we have used three different datasets. The first is a synthetic database constructed using the generator described in [3]. This uses parameters T, which defines the average number of attributes found in a record, and I, the average size of the maximal supported set. Higher values of T and I in relation to the number of attributes N correspond to a more densely-populated database. Here we show the results for the case where $T = 16, I = 8$, $N = 500$ and $D = 200,000$ (where D is the number of records).

This data, while important for comparison with published results of other methods, is relatively sparsely-populated and hence not a particularly demanding test of a method. Our second dataset is the "mushroom" available from the UCI Machine Learning Repository [12]. This is a densely populated set with $N = 129$ and $D = 7784$ (when normalised).

Finally, we have applied the methods to a "real" dataset; the "Fleet" database of an insurance company (the Royal Sun Alliance group), which records information on car use by staff. After converting to the required format, $N = 194$ and $D = 9000$. Note that this last data set, for reasons of confidentiality, is not publically available.

In each case two versions of the dataset were tested, one where the attributes were ordered according to frequency of single attributes (most frequent first), and one where the data set remained in its "raw" state. The characteristics of these data sets is summarised in Table 1.

	N	D	T	I	Size (Bytes)
T16.I8.N500.D200000	500	200,000	16	8	6,434,030
Mushroom.N129.D7784	129	7,784	-	-	358,064
Fleet.N194.D900	194	9,000	-	-	297,116

Table 1: Characteristics of test data sets

5 Results

5.1 P-tree Generation

Before examining the overall result of the association rule mining using Apriori-TFP it is appropriate to briefly consider the effect on P-tree generation. Table 2 shows the generation times and storage requirements for the three test data sets order and unordered. From the table the following can be observed:

- P-tree generation time is faster in all cases for the ordered against the unordered version of each of the data sets.

- For T16.I8.N500.D200000 and Fleet.N194.D900 the number of nodes in the P-tree increases because there are more nodes representing leading sub-strings then in the unordered case.

- In the case of Mushroom.N129.D7784 the number of nodes is reduced in the ordered case because this data set is a very dense set; therefore in the unordered form the P-tree contains many repetitions of certain sub-strings.

- In all cases the overall storage is reduced for the ordered versions, even where reordering results in more P-tree nodes, either because there were fewer nodes in the ordered version, or because the size of item-sets (i.e. the number of attributes represented by a particular item-set) stored at each node is significantly smaller. Remember that in the P-tree the attributes comprising an item set consist of the sub-string contained at the current node plus the substrings represented by its parent nodes.

- In addition, from comparison with Table 1 the overall P-tree storage for the ordered sets is less than that required for the unordered raw data, regardless of the "house keeping" overheads associated with the P-tree.

5.2 T16.I8.N500.D200000

Graphs 1 and 2 show sets of curves for time to generate the frequent sets, and the number of support-count updates involved given the T16.I8.N500.D200000 data set. Both graphs show three sets of curves: (1) Apriori-TFP using the

	T16.I8.N500. D200000		Mushroom.N129. 7784		Fleet.N194. 900	
	Unord.	Ord.	Unord.	Ord.	Unord.	Ord.
Gen. Time (mins)	9.79	8.70	0.39	0.36	0.34	0.31
Num. P-tree nodes	219,552	224,571	12,134	11,695	11,653	13744
Storage (Bytes)	6,583,844	6,374,156	204,304	181,704	304,256	265,612

Table 2: P-tree generation characteristics

ordered version of the data set, (2) Apriori-TFP using the unordered version of the data set, and (3) frequent set generation using the traditional hash tree based Apriori technique. Graph 1 plots generation time in minutes against a range of support threshold values. From this graph it can be observed that Apriori-TFP, despite the overheads associated with the interaction with the P-tree data structure to produce the T-tree, outperforms the traditional hash tree approach. It can also be noted that reordering offers a slight further execution time advantage.

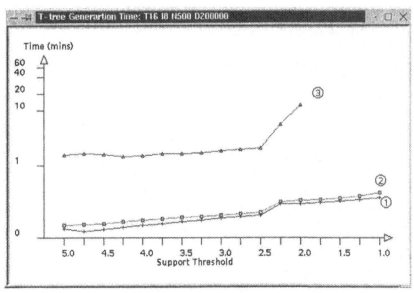

Graph 1 *Frequent set Generation time* Apriori-TFP: *(1) ordered P-tree to T-tree, (2) unordered Apriori-TFP, (3) unordered hash tree*

Graph 2 is arguably more informative in that it indicates the effectiveness of the P-tree technique and reordering in a manner independent of implementation optimisation and machine characteristics. Here, we are considering the number of support-count updates involved as the database or P-tree is scanned repeatedly. The number is lower when the P-tree is used, because of the reduced number of subsets that need be considered, as described in Section 3.

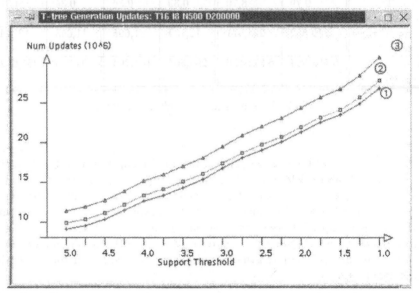

Graph 2 *Support count updates* T16.I8.N500.D200000: *(1) ordered P-tree to T-tree, (2) unordered Apriori-TFP, (3) unordered hash tree*

5.3   Mushroom.N129.D7784

Graphs 3 and 4 show similar sets of curves to those presented in the foregoing subsection but for the mushroom data set. The first graph presents data only for the P-tree to T-tree approach as the performance times for the hash tree exceeded the scale used for the graph. From this graph it can be seen that with respect to performance time reordering produces a significant advantage in this case (more so than when using T16.I8.N500.D200000). This is because the mushroom data set is densely populated, consequently the average length of an interesting set (I) is high. This also means that there are many levels in the T-tree each corresponding to an individual hash tree when using the traditional hash tree approach. (The effectiveness of the hash tree technique deteriorates as the magnitude of I increases.)

Graph 4 shows number of updates with respect to a range of support thresholds. Again, from this graph, it can be seen that reordering coupled with the P-tree to T-tree techniques offers significant advantages over the same technique used with unordered data. Note that in this case, unlike the experiments using the T16.I8.N500.D200000 data set, reordering results in a 50% gain. Similarly the Apriori-TFP algorithm significantly outperforms the hash tree approach regardless of ordering. Again the performance gains recorded when using Mushroom.N129.D7784 are a result of the dense nature of the dataset.

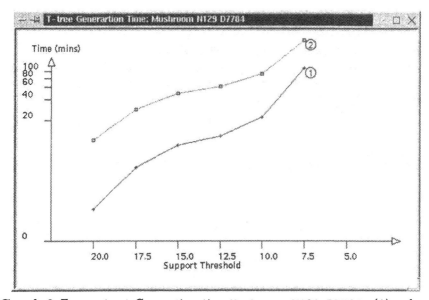

Graph 3 *Frequent set Generation time* Mushroom.N129.D7784: *(1) ordered P-tree to T-tree, (2) unordered Apriori-TFP*

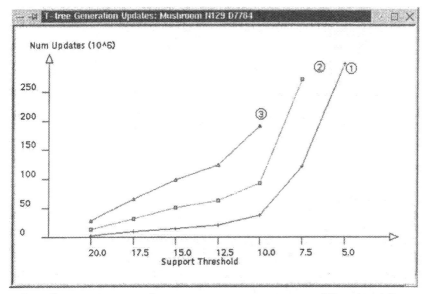

Graph 4 *Support count updates* Mushroom.N129.D7784: *(1) ordered P-tree to T-tree, (2) unordered Apriori-TFP, (3) unordered hash tree*

5.4   Fleet.N194.D900

Graphs 5 and 6 show similar sets to those presented previously for T16.I8.N500.D200000 and Mushroom.N129.D7784, but using a "live" data set provided by the Royal Sun Alliance Insurance group. Graph 5 shows that, with respect to execution time, the P-tree to T-tree technique offers significant advantages over the hash tree approach.

Interestingly, with respect to the number of updates using this data set, there was no marked improvement between the P-tree to T-tree approach against the hash tree approach until the data was reordered when a significant performance gain was realised.

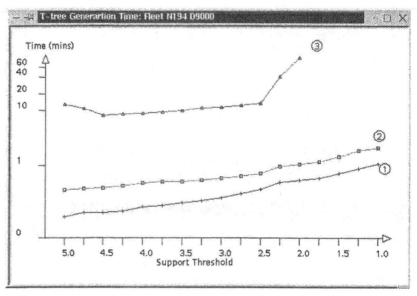

Graph 5 *Frequent set Generation time* `Fleet.N194.D900`: *(1) ordered P-tree to T-tree, (2) unordered Apriori-TFP, (3) unordered hash tree*

6 Conclusions

We have in this paper described the results of a number of experiments we have carried out to investigate the performance of methods we have developed for extracting association rules from large databases. This problem is inherently complex computationally, and there is continued interest in finding methods which overcome the exponential scaling that follows when dealing with very densely-populated data. We have shown that our method consistently outperforms the "standard" benchmark algorithm, Apriori, even on relatively sparse data. On data that is more densely-populated, which poses the greatest challenges for all methods, the performance gain is significant. We have also shown that using a simple ordering heuristic gives rise to a further improvement in performance.

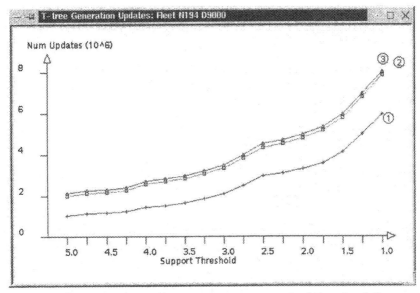

Graph 6 *Support count updates* `Fleet.N194.D900`: *(1) ordered P-tree to T-tree, (2) unordered Apriori-TFP, (3) unordered hash tree*

We observe, again, that our approach is generic in that the data structures we have described can be used as a basis for many other algorithms, and we expect that many of these will be susceptible to similar performance improvement. Investigating these algorithms is one avenue of research we are currently pursuing. A second is to further explore the use of the ordering heuristic. In particular we are investigating strategies which after ordering, partition the P-tree into regions (of different density of population) and apply different counting algorithms to each. We anticipate that hybrid strategies of this kind can give further performance gains, partly by reducing the size of partitions to a more efficiently-manageable level.

References

[1] Agarwal, R., Aggarwal, C. and Prasad, V. Depth First Generation of Long Patterns. Proc ACM KDD 2000 Conference, Boston, 108-118, 2000.

[2] Agrawal, R. Imielinski, T. Swami, A. Mining Association Rules Between Sets of Items in Large Databases. SIGMOD-93, 207-216. May 1993.

[3] Agrawal, R. and Srikant, R. Fast Algorithms for Mining Association Rules. Proc 20th VLDB Conference, Santiago, 487-499. 1994

[4] Bayardo, R.J. Efficiently Mining Long Patterns from Databases. Proc ACM-SIGMOD Int Conf on Management of Data, 85-93, 1998

[5] Bayardo, R.J., Agrawal, R. and Gunopolos, D. Constraint-based rule mining in large, dense databases. Proc 15th Int Conf on Data Engineering, 1999

[6] Brin, S., Motwani. R., Ullman, J.D. and Tsur, S. Dynamic itemset counting and implication rules for market basket data. Proc ACM SIGMOD Conference, 255-256, 1997

[7] Goulbourne, G., Coenen, F. and Leng, P. Algorithms for Computing Association Rules using a Partial-Support Tree. J. Knowledge-Based Systems 13 (2000), 141-149. (also Proc ES'99.)

[8] Han, J., Pei, J. and Yin, Y. Mining Frequent Patterns without Candidate Generation. Proc ACM SIGMOD 2000 Conference, 1-12, 2000.

[9] Rymon, R. Search Through Systematic Set Enumeration. Proc. 3rd Int'l Conf. on Principles of Knowledge Representation and Reasoning, 1992, 539-550.

[10] Savasere, A., Omiecinski, E. and Navathe, S. An efficient algorithm for mining association rules in large databases. Proc 21st VLDB Conference, Zurich, 432-444. 1995.

[11] Toivonen, H. Sampling large databases for association rules. Proc 22nd VLDB Conference, 134-145. Bombay, 1996.

[12] UCI Machine Learning Repository Content Summary. http://www.ics.uci.edu/ mlearn/MLSummary.html.

[13] Zaki, M.J., Parthasarathy, S. Ogihara, M. and Li, W. New Algorithms for fast discovery of association rules. Technical report 651, University of Rochester, Computer Science Department, New York. July 1997.

ADANNET: Automatic Design of Artificial Neural Networks by Evolutionary Techniques

D. Barrios, A. Carrascal, D. Manrique, J. Rios
Artificial Intelligence Dpt., Connectionist AI Group
Facultad de Informática, Universidad Politécnica de Madrid, Spain

Abstract

This paper describes a new evolutionary system known as ADANNET for the generation and adaptation of feed-forward artificial neural networks to solve any problem presented as a set of training patterns. ADANNET synthesizes the structure of the network that better solves the given problem and, parallelly, accomplishes the training process. Both processes use new techniques based in genetic algorithms. *Basic-architectures codification method* and a specialized crossover operator (the Hamming crossover) for this type of codification have been developed to solve the neural architecture design process, while a new a new crossover operator for real-coded genetic algorithms (*mathematical morphology crossover*) has been designed for adapting the network. Several experiments have been made to show that ADANNET obtains the smallest neural architecture that solves the given problem.

1 Introduction

The main research areas in artificial intelligence are, at the present, related to the design of auto-adaptive systems, which are able to transform themselves to solve different kind of problems [1].

Artificial neural networks (ANN) have arisen a great interest during the last years due to their properties of learning by examples, generalising to unseen data and noise filtering. These features make neural networks applicable to a wide variety of real-world tasks [2] [3]. However, the performance optimization of existing neural paradigms [4] has evolved very slowly. This is particularly true of issues such as structuring network connectivity, deciding the number of nodes in hidden layers, and setting the terms in the weight adjustment algorithm. One of the most important reasons why such advances are difficult to come by is the size and complexity of the design space available in even the best understood network models. As a result, the design of a neural network structure for a particular application is typically governed by heuristics even for the most expert practitioners [5].

To solve these problems, several approaches have been studied using different search and optimization techniques to choose the best neural architecture to solve a given problem and to speed up the training process. Some studies are focused on how model selection in neural networks can be guided by statistical procedures such as hypothesis tests, information criteria and cross validation [6], while others are based on employing linear programming [7]. The main disadvantage of such methods is their high computational cost.

A number of researchers have identified the potential synergy between genetic algorithms (GA) and artificial neural networks and have begun to combine them in various ways. Thus, there are works related to the genetic adaptation of the internal structure of the network [8]. Genetic algorithms have been used to replace completely the network learning method [9], while other researchers make this replacement in a partial way [10]. For any evolutive optimization approach chosen, the way the neural networks that make up the search space encoded is the crucial step to accomplish the task of designing them automatically. In the same way, best results in training artificial neural networks with genetic algorithms are obtained when real numbers codification, representing the weights, is employed.

There have been several approaches to obtain an efficient codification of ANNs. The first of these is the direct binary encoding of network configuration [11] where each bit determines the presence or absence of a single connection. This approach presents two major problems: first, convergence performance is degraded as the size of the network increases because the search space is much larger. Second, direct encoding methods can not prevent illegal points in the search space. Other approaches to encode ANNs are based on the binary codification of grammars [12] that describe the architecture of the network and prevent the codification of illegal neural architectures. The problem here is that one bit variation in a string results in a totally different network. This fact degrades the convergence process of the genetic algorithm that uses this codification.

There exist different techniques to train artificial neural networks with real-coded genetic algorithms: Radcliffe's flat crossover [13] chooses parameters for an offspring by uniformly picking parameter values between (inclusively) the two parents parameter values. Later, to avoid the premature convergence problems existing in this operator, BLX-α was proposed [14], which uniformly picks values that lie between two points that contain the two parents and it may extend equally on either side of the interval defined by the parents. This new method, however, is very slow when approximating to the optimum because the extension of the interval defined by the parents is determined by a static user specified parameter α fixed at the running start. Other important crossover technique for real-coded genetic algorithms is the UNDX [15]that can optimize functions by generating the offspring using the normal distribution defined by three parents. The problem here is the high computational cost required to calculate the normal distribution.

This paper presents a new system for design a train automatically artificial neural networks by genetic algorithms known as ADANNET. This systems employs a different approach of binary encoding for the design of neural architectures. This codification method, called basic-architectures codification method, is based on the definition of an Abelian semi-group with neutral element in the set neural architectures. It avoids illegal networks and needs very short encoding length, being optimum when encoding neural networks with one output. The proposed codification encodes any kind of generalised feed-forward one hidden-layer neural networks. A specialized binary crossover operator to work with the basic-architectures codification method has been also designed: the Hamming crossover (HX). This operator has better performance in searching for neural architectures than the other crossover operators.

ADANNET system trains, parallelly, the artificial neural networks obtained in the previous design step, employing real-coded genetic algorithms. To do so, a new crossover operator has been designed and called mathematical morphology crossover (MMX). It has the important feature that extends adaptively (depending on the progenitors values) the interval schemata defined by the parents, from which the offspring is obtained. The mathematical morphology crossover gives a new interpretation to the morphological gradient operation, very used in digitalized image segmentation [16] [17], to get an on-line genetic diversity measure. This measure increases the convergence speed of the genetic algorithm in the training process while avoids local optima.

2 ADANNET System

ADANNET system gives as a result the minimum neural network that is able to obtain a mean square error, which is less than a value previously established for a set of training patterns given as the system's input. The structure of ADANNET consists of two modules that work parallelly (figure 1). The *neural architecture design module* employs a genetic algorithm with the basic-architectures codification method to search for the optimum neural network that solves a problem. The *training module* receives the neural architecture to be evaluated after a decodification process. This module consists on a real-coded genetic algorithm that employs the mathematical morphology crossover to minimize the network mean square error, from which the fitness is calculated.

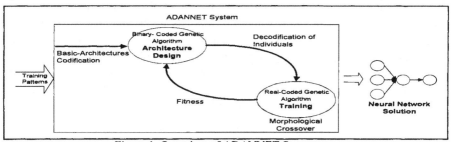

Figure 1. Overview of ADANNET Structure.

2.1 Genetic Design: Basic-Architectures Codification

Definition 2.1: A generalised feed-forward network *r* with I input neurons, H units in only one hidden layer and O output neurons is defined as $r \subset (\breve{I} \times \breve{И}) \cup (\breve{И} \times \breve{O}) \cup (\breve{I} \times \breve{O})$ whereas $\breve{I}=\{i_1, i_2, ..., i_I\}$ denotes the set of I input neurons, $\breve{И}=\{h_1, h_2, ..., h_H\}$ is the set of H units in the hidden layer and $\breve{O}=\{o_1, o_2, ..., o_O\}$ as the set of O output neurons. If $(a,b) \in r$ then the neuron a is connected to the neuron b. The cartesian product of input and hidden neurons is $\breve{I} \times \breve{И}$ that represents the set of all possible connections from the input layer to the hidden layer, $\breve{И} \times \breve{O}$ is the set of all connections from the hidden layer to the output and $\breve{I} \times \breve{O}$ represents the set of direct connections from the input to the output.

The set of all generalised feed-forward neural networks with a maximum of I input neurons, H hidden units and O output units is denoted by $R_{I,H,O}$. There is a special case, the null ANN, defined as $n=\varnothing$, where there are not connected neurons.

From the set of all existing neural networks $R_{I,H,O}$, we are only interested in the subset $V_{I,H,O}\subseteq R_{I,H,O}$ of all valid ANNs as $V_{I,H,O}$ only contains points that can solve a problem where illegal ANNs are not included.

Definition 2.2: A neural network $v\in R_{I,H,O}$ with $v\subset(\breve{I}x\breve{H})\cup(\breve{H}x\breve{O})\cup(\breve{I}x\breve{O})$ is called valid neural network, and so $v\in V_{I,H,O}$, if and only if for all $(i_r,h_s)\in\breve{I}x\breve{H}\cap v$ there exits $o_p\in\breve{O}$ such that $(h_s,o_p)\in\breve{H}x\breve{O}\cap v$ and, reciprocally, for all $(h_s,o_p)\in\breve{H}x\breve{O}\cap v$ there exists $i_r\in\breve{I}$ such that $(i_r,h_s)\in\breve{I}x\breve{H}\cap v$. It can be deduced from this definition that the null network $n\in V_{I,H,O}$.

Definition 2.3: Let be v and v' $\in V_{I,H,O}$, the superimposition operation between v and v' is defined as $v\oplus v'=v\cup v'$.

With all of these definitions it is possible to establish that the set $V_{I,H,O}$ of valid ANNs with the operation superimposition $\oplus$ is an Abelian semi-group with neutral element (the null network) $(V_{I,H,O},\oplus)$, which is easy to prove, as $\oplus$ is based on the operation union between two sets. The figure 2 shows an example of this superimposition operation between two valid neural networks.

Definition 2.4: A valid neural network $b\in V_{I,H,O}$ is called *basic neural network*, and so, $b\in B_{I,H,O}$ if and only if $\#b\leq 2$ and if $\#b=2$ then $b=\{(i_r,h_s),(h_s,o_p)\}$ with $(i_r,h_s)\in\breve{I}x\breve{H}$ and $(h_s,o_p)\in\breve{H}x\breve{O}$. $\#b$ denotes the cardinal of the set b. The subset $B_{I,H,O}\subseteq V_{I,H,O}$ of all basic ANNs has important features because they allow building any valid ANNs from these basic structures. Since basic neural networks are also valid neural networks, if $\#b=0$ then $b=\varnothing$, which corresponds to the null net. If $\#b=1$ then $b=\{(i_r,o_p)\}$, with $(i_r,o_p)\in(\breve{I}x\breve{O})$; b has only one direct connection from the input to the output layer. If $\#b=2$, then there is one connection from the input to one hidden unit, and other from this unit to the output neuron. The figure 3 shows the five basic neural networks of set $B_{2,1,1}$.

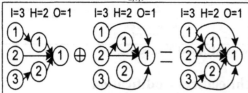

Figure 2. The superimposition operation.

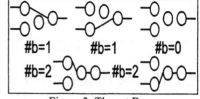

Figure 3. The set $B_{2,1,1}$.

Definition 2.5: Let be $v\in V_{I,H,O}$ and $B=\{b_1,...,b_k\}\subseteq B_{I,H,O}$. If $v=b_1\oplus...\oplus b_k$ then B is called *decomposition* of v.

Theorem 2.1: $\forall v\in V_{I,H,O}$, there exists, at least, one subset $B=\{b_1,...,b_k\}\subseteq B_{I,H,O}$ such that B is a decomposition of v. In other words, any ANN in $V_{I,H,O}$ can be obtained from superimposition of elements taken from $B_{I,H,O}$.

Proof: Let be $v\in V_{I,H,O}$ with $v\subset(\breve{I}x\breve{H})\cup(\breve{H}x\breve{O})\cup(\breve{I}x\breve{O})$. $\breve{I}x\breve{O}\cap v$ represents the set of direct connections from the input to the output neurons, so $\forall (i_r,o_p)\in\breve{I}x\breve{O}\cap v$, $\{(i_r,o_p)\}\in B_{I,H,O}$, because each $b_i=\{(i_r,o_p)\}$ is a basic neural network with $\#b_i=1$. As it was seen in the definition of valid neural networks (Definition 2.2), each pair of sets $b=\{(i_r,h_s),(h_s,o_p)\}$ is also a basic neural network with #b=2. The decomposition of the null net $v=\varnothing$ is itself. So v may be expressed as the superimposition of all basic neural networks in the way $\{(i_r,o_p)\}$ such that $(i_r,o_p)\in \check{I}x\check{O}\cap v$ with the superimposition of all basic neural networks in the way $\{(i_r,h_s),(h_s,o_p)\}$ such that $(i_r,h_s)\in \check{I}x\check{H}\cap v$ and $(h_s,o_p)\in \check{H}x\check{O}\cap v$. ∎

Corollary 2.1: If $B=\{b_1, ...,b_k\}\subseteq B_{I,H,O}$ and $B'=\{b'_1, ...,b'_k\}\subseteq B_{I,H,O}$ are decompositions of $v\in V_{I,H,O}$ then $B\cup B'$ is a decomposition of v.

Proof: $B\cup B'=\{b_1,...,b_k,b'_1,...,b'_k\}$. From the definition of decomposition $v=b_1\oplus...\oplus b_k$ and $v= b'_1\oplus...\oplus b'_k$. $\forall\ b_i\in B\cup B'$ $b_i=\{(i_r,o_p)\}$ with $(i_r,o_p)\in \check{I}x\check{O}\cap v$, or $b_i=\{(i_r,h_s),(h_s,o_p)\}$ with $(i_r,h_s)\in \check{I}x\check{H}\cap v$ and $(h_s,o_p)\in\ \check{H}x\check{O}\cap v$, so $v=b_1\oplus...\oplus b_k\oplus b'_1\oplus...\oplus b'_k$ and thus, $B\cup B'$ is another decomposition of v.

Definition 2.6: $\forall\ v\in V_{I,H,O}$, the decomposition $M\subseteq B_{I,H,O}$ is called *maximum decomposition* if and only if $M=B_1\cup B_2\cup...\cup B_n$, being $B_1,...,B_n\subseteq B_{I,H,O}$ all possible decompositions of v.

Remark 2.1: From Definition 2.6, it is clear that every $v\in V_{I,H,O}$ has one and only one maximum decomposition.

2.1.1 The Cardinal of Set $B_{I,H,O}$

The cardinal of set $B_{I,H,O}$, #$B_{I,H,O}$, subset of $V_{I,H,O}$, is now calculated. Let us consider first, the case of basic ANNs with no hidden units, #b=1: There is only one direct connection from one of the inputs to one of the outputs. So there is a total of I·O ANNs. If #b=2 then there are not direct connections, only one output is connected to one input throughout one hidden neuron, existing I·H·O possible combinations. Then, the cardinal of $B_{I,H,O}$, adding the null net, #b=0, is: #$B_{I,H,O}$ = I·O·(H+1)+1.

2.1.2 Binary Codification of Set $V_{I,H,O}$

It has been seen how it is possible to build any valid ANN from some basic structures called basic ANNs, and the existence of exactly I·O(H+1)+1 basic neural networks. The null net is unable to build more complex valid neural networks but itself because it is the neutral element in the structure defined. However, there are other I·O(H+1) basic neural networks that can be superimposed to build more complex structures. Thus, the set of basic neural networks excluding the null net: $\{b_1,...,b_{I·O(H+1)}\}$ can be combined in $2^{I·O(H+1)}$ different ways to build valid neural networks. So, there exists a one-to-one correspondence between the set of all possible decompositions of all valid ANNs and the set $V^b_{I,H,O}$ of all binary strings that encode each decomposition of valid ANNs.

With all these premises, the codification of all the points in $V_{I,H,O}$ will be based on the codification of the set of basic ANNs $B_{I,H,O}=\{b_0,b_1, b_2, ..., b_i, ..., b_{I·O(H+1)}\}$ with binary strings of I·O(H+1) bit length as following:

$b_0 \rightarrow$ 0, 0, ..., 0, ..., 0; The null net.

$b_i \rightarrow$ 0, 0, ..., 1, ..., 0; 1 is set in the ith position.

$$\cdots$$
$$b_{I \cdot O(H+1)} \rightarrow 0, 0, ..., 0, ..., 1$$

$b_0, b_1, ..., b_{I \cdot O(H+1)}$ may be ordered in any way, but from now on should preserve the same sequence that has been chosen. The null net b_0 is always encoded as a string of $I \cdot O(H+1)$ zeros. Once all basic neural networks have been encoded, it is possible to build any valid ANN included in $V_{I,H,O}$ by applying the binary-OR operator ($\vee$) to the encoded basic nets; this permits obtaining all points included in the set $V^b_{I,H,O}$.

Once the table of correspondences is stored, as shown in the example of figure 4 between basic neural networks and their binary codifications, it is easy to encode any ANN $v \in V_{I,H,O}$ by simply calculating one of the possible decompositions of v and, starting from a string of $I \cdot O(H+1)$ zeros, switching the ith bit to 1 if the ith basic neural net of the table appears in the decomposition of v. Figure 4 shows how to encode an ANN $v \in V_{2,1,1}$.

When this codification is used, the set $V^b_{I,H,O}$ has two important features: first, the search space defined with the codification proposed yields only possible solutions to the problem, that is, there are not illegal ANNs. Second, there exist several binary strings that codify the same valid ANN because the set $V^b_{I,H,O}$ encodes the set of all decompositions of all valid neural networks and, as it was shown in Theorem 2.1, any valid ANN has at least one decomposition. This feature is very desirable when working with genetic algorithms to find faster the ANN solution because, in general, several codifications of the solution are spread in the search space.

2.2 Genetic Training of Artificial Neural Networks: MMX

Mathematical morphology crossover has been designed to work on real-coded genetic algorithms. This is the case when training artificial neural networks where weights and biases are coded by the individuals of the population. A particular gene is a real number that represents the weight of a connection of the network or a bias.

Let be $D_\Re$ a point in the search space, defined by the string $s=(a_0, a_1, ..., a_{l-1})$, where $a_i \in \Re$. This operator works with each gene in the parents independently to obtain the corresponding gene in the two descendants. Let $s_1, ..., s_n$ be an odd number of strings chosen from the actual population to be crossed, the n by l progenitors matrix is defined as:

$$G = \begin{pmatrix} a_{10} & a_{11} & \cdots & a_{1l-1} \\ a_{20} & a_{21} & \cdots & a_{2l-1} \\ \cdots & \cdots & \cdots & \cdots \\ a_{n0} & a_{n1} & \cdots & a_{nl-1} \end{pmatrix} \quad \text{where } s_i = (a_{i0}, a_{i1}, ..., a_{i,l-1}), i = 1, ..., n.$$

The crossover operator works with each column $f_i=(a_{1i}, a_{2i}, ..., a_{ni})$ in matrix G obtaining genes o_i and o_i'. The result of applying the operator to matrix G is, therefore, two new descendants $o = (o_0, o_1, ..., o_{l-1})$ and $o' = (o'_0, o'_1, ..., o'_{l-1})$. The procedure employed by this crossover to generate the new offspring strings o, $o' \in D_\Re$ from the parents $s_1, ..., s_n$ in matrix G is the following:

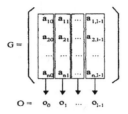

$$G = \begin{pmatrix} a_{10} & a_{11} & \cdots & a_{1,l-1} \\ a_{20} & a_{21} & \cdots & a_{2,l-1} \\ \cdots & \cdots & \cdots & \cdots \\ a_{n0} & a_{n1} & \cdots & a_{n,l-1} \end{pmatrix}$$

$$O = \quad o_0 \quad o_1 \quad \cdots \quad o_{l-1}$$

a./ The morphological gradient operator, $g_b(f_i)$: $D_{f_i} \to \Re$, is applied on each vector f_i, $i = 0, 1, .., l\text{-}1$, with a structuring element b:$D_b \to \Re$ defined as:

$$b(x) = 0, \forall x \in D_b, \ D_b = \{-E(n/2), ..., 0, ..., E(n/2)\},$$

being $E(x)$ the integer part of x; $\quad g_i$ is obtained as the value:

$$g_i = g_b \ (f_i) \ (E(n/2)+1) \quad i \in \{0, 1, ..., l\text{-}1\}$$

Just as the morphology gradient applied to images returns high values when sudden transitions in gray levels values are detected, and low values if the pixels covered by the window (structuring element) are similar; g_i gives a measure of the heterogeneity of gene i in the individuals chosen to be crossed. If value g_i is high, the population is scattered, while if it is low, that means that the values of that gene are converging.

b./ Let φ: $\Re \to \Re$ be a given function. The maximum gene is defined as:

$$g_{imax} = max(f_i) - \varphi(g_i)$$

Likewise, the minimum gene is defined as:

$$g_{imin} = min(f_i) + \varphi(g_i)$$

Those values determine the crossover interval $C_i = [g_{imin}, g_{imax}]$, from where the desired value o_i is randomly taken. The ith gene for the other descendant o'_i is obtained from inside the crossover interval using the following formula:

$$o'_i = g_{imax} + g_{imin} - o_i$$

The objective is now to obtain a rule that allows to dynamically control the range of the crossover interval to avoid falling in local minima and to get a high convergence speed. When the individuals to be crossed are diverse (which implies a high value of the gradient) the crossover interval is made narrower according to the values $max(f_i)$ and $min(f_i)$, thus allowing to explore its interior searching for the optimum much faster. On the other hand, if the individuals to be crossed are very similar (gradient close to zero), which means that the population is converging, then it is advisable to expand the interval $[min(f_i),max(f_i)]$ to allow the exploration of new points in the domain, thus avoiding the possible convergence to a local optimum.

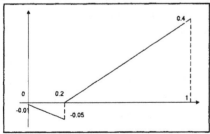

$$\varphi(g_i) = \begin{cases} -(0.2 \cdot g_i) - 0.01 & \text{if} \ \ g_i \le 0.2 \\ (0.5 \cdot g_i) - 0.1 & \text{otherwise} \end{cases}$$

Figure 4. Function φ used by the mathematical morphology crossover.

This possibility of expanding or narrowing the crossover interval depending on the value of the gradient g_i, is given by the function φ, which is shown in figure 4. It is defined in domain $[0,1]$, so the population had to be normalized in the same range. This function only performs one multiplication, so its application in the crossover operator described is very efficient, as it allows the generation of a new individual with only 1 multiplications. $\varphi(g_i)$ is positive when gi is strictly greater than 0.2, making the crossover interval narrower in this case. The greatest narrowing takes place in $\varphi(1)=0.4$. On the other hand $\varphi(g_i)$ takes negative values if $g_i \leq 0.2$, that is, the crossover interval is expanded, and the maximum expansion is produced in $\varphi(0.2)= -0.05$. Starting from this point the function takes values each time smaller as the gradient value diminishes, until reaching value -0.01 in $g_i=0$. Otherwise the crossover interval would be too much wide compared with the interval $[g_{imin}, g_{imax}]$.

3 The Hamming Crossover

The basic-architectures codification method has the following feature: given a binary string that represents a valid neural architecture, the variation of one bit in such string results in a very similar neural architecture. These two architectures are only differenciated by the basic neural architecture represented by the modified bit. Thus, only one or connections and one neuron have changed. This feature is very important when working with genetic algorithms because its local search capability is potentiated. The Hamming crossover has been especially designed to make use of this characteristic.

The Hamming crossover works with binary strings of length l, and it is based on the definition of Hamming distance [18], $d_H(s,s')$, between two binary strings $s=(a_0, a_1, ..., a_{l-1})$ and $s'=(a_0', a_1', ..., a_{l-1}')$, where $a_i, a_j \in \{0,1\}$. From the set $G=\{s_1, ..., s_n\}$ of progenitor strings, which have been chosen from the actual population, two new descendants are obtained, o and o', through the application of the following steps:

a./ The maximum Hamming distance, h, between two progenitor strings is calculated: if $s_{min}, s_{max} \in G$ are such that $d_H(s_{min}, s_{max}) \geq d_H(s_i, s_j) \ \forall \ s_i, s_j \in G$, then $h=d_H(s_{min}, s_{max})$.

b./ The genetic diversity measure of the population, g, is calculated:
$$g = \frac{h}{l}, g \in [0,1].$$

c./ The offspring is obtained: as it happened in the case of MMX, the genetic diversity measure, g, guides the behavior of the Hamming crossover adaptatively. If g takes values near to zero, the genetic diversity of the population is increased to avoid falling in local minima. In the other hand, if g takes larger values, then the local search capability is increased by generating new strings *similar* to the progenitors in terms of Hamming distance. This feature is got by employing the function φ, as it was used in the mathematical morphology crossover and shown in figure 2. Function φ gives the maximum number of bits, n, to be modified in the two descendants using the following formula:

$$n = E[l \cdot \varphi(g)]$$

Given $h = d_H(s_{min}, s_{max})$, the *minimum strings set*, denoted by G_{min}, is defined as the set of binary strings at a Hamming distance $|n|$ from s_{min}, and $h - n$ from s_{max}:

$$G_{min} = \{s_1, ..., s_m\}, d_H(s_{min}, s_i) = |n| \text{ y } d_H(s_{max}, s_i) = h - n, \forall s_i \in G_{min}$$

In the same way, the *maximum strings set*, denoted by G_{max}, is defined as the set of binary strings at a Hamming distance $|n|$ from s_{max} and $h - n$ from s_{min}:

$$G_{max} = \{s_1', ..., s_m'\}, d_H(s_{max}, s_i') = |n| \text{ y } d_H(s_{min}, s_i') = h - n, \forall s_i' \in G_{max}$$

The so defined sets G_{min} and G_{max} assure that:

$$\forall s_i \in G_{min}, \forall s_i' \in G_{max}, d_H(s_i, s_i') = h - 2n$$

Let be $m \in \{0, ..., h-2n\}$, the *offspring set*, $O_m = \{o_1, ..., o_p\}$, is defined as the sett of binary strings such that:
1. $\forall s \in G_{min}, \forall s' \in G_{max}: d_H(o_i, s) = m, d_H(o_i, s') = h-2n-m$, with $o_i \in O_m$, or,
2. $\forall s \in G_{min}, \forall s' \in G_{max}: d_H(o_i, s) = h-2n-m, d_H(o_i, s') = m$, with $o_i \in O_m$.

Given the offspring set $O_m = \{o_1, ..., o_p\}$, the *symmetric offspring set*, $O_m' = \{o_1', ..., o_q'\}$, is defined as the set of binary strings such that:
1. If for any string $s'' \in G_{min}, d_H(o_i, s'') = m$, with $o_i \in O_m$, then $\forall s \in G_{min}, \forall s' \in G_{max}: d_H(o_i', s) = h-2n-m, d_H(o_i', s') = m, \forall o_i' \in O_m'$.
2. If for any string $s \in G_{min}, d_H(o_i, s) = h-2n-m$, with $o_i \in O_m$, then $\forall s \in G_{min}, \forall s' \in G_{max}: d_H(o_i', s) = m, d_H(o_i', s') = h-2n-m, \forall o_i' \in O_m'$.

The Hamming crossover operator randomly chooses an offspring set O_m, from which one of its strings, o, is taken as the first descendant individual. Then, the symmetric offspring set, O_m', is calculated, from which one of its strings, o', is randomly selected as the second descendant individual. These two descendants constitute the result given by this operator.

4 Results

The experimental results accomplished to illustrate ADANNET system are related to the convergence speed, size of the networks given as solution and probability of falling in local optima. These tests are sorted in three types:
1. The mathematical morphology crossover, employed in the training module, has been compared to gradient backpropagation method with momentum in terms of convergence speed and probability ob being trapped in local minima.
2. The basic-architectures codification method with the Hamming crossover, employed in the architectures design module, has been compared to the direct and grammar codification methods referred to the speed of convergence and size of the networks given as solutions.
3. The perfomance of the Hamming crossover operator is compared to the generalized crossover, one point, two points and uniform crossovers [19]. In all cases, the basic architectures method has been used.

4.1 Results with the Mathematical Morphology Crossover

Training a full-connected 2-4-1 feedforward neural network with MMX has been tested to solve the two-spirals problem. This is one of the standard benchmarks for neural network learning algorithms, which for each 400 training points belonging to one of two interwined spirals, the network must tell in which spiral a given point belongs to. This is a hard task for backpropagation due to its complicated error landscape, and enable us to test the high speed of convergence of MMX when training neural networks without being trapped in any local optima. Each of the real numbers of the individuals in the population, which represent the weights of the connections of the network, are randomly generated in the range of ±15.0 at the initialisation of the genetic algorithm. The size of population is 30, which is quite small, allowing higher efficiency in computational terms. To evaluate the fitness of each individual, feedforward computation is performed by presenting the patterns of one epoch. The fitness of an individual is the mean square error (MSE). MMX is performed by taking five parents from the population by the Roulette-Wheel method, and obtaining an offspring of two new individuals that replace the worst two networks of the population. Mutation probability has been set to 0% in order to show better the performance of MMX. Convergence speed and performance of MMX in training neural networks has been compared to backpropagation with momentum (BPM) in terms of the number of floating point operations (FLOPS) employed by each method to reach the optimal solution.

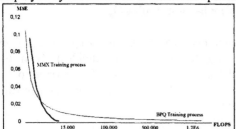

MSE	Averaged FLOPS (BPQ / MMX)	Failed Trials (BPQ /MMX)
10^{-3}	1,2E6 / 12.235	53% / 0%
10^{-4}	1,5E6 / 15.085	57% / 0,2%

Figure 5. Comparison between MMX and BPQ in terms of speed of convergence.

Table 1. Averaged number of FLOPS and failed trials occurred to solve the two-spirals problem after 1000 trials.

For each learning method, we ran 1000 trials, and the average value of the number of FLOPS employed to reach a MSE of 10^{-3} and 10^{-4} was computed to compare the speed of convergence and stability of each method. The results are shown in table 1, where it can be seen from the second column the averaged number of FLOPS needed to train the neural network by each of the two learning approaches. MMX is much better than BPM reaching a MSE of 10^{-3} and 10^{-4}. Third column of table 1 shows the number of failed trials. MMX never fails in any local minima as it happens to BPQ when the MSE to be reached is 10^{-3}. MMX can not reach an MSE of 10^{-4} only the 0,2% of the cases executed, while this happens the 57% when BPM is run.

Figure 5 shows typical convergence curves of the evolution of the MSE in the training process using both MMX and BPM. It can be seen how MMX convergence is much faster than BPM even when approaching to the optimum.

4.2 Results with the Basic-Architectures Codification

ADANNET systems employs the basic-architectures codification method to design neural architectures. The coder/decoder problem has been studied to show the speed of convergence and the size of the neural architectures obtained as solutions to these problems when the codification method proposed is used in comparison to the direct and grammar encoding methods. Similar genetic settings have been chosen for the three different encoding methods. Thus, we used a proportional reproduction strategy in which reproduction probability is decided according to the fitness of each individual. The probability of mutation has been set to 5%, and the Hamming crossover operator has been used with a probability of 60%. For each experiment we ran 100 trials of 1000 generations and the mean value calculated. The fitness of each neural network of the population is calculated as:

$$f = MSE_{It} \frac{C_a}{C_t} \tag{1}$$

being C_a the number of connections existing in the actual neural network and C_t the maximum number of connections allowed by the codification. MSE_{it} is the mean square error given by the network after *it* learning iterations have been run. Mathematical morphology crossover have been employed as the learning algorithm.

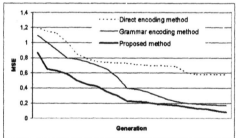

	Direct encoding	Grammar encoding	Proposed Method
4-0-4	42%	58%	74%
4-1-4	41%	32%	15%
4-2-4	17%	10%	11%

Figure 6. Convergence process in the coder / decoder problem.

Table 2. Final solutions of the coder /decoder

Figure 6 shows the results of the experiments for this problem. The averaged MSE after it=50,000 learning iterations of the ten best individuals of the population is plotted against the generation. The three lines show this evolution for the three compared methods when encoding architectures of a maximum of four input and output units and up to 8 hidden neurons. Apart from the fact that the proposed method clearly outperforms the other methods, it is important to notice that, in these experiments, the evolution line of our model tends to converge much faster after several iterations have occurred. The table 2 shows the final solutions given by each method. From this table, it can be observed that the proposed method not only converges faster, but also gets smaller neural networks. Using the proposed method, architectures without hidden neurons (4-0-4) are obtained in the 74% of the executions. Obtaining small neural networks is very desirable when they are working as part of an intelligent system to solve the problem they are designed to.

4.3 Results with the Hamming Crossover

The Hamming crossover operator is used by the architecture design module to increase the convergence speed and to avoid falling in local optima with respect to other crossover operators when basic-architectures codification is employed. Test results are shown in solving the coder / decoder problem, encoding architectures of a maximum of four input and output units and up to 8 hidden neurons. The genetic parameters are similar the ones used in previous section. Figure 5 shows the convergence process of ADDANET towards the optimum neural network using Hamming, one point, two points, uniform and generalized crossover operators. For each of them, the averaged fitness (formula 1) after it=5,000 learning iterations of the ten best individuals of the population is plotted against the generation. As it can be seen, the application of the Hamming crossover operator, not only obtains the optimum neural network, but also it takes less time than the other operators.

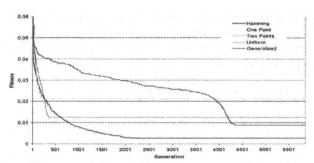

Figure 5. Convergence process in the coder / decoder problem using different crossovers.

	Hamming	One point	Two points	Uniform	Generalized
4-0-4	74%	0%	0%	0%	38%
4-1-4	15%	0%	0%	0%	30%
4-2-4	11%	0%	0%	6%	18%
4-3-4	0%	0%	0%	13%	12%
4-4-4	0%	19%	23%	26%	2%
Others	0%	81%	77%	55%	0%

Table 3. Final solutions of the coder /decoder for each of the five crossover operators.

Table 3 reports the neural networks obtained with each of five crossover operators used with the basic-architectures codification method. The Hamming crossover clearly outperforms the other operators. 84% of the executions run with the Hamming crossover gave as a result 4-0-4 and 4-1-4 neural networks. The generalized crossover, which gave second better results, obtains the two best architectures the 68% of the cases.

5 Discussion

ADDANET is a system capable of designing and training one-hidden layer generalized feedforward neural networks. The basic-architectures codification method proposed to be used in the architecture design module allows a neural network topology to be represented through elemental structures known as basic neural architectures. This approach, in contrast to grammar and cellular encoding exhibits several advantages. Firstly, it provides a clear representation of the structure of the networks encoded. The proposed scheme requires short codification length, being the optimum when one output neural networks are encoded. This is due, partially, to the fact that illegal neural networks are not codified and so, the search space is smaller. Finally, the proposed approach generates regular patterns, preserving the meaningful subcircuits discovered to improve the networks existing in the population. This is possible because one bit variation of the binary string results in a very similar neural architecture where only one or two connections have been changed. This feature is potentiated by employing the Hamming crossover, which generates the offspring near the progenitors in terms of the definition of Hamming distance, improving the fine local search near the optimum architecture and, this way, increasing the speed of convergence and reducing the size of the networks obtained as solutions.

The training module of the ADANNET system implements real-coded genetic algorithms through the morphological crossover. This operator can be applied on any optimization problem. In particular, it is used by ADANNET to minimize the MSE in the training process of the networks generated by the design module. Morphological gradient operation has been reinterpreted to build this crossover, giving a heterogeneity measure of the population in order to, dynamically, extend or make narrower the interval defined by the parents. This effect balances adequately the exploration and explotation capabilities of the genetic algorithm, allowing high speed searching and avoiding falling in local optima.

6 Conclusions

This paper has presented ADANNET, a system that automatically designs and trains artificial neural networks to solve a problem given as input as a set of training patterns. ADANNET obtains the smallest neural architecture that solves the problem. This feature implies the following: firstly, smaller networks have higher generalization capability than larger ones. Run-time response speed is also higher in small networks because they have less number of processing elements, and finally, it is possible to remove all those input variables that do not affect to the output. In other words, ADANNET accomplishes sensitivity analysis in an indirect way. These features ensure better scalability and the possibility to generate very complex networks for more difficult real-world tasks. In particular, using ADANNET to build automatically an intelligent system based on artificial neural networks for the early diagnosis of breast pathologies is now in progress.

References

1. Konar A.. Artificial Intelligence and Soft Computing. CRC Press, Boca Raton, Florida, 2000
2. Mars P., Chen J.R., Nambiar R. Learning Algorithms: Theory and Applications in Signal Processing, Control and Communications. CRC Press, New York, 1996.
3. Linggard R., Myers D.J., Nightingale C. Neural Networks for Vision, Speech and Natural Languaje. Chapman and Hall, London, 1992.
4. Principe J. C., Euliano N. R., Lefebvre W. C. Neural and adaptive systems, fundamentals through simulations. Wiley & Sons, New York, 2000
5. Manrique D. Neural networks design and new optimization methods by genetic algorithms. PhD thesis, Universidad Politécnica de Madrid, Madrid, 2001.
6. Anders U., Korn O. Model selection in neural networks. Neural Networks 1999; 12:309-323.
7. Sweatman C., Mulgrew B., Gibson G. Two algorithms for neural-network design and training with application to channel equalization. IEEE Transactions on Neural Networks 1998; 9 (3): 533-542
8. Braun H. On optimizing large neural networks (multilayer perceptrons) by learning and evolution. Zeitschrift für Angewandte Mathematik und Mechanik 1996; 76 (1):211-214.
9. Barrios D., Carrascal A., Manrique D., Ríos J.: Neural network training using real-coded genetic algorithms. Proceedings of the 5th Ibero-American Symposium on Pattern Recognition, 2000, pp 337-346, Lisbon, Portugal.
10. Gonzalez J.: A genetic algorithm as the learning procedure for neural networks. International Joint Conference on Neural Networks 1992 (1): 835-840
11. Dorado J. Cooperative Strategies to Select Automatically Training Patterns and Neural Architectures with Genetic Algorithms. PhD Thesis, University of La Coruña, Spain, 1999.
12. Kitano H. Designing neural networks using genetic algorithms with graph generation system. Complex Systems 1990; 4:461-476.
13. Radcliffe N. J. Genetic neural networks on MIMD computers. PhD thesis, University of Edinburgh, Edinburgh, UK, 1990
14. Eshelman L. J., Schaffer J. D. Real-coded genetic algorithms and interval-schemata. Foundations of Genetic Algorithms 1993; 2:187-202
15. Ono I., Kobayashi S. A real-coded genetic algorithm for function optimization using unimodal normal distribution crossover. Proceedings of 7th International Conference on Genetic Algorithms, 1997, pp 246-253
16. Crespo, J. Morphological connected filters and intra-region smoothing for image segmentation. PhD thesis, Georgia Institute of Technology, Atlanta, 1993.
17. D'alotto L. A., Giardina C. R. A unified signal algebra approach to two-dimensional parallel digital signal processing. Marcel Dekker, New York, 1998.
18. Hamming R.W. Error Detecting and Error Correcting Codes. Bell System, Technical Journal 1950; 29:147-160.
19. Michalewicz Z. Genetic Algorithms + Data Structures = Evolution Programs. Springer-Verlag, New York, 1999.

SESSION 2:

MACHINE LEARNING 2 /

CONSTRAINT SATISFACTION

Informed Selection of Filter Examples for Knowledge Refinement

Nirmalie Wiratunga and Susan Craw

School of Computer and Mathematical Sciences
The Robert Gordon University,
St Andrew Street, Aberdeen AB25 1HG, Scotland, UK
Email: nw|smc@scms.rgu.ac.uk

Abstract

Refinement tools aim to incrementally modify knowledge based systems (KBSs) by identifying and repairing faults that are indicated by training examples for which the KBS gives an incorrect solution. These tools generally employ greedy hill climbing to search the space of possible refinements. Typically refinement algorithms are iterative and at each iteration chooses a fix having the best impact on the faulty KBS. This impact is ascertained by an accuracy measure taken over a subset of training examples. An informed selection of examples will help direct the search to useful areas of the refinement search space thus reducing the need to backtrack to previous refinement states. Therefore the availability of a representative set of examples is important for refinement tools. However, in real environments it is often difficult to obtain a large set of examples since each problem-solving task must be labelled with the expert's solution. Even if a large set is available a careful selection of examples will help reduce computational costs. This paper investigates clustering and committee based approaches as a means to select a representative set of examples upon which an accuracy measure can be based. Of those selected only the subset of unlabelled examples requires to be labelled. Experiments in two domains show a reduction in the number of times previous refinements states need to be re-visited. Moreover, this reduction is possible without affecting the accuracy of the final refined KBS.

1 Introduction

Knowledge refinement is incremental learning, where the learning must adapt existing knowledge in a Knowledge-Based System (KBS). Refinement tools aid knowledge engineers by assisting with the knowledge debugging and maintenance phases in the Knowledge-Based Systems development cycle [4, 10, 11]. In common with other learning algorithms, the tasks and the expert's solutions are maintained as training examples. KBS faults are identified when the system's and expert's solution for a given task are inconsistent. This is the primary role of training examples to drive the refinement process. A secondary role is to provide a test bed upon which generated refinements can be ranked by accuracy, thereby identifying the best refinement. We refer to this as the filtering task and the set of examples forming the test bed are the filter examples.

The choice of training examples in each of its refinement roles becomes important when one of the constraints on the refinement process is a limited number of labelled training examples. This is a relatively common problem in a real environment, where labelling many problem-solving tasks with the expert's solution may require significant interaction with a busy expert. Unlabelled training examples can often be generated by using domain knowledge already embodied in the KBS or meta-knowledge [14]. Therefore, unlike the labelling task, generating unlabelled examples does not typically require the expert. Previous work looked at a clustering mechanism as the basis for selecting examples for driving the refinement process [13]. The goal of the work described in this paper concentrates on performing an informed selection of training examples for the filtering task. Selected examples that are unlabelled must subsequently be labelled, thereby reducing the demand on the expert.

The problem of unavailability of labelled training examples and sample selection of relevant examples from a set of unlabeled examples falls under the paradigm of active learning and more specifically, selective sampling. We adopt the common approach of partitioning the available examples into clusters [6]. For this purpose we exploit the relationship between the examples and how they are solved by the faulty KBS. As a result our clusters will contain examples that trigger similar problem solving behaviour in the KBS. These clusters are further exploited to identify examples that are affected by proposed refinements with the aim of identifying a representative set of filter examples. We have found the cluster based selection approach to be effective but computationally costly. A different approach exploiting the disagreement amongst generated refined KBSs is introduced as a means to select a sample of filter examples. With both approaches we have developed heuristics that identify those examples that are most likely to be affected by the proposed refinements and thus are good candidates upon which the accuracy ranking can be based.

Section 2 introduces iterative refinement by describing the process undertaken by a particular family of refinement tools. Details of the filtering task itself is presented in Section 3. The cluster based and committee based filter example selection heuristics appear in Sections 4 and 5. Experimental results from evaluating the selection heuristics on two problem domains are presented in Section 6 followed by conclusions in Section 7.

2 Refinement with KRUSTtools

The KRUSTWorks project has developed a generic knowledge refinement framework. Given a specific rule-base shell, this framework is used to generate a refinement tool, a KRUSTTool, by re-using core refinement modules [4]. Incremental refinement is triggered when fault evidence is provided by labelled training examples. A labelled training example e is a task-solution pair $\langle [f_1, \ldots, f_m], goal \rangle$; the observables $f_1, \ldots, f_m$ are the facts that initialise the problem-solving task, and its solution $goal$ is the example's label acquired from the expert. The KRUSTTool's refinement process is iterative with labelled train-

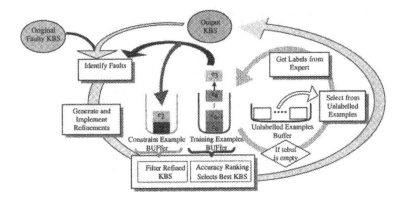

Figure 1: The KRUSTTool Process.

ing examples $e_1, \ldots, e_n$, utilized one at a time (Figure 1). The input KBS for each iteration is the best refined output KBS from the previous iteration, or the original faulty KBS in the first iteration. The training examples buffer (tebuf) contains labelled examples that are yet to be used by the KRUSTTool. For each iteration, the top example in tebuf is chosen as the refinement example to drive that refinement cycle. If the refinement example is correctly solved by the input KBS then refinement is not required, otherwise the fault evidence is employed to allocate blame. The refinement algorithm then identifies various ways by which the required target solution can be attained and generates several potential refinements and implements them as refined KBSs. Once used, the refinement example is then transferred into the constraint examples buffer (cebuf), which is simply the buffer that keeps track of examples previously solved by the KRUSTTool. The refined KBSs are then subjected to a filtering process with the aim of rejecting those less promising. Any remaining refined KBSs are ranked by accuracy on the tebuf, and the refined KBS with the highest accuracy is the output KBS for this iteration.

With learning algorithms it is important that training examples are selected with its usage in mind this is also true with knowledge refinement systems. Selecting examples for the accuracy ranking is an important task, because *good* selection criteria will help guide the KRUSTTool to promising parts of the refinement search space. Notice that active selection is initiated only when tebuf is empty (provided that expert interaction is possible). However it makes sense to enable active selection for the accuracy ranking task as well so that filter example selection can be focused on the filtering role. Ensuring that the tool has access to filter examples that help identify the best refined KBS will result in improved accuracy of the final output KBS thereby improving overall effectiveness. Improving efficiency involves reducing the need to re-visit previous refinement states thereby reducing the number of refinement iterations and considerable savings on computational costs.

3 Active Accuracy Filter

The KRUSTTool's refinement algorithm employs the *Consistency Filter* to ensures that consistency is maintained with previously solved examples in cebuf [12]. When all refined KBSs fail to pass the consistency filter the KRUST-Tool will backtrack to a previous refinement state, selecting the next best refined KBS that was rejected then. When two or more refined KBSs successfully pass the consistency filter the KRUSTTool must select the best one. Selecting the best KBS involves an *Accuracy Filter* that makes judgments about the quality of proposed refinements based on accuracy rankings. The difficulty with the *Accuracy Filter* is in identifying a relevant subset of examples upon which the ranking can be based. An obvious strategy is to rank refined KBSs on the accuracy over labelled examples in tebuf. Obvious disadvantages in such a scheme include: high processing costs when tebuf is large; insufficient evidence for judgment when tebuf is small; and duplication bias, where a large number of similar examples may incorrectly suggest high (or low) accuracy. Even if the number of training examples in tebuf is not too extreme, using all training examples is not sensible as proposed refinements may have affected only a subset of these examples. Needless to say, using unaffected examples for judgment purposes will not contribute additional information towards ascertaining whether a proposed refinement is *good* or bad, but instead will increase processing costs. Moreover, confining the role of filtering to just labelled examples may mean that other relevant unlabelled examples are not able to influence this ranking.

The functionality of the accuracy filter needs to be extended to one that is able to actively select (from both labelled and unlabelled) relevant examples that are testing of the proposed refined KBSs, we refer to such a filter as the *active accuracy filter*. We aim to incorporate active selection of filter examples in this manner to facilitate: the selection of few yet *good* examples, reducing needless processing and minimising labelling cost; efficiency gains by improved guidance through the space of possible refinements, thereby avoiding local maxima and reducing the need to backtrack; and accuracy gains by moving refinement search to parts of the search space containing more promising refined KBSs. To achieve these goals, the active accuracy filter needs to select examples that are affected by the proposed refinement. *Affected examples* are those examples that as a result of refinement get solved differently; for instance an example previously correctly solved is now incorrectly solved or vice versa; or its solution is reached through a different reasoning path. However, things are more complicated than that, as some of the effects are to be expected while others are not. This means that the active accuracy filter must not only identify affected examples, but select only those examples that should not have been affected the way they have. Additionally, example selection by the active accuracy filter must not be based on techniques that simply compare the system and expert solutions, because active selection of filter examples must also extend to the set of examples where labelling has not yet occurred.

4 Cluster-Based Filter Example Selection

Previous work shows that clustering examples according to the input KBS's problem solving behaviour, enabled the selection of a representative set of refinement examples covering the range of faults in the KBS [13]. Essentially examples that exercise similar parts (or rules) of the KBS are clustered together. Here, we extend this clustering framework to assess changes in problem solving behaviour, before and after the proposed refinement. Changes in problem solving behaviour are captured by analysing changes in cluster membership. Examples that get clustered differently as a result of the implemented refinement are likely to have been affected by the refinement.

---

1. Cluster examples by problem solving behaviour of the input KBS.

2. For each refined KBS that passed the consistency filter:
   (a)   Repeat step 1, but this time based on problem solving behaviour of the refined KBS.
   (b)   Compare example clusters formed with the input KBS to those formed with the refined KBS in step 2(a), analysing changes to cluster membership.
   (c)   Identify those examples with changed cluster membership, noting them as affected examples.

3. Select filter examples from those noted as affected.

Figure 2: Algorithm for the Cluster-Based Approach.

Figure 2 outlines the steps involved in the cluster-based approach. In step 1, labelled (in tebuf) and unlabelled examples are clustered with respect to the input KBS's problem solving behaviour. The example clusters thus formed are compared with example clusters formed according to problem solving behaviour of each refined KBS in step 2. The goal of this comparison is to identify affected examples by analysing changes in cluster membership. However, a refinement can cause significant changes in cluster content thus making the comparison difficult. Therefore, a more tractable method localises the comparison to changes relative to the original cluster in which the refinement example was a member by considering only those changes affecting the cluster from which the refinement example was selected. In step 3, filter example selection heuristics, select from example subsets that are noted as affected.

Figure 3 illustrates a fictitious scenario where 35 examples are clustered based on problem solving behaviour of an input KBS, K. Affected examples are identified by comparing cluster content of a containing the refinement example (striped) with each of the refined KBS's clusters. Affected examples are those contained in clusters marked in bold. Therefore, the affected examples with refined KBS K_1 will be all examples in clusters x, y and z, because the initial examples clustered together in a are now distributed amongst these 3

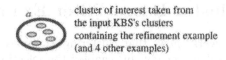

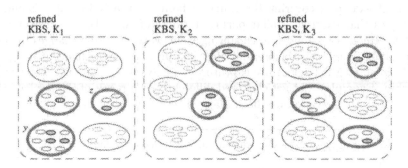

Figure 3: Analysing Changes in Cluster Content.

clusters. Generally, analysing the difference between clusters before and after refinement helps identify examples that were affected by the refinement but more importantly it identifies examples that were affected in a similar manner.

4.1 Selection from Clusters

Given a set of M proposed KBSs $\{K_1, \ldots, K_M\}$, we can identify M affected example sets $\{\epsilon_1, \ldots, \epsilon_M\}$. The simplest heuristic KFILTER randomly selects k examples from each ϵ_i, resulting in $M * k$ filter examples. Any resulting duplicates are removed. A further possibility is to select the $M * k$ most frequently seen examples in $\{\epsilon_1, \ldots, \epsilon_M\}$, and we refer to this filter example selection heuristic as, FQFILTER. The advantage of both these heuristics is simplicity.

Selecting the best refined KBS also means that filter examples must be able to filter out refined KBSs that are too extreme, i.e. over-generalised or over-specialised. For this purpose a more targeted example selection approach is necessary, where examples although affected must only be selected as filter examples if normally they should *not* have been affected. With such a sample of filter examples refined KBSs that are over specialised or over generalised will have a low accuracy ranking and be correctly rejected. The notion of selecting *awkward examples* to ensure that refined KBSs are evaluated on examples relevant to the refined KBSs being evaluated is presented in [8]. There relevant examples were those that get solved differently as a result of refinement that is too extreme. However, the identification of such examples involves a rigorous process of analysing changes in rule activations, fact assertions and system solutions. This can be impractical when dealing with KBSs with large numbers of rules and facts, furthermore all examples need to have already been labelled. Here we present a generic approach to selecting examples that will help discover over-generalisation and/or over-specialisation.

4.2 Effects of Refinement Operators

The KRUSTTool records the problem-solving behaviour that is undertaken by a KBS for an example in a graph structure. This consists of the rule activations and the order in which these activations occur. Figure 4 illustrates problem-solving behaviour of a fictitious faulty input KBS K containing rules $R_1, \ldots, R_{10}$ and its corresponding refined KBS K_1, when separately executed on example $e = \langle [f_1, \ldots, f_5], goal_e \rangle$. The ovals represent observables, derived facts and the final system solution. Assume that e is a member of K_1's affected example set, ϵ_1, where K_1 is a refined KBS that fixes a fault (or faults) in K. Differences between K's reasoning and K_1's reasoning can be captured by examining the corresponding rule activations.

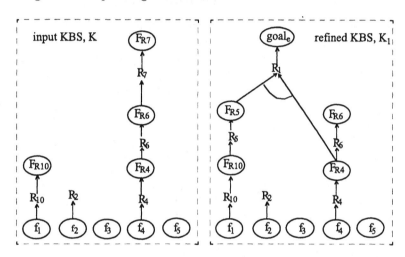

Figure 4: Observable usage before and after specialisation and generalisation.

A generalised KBS, typically results in new fact assertions (like F_{R5}) because generalisation tries to enable rule activations which, prior to refinement would not have activated. Often this amounts to weakening rule conditions so that they are satisfied by other rule conclusions (or observables). Specialisation has the opposite effect to generalisation, where previously derived facts are absent after refinement (like F_{R7}). Here, instead of weakening a rule's conditions they are strengthened so that other rule conclusions (or observables) will not satisfy one or more of the rule's conditions. With both refinement operations, given an input KBS, K, and a set of proposed KBSs K_i, we note observables that are being used differently with each proposed refined KBS, K_i, when compared to K. With each such observable consisting of attribute-value pairs we maintain the attribute-parts in a list, the *affected attributes* list, κ_i. For instance with K, the activation of the end rule R_7 has incorrectly concluded with system solution, F_{R7}. This is fixed in K_1 by disabling rules that lead to the conclusion of F_{R7}, and enabling rules that should instead lead to the target goal, $goal_e$. Consequently, we can identify several changes in observable usage with K_1 not seen with K: f_1 indirectly contributes to the activation of R_5 and so R_1; f_4 indirectly contributes to the activation of R_1; and f_4 as a result of specialisation does not contribute to the activation of R_7. Accordingly, K_1's affected attribute list κ_1 will contain f_1's and f_4's attribute-parts.

Once affected attribute lists are identified we need to select from K_i's affected example set, ϵ_i, examples that are *atypical* (dissimilar in values) with respect to their values for attributes in κ_i. The underlying intuition is that extreme refinements might be exposed by examples that have atypical values corresponding to observables that are utilised differently by the proposed KBS as a result of the refinement.

4.3 Selection by Atypical Example Scores

For each proposed refined KBS, the examples in its affected example set $\epsilon = \{e_1, \ldots, e_N\}$ are each given an Atypicalilty score by calculating the Cartesian distance between e_i and the remaining examples in ϵ. The distance calculation need only consider values for those attributes in the affected attribute list κ, because attributes not in κ are associated with observables that have not contributed to the changes in problem-solving behaviour as a result of the implemented refinement.

With refinements that are too extreme, it is most likely that examples with high atypical scores will be incorrectly solved by the refined KBS. Such examples have extreme values for observables that get used differently by the refined KBS as a result of the implemented refinement. Selection heuristic *FILTER, selects from each proposed refined KBS's affected example set (ϵ), k examples with highest *Atypical* scores as filter examples.

5 Committee-Based Selection

Although cluster-based filter example selection is able to identify affected examples and their degree of affectedness, it is computationally very demanding. The use of a committee to identify and eliminate noisy examples without the need for clustering is discussed in [3]. Noisy examples are those that the committee of learning algorithms finds hardest to solve. However for filtering purposes it is the committee of refined KBSs that might be *noisy*, therefore any examples that they find hard to solve are good candidates for the accuracy ranking. For this purpose system solutions of committee members are combined into a vote for or against selecting an example for filtering. Typically, we want to select examples where a majority of members are in disagreement. The credibility of this approach depends on the goodness of the committee, where members have an error rate of better than random guessing, and disagreement between members are uncorrelated [5]. For filtering purposes, although the committee is formed by refined KBSs originating from a single input KBS, differences in system solutions is due to differences between implemented refinements alone. We consider two alternative approaches to ascertaining disagreement: a vote-based heuristic; and a disagreement score suggested in [1].

For the voting approach the system solutions for each example are compared noting the majority vote, which is the highest number of refined KBSs agreeing on a system solution, and the minority vote, which is the least number of refined KBSs in agreement. With heuristic VOTEFILTER, the k examples with lowest minority vote are selected and any ties are resolved by favouring examples with lower majority votes. Establishing a majority or minority vote is difficult when one or more committee members fail to classify an example into any class. This can happen when proposed refined KBSs are too specialised. In such situations we could choose to ignore votes by refined KBSs that fail to classify examples. However, this may influence the selection of examples that are not necessarily ideal for filtering purposes. Instead, we allow the votes of these members on the basis of derived facts (in the absence of end facts).

A disagreement score $D(e)$, for example e, using a committee with M members, that classifies the example into one or more classes in C, is calculated by the entropy of the distribution of classes voted for by the committee [1]. Given the number of committee members classifying e in class c, where $c \in C$, denoted by $votes(c, e)$, the normalised vote entropy is:

$$D(e) = -\frac{1}{\log \min(M, |C|)} \sum_{c \in C} \frac{votes(c, e)}{M} \log \frac{votes(c, e)}{M}$$

Again when refined KBSs fail to classify an example into a class, derived facts are considered instead. Therefore, the cardinality of C can change from example to example, depending on how specialised members are, and depending on the concepts (or sub-concepts) concluded. Notice that the number of members is not fixed and will change from one refinement iteration to another. The vote entropy has value 1 when all committee members are in disagreement, and value 0 when all are in agreement, taking on intermediate values when in partial agreement. With selection technique NTROPYFILTER, k examples with highest normalised entropy vote are selected.

6   Experiments

The data set and rule-base for the binary class student loans, and the data set for the multi class soybean was taken from the UCI repository [2]. The student loans consists of 1000 labelled examples. We heavily corrupted the student loans KBS by introducing 5 faults to the 20 rules. The soybean data set of 337 labelled examples was formed by merging the large and small soybean data sets and selecting those examples classified in the first 15 classes. A soybean KBS with 44 rules was created by incorporating rule chaining into the rule set generated by c4.5rules [9]. This KBS was then corrupted in 13 places, by adding and modifying antecedents in rules covering 4 of the 15 classes. The soybean KBS tends to have a flatter structure when compared to the more straggling Student Loans KBS. The reason for this is that the flat structure characteristic of induced rules was inherited as a result of c4.5rules.

For the student loans domain, a set of 100 training examples and a further 100 evaluation examples are randomly selected. The KRUSTTool is run with increasing subsets of the 100 training examples. The graphs show results averaged over 10 runs for each training set size. However, with the Soybean domain the high computational costs due to the cluster-based method makes it impractical to have many repeated test runs. Instead, results are based on 20 test runs with 100 training and 100 evaluation examples. Although all examples in the data set are labelled for experimentation purposes, these labels are ignored until examples are selected from the training set for the refinement task. Significance results are based on a 95% confidence level and apply the Kruskal Wallis [7] non-parametric test as some results are not normally distributed.

Informed filter example selection heuristics KFILTER, FQFILTER, *FILTER and the committee-based techniques are compared against: NOFILTER where filter examples are those yet to be processed in tebuf, and unlabelled examples are never selected for filtering; and RNDFILTER where k filter examples are randomly selected from both labelled and unlabelled examples. The experiments investigate whether active accuracy filtering employing informed selection heuristics is able to reduce backtracking by guiding the KRUSTTool through the space of possible refinements. The fewer the number of backtracks the better the filtering heuristic at guiding refinement search. Additionally, fewer re-visits to previous refinement states, results in reduced iterations.

The experiments also evaluate the effect of the active accuracy filter on the error-rate of the final output KBS. It is hoped that improved guidance will move the search to parts of the refinement space resulting in higher accuracy. The contents of tebuf are selected manually at the start of each test run to ensure that any improvements are not influenced by this initial selection of examples. This ensures that all filter example selection heuristics will have equal refinement opportunity and that experimental results reflect the effect of filter example selection on the refinement process, decoupled from benefits from refinement example selection (in [13]).

6.1 Student Loans Domain

Figure 5 shows the error rate of the final refined KBS. Clearly, active selection of filter examples is important; even random selection is able to significantly reduce error-rate compared to the passive NOFILTER (p=0.001). So, can a more informed selection improve on RNDFILTER's performance? Heuristics *FILTER, KFILTER and FQFILTER have significantly lower error-rates than RNDFILTER (p=0.006). The results from the committee-based techniques have not been plotted as they did not improve on RNDFILTER. The reason for poor performance in this domain is that disagreement amongst committee members is similar for most examples, therefore, ties are broken randomly, reducing the performance of the committee based techniques to random.

*FILTER undertakes the most targeted selection procedure, therefore it was surprising that there was no significant difference in error-rate between it, the KFILTER and the FQFILTER. Close examination of test runs showed that the

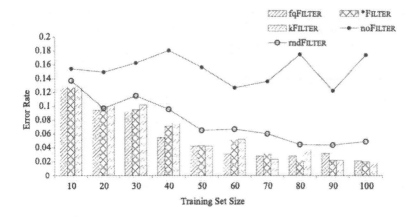

Figure 5: The Effects of Filter Example Selection on Error Rate.

initial manual selection of refinement examples was proving beneficial for refinement, resulting in an insignificant difference in error-rates. A further set of experiments consisting of 20 test runs with half the number of refinement examples was carried out. Of the 20 runs, the first ten involved a training and evaluation set size of 50 and the second ten a set size of 100. The results from these 20 runs indicate that *FILTER had significantly lower error-rates (p=0.03) compared to both KFILTER and FQFILTER. However, there was no significant difference between KFILTER and FQFILTER. Essentially, this suggests that atypical examples selected by *FILTER are not only well suited for filtering, but are also suited for driving refinement.

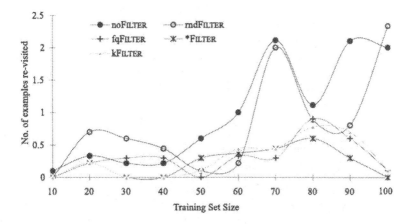

Figure 6: The Effects of Filtering on Backtracking.

Figure 6 plots the number of times backtracking is triggered. The committee-based approaches are not plotted as they did not improve on RNDFILTER. Number of backtracks triggered is significantly less with the informed selection heuristics compared to NOFILTER and RNDFILTER (p = 0.001). The targeted selection of cluster-based approaches has guided the KRUSTTool through the refinement search space, reducing the need to revisit previous states.

6.2 Soybean Disease Domain

In this domain, any actively selected filter examples once utilised for filtering, are never moved into tebuf or cebuf, therefore, filter examples do not get the opportunity to drive refinement. The informed selection heuristics (except FQ-FILTER) were compared with RNDFILTER and NOFILTER. FQFILTER is not used because it did not perform any better or worse than KFILTER with the student loans domain. All selection heuristics had significantly lower error-rates when compared to NOFILTER (p=0.007). However, the difference between VOTE-FILTER, NTROPYFILTER, *FILTER, KFILTER and RNDFILTER is not significant.

The number of backtracks triggered was significantly reduced by the informed selection heuristics compared to RNDFILTER and NOFILTER (p=0.009). With increased backtracking, re-visits to previous refinement states increases. This can have drastic effects on the number of iterations. For instance, in one run the number of times backtracking is triggered with VOTEFILTER, NTROPY-FILTER, *FILTER, KFILTER and RNDFILTER is 0, 0, 1, 28 and 69, while the corresponding number of iterations is 8, 8, 10, 43 and 208. Close examination reveals that the number of refined KBSs that pass the consistency filter can sometimes be in excess of 30. This means for RNDFILTER in the worst case, the best refined KBS will be selected only after 29 re-visits. What is interesting here is that there was no significant difference in the number of backtracks triggered between *FILTER and the committee-based techniques. Unlike the student loans domain here, the committee selection fared well, because differences between committee members were not localised to common problem solving areas. Consequently, the committee consisted of a sufficient mix of members agreeing and disagreeing about solutions for affected examples. This is always more encouraging than with similar levels of disagreement for all affected examples. Both VOTEFILTER and NTROPYFILTER have similar results. Processing requirements for *FILTER and KFILTER are on average 45% greater than that for VOTEFILTER and NTROPYFILTER.

7 Conclusion

Incremental refinement involves a search for the best refined KBS through the space of possible refinements. Generally refinement tools resort to hill-climbing search by either attempting to fix the outstanding fault indicated by the largest number of incorrectly solved examples, or by selecting the refinement that correctly solves the largest number of examples from a set of potential refinements. KRUSTTool adopts the latter approach, where the selected KBS has the highest accuracy over a subset of examples (referred to as filter examples). The emphasis of this paper is improving the accuracy ranking by informed selection of filter examples with a view to guiding the hill-climbing search.

The accuracy ranking can be adversely affected when it is based on a non-representative set of examples, particularly consisting of examples unaffected by the potential refined KBSs, or a large set of examples consuming considerable computational resources and expert labelling costs. The cluster-based selection methods aim to identify examples that are affected by the refinement and are correctly solved only by promising refinements. This involves clustering examples according to problem solving behaviour of the input KBS and analysing changes to cluster membership once examples are re-clustered according to the problem solving behaviour of each potential refined KBS. The changes can be difficult to track and this is tackled by considering only those changes that affect the cluster from which the refinement example was selected. The Cartesian distance between affected examples provides a score reflecting the degree of affectedness. The higher the score the greater the impact of refinement on the problem solving behaviour associated with that example. However, the high computational cost associated with clustering is a drawback. Future work will concentrate on improving the clustering algorithm so that it scales better to larger real-world KBSs. The committee-based approach selects examples that are solved most differently by potential refined KBSs without the need to cluster examples. This involves a measure of disagreement, reflecting consensus about how the example was solved.

Experimental results show that even a random selection from both the labelled and unlabelled sets was able to improve effectiveness and efficiency, compared to an accuracy filter with just the labelled examples in tebuf. Clearly this highlights the need to incorporate unlabelled examples in the accuracy ranking. The cluster-based heuristics managed to select few yet relevant examples thereby guiding refinement to promising parts of the search space resulting in significantly lower error rates and fewer re-visits to previous refinement states. There is also evidence that examples selected in this manner can be useful not only for the filtering task but also for driving refinement. The committee-based approach is not computationally demanding and on one domain achieved similar results to cluster-based heuristics. With student loans the potential for diversity amongst generated refined KBSs can be low reducing committee-based to random selection. This suggests a hybrid approach where cluster-based is adopted when diversity is low and committee-based otherwise.

The accuracy ranking guides refinement search by enabling selection of the best refined KBS from a set of potential refined KBSs. Effective guidance reduces the need to backtrack to previous refinement states thus improving overall efficiency. Informed selection of filter examples presented in this paper addresses this issue and achieves it without increasing the demand on the expert and the error rate of the final KBS.

Acknowledgments

The KRUSTWorks project is funded by EPSRC grant GR/L38387 awarded to Susan Craw.

References

[1] Shlomo Argamon-Engelson and Ido Dagan. Committee-based sample selection for probabilistic classifiers. *JAIR*, 11:335–360, 1999.

[2] C. Blake, E. Keogh, and C.J. Merz. UCI repository of machine learning databases, 1998. http://www.ics.uci.edu/~mlearn/MLRepository.html.

[3] C. E. Brodley, and M. A. Friedl. Identifying and eliminating mislabelled training instances. *Proceedings of the Thirteenth National Conference on AI*, pages 799–805, Portland, Oregon, 1996. AAAI

[4] Susan Craw and Robin Boswell. Representing problem-solving for knowledge refinement. In *Proceedings of the Sixteenth National Conference on AI*, pages 227–234, Menlo Park, California, 1999. AAAI Press.

[5] Thomas G. Dietterich. Ensemble methods in machine learning. In J. Kittler and F. Roli, editors, *First International Work Shop on Multiple Classifier Systems*, pages 1–15, New York, 2000. Springer Verlag.

[6] Andrew McCallum and Kamal Nigam. Employing EM in pool-based active learning for text classification. In *Proceedings of the Fifteenth International Conference on Machine Learning*, pages 359–367, 1998.

[7] William Mendenhall and Terry Sincich. *Statistics for the Engineering and Computer Sciences*. Collier MacMillan, London, 1988.

[8] Gareth J. Palmer and Susan Craw. The role of test cases in automated knowledge refinement. In *Proceedings of the BCS Expert Systems '96 Conference*, pages 75–90, Cambridge, UK, 1996. SGES Publications.

[9] J. R. Quinlan. *C4.5: Programs for Machine Learning*. Morgan Kaufmann, San Mateo, 1993.

[10] B. Richards and R. Mooney. Automated refinement of first-order horn-clause domain theories. *Machine Learning*, 19:95–131, 1995.

[11] Marcelo Tallis and Yolanda Gil. Designing scripts to guide users in modifying knowledge based systems. In *Proceedings of the Sixteenth National Conference on Artificial Intelligence*, pages 227–234, Menlo Park, California, 1999. AAAI Press.

[12] Nirmalie Wiratunga and Susan Craw. Incorporating backtracking search with knowledge refinement. In *European Symposium on Validation and Verification*, pages 193–205, Oslo, Norway, 1999. Kluwer.

[13] Nirmalie Wiratunga and Susan Craw. Informed selection of training examples for knowledge refinement. In *Proceedings of the EKAW2000*, pages 233–248, Juan-les-Pins, France, 2000. Springer.

[14] N Zlatareva and A Preece. State of the art in automated validation of KBSs. *Expert Systems with Applications*, 7:151–167, 1994.

Competence-Guided Case Discovery

Elizabeth McKenna[1] and Barry Smyth[1,2]

[1] Smart Media Institute, University College Dublin, Dublin, Ireland.
{Elizabeth.McKenna@ChangingWorlds.com}
[2] ChangingWorlds, South County Business Park, Leopardstown, Dublin 18, Ireland.
{Barry.Smyth@ChangingWorlds.com}

Abstract. The performance of a case-based reasoner depends critically on the cases in its case-base. Research to date has focused on those cases that are present in case-bases, with little or no direct attention given to the *holes* that exist in every case-base, and that ultimately limit the competence of real systems. In this paper we argue that modeling these *competence holes* is necessary to fully understand the potential of a case-base. We present and evaluate a novel technique for identifying, mapping and filling these competence holes by pro-actively discovering new cases that enhance the competence of the evolving case-base.

1 Introduction

Case-Based Reasoning (CBR) systems solve new problems by reusing the solutions of previous problem solving experiences stored as cases in a case-base, and performance depends critically on these cases. Recent work has focused on understanding and modeling the performance contributions of available cases in an attempt to better understand and optimise the competence and efficiency of CBR systems ([3, 7, 11–13, 15]). However, to date there has been little attention given to what might be termed the *competence holes* in a case-base; that is, those regions of the problem space that are not covered by cases.

In this paper we argue that understanding and modeling these competence holes should not be neglected. We present a new technique for identifying, mapping and evaluating the competence holes in a case-base. We show how this technique can be used as the basis for a novel *case discovery* algorithm capable of suggesting new cases to an author that actively fill important competence holes to enhance the coverage characteristics of the evolving case-base.

2 Related Work

Of course researchers have always *implicitly* recognised the presence of holes within case-bases, and have actively sought ways of filling these holes. After all, the primary goal of adaptation knowledge is to allow for holes within the case space, which correspond to target problems, to be bridged by adapting the solution of a nearby case. Until recently though, there has been little *explicit* attention given to the problem of holes within the case-base until researchers began to investigate the so-called *case discovery problem*, that is the problem of identifying new cases to drive the authoring process.

It must be pointed out that case discovery is quite different from work on case-base editing and case learning. Case-base editing involves identifying and eliminating redundant or harmful cases from a larger space of cases that are known *a priori*; for example, by selecting only high-quality cases from an existing case-base ([1,6,11]). Similarly, traditional case learning involves the acquisition of new cases as a result of successful problem solving sessions, in other words, the acquisition of new cases that are target-focused adaptations of existing cases within the case-base. In contrast, case discovery is not about selecting cases from a set of known cases or from a set of possible adaptations of known cases. Rather, case discovery is about recognising regions of a problem space that are not yet covered by the case-base at all, and subsequently formulating descriptions of the cases that might fill these uncovered regions or competence holes, so that these new case descriptions may be suggested to the case author.

Of course, whether these new cases prove to be a valid or valuable addition to an evolving case-base depends on whether the competence holes they are designed to fill correspond to *active* or *inactive* regions of the target problem space. Active regions correspond to likely future target problems whereas inactive regions correspond to regions of the problem space that relate to invalid attribute-value combinations (see also ([4,5]). Identifying active competence holes, and the cases that fill them, is obviously of immediate benefit to a case author, and information about *inactive competence holes* and their corresponding attribute-value sets may inform authors about domain constraints that were previously undocumented.

2.1 Case Discovery *á là* CaseMaker

McSherry's work on the CaseMaker system is particularly relevant here as it is one of the first attempts to clearly define and address the case discovery problem ([8,9]). Case-Maker uses a discovery technique that enumerates a complete set of uncovered cases (by searching the space of allowable feature combinations), and prioritises these cases by their potential coverage contributions. Recent enhancements enable CaseMaker to ignore cases that fall into inactive competence holes, by exploiting available domain knowledge, and therefore focus the discovery process on valid attribute-value combinations only. Results indicate that under certain conditions (where suitable domain knowledge is available and accurately evaluating the coverage of new cases is possible) CaseMaker is capable of discovering highly competent new cases.

2.2 Discovering Holes in Data

Related research in machine learning and data mining has begun to explore hole discovery in data sets, and this research has some bearing on our current endeavours in CBR. Early attempts focused on identifying empty regions in two-dimensional data-sets [2, 10], but more recent work by Lui et al [4,5] has resulted in a progression of hole discovery techniques that are well suited to discovering holes in k-dimensional relational data such as many traditional databases and indeed case-bases.

Lui et al focus on locating maximal empty hyperrectangles within a data set; that is hyperrectangles that do not contain any known data points. Recent enhancements [5] include an algorithm that is capable of locating maximal hyperrectangles within continuous and discrete feature spaces, and the restriction that the hyperrectangle must be empty can be relaxed to allow for the presence of anomolous outliers within the proposed hole. As it stands their approach requires two types of user intervention: (1) the user must provide an *interestingness threshold*, which corresponds to a lower-bound on the size of a hyperrectangle before it is considered interesting as a hole; (2) a *case density threshold* as an upper-bound on the density of data points within a hyperrectangle, below which it is considered to be empty. Generally speaking these parameters must be defined empirically according to the data set being examined.

2.3 Discussion

In this paper we are primarily interested in the case discovery problem and we suggest that solutions to this problem are necessarily made up of two main components: (1) a *hole discovery* component for identifying interesting competence holes within a case-base; and (2) a *case creation* component for suggesting cases to fill these holes. Furthermore, we suggest that ideally a case discovery algorithm should work to maximise the competence gain due to new cases. As such the algorithm must be capable of prioritising competence holes according to their importance from a competence viewpoint, and also of prioritising case creation to create cases with maximal competence properties.

The related work introduced above goes part of the way to fulfilling these important properties. For example, McSherry's CaserMaker algorithms focus on the case creation process, and actively prioritise cases according to their measurable coverage properties. However, these algorithms do not attempt to explicitly identify distinct competence holes or to prioritise these holes prior to case creation. In contrast, Lui et al focus exclusively on the hole discovery process and do not address the case creation issue at all. In addition, hole discovery must be fine-tuned by an external source (human engineer) in order to appropriately set the various thresholds for a given data-set.

In the remainder of this paper we will describe a novel approach to case discovery that combines a competence-guided hole discovery process and a case creation process and that does not rely on any tuning parameters or human intervention.

3 Competence-Guided Case Discovery

The inspiration for our competence-guided approach to case discovery is drawn from the competence modeling work of Smyth and McKenna [7, 12, 13]. Very briefly, Smyth and McKenna have developed a competence model for CBR systems in which the competence properties of individual cases, groups of related cases (called *competence groups*), and ultimately an entire case-base, can be accurately and efficiently predicted. In addition, they have shown how this model can be used to drive a variety of innovative solutions to a number of important CBR problems including, case retrieval [14], case learning [6], and case-base visualisation [12, 7].

An essential point about the Smyth and McKenna competence model is their proposal that the *fundamental unit of competence* for CBR systems is not the individual case but rather, well defined groups of related cases called *competence groups* that individually make independent contributions to global competence [7, 12]. Large competence groups then correspond to the competence rich areas of the case-base and the empty regions between groups correspond to competence holes.

3.1 Hole Discovery

According to Smyth and McKenna, as a case-base develops its competence groups and the holes between them evolve in a well defined manner [7]. In particular, one important evolutionary phase that exists for all case-bases occurs after the early growth stages, when new cases that contribute positively to competence tend to fall between nearby competence groups often causing these groups to coalesce to form a single group. These cases correspond to so-called *spanning cases* [11] and it should be highlighted that although these spanning cases do not contribute *directly* to competence in the same way that *pivotal* cases do, they do nonetheless have a positive indirect impact. Of course during this phase some cases do also fall within existing group structures but these cases tend to make only minor competence contributions.

This suggests a strategy for identifying *interesting* competence holes, holes that when filled are likely to have a significant impact on overall case-base competence: interesting competence holes exist between *nearest-neighbour* competence groups since these groups are most likely to be separated by the absence of a genuine competence-rich case. On the other hand, holes that exist between distant competence groups are less interesting as these groups are unlikely to be related and therefore useful, competence-rich cases are unlikely to exist in the spaces between these groups.

Thus, our hole discovery algorithm identifies nearest-neighbour competence groups, and subsequently our case creation algorithm aims to propose new cases that are most likely to cause a set of nearest-neighbour groups to merge.

Boundary Cases To identify nearest-neighbour groups we need a way of measuring the similarity between two groups. Our approach is to focus on the cases that lie on the boundaries of competence groups, and in particular, for each pair of groups we identify a pair of *boundary cases*, one from each group, that display maximal similarity (see Equation 1). Thus, in a case-base of g groups, each group has a set of *g-1 boundary pairs* (BPs).

$$For\ c_i \in G_1, c_j \in G_2,\ BP(c_i, c_j) if f$$
$$\nexists c_k \in G_1,\ c_l \in G_2 : Sim(c_k, c_l) > Sim(c_i, c_j) \quad (1)$$

For example, Figure 1 shows a case-base with 3 competence groups G, H and I. If we compare every case in group G to every case in Group H we can see that cases g_H and h_G are the most similar and hence are selected as a boundary pair for group G and H. Likewise, (g_I, i_G) and (i_H, h_I) also form boundary pairs. Of course this diagram is for illustrative purposes only and should not be interpreted as meaning that a case-base has just a single competence hole consisting of all possible cases not yet in the case-base. A typical case-base can have many distinct competence holes which represent real

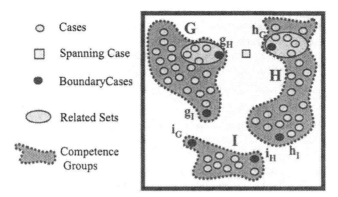

Fig. 1. Competence Groups & Boundary Pairs

target problems. The point we make in this paper is that the useful competence holes are likely to be located between nearby competence groups.

Nearest-Neighbour Groups The more similar two groups are, the higher the probability that they will merge. Hence, we are more interested in the holes that lie between nearest-neighbour groups (NNGs). For each group G_1 we identify its NNG G_2 such that the boundary pair for G_1 and G_2 displays maximal similarity (see Equation 2).

$$For\ G_1 = \{c_1, ..c_n\} \subseteq C,\ NNG(G_1, G_2)\ iff$$
$$G_2 \subseteq C - G_1 \wedge \exists c_i \in G_1, c_j \in G_2 : BP(c_i, c_j)$$
$$\wedge\ \not\exists\, G_3 \subseteq C - (G_1 \cup G_2) : c_k \in G_1, c_l \in G_3 \wedge$$
$$BP(c_k, c_l) \wedge Sim(c_i, c_j) < Sim(c_k, c_l)\quad (2)$$

Thus, for a case-base with g competence groups we can produced a prioritised list of up to g competence holes, one per group, and each represented by a pair of boundary cases that correspond to the extreme points of the holes. As we shall see in the next section, for each competence hole, the boundary pair cases act as reference points for the case creation process.

3.2 Case Creation

Given a pair of boundary cases that correspond to the extremes of a competence hole, the case creation task comes down to creating a case that lies midway between the boundary cases in the problem space (see Figure 1). One simple way to achieve this is to construct the new case so that its feature values correspond to the mean of the features values of the boundary cases.

In computing these means across continuous and discrete features we could use the feature value distribution across the case-base as a whole. However, this strategy is flawed as it would tend to produce the same mean case irrespective of the boundary pair. A better strategy is to base case creation on only those cases that are in the region

```
NewCase ← empty case
CreateCase(c₁, c₂)
 RSs ← RS(c₁) ∪ RS(c₂)
 For each attribute i ∈ NewCase
  if attribute i is continuous
   NewCase{i} ← Average value of i in RSs

  else if attribute i is nominal
   NewCase(i) ← Majority value of i in RSs
 End For
Return NewCase
```

Fig. 2. Case creation algorithm (RS = RelatedSet)

of the boundary pair cases. More precisely, we compute the feature values of the new case from the mean feature values of the cases in the *related sets* of the boundary pair (see Figure 1). Very briefly, Smyth and McKenna [7, 12] define the related set of a case to be the union of its coverage and reachability sets [11] and as such can be computed directly from the case-base competence model; the related set of a case is essentially the set of cases that can solve it, or that it can solve. This leads to the case creation algorithm shown in Figure 2.

3.3 Discussion

Earlier we proposed that a complete case discovery algorithm should be capable of: (1) identifying and prioritising interesting competence holes within a case-base according to their competence implications; and (2) prioritising case creation in order to create new cases that maximally benefit the competence of the evolving case-base.

A new two-stage competence-guided case discovery algorithm that achieves both of these goals has been outlined and is now presented as Figure 3. During phase one it identifies and prioiritises competence holes that lie between nearby competence groups, and that, according to the case-base competence model, are likely to offer significant opportunities for competence improvement should they be filled with the appropriate new cases. During phase two, new cases are created to fill each of these competence holes. The new cases are created to lie at the midpoint between the competence groups that border the competence hole in question.

```
C ← Case-Base
CM ← Competence Model
CaseDiscovery(C,CM)
 For each competence Group G ⊆ C
  (c₁, c₂) ←  BP of G and NNG(G)
  spanningCase ← CreateCase(c₁, c₂)
  newCases ← newCases ∪{spanningCase}
 End For
Return NewCases
```

Fig. 3. The Case Discovery algorithm.

At this point it is important to make an important observation in relation to our case discovery process. The idea of merging competence groups, to many, may not necessarily seem like a good thing from a competence viewpoint. Indeed one could certainly conceive of scenarios where merging two groups would increase competence only minimally (by the single spanning case). While this is true in theory, there is good evidence to hope for better results in practice, especially during the growth of mature case-bases; see [7].

4 Experimental Evaluation

Of course, ultimately, the competence-guided case discovery algorithm described in Section 3 is only likely to be useful if we can demonstrate that it actively discovers new cases that are seen to significantly improve the competence of an evolving case-base. In this section we describe some of the results obtained from an extensive experimental study.

4.1 Experimental Setup

The competence-guided case discovery algorithm is compared to three other discovery algorithms across a range of sample case-bases and experimental conditions.

Data-Sets The Travel (available from AI-CBR) and Property (available from the UCI ML Repository) case-bases are used to provide the raw case data for our discovery experiments. These case-bases are processed to produce a range of different case-base sizes and test sets. In total we use 1000 cases from the Travel domain to produce 4 case-base sizes, ranging from 100 cases to 400 cases, with the remaining cases used to form the test sets. For the Property domain, with a total of 500 cases, we produce 5 case-base sizes from 50 to 250 cases and once again the remaining cases are used as test sets. In each domain, and for each case-base size n, we produce 30 different random case-bases and test sets to give 120 case-bases and test sets for the Travel domain and 150 case-bases and test sets for the Property domain. There is never any direct overlap between a case-base and its associated test set.

We compare four different case discovery algorithms. The algorithms are all similar in that they each select two cases from the case-base (reference cases) and use the related sets of the chosen cases to create a new case as described above. However, the techniques vary in the way the two initial reference cases are selected:

- **Random** - selects two cases at random from the case-base.
- **Min** - selects the two most similar cases in the case-base (min here refers to minimum distance).
- **Max** - selects the two least similar cases in the case-base (max here refers to maximal distance).
- **Boundary** - selects the boundary pair from the most similar pair of nearest-neighbour competence groups as described in Section 3.1.

Thus, the boundary method corresponds to our competence-guided case discovery algorithm described in the previous section, whereas the Random, Min, and Max all correspond to somewhat more naive, but nonetheless valid, discovery techniques.

Earlier we claimed that our case discovery technique could be used to discover cases without the need for human intervention. While this is true, we nevertheless believe that the ideal scenario is to include the author in order to validate or tweak the case recommendations. In the following experiments each of the discovery algorithms will discover different cases, which correspond to the cases that would be suggested to the case author in a real-life setting. We believe it is more realistic to model the situation whereby the author accepts a new candidate case as a *suggestion*, but actually adds a slight variant of the candidate to the case-base. Thus we are not relying on the discovery algorithm to fully automate the authoring process, but rather as a support tool for the author. To simulate this we propose to use candidate cases as probes into the test set, and the actual cases that are added to the case-base (the assumed real cases that the author would pick) are the k nearest cases in the test set to each candidate. In our experiments we set k = 3. We go on to evaluate the coverage of these k cases in order to measure the value of the case suggested to the author.

4.2 Existing Coverage

In this experiment we examine the basic coverage properties of the four case discovery algorithms in the Travel and Property domains.

Method: For both domains, and for each case-base of size n, we use each of the four case discovery methods to suggest new *candidate cases* for the competence holes identified by each method, where each competence hole is defined by the case pair selected by the appropriate algorithm, Boundary, Min, Max, and Random. That is, during each case creation run, the Boundary method creates a candidate case using the next most similar boundary pair; the Min method uses the next set of most similar cases in the case-base; the Max method uses the next set of least similar cases; and the Random method simply selects two reference cases at random. The experiment terminates when a candidate has been created for each of the boundary pairs in the case-base, and by design each of the four algorithms will produce the same number of candidate cases.

Each candidate case is used to select its k nearest cases (called *target cases*) from the appropriate test-set (k=3) and the coverage of each target case is measured by computing the number of remaining test cases that each target can be used to solve. For each of the case discovery algorithms we note the cumulative coverage of their target cases. This is repeated over all 30 data-sets for each case-base of size n to produce a mean overall coverage value for each discovery algorithm.

Results: The results are shown in Figure 4 as overall coverage versus case-base size, for the Travel and Property domains respectively. Interestingly, in both domains our competence-guided, Boundary method appears to perform poorly, generating cases with reduced coverage characteristics when compared to the Min, Max, and Random methods.

Discussion: While these results are disappointing, we must point out a potential flaw in this experiment. When measuring the coverage properties of the target cases, we considered the coverage of these cases with respect to the test set, preferring those

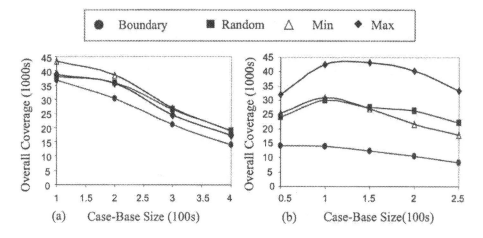

Fig. 4. Coverage properties of the newly created cases.

target cases that cover more test cases. However, the flaw is that these covered test cases may be already covered by the existing case-base. Thus, a newly discovered target case may cover many test cases, but if these test cases are already covered by the existing case-base then there has been no real competence gain. Thus, it is not enough to just consider the coverage of each newly discovered case, we must consider the unique new coverage offered by each case.

4.3 Unique Coverage

As discussed above an important feature of any case discovery algorithm is its ability to suggest candidate cases that will *add* to the coverage (i.e. the competence) of a case-base. Hence, the algorithm should generate cases with high unique coverage contributions - cases that cover new problems that were previously not covered by the case-base. In this experiment we will look at the unique coverage properties of the target cases generated by the four case discovery algorithms.

Method: For each of the target cases selected in the previous experiment we note how many of their covered cases in the test set are otherwise unsolved by the existing case-base. This new coverage value represents the unique coverage of the target cases. As before, for each technique we note the cumulative unique coverage over all target cases and for each case-base size across the Travel and Property domains.

Results: The results are shown in Figure 5 as unique coverage versus case-base size. This time the unique coverage properties of the target cases generated by the various techniques are quite different to the coverage properties shown in Figure 4. During the early stages of case-base growth the Max technique generates cases with slightly higher unique coverage than the Boundary technique; the addition of spanning cases is really only suitable if the case-base is in the coalescence phase and not during the early growth stages. However, as the case-base grows the Boundary method succeeds in consistently producing cases that provide higher unique coverage than any of the other techniques. This can be seen after the 200 case mark in the Travel domain and the 100 case mark in the Property domain - the respective case-bases have entered their coalescence phases where the addition of new spanning cases now significantly increases overall case-base competence.

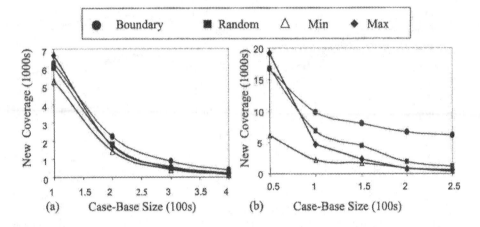

Fig. 5. Unique coverage provided by the candidate cases.

Discussion: The reason for the success of the Boundary method is that it uses a competence-guided approach to locating the interesting competence holes that lead directly to the discovery of competence-rich spanning cases. Locating these spanning cases is impossible using the Random, Max and Min techniques. For example, the Min approach selects reference cases that are very similar to each other and uses their related sets to generate new cases. These new cases are likely to fall into the same competence group as the reference cases, and are thus likely to be redundant (i.e. already solvable by the case-base). In short, the Min technique tends to produce competence-poor auxilliary cases [11]). Similarly, the Max and Random methods suffer from relatively unfocussed discovery strategies that are unlikely to locate many competence-rich cases.

4.4 Coverage Gain

In this final experiment we look at the benefit of the competence-guided Boundary case discovery method more closely by examining the *unique coverage gain* due to this method in comparison to Min, Max, and Random.

Method: The formula described in Equation 3 is used to compute the coverage gain of the Boundary approach relative to the Random, Min and Max techniques. For both the Travel and Property domain we compute the unique coverage gain over all case-base sizes using the data generated in the previous experiment.

$$\frac{UniqueCoverage_{Min/Max/Random}}{UniqueCoverage_{Boundary}} \tag{3}$$

Results: Figure 6 shows the results for both domains and indicates that, over time, the Boundary method is successful at discovering cases that have up 2.6 (in the Travel domain) and 15 times (in the Property domain) the unique coverage characteristics of cases generated by the Random, Min and Max techniques.

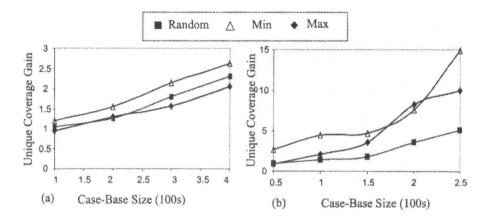

Fig. 6. New coverage gain provided by the candidate cases.

Discussion: The ultimate benefit of the Boundary technique as a case authoring guide is now clear as it promises to suggest cases that are likely to result in the addition of new cases that have many times the competence contributions of cases suggested by the Min, Max, and Random methods.

Finally, in our experiments, when selecting the target cases we have chosen the k=3 nearest-neighbours from the test set. Similar results are found for different settings of k (k = 1, 5, 7 for example).

5 Conclusions

It is perhaps unusual, given the central role that cases play in CBR, that to date there has been little support for case authors. In our research we have attempted to remedy this by proposing a competence-guided case discovery algorithm that seeks out interesting competence holes within a case-base, and suggests cases to fill these holes, and thus improve overall case-base competence.

This competence-guided case discovery algorithm is designed to discover competence-rich spanning cases, which are appropriate during a specific stage in the evolution of a case-base. This algorithm is appropriate for relatively mature case-bases but is less appropriate during other stages of case-base development, for example, during early developmental stages *pivotal cases* [11], and not spanning cases, are the main source of competence. This work is still in its infancy and our future research will focus on investigating complementary discovery strategies for these other developmental stages as we move toward a complete case discovery framework.

References

1. D.W. Aha, D. Kibler, and M.K. Albert. Instance-Based Learning Algorithms. *Machine Learning*, 6:37–66, 1991.
2. B. Chazelle, R.L. Drysdale, and D.T. Lee. Computing the largest empty rectangle. In *SIAM Journal of Computing*, pages 300–315, 1986.

3. D. Leake and D. Wilson. Remembering Why to Remember: Performance-Guided Case-Base Maintenance. In Enrico Blanzieri and Luigi Portinale, editors, *Advances in Case-Based Reasoning. Lecture Notes in Artificial Intelligence*, pages 161–172. Springer Verlag, 2000.

4. B. Liu, L.P. Ku, and W. Hsu. Discovering Interesting Holes in Data. In *Proceedings of the International Joint Conference of Artificial Intelligence*, pages 930–735, 1997.

5. B. Liu, K. Wang, L-F Mun, and X-Z Qi. Using Decision Tree Induction for Discovering Holes in Data. In *Proceedings of the Pacific Rim International Conference on Artificial Intelligence (PRICAI-98)*, 1998.

6. E. McKenna and B. Smyth. Competence-guided Editing Methods for Lazy Learning. In Werner Horn, editor, *Proceedings of the 14th European Conference on Artificial Intelligence*, pages 60–64. IOS Press, 2000.

7. E. McKenna and B. Smyth. An Interactive Visualisation Tool for Case-Based Reasoners. *Applied Intelligence: Special Issue on Interactive Case-Based Reasoning*, 14(1), 2001.

8. D. McSherry. Automating case selection in the construction of a case library. In *Knowledge Based Systems*, pages 133–140. Elsevier, 2000.

9. D. McSherry. Intelligent Case-Authoring Support in CaseMaker-2. In *Proceedings of the 5th European Workshop on Case-Based Reasoning*, pages 198–209. Springer Verlag, 2000.

10. M. Orlowski. A new algorithm for the largest empty rectangle problem. In *Algorithmica*, pages 65–73, 1990.

11. B. Smyth and M.T. Keane. Remembering to Forget: A Competence Preserving Case Deletion Policy for CBR Systems. In Chris Mellish, editor, *Proceedings of the 14th International Joint Conference on Artificial Intelligence*, pages 377–382. Morgan Kaufmann, 1995.

12. B. Smyth and E. McKenna. Modelling the Competence of Case-Bases. In B. Smyth and P. Cunningham, editors, *Advances in Case-Based Reasoning. Lecture Notes in Artificial Intelligence*, pages 208–220. Springer Verlag, 1998.

13. B. Smyth and E. McKenna. An Efficient and Effective Procedure for Updating a Competence Model for Case-Based Reasoners. In R.L de Mantaras and E. Plaza, editors, *Proceedings of the 11th European Conference on Machine Learning*, pages 357–368. Springer Verlag, 2000.

14. B. Smyth and E. McKenna. Incremental Footprint-Based Retrieval. In M. Bramer, A. Preece, and F. Coenen, editors, *Proceedings of Expert Systems 2000*, pages 89–101. Springer Verlag, 2000.

15. J. Zhu and Q. Yang. Remembering to Add: Competence Preserving Case-Addition Policies for Case-Base Maintenance. In *Proceedings of the 16th International Joint Conference on Artificial Intelligence*, pages 234–239, 1999.

The Inseparability Problem in Interactive Case-Based Reasoning

David McSherry

School of Information and Software Engineering, University
of Ulster, Coleraine BT52 1SA, Northern Ireland

Abstract

In applications of interactive case-based reasoning (CBR) such as help-desk support and on-line decision guides, a problem that often affects retrieval performance is the inability to distinguish between cases that have different solutions. For example, it is not unusual in a recommender system for two distinct products or services to have the same values for all attributes in the case library. While it is unlikely that both solutions are equally suited to the user's requirements, the system cannot help the user to choose between them. This problem, which we refer to as *inseparability*, can also arise as a result of incomplete data in the target problem presented for solution by a CBR system. We present an in-depth analysis of the inseparability problem, its relationship to the problem of incomplete data, and its impact on retrieval performance.

1 Introduction

In interactive CBR applications such as fault diagnosis, help-desk support, and on-line decision guides, each of the faults to be identified, or products to be selected, is often represented by a single case in the case library [1,3,5,6,9]. A case library in which all cases have unique solutions is *irreducible* in the sense that the deletion of a single case means that the corresponding product or fault is no longer represented in the case library [5,6]. A problem that often affects retrieval performance in interactive CBR is the inability to distinguish between certain cases. For example, it is not unusual in a recommender system for two distinct products to have the same values for all attributes including price range [3]. While it is unlikely that both products are equally suited to the requirements of the user, the system cannot help the user to choose between them.

We say that two cases are *inseparable* if they have the same values (or both have missing values) for all attributes in the case library [6]. Inseparability can be caused by inadequacy of the attributes used to index cases. A better understanding of its effects may therefore be of major benefit in case-base construction and maintenance. In this context, the problem is analogous to the inadequacy of attributes in a data set to distinguish between training examples in decision-tree learning [8]. In interactive CBR, inseparability can also arise as a result of incomplete data in the target problem presented for solution. Obtaining data required for retrieval in fault diagnosis, for example, may involve difficult or expensive tests that the user is unable or reluctant to perform [4]. In a recommender system, a user may decline to specify a preferred value for an attribute that she considers to be of no importance. Incomplete data effectively reduces the number of attributes available for retrieval, with the result that certain cases may no longer be distinguishable.

In previous work, we showed that the *separability* of an irreducible case library, conceptually the opposite of inseparability but easier to quantify, provides an upper bound for the level of precision that can be achieved by any retrieval strategy [6]. In this paper, we present an in-depth analysis of the inseparability problem, its relationship to the problem of incomplete data, and its impact on retrieval performance.

In Section 2, we examine possible retrieval strategies for irreducible case libraries and techniques for their evaluation in terms of retrieval performance. In Section 3, we examine the relationship between separability and precision, and identify conditions in which separability not only provides an upper bound for precision, but actually determines the level of precision that can be achieved by any retrieval strategy. In Section 4, we show that the separability of an irreducible case library can be at least partially evaluated from a decision tree. In Section 5, we examine the effects on separability and precision of increasing levels of incomplete data and the choice of attributes used to index cases in an irreducible case library. Our conclusions are presented in Section 6.

2 Retrieval Strategies

In this section we examine possible retrieval strategies for irreducible case libraries, and identify conditions for a retrieval strategy to be regarded as "well behaved". We also describe the empirical techniques on which our approach to the evaluation of retrieval performance is based.

2.1 Inductive Retrieval and Nearest-Neighbour Retrieval

When a target problem is presented to a CBR system for solution, the cases retrieved depend on the data provided in the target problem, the available cases, and the retrieval strategy used by the system.

Definition 1. *Given a case library L, target case C_t, and retrieval strategy S, we denote by rCases(C_t, S, L) the set of cases that are retrieved when S is applied to L with C_t as the target case.*

Common retrieval strategies include inductive retrieval and nearest-neighbour (NN) retrieval [12], either of which can be applied to an irreducible case library [6]. We assume that when NN retrieval is applied to an irreducible case library:

1. the retrieved cases are those that are maximally similar to the target case
2. two cases that differ in the values of one or more attributes are less similar than two cases that have the same values for all attributes
3. two cases that have the same values for all attributes are equally similar to any other case

As each case in an irreducible case library has a unique solution, it is not possible to apply the k-NN technique [7] of selecting a majority class from the k most similar cases. On the other hand, two or more library cases may be maximally similar to a target case, and therefore equally eligible for retrieval. In inductive retrieval, a decision tree induced from stored cases is used to guide the retrieval process [12]. The cases retrieved for a target case are those at the leaf node, if any, of the decision tree reached by following the path determined by the attribute values in the target case. As in NN retrieval, more than one case may be retrieved.

2.2 Admissible Retrieval Strategies

A property shared by inductive retrieval and NN retrieval is that if one of two inseparable cases is retrieved, then the other is also retrieved. We say that a retrieval strategy is *consistent* if it has this property [6], and *dynamic* if only the attributes whose values are known for the target case contribute to the retrieval process. NN retrieval is dynamic provided the assessment of similarity is based only on the attributes whose values are known for a target problem. An example of a retrieval strategy that is not dynamic is inductive retrieval based on a fixed decision tree. Such a decision tree is typically constructed *off line* by an algorithm that assumes all attributes in the case library, or as many as required to build the decision tree, will be available for retrieval. One drawback of the approach is that retrieval failure may occur if some of the attributes in the decision tree are unknown for a target case [12]. On the other hand, inductive retrieval based on a decision tree constructed at run time only from attributes whose values are known for the target case is dynamic. In practice, only a single path in a virtual decision tree is constructed in the approach, which is often referred to as *lazy* induction [3,4,10].

The retrieval strategies on which we focus in this paper are assumed to be both consistent and dynamic, and so *admissible* according to the following definition.

Definition 2. *A retrieval strategy S is said to be admissible if it is both consistent and dynamic.*

2.3 Evaluation of Retrieval Performance

While many CBR systems are appropriately evaluated in terms of classification accuracy, this is not possible if all cases have unique solutions as in the irreducible case libraries that are common in interactive CBR. The problem with the standard technique of using a subset of the cases in a case library as a test set is the assumption that the outcome classes to be predicted in the test set are represented among the remaining cases in the case library. This assumption is clearly violated in an irreducible case library. Evaluation in terms of classification accuracy is similarly compromised in conversational CBR, in which it is often the case that most (or all) cases in the case library have unique solutions. Aha *et al.* [1] have proposed an approach to evaluating retrieval performance in conversational case libraries called *leave-one-in*. In this approach, each case in the case library is used as a test case but without removing it from the case library during testing. In [1], retrieval performance is assessed in terms of the number of times the solution for the most similar case matches the solution for the test case.

In this paper, our approach to the evaluation of retrieval performance is based on a modified version of leave-one-in that simulates the problem of incomplete data in the target cases presented for solution by a CBR system. When a test case is presented for solution, the attributes available for retrieval are restricted to a non-empty subset A of the attributes whose values are known for the test case. Given a test case C, we denote by C_A the incomplete version of C that is presented as a target problem to the CBR system.

As the following proposition shows, a left-in case is always retrieved provided the attributes available for retrieval include at least one attribute whose value for the test case is known.

Proposition 1. *For any irreducible case library L, admissible retrieval strategy S, test case* $C \in L$, *and non-empty subset A of the attributes whose values are known for C,* $C \in rCases(C_A, S, L)$.

Proof. In NN retrieval, C cannot fail to be retrieved as no case can be more similar to C_A than C with respect to the attributes in A. In dynamic induction, C cannot fail to appear at the leaf node of a decision tree constructed from the attributes in A.

However, a point we would like to emphasise is that a test case is not necessarily retrieved in the version of leave-one-in used in [6] to investigate the effects of missing values in the case library on retrieval performance. In that approach, any missing values in a test case were "filled in" before it was presented as a target problem for solution, thus simulating the retrieval failures that may occur in practice if an attribute whose value is missing for a test case is known for the target problem.

Our technique of restricting the attributes available for retrieval in leave-one-in can be used to investigate the effects on retrieval performance not only of incomplete data but also of the choice of attributes used to index cases in an irreducible case library.

3 Separability and Precision

Our previous definition of inseparability [6] did not take account of the attributes available for retrieval. In practice, the attributes available for retrieval may vary depending on the attributes used to index cases or as a result of incomplete data. Here we say that two cases are inseparable with respect to a given set of attributes A if they have the same value, or both have missing values, for every attribute in A.

Inseparability with respect to a given set of attributes can be seen to define an equivalence relation among the cases in a case library. As Figure 1 illustrates, the equivalence class, or partition, containing a given case C is the set of cases from which C is inseparable.

Definition 3. *Given an irreducible case library L, and non-empty subset A of the attributes in L, then for any $C \in L$ we define iCases(C, L, A) = $\{C^\circ \in L: C$ and C° are inseparable with respect to A}.*

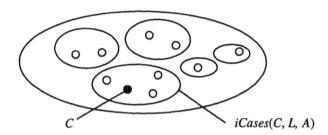

Figure 1. Inseparability partitions a case library into groups of inseparable cases

3.1 Separability

Conceptually the opposite of inseparability, separability is easier to quantify than inseparability. In previous work, we showed that separability, defined as a measurable characteristic of a case library, provides an upper bound for the level of precision that can be achieved by any retrieval strategy [6]. However, our previous definition did not take account of the attributes available for retrieval. Below we define the separability of an irreducible case library with respect to a given set of attributes.

Definition 4. *Given an irreducible case library L, and non-empty subset A of the attributes in L, we define*

$$separability(L, A) = \frac{\sum_{C \in L} \frac{1}{|iCases(C,L,A)|}}{|L|} \times 100$$

For the example case library in Fig. 1,

$$separability(L, A) = \frac{\frac{1}{2}+\frac{1}{2}+\frac{1}{4}+\frac{1}{4}+\frac{1}{4}+\frac{1}{4}+\frac{1}{2}+\frac{1}{2}+1+1}{10} \times 100 = 50$$

The separability of the example case library is therefore 50%. It is worth noting that our measure of separability is equivalent to the number of distinct groups of inseparable cases as a percentage of the number of cases in the case library. The following proposition shows how inseparability affects the number of cases retrieved when a test case is presented as a target case for solution in leave-one-in.

Proposition 2. *For any irreducible case library L, admissible retrieval strategy S, test case C ∈ L, and non-empty subset A of the attributes whose values are known for C, iCases(C, L, A) ⊆ rCases(C_A, S, L).*

Proof. By Proposition 1, $C ∈ rCases(C_A, S, L)$. As S is admissible, it follows that $C° ∈ rCases(C_A, S, L)$ for any $C° ∈ iCases(C, L, A)$.

3.2 Precision

In the context of information retrieval, precision is defined as the percentage of retrieved documents that are relevant [11]. In CBR, the aim is usually to retrieve a single case that solves a target problem rather than a set of relevant documents as in information retrieval. Moreover, there is often only one case in a case library that can provide the correct solution for a target problem. In fault diagnosis, for example, most or all cases may have unique solutions. In a recommender system, there may be only one product or service that ideally meets the requirements of the user.

In CBR, one way to ensure that the "right" case, if it exists, is retrieved would be to retrieve *all* cases in the case library. Of course, such a strategy would be unacceptable in practice. While it is not always possible to retrieve the right case and *only* the right case, an effective retrieval strategy should minimise the number of "unwanted" cases, on average, that are also retrieved. It is this aspect of retrieval performance in interactive CBR that we refer to as precision [6].

The leave-one-in technique proposed by Aha *et al.* [1] provides an empirical basis for the evaluation of retrieval performance in which every case in the case library is used as a test case. We use a modified version of leave-one-in in which the attributes available for retrieval are restricted to a subset A of the attributes in the case library that is the same for all test cases. By Proposition 1, a test case is always retrieved provided the attributes available for retrieval include at least one attribute whose value is known for the test case. Thus *no* test case can fail to be retrieved in leave-one-in provided every case in the case library has a known value for at least one of the attributes that are available for retrieval. We refer to such a subset of the attributes in a case library as a *covering* set of attributes.

Definition 5. *A subset A of the attributes in an irreducible case library L is a covering set of attributes if every case in L has a known value for at least one of the attributes in A.*

Attempting to solve problems for which no data is available is of course an unrealistic scenario that can only result in retrieval failure with any retrieval strategy. For the purpose of evaluating retrieval performance over all test cases in leave-one-in, it is therefore reasonable to insist that the set of attributes available for retrieval is a covering set. The fact that all test cases are retrieved in the version of leave-one-in used in this paper enables the definition of precision used in [6] to be simplified. Our revised definition also takes account of the attributes that are available for retrieval.

Definition 6. *For any irreducible case library L, retrieval strategy S, and covering subset A of the attributes in L, we define*

$$precision(S, L, A) = \frac{\sum\limits_{C \in L} \frac{1}{\left| rCases(C_A, S, L) \right|}}{\left| L \right|} \times 100$$

As we have shown in previous work, the separability of a given case library provides an upper bound for the level of precision that can be achieved by any admissible retrieval strategy [6]. This result can easily be generalised to take account of the attributes that are available for retrieval.

Proposition 3. *For any irreducible case library L, admissible retrieval strategy S, and covering subset A of the attributes in L, precision(S, L, A) ≤ separability(L, A).*

3.3 Missing Values

Missing values in the case library is a common cause of imperfect precision in interactive CBR and can also result in retrieval failure [1,6]. Though related to the problem of incomplete data, missing values occur for different reasons. In fault diagnosis, for example, an attribute's value may not be recorded in a case because it played no part in the solution of the problem, not because the information was unobtainable. In our view, missing values and incomplete data are different problems that require different solutions. In previous work we investigated the effects of increasing levels of missing values on retrieval performance, using a version of leave-one-in designed to simulate the retrieval failures often caused by missing values [6]. A comparison of several retrieval strategies showed some to be more tolerant of missing values than others.

While incomplete data can only reduce separability, missing values may either increase separability (though without necessarily increasing precision) or decrease separability. If two cases differ only in the value of an attribute whose value is missing in both cases, the two cases are rendered inseparable by the missing values. On the other hand, two cases that would otherwise be inseparable will lose this status if one has a missing value for an attribute for which the other has a known value. As we now show, the relationship between separability and precision is greatly simplified in the absence of missing values. In fact, the separability of an irreducible case library in which there are no missing values determines the precision that can be achieved by any admissible retrieval strategy.

Theorem 1. *If L is an irreducible case library in which there are no missing values, then for any test case C ∈ L, non-empty subset A of the attributes whose values are known for C, and admissible retrieval strategy S, rCases(C_A, S, L) = iCases(C, L, A).*

Proof. By Proposition 2, it suffices to show that $rCases(C_A, S, L) \subseteq iCases(C, L, A)$. If $C^o \in L$ is such that $C^o \notin iCases(C, L, A)$ then C^o has a different value from C for at least one of the attributes in A. With no missing values in the case library, this is enough to ensure that C^o is not retrieved by inductive retrieval when C_A is presented as a target problem for solution; that is, $C^o \notin rCases(C_A, S, L)$. In NN retrieval, it is also enough to ensure that C is more similar to C_A than C^o. Again it follows that $C^o \notin rCases(C_A, S, L)$.

Corollary. *If L is an irreducible case library in which there are no missing values, then for any admissible retrieval strategy S, and covering subset A of the attributes in L, $precision(S, L, A) = separability(L, A)$.*

It follows from the above theorem and corollary that for an irreducible case library in which there are no missing values, precision is the same for any admissible retrieval strategy. It also follows that in the absence of missing values, the only source of imperfect precision, at least as detected by leave-one-in, is inseparability, whether caused by incomplete data or inadequacy of the attributes in the case library. However, a possible source of imperfect precision that leave-one-in is unable to detect is *noise* [6]. While we assume the absence of noise in this paper, its impact on retrieval performance in interactive CBR is an important issue to be addressed by further research.

4 Identification Trees

We refer to a decision tree used to guide retrieval from an irreducible case library as an *identification* tree [5,6]. By Theorem 1, the precision provided by an identification tree dynamically constructed from an irreducible case library that contains no missing values is independent of the splitting criterion used to construct the tree. On the other hand, retrieval efficiency, as measured by the average path length of the identification tree, very much depends on the splitting criterion. In previous work we have shown that in the absence of missing values, information gain [8] tends to produce more efficient identification trees than other splitting criteria [5]. In this paper, we focus on the use of identification trees as a means of evaluating, or partially evaluating, the separability of an irreducible case library.

Proposition 4. *If L is an irreducible case library in which there are no missing values, then the groups of cases at the leaf nodes of an identification tree for L are the groups of cases that are inseparable in L.*

As noted in Section 3.1, separability is the number of groups of inseparable cases as a percentage of the number of cases in the case library. The separability of an irreducible case library that has no missing values can therefore be evaluated simply from the size of the case library and the number of leaf nodes of an identification tree. Separability with respect to a given set of attributes can similarly be evaluated from an identification tree constructed from those attributes.

Table 1. Example case library

mpg	cyl	disp	hp	wt	acc	yr	or	Solution
30-34	4	< 100	50-99	<2000	20+	74	3	*toyota corolla 1200*
10-14	8	400+	200+	4000-4499	<10	70	1	*chevrolet impala*
25-29	4	100-149	50-99	2000-2499	10-14	74	2	*fiat 124 tc*
30-34	4	<100	50-99	2000-2499	15-19	80	2	*audi 4000*
20-24	4	100-149	50-99	2500-2999	20+	72	2	*peugeot 504 (sw)*
15-19	6	250-299	100-149	3500-3999	15-19	75	1	*amc matador*
20-24	4	150-199	50-99	3000-3499	20+	80	1	*amc concord*
15-19	8	350-399	150-199	3500-3999	10-14	79	1	*chrysler lebaron t & c (sw)*
25-29	4	100-149	50-99	2500-2999	10-14	78	3	*toyota corona*
30-34	4	<100	50-99	<2000	15-19	82	3	*mazda glc custom*
10-14	8	400+	200+	4000-4499	<10	70	1	*plymouth fury iii*
15-19	6	250-299	100-149	3500-3999	15-19	75	1	*chevrolet chevelle malibu*
30-34	4	<100	50-99	<2000	15-19	82	3	*honda civic (auto)*

Table 2. An incomplete version of the test case *toyota corolla 1200*

mpg	cyl	disp	hp	wt	acc	yr	or	Solution
30-34	4	< 100		<2000				?

For an irreducible case library that does contain missing values, separability can still be partially evaluated by constructing an identification tree from the intact cases in the case library; that is, those cases that do not have any missing values. Since an intact case cannot be inseparable from another case that has missing values, the cases at the leaf nodes of such an identification tree are the groups of intact cases that are inseparable in the whole case library. Moreover, the number of leaf nodes as a percentage of the number of cases in the case library can be seen to provide a *lower bound* for the separability of the case library.

To illustrate the approach, we use an irreducible case library containing 13 cases from the AutoMPG data set [2]. The example case library is shown in Table 1. Many of the attributes in the case library resemble those that one might expect to see in a CBR system for recommending previously-owned automobiles. Three of the attributes (*cylinders*, *year* and *origin*) have discrete values. Continuous attributes in the data set (*mpg*, *displacement*, *horsepower*, *weight* and *acceleration*) were discretised by splitting their ranges into intervals that seemed most natural for the expression of user preferences. Often in interactive CBR there is a trade-off between maximising the separability of cases and minimising the number of values from which the user is required to select. Table 2 shows an incomplete version of the test case *toyota corolla 1200* in which the values of 4 of the attributes in the case library are unknown.

Figure 2 shows an identification tree for the example case library. The splitting criterion used to construct the tree was a simplified form of the information gain criterion [8] for irreducible case libraries [5]. There are 10 leaf nodes in the identification tree and therefore 10 distinct groups of inseparable cases among the 13 cases in the case library. Separability of the cases in the example case library is therefore 77%. As there are no missing values in the case library, this is also the precision provided by any admissible retrieval strategy when applied to the case library.

year = 70 : *chevrolet impala* or *plymouth fury iii*
year = 72 : *peugeot 504 (sw)*
year = 74
    acceleration = 10 to 14 : *fiat 124 tc*
    acceleration = 20 or more : *toyota corolla 1200*
year = 75 : *chevrolet chevelle malibu* or *amc matador*
year = 78 : *toyota corona*
year = 79 : *chrysler lebaron t & c (sw)*
year = 80
    acceleration = 15 to 19 : *audi 4000*
    acceleration = 20 or more : *amc concord*
year = 82 : *mazda glc custom* or *honda civic (auto)*

Figure 2. Identification tree for the example case library

The example identification tree illustrates the limitation of inductive retrieval based on a fixed decision tree to which we referred in Section 2.2. With the incomplete version of the test case *toyota corolla 1200* from Table 2 as the target problem, the tree is useless for retrieval as *year* and *acceleration* are unknown. Figure 3 shows an identification tree based on the four attributes (*mpg*, *cylinders*, *displacement*, and *weight*) whose values are known for the example problem. In practice, only a single path in the identification tree would be constructed, leading to the retrieval of the test case *toyota corolla 1200* along with two other cases. It can be seen from Figure 2 that only the test case would be retrieved if *acceleration* and *year* were known for the target problem. Thus the price paid for incomplete data is a considerable loss of precision in the query result.

The identification tree in Figure 3 can also be used to assess the impact that deletion of the attributes *year* and *acceleration* from the case library would have on retrieval performance. As the new identification tree has only 9 leaf nodes, the separability of the case library, and hence the precision provided by any admissible retrieval strategy, is reduced from 77% to 69%.

weight = 2000 to 2499
    displacement = 100 to 149 : *fiat 124 tc*
    displacement = less than 100 : *audi 4000*
weight = 2500 to 2999
    mpg = 20 to 24 : *peugeot 504* (sw)
    mpg = 25 to 29 : *toyota corona*
weight = 3000 to 3499 : *amc concord*
weight = 3500 to 3999
    cylinders = 6 : *chevrolet chevelle malibu* or *amc matador*
    cylinders = 8 : *chrysler lebaron t & c (sw)*
weight = 4000 to 4499 : *chevrolet impala* or *plymouth fury iii*
weight = less than 2000 : *toyota corolla 1200* or *mazda glc custom* or *honda civic (auto)*

Figure 3. Identification tree based on the attributes in the target problem

5 Experimental Results

We now present the results of experiments in which we examine the effects on separability and precision of incomplete data and the choice of attributes used to index cases in an irreducible case library. The irreducible case library used in our experiments was created by removing the 6 examples in the AutoMPG data set [2] that have missing values to provide a case library containing 392 cases. Separability of this case library with respect to the complete set of 8 attributes is 84%. As there are no missing values in the case library, it follows from Theorem 1 that the precision provided by any admissible retrieval strategy with all eight attributes available for retrieval is 84%. Similarly, the precision provided by any admissible strategy when only a subset of the attributes in the case library is available for retrieval is determined by the separability of the case library with respect to the available attributes. The absence of missing values also means that any non-empty subset of the eight attributes in the case library is a covering set.

5.1 How Does Incomplete Data Affect Precision?

Our first experiment examines the effects of increasing levels of incomplete data on precision in the AutoMPG case library. The impact on precision depends not only on the number of attributes whose values are unknown but also on which attributes are unknown. For example, the number of combinations of 3 unknown attributes from the 8 attributes in the case library is $^8C_3 = 56$. For numbers of unknown attributes ranging from 0 to 7, Figure 4 shows the maximum, minimum and average precision provided by any admissible retrieval strategy over all combinations of unknown attributes.

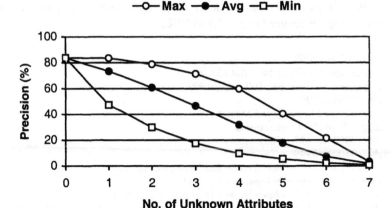

Figure 4. Effects of incomplete data on precision

Precision can be seen to have fallen as the number of unknown attributes increased. In the worst case, even one unknown attribute reduces precision to below 50%, which equates to the retrieval of one additional case with every test case. On the other hand, maximum and average precision remain above the 50% level until the number of unknown attributes reaches five and three respectively.

5.2 Attribute-Selection Strategies

Our second experiment compares the effectiveness of two possible approaches to the selection of attributes to index cases in an irreducible case library with the aim of maximising separability. First we removed all eight attributes from the case library used in the first experiment. The attributes were then selected for (re-)addition to the case library by three sequential strategies. The first strategy (Max-S) selects attributes in order of maximum increase in separability, and hence precision as there are no missing values in the case library. The second strategy (Max-N) gives priority to attributes that have most values, with ties between attributes with the same number of values broken randomly. In the third strategy (Rand), attributes were added to the case library in random order. Attribute selection continued in each strategy until the supply of available attributes was exhausted.

Figure 5 shows the cumulative effects on separability of the eight attributes in order of selection by each strategy. The results for Max-S are consistent with the pattern we expected to see. Separability can be seen to have risen rapidly with the addition of the first four attributes and less rapidly from that stage onwards. The addition of the last attribute has little impact on separability. While attributes with most values tended to have the most favourable impact on separability, this was not invariably the case. The fifth and sixth most useful attributes according to Max-S were *acceleration* and *origin*, although these attributes have fewer values (4 and 3) than the seventh and eighth most useful attributes, *horsepower* (5) and *cylinders* (5). That attributes with most values do not always give the greatest increases in separability is also reflected by the relatively weak performance of Max-N in comparison with Max-S, although it produced much better results than the random strategy.

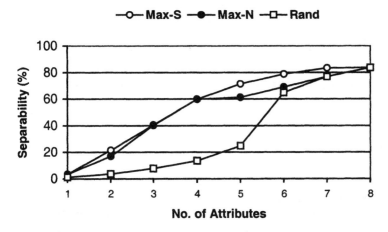

Figure 5. Comparison of three attribute-selection strategies

The experiment produced another interesting result. Given its sequential (or greedy) approach to attribute selection, Max-S cannot be expected to give optimal results. However, it did in fact give optimal results at every stage of the selection process. This was verified by determining the maximum separability over all possible combinations of attributes at each stage. For example, separability with respect to the first four attributes selected by Max-S (60%) is the maximum possible separability over all seventy combinations of 4 from the 8 available attributes. Of course, it does not follow that selecting attributes in order of maximum increase in separability will always give optimal results.

6 Conclusions

Our analysis of the inseparability problem in interactive CBR builds on previous work which showed that the separability of an irreducible case library provides an upper bound for the precision that can be achieved by any retrieval strategy [6]. One source of inseparability is inadequacy of the attributes used to index cases in a case library. Inseparability can also arise as a result of missing values in the case library or incomplete data in the target problem presented for solution by a CBR system. We have shown that incomplete data does not cause retrieval failure unless there is no data available for retrieval. However, it effectively reduces the number of attributes available for retrieval, thus reducing separability and hence precision.

We have shown that the relationship between separability and precision is greatly simplified in the absence of missing values. In fact, the separability of an irreducible case library in which there are no missing values determines the precision that can be achieved by any admissible retrieval strategy.

Our approach to the evaluation of retrieval performance is based on a modified version of leave-one-in [1] which is designed to simulate the problems caused by incomplete data or inadequacy of the attributes used to index cases in an irreducible case library. Our experimental results confirm the hypothesis that incomplete data may result in a considerable loss of precision. We have also compared possible approaches to attribute selection in the construction of an irreducible case library with the aim of maximising separability. Our results suggest that selecting attributes in order of maximum increase in separability may be better than simply giving priority to attributes that have most values.

References

1. Aha, D.W., Breslow, L.A., Muñoz-Avila, H.: Conversational Case-Based Reasoning. Applied Intelligence 14 (2001) 9-32
2. Blake, C., Merz, C.: UCI Repository of Machine Learning Databases. Department of Information and Computer Science, University of California, Irvine, California (1998)
3. Doyle, M., Cunningham, P.: A Dynamic Approach to Reducing Dialog in On-Line Decision Guides. In: Blanzieri, E., Portinale, L. (eds): Advances in Case-Based Reasoning. LNAI, vol 1898. Springer-Verlag, Berlin Heidelberg (2000) 49-60
4. McSherry, D.: Interactive Case-Based Reasoning in Sequential Diagnosis. Applied Intelligence 14 (2001) 65-76
5. McSherry, D.: Minimizing Dialog Length in Interactive Case-Based Reasoning. Proceedings of the Seventeenth International Joint Conference on Artificial Intelligence. International Joint Conferences on Artificial Intelligence (2001) 993-998
6. McSherry, D.: Precision and Recall in Interactive Case-Based Reasoning. In: Aha, D.W., Watson, I. (eds): Case-Based Reasoning Research and Development. LNAI, vol 2080. Springer-Verlag, Berlin Heidelberg (2001) 392-406
7. Mitchell, T.: Machine Learning. McGraw-Hill (1997)
8. Quinlan, J.R.: Induction of Decision Trees. Machine Learning 1 (1986) 81-106
9. Shimazu, H., Shibata, A., Nihei, K.: ExpertGuide: A Conversational Case-Based Reasoning Tool for Developing Mentors in Knowledge Spaces. Applied Intelligence 14 (2001) 33-48
10. Smyth, B., Cunningham, P.: A Comparison of Incremental Case-based Reasoning and Inductive Learning. In: Haton, J.-P., Keane, M., Manago, M. (eds): Advances in Case-Based Reasoning. LNAI, vol 984. Springer-Verlag, Berlin Heidelberg (1994) 151-164
11. van Rijsbergen, C.J.: Information Retreival. Butterworth & Co, London (1979)
12. Watson, I.: Applying Case-Based Reasoning: Techniques for Enterprise Systems. Morgan Kaufmann, San Francisco (1997)

Preprocessing Algorithms for non-binary Disjunctive Constraint Satisfaction

Miguel A. Salido[1], Adriana Giret[1], Federico Barber[1]

[1] Dpto. Sistemas Informáticos y Computación
Universidad Politécnica de Valencia, Camino de Vera s/n 46071
Valencia, Spain
{msalido, agiret, fbarber}@dsic.upv.es

Abstract. Some constraint languages are more powerful than others because they allow us to express a larger collection of problems. More generally, the finite constraint satisfaction problem (CSP) with arbitrary constraints (non-binary), is known to be NP-complete [9], whereas many families of restricted constraints have been identified like tractable subproblems [1][7]. We propose two preprocessing algorithms in order to study the consistency check (*the consistency algorithm*) when a new non-binary constraint is inserted into the system and to reduce the variable domains (*the reduction algorithm*) that participate in these non-binary disjunctive temporal constraints. Following, we can apply some of the techniques to solve this CSP. Thus, we can manage more complex and expressive constraints that many real problems must deal with.

1   Introduction

Nowadays many researchers are working on non-binary constraints [2],[3] and are mainly influenced by the growing number of real-life applications. Modelling a problem with non-binary constraints has several advantages: it facilitates the expression of the problem, it enables more powerful constraint propagation as more global information is available, etc.

Many real problems require more complex temporal constraints that the system must manage efficiently. These problems are also frequently dynamic problems whose constraints can be dynamically inserted or deleted.

In this paper, we extend the framework of simple temporal problems studied originally by Dechter, Meiri and Pearl [4] to consider non-binary disjunctive temporal constraints of the form $\sum_{i=1}^{n} p_i x_i \leq b$, where x_i are variables (time points) ranging over disjunctive intervals and $n \geq 2$.

The consistency of these problem types may be solved by means of techniques based on constraint satisfaction problems (CSPs) and techniques based on closure processes. These two techniques have a similar graphic representation, (a directed graph), but they have different goals.

- CSP has been widely studied in the Artificial Intelligence community for many years. It has been recognised that CSPs have practical significance because many problems arising in scheduling, in operational research and other real problems, can be represented as CSPs. The main goal of a CSP is to find one or several solutions in a previously consistent system.
- We can also solve these problems by means of the closure processes. The main aim of closure techniques is to guarantee the consistency of the existing constraints, which may be included and/or excluded by means of a dynamic behaviour. There exist several levels of consistency depending on the solution exigency, from the lowest levels (path consistency [10]) to the most demanding ones (global consistency [5]).

Both techniques may have a common graphic representation by means of a disjunctive temporal constraint network, where nodes represent temporal points and arcs represent binary disjunctive temporal constraints between two temporal points. Arc and node consistency work well for pruning the domains in networks of this kind. However, they do not work well if the problem contains primitive constraints that involve more than two variables (non-binary) since such primitive constraints are ignored when performing consistency checks.

In order to improve this deficiency, we propose two algorithms: *the consistency algorithm* performs a consistency check when a new non-binary temporal constraint is dynamically inserted into the system and *the reduction algorithm* may reduce the variable domains that participate in this non-binary temporal constraint.

In Fig. 1, we can see the application order of the algorithms.

In proposition 1 we prove the new domain consistency with the existing domains, so the closure graph maintains consistency.

We will focus this paper on dynamic constraint satisfaction problems and make the following contributions:
- In order to manage these non-binary constraints we present an algorithm called *the consistency algorithm* that studies whether the new inserted non-binary constraint is consistent with the existing binary ones.
- If the new non-binary constraint is consistent with the existing binary ones, a new and simple algorithm, *the reduction algorithm,* might be applied to reduce the variable domains that participate in this non-binary constraint in order to make the CSP solving process more efficient.

In section 3, we specify these two algorithms in order to apply them to non-disjunctive domain problems. Following, in section 4 we extend these two algorithms to disjunctive domain problems.

Finally in future works, we will consider non-linear constraints that permit us to represent other types of more complex frameworks. Both algorithms can be applied to problems with these types of constraints.

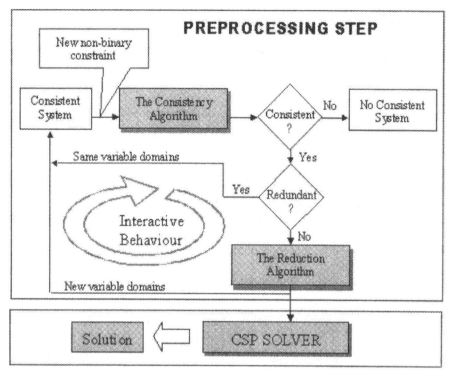

Fig. 1. Application Ordering of Algorithms.

2 Preliminaries

Briefly, a constraint satisfaction problem (CSP) consists of a set of *variables* $X = \{x_1, \ldots, x_n\}$ where each variable $x_i \in X$ has got a finite set D_i of possible values (its *domain*) and a finite collection of *constraints* $C = \{c_1, \ldots, c_p\}$ restricting the values that the variables can simultaneously take. Each constraint c_i is a pair (s_i, R_i), where s_i is a list of variables of length m_i, called *the constraint scope*, and R_i is an m_i-ary relation, called *the constraint relation*.

The tuples of the constraint relation R_i indicate the allowed combinations of simultaneous values for the variables in the corresponding scope s_i. The length of the tuples will be called the *arity* of the constraint. Non-binary CSPs are CSPs that contain constraints with arity greater than 2. In particular, we will classify the constraints by means of the arity. We denote R_i as (:) to make the notation easier:

- *Unary constraint:* specify the allowed values for a variable, $a : x_i : b : a, b \in Z$.
- *Binary constraint:* specify the allowed combinations of values for a pair of variables. We can classify *binary constraints* into two types:

a) *Standard binary constraint*: $a : x_i - x_j : b : a, b \in Z$.

b) *Non-standard binary constraint*: is a *2-ary* constraint.

- *n-ary constraint*: specifies the allowed combinations of values for n variables:

$$a \leq \sum_{i=1}^{n} p_i x_i \leq b : a, b, p_i \in Z.$$

We denote x_0 as "The beginning of the world" where $x_0 = 0$. Thus, all *unary constraints* can be expressed by means of a *standard binary constraint* adding x_0.
For instance: $a : x_i : b = a : x_i - x_0 : b$.

We consider *non-standard binary constraints* as *n-ary constraints*. Therefore, we only have two different types of constraints: *standard binary constraints* and *n-ary constraints* (from now on "*non-binary constraints*").

A solution to a CSP is an assignment of a value from its domain to every variable in such a way that every constraint is satisfied.

Our objective may be:
- to get only one solution, with no preference as to which one;
- to get all solutions;
- to get an optimal, or at least, a good solution by means of an objective function defined in terms of some variables [6].

Solutions to CSPs are found by searching systematically through the possible assignments of values to variables, usually guided by heuristics. The *consistency* and *reduction reductions* study the consistency and reduce the variable domains in order to reduce these search processes and make these heuristics more efficient.

3 Specification of the Algorithms

Both the *consistency* and *reduction algorithms* are presented in this section. We will represent our problem by means of a *Temporal Network* (TCSP). This network is represented by a *directed constraint graph*, where nodes represent time points (variables), and arcs represent disjunctive temporal constraints between two temporal points. Thus, both algorithms will be applied to non-binary constraints:

$$a \leq \sum_{i=1}^{n} p_i x_i \leq b, \text{ where } x_i \text{ are temporal points, } p_i \text{ is the coefficient of } x_i \text{ variable.}$$

We introduce the time point x_0 ($x_0 = 0$) in order to represent all *unary constraint* by means of a *standard binary constraint* $a : x_i - x_0 : b$. In Fig.2 the new arcs joining all temporal points with x_0 are represented.

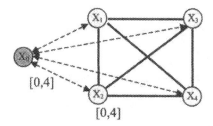

Fig. 2. An example adding the null variable x_0

Definition 1[4]

Let I_i and I_j be two temporal intervals. The *composition of* I_i and I_j, denoted by $I_i \otimes I_j$, admits only values r for which there exist $t \in I_i$ and $s \in I_j$, such that $t + s = r$, (i.e) if $I_i = [a,b]$ and $I_j = [c,d]$, then $I_i \otimes I_j = [a+c, b+d]$.

Definition 2[4]

Let I_i and I_j be two temporal intervals. The *intersection of* I_i and I_j, denoted by $I_i \oplus I_j$, admits only values that are allowed by both of them.

Definition 3

Let p_i be the coefficient of the variable x_i. We denote $sig(p_i)$ like the sign of p_i.

3.1 The Consistency Algorithm

The main goal of our *consistency algorithm* is to determine whether a non-binary constraint is consistent with the existing binary ones. Therefore, we start from a consistent system. When a *new non-binary constraint* is asserted into the system, the algorithm checks its consistency with the existing *standard binary constraints*. If the new constraint is consistent, then we will apply the *reduction algorithm* only in the case that the constraint intersects its variable domains. If the *non-binary* constraint has only one inequality in the upper bound ($\sum_{i=1}^{n} p_i x_i \leq b$ as usual) and this constraint is consistent with the existing ones, then, *the consistency algorithm* assigns (a) to the lower bound ($a \leq \sum_{i=1}^{n} p_i x_i \leq b$). Analogously $a \leq \sum_{i=1}^{n} p_i x_i \Rightarrow a \leq \sum_{i=1}^{n} p_i x_i \leq b$. In Fig 3. the consistency algorithm is represented.

Let $a \leq \sum_{i=1}^{n} p_i x_i \leq b$ be a *n-ary constraint*, where $a, b, p_i \in Z : i = 1..n$, and x_i are variables (time points).

Step1. We transform this *n-ary constraint* to the form:

$$a \leq \sum_{i=0}^{n} \sum_{j=1}^{|p_i|} sig(p_i) x_i \leq b : p_0 = -\sum_{i=1}^{n} p_i .$$

Step2. We make two disjunct sets, where each set is composed by the same sign variables.

Step3. We make all possible combinations among elements of both sets.

Step4. For each generated combination among variables, we make the multi-binary constraint (composition of standard binary constraints) with the same relation and same independent term.

Step5. For each standard binary constraint, we assign its original temporal domains.

Step6 We intersect all the resulting intervals corresponding to all the possible combinations obtaining the minimal domain $([d_1, d_2])$ where the *n-ary constraint* could be consistent.

Step7. We intersect the interval $([d_1, d_2])$ with the original n-ary interval [a,b].

We can distinguish several different situations (see Fig 4a):

1.- If $[d_1, d_2] \oplus [a, b] = \phi$, then the n-ary constraint is not consistent. (stop).

2.- If $[d_1, d_2] \oplus [a, b] \neq \phi$, then the n-ary constraint is consistent with the binary ones. We can also study:

> **2.1** If $[d_1, d_2] \oplus [a, b] = [d_1, d_2]$ then, the n-ary constraint is consistent. We will not apply *the reduction algorithm* because we are not going to reduce the variable domains. We do not label these variables and we delete this constraint because it is redundant. (stop).

> **2.2** If $[d_1, d_2] \oplus [a, b] \subset [d_1, d_2]$ then we must apply *the reduction algorithm* in order to reduce the variable domains.

Fig.3.The Consistency Algorithm.

Example

Let´s take a simple example in R^2 where we can see the behaviour of the *consistency algorithm*. We represent all the constraints graphically. We study a non-binary constraint that will be consistent with the binary ones.

Let the following initial binary constraints be:

$$2 \leq x_1 - x_0 \leq 6 \rightarrow x_1 \in [2,6]_{[\ ]}$$
$$0 \leq x_2 - x_0 \leq 4 \rightarrow x_2 \in [0,4]_{[\ ]}$$
$$-6 \leq x_2 - x_1 \leq 2$$

Let´s see if the non-binary constraint $c_1 : 2x_1 - x_2 : 2$ is consistent with the existing ones. Fig. 4b. represents the variable domains and the binary constraints.

Step1. $2x_1 - x_2 : 2 = x_1 + x_1 - x_2 - x_0 : 2$

Step2. Positive variables set: $\{x_1, x_1\}$, negative variables set: $\{x_2, x_0\}$

Step3. Possible combinations. Only one possible combination: $\{(x_1, x_2) \wedge (x_1, x_0)\}$

Step4. $x_1 + x_1 - x_2 - x_0 : 2 = (x_1 - x_2) + (x_1 - x_0) : 2$

Step5. We assign its corresponding intervals: $[-2, 6] \otimes [2, 6] = [0, 12]$

Step6. We have only one possible combination: $[d_1, d_2] = [0, 12]$

Step7. $[a, b] = [-\infty, 2]$, so $[0, 12] \oplus [-\infty, 2] = [0, 2] \neq \phi$.

Therefore, the non-binary constraint c_1 is consistent with the standard binary ones, and also $[0, 12] \oplus [-\infty, 2] = [0, 2] \subset [0, 12]$, so we must apply the *reduction algorithm* in order to reduce the variable domains. We can also observe that the lower bound of the non-binary constraint is zero: $0 : 2x_1 - x_2 : 2$. (see Fig. 4c).

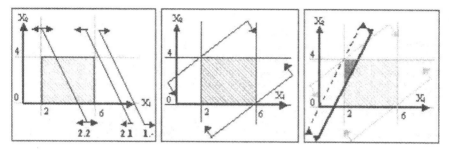

Fig. 4. a) Different situations in step7. b) Example graphic. c) Graphic with the non-binary one

Graphically, we can observe that the variable domain generates a quadratic polyhedron by means of Cartesian Product of the domains.

The non-binary constraint is consistent because it intersects the quadratic polyhedron of possible solutions. Also, it can be observed that the variable domains can be reduced significantly because the minimal quadratic polyhedron that includes the new valid region is included strictly in the original polyhedron. This will be seen in the *reduction algorithm*

3.2 The Reduction Algorithm

The reduction algorithm is only applied when the section (2.2) of *the consistency algorithm* is reached. *The reduction algorithm* only affects some of the variables that participate in the *non-binary* constraint reducing the domain size. In Fig. 5 the pseudo-code of *The reduction algorithm* is presented.

Let the *n-ary* constraint be: $\sum_{i=1}^{n} p_i x_i \leq b$, where $b, p_i \in Z : i = 1..n$

For each variable x_i that participates in the non-binary constraint do the following:

Step1. Fix all the positive variables of the *n-ary* constraint to their lower bound and all the negative variables of the *n-ary* constraint to their upper bound, except x_i, and substitute them in the *n-ary* constraint, obtaining a *unary constraint*: $\pm x_i \leq \lfloor u'_i \rfloor = u_i$. We obtain a real number u'_i and round it down to the nearest integer u_i.

Step2. If $sig(x_i)$ is positive, we verify if the resulting unary constraint can be reduced in its original upper bound. If $sig(x_i)$ is negative, we verify it in its lower bound. In the case that this unary constraint is not upper bounded (or lower) then this new bound is added to the unary constraint.

Fig.5. The Reduction Algorithm.

Example

Let's continue with the previous example in order to study *the reduction algorithm* in the non-binary constraint: $c_1 : 2x_1 - x_2 : 2$.

We are going to study the x_1 domain:

Step1. We fix $x_2 = 4$.

Step2. $2x_1 - 4 : 2 = x_1 : \lfloor 6/2 \rfloor = 3$. The x_1 domain is reduced to $x_1 \in [2,3]_{[c_1]}$.

We are going to study x_2 domain:

Step1. We fix $x_1 = 2$.

Step2. $4 - x_2 : 2 = x_2 \geq \lfloor 2 \rfloor = 2$. The x_2 domain is reduced to $x_2 \in [2,4]_{[c_1]}$.

Example

Now let's look at the same example in which the non-binary constraint is not consistent with the existing ones. Let the non-binary constraint be: $2x_2 + x_1 : 0$.

We can observe graphically (Fig. 6a) that the non-binary constraint is not consistent with the existing ones. By means of *the consistency algorithm*, it can be seen that this constraint is really not consistent.

Step1. $2x_2 + x_1 : 0 = x_2 + x_2 + x_1 - x_0 - x_0 - x_0 : 0$

Step2. Positive variables set: $\{x_2, x_2, x_1\}$, negative variables set: $\{x_0, x_0, x_0\}$

Step3. Only one possible combination: $\{(2,0) \wedge (2,0) \wedge (1,0)\}$

Step4. $x_2 + x_2 + x_1 - x_0 - x_0 - x_0 : 0 = (x_2 - x_0) + (x_2 - x_0) + (x_1 - x_0) : 0$

Step5. We assign its corresponding intervals: $[0, 4] \otimes [0, 4] \otimes [2, 6] = [2, 14]$

Step7. $[-\infty, 0] \oplus [2, 14] = \phi$, so the constraint $2x_2 + x_1 : 0$ is not consistent.

Therefore, the problem with this non-binary constraint does not have a solution.

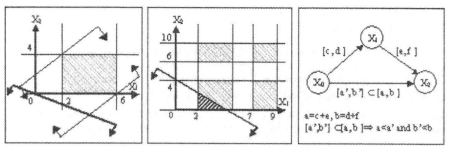

Fig. 6. a) No consistent constraint. b) Constraint in disjunctive domains. c) Closure graph. [a',b'] is the new interval between x_0 and x_2. [c,d] and [e,f] are the previous closure domains.

Proposition 1.
Let G be a closure graph. We assume that a new non-binary constraint is inserted into the system and reduce the domain of any binary constraint. Then, the new domain is consistent with the previous closure graph. (See, fig.6c).

Proof:

We must prove $[c,d] \cap ([a',b'] \otimes [-f,-e]) \neq \phi$.

We assume $[c,d] \cap ([a',b'] \otimes [-f,-e]) = \phi = d < a'- f \vee b'- e < c$.

If $d < a'- f = d < a'- f = a'\dashv d - b = d < a'\dashv d - b = b < a'< b'= b < b'$ false.

If $b'- e < c = b'\dashv c - a < c = b'< a < a'= b'< a'$ false.

4 Application to disjunctive problems

A problem with disjunctions in its variable domains is a very complex problem because the difficulty increases exponentially with the number of disjunctions (l). A variable has a disjunctive domain if its possible values are enclosed in disjunctive intervals, for example $x_1 \in [2,6] \cup [7,9]$. However, we can apply both *consistency* and *reduction reduction*s to non-disjunctive problems in an analogous way.

We only need to modify step5 of the *consistency algorithm*. Instead of assigning only the original temporal domain, we generate all the alternative possible domains according to all possible combinations among the variable intervals.

If at least one of the possible combinations is valid, then the original constraint is consistent. Otherwise, the original constraint is not consistent. We must take into account that the complexity increases exponentially because we have a non-disjunctive problem for each possible combination. In *the reduction algorithm*, we might initially reduce the variable domains by means of a new step called *step0* which reduces the intervals that do not participate in the valid combinations. First, we observe the variable intervals that only participate in invalid combinations. In this case, these intervals can be directly eliminated. Afterwards, we will apply the following steps of *the reduction algorithm*.

Let´s see an example to clarify this property.

We assume a problem with only two variables x_1, x_2 with two disjunctions $(l = 2)$ in the variable domains.

$$x_1 \in [2,6] \cup [7,9]; \ x_2 \in [0,4] \cup [6,10]$$

Thus the set of possible solutions is formed by disjunct polyhedrons.

Let's see the consistency of the non-binary constraint: $x_1 + 2x_2 : 6$ (Fig. 6b.) in the last problem. The non-binary constraint is consistent with the existing ones and three of the four polyhedrons are inconsistent with the new constraint. So, we can eliminate these three polyhedrons. This implies deleting the intervals that do not participate in the valid polyhedron. Let's see how the *consistency reduction* changes.

Step4. $(x_2 - x_0) + (x_2 - x_0) + (x_1 - x_0) : 6$

Step5. $[0, 4] \ \otimes \ [0, 4] \ \otimes \ [2, 6] \ = [2, 14]$ **valid**
        $[0, 4] \ \otimes \ [0, 4] \ \otimes \ [7, 9] \ = [7, 17]$ **invalid**
        $[6, 10] \ \otimes \ [6, 10] \ \otimes \ [2, 6] \ = [14, 26]$ **invalid**
        $[6, 10] \ \otimes \ [6, 10] \ \otimes \ [7, 9] \ = [19, 29]$ **invalid**

We can observe that the intervals $[6, 10]$ and $[7, 9]$ only participate in invalid combinations, so these intervals are directly eliminated by the *step0* of *the reduction algorithm*. Thus, applying the following steps over the new domains: $x_1 \in [2,6]$; $x_2 \in [0,4]$, we will reduce these domains to: $x_1 \in [2,6]; \ x_2 \in [0,2]$

5   Computational Cost

The computational cost depends on the number of variables that participate in the non-binary temporal constraint. Generally, constraints of this type do not have more than four variables in an attempt to represent durations by means of temporal points [8]. So, Thus, it is very common for constraints such as $d_i + d_j : 4$ (duration i plus duration j is less than 4) can be translated to $(x_{i_1} - x_{i_2}) + (x_{j_1} - x_{j_2}) : 4$ and managed by the *consistency* and *reduction* reductions. Let's see the computational cost of the algorithms where k is the number of variables that participate in the non-binary constraints and l is the mean number of disjunction:

Computational cost in the consistency algorithm:

- Non-disjunctive constraints: The computational cost in the worst case is $(k/2)!$.

- Disjunctive non-binary constraints: The computational cost in the worst case is $l^k (k/2)!$.

This computational cost is due to the number of possible combinations, however this number can be reduced because of many combinations are repeated.

Computational cost in the reduction algorithm:

- The computational cost is $O(k)$ in disjunctive and non-disjunctive constraints.

6 Conclusion and Future Works

In this paper, we have proposed a new technique for the study of consistency and domain reduction in problems with non-binary constraints. *The consistency algorithm* makes a study of the consistency when a new non-binary constraint is inserted into the system. If the new non-binary constraint is consistent with the binary ones, its consistency must be checked with the previous non-binary constraints inserted into the system by means of linear programming techniques. *The reduction algorithm* takes place when the non-binary constraint is consistent with the previously existing ones. In this case, it makes a reduction of the variable domains that participate in this non-binary constraint. These algorithms are applied in a pre-processing step. Therefore, when the non-binary constraint is consistent with the existing ones, some of the techniques can be applied to solve these reduced problems. Furthermore, we can manage non-binary constraints and study the management of consistency in systems with disjunctive temporal constraints.

As future work, the *consistency algorithm* could also be applied to non-linear problems where some variables can be pondered by a non-integer factor. Problems of this type may permit us to represent other types of situations like the following example: *"John(x_1) takes two to five times longer to go to the university than Michael(x_2) does"*. This non-linear constraint will be represented by: $x_1 = [2,5]x_2$, where x_1 and x_2 can be disjunctive intervals. The consistency of constraints of this kind could be partial because these constraints can only be consistent in a subinterval of the original one. In this case, we can obtain the subinterval in which this constraint is consistent.

References

1. Cooper, M.C., Cohen, D.A., Jeavons, P.G.: Characterizing tractable constraint. Artificial Intelligence 65 (1994) 347-361
2. Bessière, C., Meseguer, P., Freuder, E.C., Larrosa, J.: On forward checking for non-binary constraint satisfaction. In Proceeding CP'99, Alejandria VA, (1999)
3. Gent, I.,Stergiou, K., Walsh, T.: Descomposable constraints, Artificial Intelligence 123. (2000) 133-156
4. Dechter, R., Meiri, I., Pearl, J,: Temporal Constraint Network, Artificial Intelligence 49, (1991) 61-95
5. Dechter, R.: From Local to Global Consistency, Artificial Intelligence 55, (1992) 87-107
6. Eiben, A.E., Ruttkay, Zs.: Constraint satisfaction problems, Handbook of Evolutionary Computation, IOP Publishing Ltd. and Oxford University Press, (1997) C5.7:1-C5.7:8.
7. Jeavons, P. G., Cooper, M. C.: Tractable constraints on ordered domains. Artificial Intelligence 79, (1996) 327-339
8. Jonsson, P., Bäckström, C.: A Unifying Approach to Temporal Constraint Reasoning. Artificial Intelligence 102(1). (1998) 143-155
9. Mackworth, A. K.: Consistency in Network of Relations, Artificial Intelligence 8. (1977) 99-118
10. Montanari, U.: Networks of constraints: fundamental properties and applications to picture processing. Information Sciences 7. (1974) 95-132

SESSION 3:

AGENTS

A Study of Autonomous Agent Navigation Algorithms in the ANIMAT Environment

Arthur Pchelkin and Arkady Borisov
Riga Technical University, Riga, Latvia

Abstract

This paper deals with the examination of possibilities of the algorithm of autonomous agent navigation. The ANIMAT problem was developed to study the possibilities of ZCS classifier system learning. A ZCS classifier system is purely reactive. For this system it is essential to have a possibility to identify the global state of the environment by the input message. This reduces the application area of the system and its ability to solve complex tasks. The present paper proposes to build an alternative learning algorithm that would be able to cope with the above mentioned problems. The effectiveness of the suggested algorithm is tested via practical experiments. In the experiments performed the algorithm has demonstrated its essential superiority over a classifier system with temporary memory.

1 Introduction

Classifier systems [1] are a class of learning systems that are able to generate the corresponding response to environment messages received with the help of sensors. A classifier system that includes a production system is able to solve tasks according to the black box principle. Here, input and output messages are known, while the structure of internal rules is unknown because it varies and improves in the course of learning. A system of this type learns by producing its own rule list. The rules are stored in the form of classifiers. Each classifier consists of two parts: condition part and action part.

The ANIMAT (abbreviation from animat and robot) problem [2] was first introduced to enable a better study of a zeroth level classifier system (ZCS) learning capability. A ZCS classifier system has no memory and it cannot respond to the environment messages taking into account the history of operation. It is necessary for this system to be able to identify the global state after the input message. This narrows the application area of this system and ability to solve complicated tasks. Due to this in [3] it was decided to extend a ZCS system with temporary memory. Since then it has been called the zeroth level classifier system with memory (ZCSM) classifier system.

In further papers [4] experiments were performed with this system employing the ANIMAT problem in order to check the effectiveness of the classifier system. It was shown that the use of memory allows the classifier system to cope with tasks in which learning without memory yields completely negative results. However, further negative results were determined.

Through a number of experiments performed to examine the suggestion of temporary memory application [3], researchers have found that in cases when it is necessary to produce long classifier strings, learning becomes very unstable and unpredictable. It was mentioned that sometimes one may arrive at a completely unpredictable fall in agent performance.

Due to the above reasons, Wilson [5] proposed modifying the ZCS classifier system. The modification was called XCS. It was then complemented by temporary memory [6] and called XCSM [5]. In [6] the results of the experiments performed showed the superiority of XCSM over ZCSM. At the same time it was found that XCSM successfully copes with simple environments whereas in the complicated ANIMAT environments it produces rather negative results. Moreover, all the experiments were performed in comparatively simple environments where the number of similar states (according to locally available information) was small.

All the described above negative results demonstrate that the ANIMAT learning problem is not trivial in the case of non-Markov environment and when an agent has to make a lot of steps to solve the task. On the other hand, the ANIMAT problem is topical and important because it is related to artificial intelligence as a whole [7]. Due to this, it is decided to develop an alternative agent learning algorithm that would be able to cope with the above mentioned problems. This paper proposes constructing this kind of algorithm by employing inference of finite automata using homing sequences [8].

2 ANIMAT Environment

To better examine the possibilities of classifier system learning, in 1985 Wilson formulated the ANIMAT learning problem [2]. The essence of this problem is searching for immovable objects in a labyrinth. The agent' s life consists of several cycles: it is placed in a random place, after which the agent has to find the object searched with the least possible number of steps. Initially the agent has no any knowledge on the environment. Hence, in the course of cycle execution the agent has to learn to quickly find food in the labyrinth. Each cycle can be treated as a task solved by the agent. The present paper makes use of this task. However, it was slightly changed. To extend this learning task, several specific assumptions were relinquished, for example, an assumption about the specific environment geometry. The only remaining assumption about the structure of the environment was this: the environment is deterministic. Two motivations have been employed: to extend the ANIMAT environment and at the same time enable possible application of methods of finite deterministic automata inference.

Let us consider the following problem: the agent's moving along the finite directed graph (see Fig. 2.1.). At any one time, the agent can stay in one of the nodes and is able to read its denotation (symbol). Similarly, each edge has denotations out of the alphabet the agent is familiar with. When the agent selects one of those edge denotations, it moves along the corresponding edge (in the direction of the edge). A single labelled edge is associated with each node.

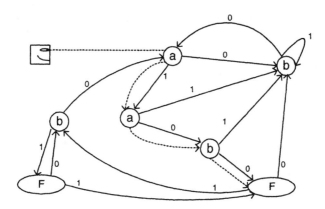

Figure 2.1 Example of the ANIMAT environment

The graph may also contain one or more nodes with special denotations that designate "food" with symbol F. Nodes of this kind can be treated as target states. The task of the agent is to find any of these target states-nodes within the least possible number of states starting from any randomly selected node. In Fig. 2.1 the dotted line shows a possible sequence of actions (moves along the graph) as a result of which the agent reaches the target state (the node with symbol F). This environment is similar to the finite state deterministic automaton in which graph nodes represent states but graph edges stand for transitions between the states. Due to that, when moving along the graph edges, the agent is able to recognise this environment as a finite-state deterministic automaton by employing finite automata inference methods.

This learning problem can be divided into two sub-problems:
1) The graph is known but the agent's location is not.
2) The agent does not know the graph but it is known that the graph does not vary.

It should be noted that the second problem includes the first one and also the problem of finite deterministic automata inference. The next section will therefore examine the first problem and the section that follows will consider the second problem.

3 Navigation algorithm

This section deals with studying agent navigation possibilities in the case when the model of the environment is known to the agent, whereas its specific location in the environment is unknown (it should be noted that the process of agent learning is not examined in this part). At the beginning of this task the agent is located in a randomly selected place but in the end the agent finds the target state.

Generally speaking, this problem is a special case of partially observable Markov decision processes, POMDP [9]. Various algorithms [10] exist that are designed to solve this problem. All of them, however, provide only an approximate solution when searching for the optimal strategy. Moreover, all these algorithms are dynamic: while seeking the optimal strategy, the solution only approaches the optimum through multiple iterations. Due to that, in this study we propose employing a simpler algorithm [11] that would enable accurate calculation of the optimal strategy by one iteration only, making use of the specifics of the task.

The algorithms that solve POMDP usually calculate the optimal value function [9] to produce an optimal policy. The optimal value function represents belief states that define the probability of the agent's staying in each environment's state with respect to the corresponding optimal values. To calculate the optimal value function, these algorithms usually only search for approximate solution by several iterations. When the environment is deterministic (this is the case in this study), an opportunity appears to accurately calculate this optimal value function by one iteration employing the specifics of the structure of the belief state set. Let us outline this structure.

Let us define the number of states for each belief state in which the agent can stay at the moment. Employing this number makes it possible to order belief states at various levels so that at the top there are states with the largest number and on the bottom those with the least number of states. Transitions between belief states can be either deterministic when only a single perception is expected from the environment or non-deterministic when several perceptions are expected. Inside each level all the transitions are deterministic whereas non-deterministic ones go to the bottom.

The deterministic transitions are fairly essential since they sufficiently simplify the calculation of the optimal value function. For example, if all the transitions were deterministic, it would be possible to calculate this function as the length of the shortest path between the current belief state and those in which it is known for sure that the agent is in the target state.

The suggested algorithm calculates the optimal value function by one iteration as follows. First, optimal values are calculated for the lowest level. After that optimal values are calculated starting from the bottom in the direction of the top. For each level, optimal values are calculated employing previously calculated values for the lower levels and lengths of the shortest deterministic paths inside the level. In [11] it was proved that this algorithm calculates the optimal policy according to the polynomial time dependence on the size of the environment (number of perceptions, number of actions and number of states) and the number of belief states.

It was not confirmed in this study that a set of belief states is in the polynomial dependence on the number of states in the environment. However, it was proposed to experimentally test the size of this set. Before making experiments, a hypothesis was suggested stating that normally this set is polynomially large. To check this hypothesis, it was decided to experimentally evaluate the size of the set of belief states. For this, *80000* random ANIMAT environments with the number of states from *10* through *100* were generated. For each environment, the size of the belief set was evaluated. After that the average size for every number of states was calculated. Fig. 3.1 depicts the results of that experiment. The experiment showed that the size of the set of belief states grows rather slowly: intuitively it seems to proceed a bit faster than the linear function.

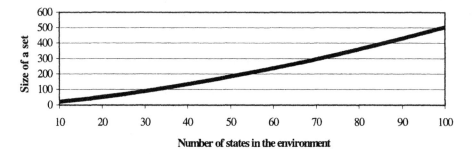

Figure 3.1 Dependence of the size of a set of belief states
on the number of states in the environment

4 Learning Algorithm

It is decided to develop the agent learning algorithm using finite automata inference methods [12] and the navigation algorithm that was described in the preceding section. The navigation algorithm supplies the agent with the optimal policy when the environment model is known. The task of automata inference methods is to enable the elaboration of this model.

In [13] it is described how to recognise the finite deterministic automaton effectively. The proposed L^* algorithm employed the minimally adequate teacher. The teacher is able to respond to queries of two types:

- membership query: the teacher answers the question: "Is the given symbol string recognised by the unknown automaton?"
- equivalence query: the teacher says "Yes" if the unknown automaton is isomorphic to the recognised one and offers a counterexample if it is not.

Angluin's algorithm has one essential shortcoming. It cannot be used directly to recognise the ANIMAT environment as this algorithm employs the *reset* command (this command resets finite automata to the start state) whereas in the ANIMAT environment this command is not available. Due to that, another algorithm was used [8] that can recognise the environment model without the *reset* command. This algorithm is based on the previous one. It simulates several copies from L^* and constructs a homing sequence with whose help the *reset* command can be simulated. Homing sequence is a sequence of actions that helps determine where the agent is located after its execution (in the environment, an action is treated as a move along the graph.

The previous automata inference algorithm employs a teacher that can make equivalence queries: it says "Yes" if the developed model is equivalent to the automaton and supplies the algorithm with a counterexample if it is not equivalent. In practical implementation, the teacher can be replaced by randomly generated action sequences [8]. This, however, can help supply the algorithm with counterexamples only if they exist. To make sure that the model is equivalent, it is recommended to use an additional parameter, *the maximal number of tests (generated action sequences)*. This parameter ensures that the recognition of the environment has finished and the environment is recognised correctly. Note that it is essential to extend the length of tests when generating them to ensure that any state can be reached.

The suggested learning algorithm consists of two parts:
1) the environment model is recognised through experiments;
2) an optimal policy to search for the target state is elaborated.

To ensure that the agent's ability to find a target state is satisfactory even at the start of learning, it was decided to record the shortest path to the target state at the end of each test (action sequence). Two positive results can be achieved in this way: the agent will either find the target state or the present test will reveal the contradiction between the model developed and the environment, and that could be used as a counterexample for the automata inference algorithm.

5 Experiments

The previous sections described the learning algorithm. This section proposes testing its effectiveness in the ANIMAT learning problem (see Fig. 5.1). The ANIMAT problem consists of a two-dimensional plane divided into equal cells. Each cell may contain an empty space, trees or food. The task of the agent in this artificial forest is to move along the cells so as to find food. The following cell denotations were introduced: "F" - food, "T" – tree, " " – empty space.

The life of an agent, an artificial animal, consists of problems it has to solve. The agent is placed randomly in a place on the plane. Then it has to find the searched object, food, by making the least possible number of steps. The agent is able to move in all 8 possible directions. It can, however, only move through empty spaces. When it tries to climb a tree, it remains in the same position and nothing happens. This feature was introduced specially to make orientation in the environment more complicated for the agent. Otherwise, it could serve as additional information that could be used by the agent in the course of learning. It should be noted that the agent has no special knowledge of the environment's geometry.

To compare the suggested algorithm with XCSM with regard to effectiveness, it can be tested in relatively complicated environments such as Maze7 (see Fig. 5.1(a)) and Maze10 (see Fig. 5.1(b)). In [6] XCSM was tested in Maze7 and the negative results were derived. Maze10 is similar to Maze7 but is more complicated. Additionally, the proposed algorithm was studied in the Lab1 environment (see Fig. 5.4). The first two environments have the same feature: the food the artificial animal searches for is not hidden. The last environment is non-

Markov, like the two previous ones, but it contains more states. This complicates agent learning. Besides, this environment was constructed so that food is hidden and is difficult to find.

T	T	T	T	T
T				T
T		T		T
T		T		T
T		T		T
T	F	T	T	T

(a)

T	T	T	T	T	T	T	T	T
T								T
T		T		T		T		T
T		T		T		T		T
T		T	F	T		T		T

(b)

Figure 5.1 Environments `Maze7` (a) and `Maze10` (b)

The suggested learning algorithm employs one empirical parameter, *the maximal number of tests*. To perform experiments, it was decided to select this parameter as follows. The `Maze7` environment is simple enough and it suffices that this parameter is equal to 10. Other environments are more complicated. That is why we propose using the value of this parameter equal to 100 for each of the environments. Figures 5.2, 5.3 and 5.5 show the results of these experiments. In each environment the experiment was performed 40 times and the results depicted are the average of 40 experiments.

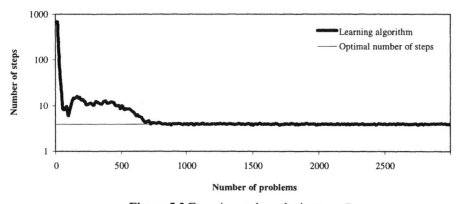

Figure 5.2 Experimental results in `Maze7`

In the course of the experiments, the process of agent learning was studied. After each problem was solved (when the agent looked for food), the number of steps made by the agent to find the food was calculated. From the graphs it can be seen how the number of steps varies depending on the number of problems solved.

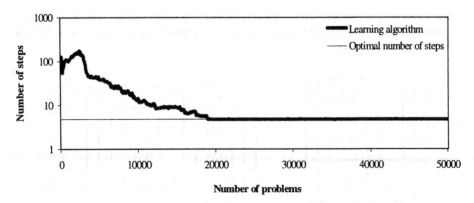

Figure 5.3 Experimental results in Maze10

T	T	T	T	T	T	T	T	T	T	T	T	T	T	T
T											T		T	T
T	T		T		T	T	T	T		T	T			T
T			T										T	T
T		T	T		T	T	T	T	T	T	T		T	T
T			T		T		T	F		T			T	T
T	T		T				T	T		T				T
T			T		T	T				T				T
T			T			T	T	T	T	T	T		T	T
T	T		T	T			T							T
T					T			T			T	T		T
T	T	T	T	T	T	T	T	T	T	T	T	T	T	T

Figure 5.4 Environment Lab1

Algorithm learning results can be compared with the optimal number of steps that is shown separately on each graph. In all the experiments, the agent has achieved the theoretical optimum with respect to searching the target states by employing the suggested learning algorithm. However, in the last two environments it took more time. It should be noted that in Maze7 even the modified classifier system XCSM exhibits negative learning results [6]. The fact that environments Maze10 and Lab1 for the suggested algorithm turned out to be similar as to the complexity cannot be due to the fact that they are really similar but because the same value of parameter *maximal number of tests* was used. Note the specifics of automata recognition methods: it is testing that takes most of the automata recognition time.

In analysing the experimental results one can observe that all graphs have the same feature. At the beginning, a sufficiently good result is achieved. It then becomes worse and only improves later. This illustrates the specifics of the learning algorithm. At the beginning of learning, an approximate environment model is created and the agent can search for food fairly well, employing this model. After that, tests generation starts (action strings) and their length is extended, which increases the number of steps made.

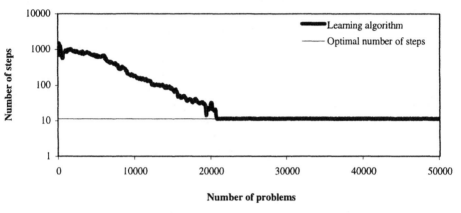

Figure 5.5 Experimental results in Lab1

Fig. 5.6 shows a summary of experimental results. Additional statistics is also shown that could be effective to analyse the results. The results presented are the average of 40 experiments in each case. On the graph, the learning algorithm reaches the optimum only when it is achieved in all the experiments: it can also be seen in column *maximum* (see Fig. 5.6).

Environment	Optimal number of steps	The optimal policy was developed by (problems)		Number of states in the environment	Number of belief states
		Maximum	**On average**		
Maze7	3,9000	720	239	10	11
Maze10	4,7895	19 000	6 568	19	28
Lab1	11,3544	20 800	9 941	79	97

Figure 5.6 Summary of experimental results

But on average, the learning algorithm reaches the theoretical optimum much earlier. It can be seen from column *average*. In the first two environments the target state can be reached by approximately 4 steps on average, but in the last environment the food is well hidden. So the necessary number of steps on average is 11. This is also represented in the graphs. If at the beginning of learning in the `Maze7` environment the agent needs 6 steps to find food, in `Maze10` it makes 55 steps whereas in `Lab1` more than 550 steps are required.

6 Conclusions

This paper has described an agent navigation algorithm able to provide an agent with the optimal policy for target state searching. An algorithm for agent learning has also been developed that is based on the navigation algorithm and the finite deterministic automata learning algorithm. The suggested learning algorithm employed various assumptions regarding the environment, the main one being that the environment is deterministic by structure. Via a series of experiments, the suggested agent learning algorithm was tested in those tasks where the XCSM classifier system produced negative results. In addition, the algorithm was tested in a rather complicated task in which a lot of similar states were observed. In that task, the target state was not only located far from the agent (the agent was forced to make a large number of steps to reach this state) but was quite sufficiently hidden in the environment. In all the experiments the agent reached the theoretical optimum as regards target state searching. This confirms that the proposed learning algorithm is able to work effectively in the ANIMAT environment.

Acknowledgement This research has partly been supported by the Latvian Education Foundation Programme *A/S DATI to Education, Science and Culture.*

References

1. Holland, J. H. Adaptation. In R. Rosen & F.M. Snell (Eds.), *Progress in theoretical biology*, 4. New York: Plenum, 1976
2. Wilson, S. W. Knowledge growth in an artificial animal. *Proceeding of the First International Conference on Genetic Algorithms and Their Applications* (pp. 16-23). Hillsdale, New Jersey: Lawrence Erlbaum Associates, 1985
3. Wilson, S. W. ZCS: a zeroth level classifier system. *Evolutionary Computation* 2(1): 1-18, 1994
4. Cliff, D. & Ross, S. Adding temporary memory to ZCS. *Adaptive Behavior* 3(2), 101-150, 1994
5. Wilson, S. W. Classifier fitness based on accuracy. *Evolutionary Computation* 3(2): 149-175, 1995
6. Lanzi, P. L. Adding Memory to XCS. In: *Proceedings of the IEEE Conference on Evolutionary Computation*. IEEE Press, 1998
7. Wilson, S. W. The Animat Path to AI. In *From Animals to Animats: Proceedings of The First International Conference on Simulation of Adaptive Behavior* (pp. 15-21), J.-A. Meyer and S.W. Wilson, eds., Cambrige, MA: The MIT Press, Bradford Books, 1991

8. Rivest, R. L. & Schapire, R. E. Inference of finite automata using homing sequences. *Information and Computation* 103(2): 299-347, 1993
9. Cassandra, A. R. Optimal policies for partially observable Markov decision processes. Technical Report CS-94-14, Brown University, Department of Computer Science, Providence RI, 1994
10. Cassandra, A. R. & Kaelbling, L. P. & Littman, M. L. Optimal policies for partially observable stochastic domains. In *Proceedings of the Twelfth National Conference on Artificial Intelligence*, Seattle, WA, 1994
11. Pchelkin, A. A study of autonomous agent navigation possibilities in the Animat environment. Master's Thesis, The University of Latvia, supervised by Prof. Arkady Borisov, 2001
12. Balcázar J. L. & Díaz, J. & Galvaldà, R. & Watanabe, O. Algorithms for Learning Finite Automata from Queries: A Unified View. *Technical Report TR96-0017*. Department of Computer Science, Tokyo Institute of Technology, 1996
13. Angluin, D. Learning regular sets from queries and counterexamples. *Information and Computation* 75:87-106, 1987

Intelligent Agents for Resource Management in Third Generation Mobile Networks

Damian Ryan, John Bigham, Laurie Cuthbert, Laurissa Tokarchuk
Electronic Engineering, Queen Mary, University of London
London, UK

Abstract

In 3G mobile networks, management of the radio resource is more complex than in existing 2G networks: higher bandwidth services requiring better QoS, liberalisation of the marketplace and technical issues with the radio access method (WCDMA) all contribute to this problem. This paper discusses an architecture for the use of intelligent agents as an efficient, scaleable and robust solution in the realistic context of a deregulated marketplace containing several service providers, network operators and customers. The aim is to bring financial benefits to all parties through improved efficiency: by competition between service providers, between network operators, and by more efficient management of radio resou ce.

1 Introduction

Resource management is increasingly important as mobile networks become more complex and applications need more bandwidth. Customers are also demanding better performance. It is possible to provide this level of performance by over-dimensioning networks with extra radio transmitters (base stations) but this approach leads to higher prices passed onto the user, and this is a heavy deterrent to the take-up of the new services under development. This is exacerbated in mobile networks where resources at the air interface are necessarily limited.

Third Generation (3G) mobile systems are seen as the technology to bring users the new broadband services being developed for the Internet. Providing flexible, higher bandwidth services in a mobile environment, however, complicates resource management and control, because of the variable bandwidth requirements of the services, the wideband code division multiple access (WCDMA) radio architecture, and the varying demands on the fixed part of the network infrastructure. Such complexity necessitates sophisticated control and management techniques. Resource control is seen as a short-term response to events whereas management is seen as a longer-term mechanism.

The situation is further complicated by deregulation of mobile networks: an "any-to-any" marketplace is envisaged, where users may buy services from any service provider, and where service providers, in turn, may buy capacity from any network operator. Management of resources is therefore inextricably linked to the business strategies of both service and network providers.

Intelligent agents have been used in several domains, from the design of industrial buildings, through knowledge management for disaster and emergency response professionals to buying and selling on the Internet. Agent technology has been used in the management of telecommunications systems [1-3] to address the problem of distributed resource control and management, as well as to incorporate the "business dimension" with different service providers [4, 5]. Much of this work has dealt with fixed ATM networks but the concepts can be extended to a wireless network.

The extra dimension in a wireless network is the allocation of radio bandwidth to radio cells to avoid local congestion or degradation in QoS. Recent work by Bodanese [6-8] has resulted in a distributed resource allocation scheme for first generation mobile networks using intelligent agents: this scheme offers an efficient approach to resource allocation under moderate to heavy loads.

The rationale for using intelligent agents is to give greater autonomy to small groups of radio cells (base stations) in the mobile network. This autonomy gives an increase in flexibility to deal with new situations in traffic load, and the potential to decrease the signalling overhead on the network. The agent framework combines the requirements for real-time connection-by-connection control with longer-term planning, which may be partially dictated by business considerations. This is achieved by provision of a reactive component within the agents (for rapid response to unplanned conditions) and a planning component (for longer-term optimisation of allocation among cells).

To provide separate communication channels, second generation (2G) networks use one or a combination of access techniques called time division multiple access (TDMA) and frequency division multiple access (FDMA). TDMA allocates channels to separate mobile users in sequential time slots, so that, at any given time, only one user is transmitting. This is analogous to several people in one room taking turns to speak. FDMA allocates channels to users at different frequency bands, so that, at any given time, several users are transmitting, but each at a different frequency. This is analogous to several rooms, each containing two people having a private conversation. Both TDMA and FDMA provide a fixed, finite number of channels, and resource control in a 2G system concentrates on optimal allocation of these channels to users. In 3G networks, however, WCDMA is used to allow multiple access to the radio resource. WCDMA allows all users to transmit simultaneously, and in the same frequency band; it distinguishes users by encoding each user's signal with a unique tag. This is analogous to several people in one room, simultaneously talking in pairs, but each in a different language (encoding). WCDMA is much more flexible for channel allocation but brings with it much more complexity in areas such as congestion control than in TDMA/FDMA systems. As all users share a common frequency, the issue with WCDMA is one of controlling interference rather than assigning frequencies or time slots. The EU IST project "SHUFFLE" aims to implement intelligent agents to address these issues, to control and manage both the business interactions of the service providers and network operators, and the radio resource of 3G networks.

2. Functional Architecture

Figure 1 depicts the general case of relationships between service providers (SPs) and network providers (NPs). Users may choose between a number of SPs from which to buy services, and, in turn, SPs may choose between a number of NPs from which to buy capacity to deliver those services. This contrasts with the simpler model of existing 2G networks where generally the user is restricted to only one SP, and SP and NP are typically the same organisation. This latter situation may also be the case in our scenario but the business roles are allowed to be separated.

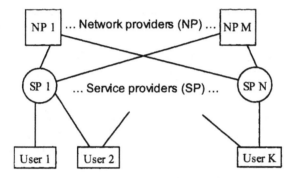

Figure 1. General interaction

Combining the agent control of both user-SP and SP-NP interactions leads to an outline functional architecture as shown in Figure 2.

This model describes two separate interactions: (1) setting up a connection (used loosely here to encompass both circuit-based services such as voice, and connection-oriented services such as TCP/IP), and (2) negotiation of a Service Level Agreement (SLA) between a user and a SP, and between a service provider and a network provider.

2.1 Connection Set-up

When a user wishes to make a connection for a particular type of service (a voice conversation, for example) the User Agent (UA), which has a client interface in the user's mobile terminal, contacts the Resource Agent of some chosen service provider (SPRA). The service provider may have been chosen manually by the user, via the terminal's interface, or by gate-keeping intelligence within the UA. This initial request for a connection may be carried over any available network provider's network. The sequence of events is thus:

1. Either the user, or the UA, on behalf of the user, chooses a service provider;
2. The UA sends a request for a connection to the SPRA of that service provider (solid arrow from UA to SPRA in Figure 2) over any available network;
3. The SPRA "chooses" a network provider to physically carry the connection over its radio network. The choice may be made based on such factors as price and reputation (discussed below);
4. The reactive component of the SPRA relays the connection request to the NPRA of its chosen network provider (solid arrow from SPRA to either NPRA1 or NPRA2 in Figure 2);
5. The reactive component of the NPRA determines if it has the required radio resource to carry the requested connection. It signals the result of this determination back to the SPRA, in either event (solid arrow from NPRA back to SPRA in Figure 2);
6. The SPRA receives the "yes/no" decision from the NPRA. If the answer is "no," the SPRA may contact an alternative NP to request the connection, or it may immediately report back failure to the UA, depending on circumstances.
7. If the answer is "yes," the SPRA relays this back to the UA and tells the UA which network the terminal should connect to for that connection (solid arrow back from SPRA to UA in Figure 2);
8. The connection is set up.
9. When the user terminates the connection, the UA contacts the NPRA (solid arrow from UA to either NPRA1 or NPRA2 in Figure 2), the connection is torn down, the network provider bills the service provider for the bandwidth (radio resource) used, and the service provider bills the user for the service used over the radio resource.

It should be noted that all of this activity takes place within the resource plane, completely separate from negotiation activity, which is now described.

2.2 Negotiation

Negotiation occurs under at least two circumstances: composition of Service Level Agreements (SLAs) between parties, and set-up of bandwidth-intensive services (for example, video conference calls).

2.2.1 Service Level Agreements

SLAs are contracts for expected reasonable behaviour between interested parties (users, service providers and network providers). When a user subscribes to a service provider, some kind of SLA will be negotiated between the two, specifying the user's required level of service (their class), what types of service are required, prices to be paid for those services, penalties for failing to deliver agreed levels of service, etc. This list is not exhaustive.

Because of the scarcity of radio resource, unlike fixed resource in, say, an ATM network (for example, IMPACT, [4]) it is not possible for service providers to reserve capacity from a network provider ahead of time.[1] Instead, the service providers lease a "right to access capacity". This right forms part of the SLA between a service provider and a network provider, along with other parameters such as price, and penalties for conformance failure.

Although SLAs are necessarily agreed between parties at the initiation of a relationship (for example when a user first subscribes to a service provider, or when a service provider first negotiates terms of business with a network operator) it is not required that they remain fixed. SLAs may be dynamically renegotiated in light of changing requirements, market conditions, business strategies, etc. This provides additional flexibility.

SLAs are written to be legally binding (and hence capable of interpretation by a lawyer, should the need arise) but can be specified in electronic form (using XML, for example) for use by the agents representing the relevant parties. The definition and implementation of SLAs is part of the work of the SHUFFLE project, but is beyond the scope of this paper. These topics are yet to be fully addressed within the project. The following section outlines progress on negotiation in the context of runtime connection admission.

2.2.2 Negotiation for Bandwidth-intensive connections

Under ordinary circumstances, the services that users require can be handled purely in the resource plane, by the reactive components of the relevant resource agents, which attempt to allocate resources to meet their SLAs. However, from time to time, a user may want a service that requires very high bandwidth, such as streaming delivery of video media. Depending on the type of cell in which the user is situated, the required bandwidth may represent a significant proportion of that available to carry all connections, or it may even exceed this amount. Under this circumstance, if the service is important enough to the user, the request may be flagged as being willing to submit to negotiation for its connection.

The trade-off is in terms of time against probability of success of the connection. In general, users want rapid response to their requests for connections, measured in terms of milliseconds. However, a user wanting a resource-hungry service may be willing to accept a small delay (of the order of a few seconds) if this leads to a greater likelihood that the connection will succeed. This delay gives the service provider the leeway to negotiate, both with the UA (in terms of acceptable QoS measures for the service, such as bit rate), and with several network providers (which may competitively bid to carry the connection). The constraints on the terms of negotiation are set out in the relevant SLAs. In this instance, negotiation may permit a connection that would otherwise not succeed to be set up. This is desirable from the user's point of view, and from both service and network providers' points

---

[1] A simple calculation shows that if there are four service providers, each reserving the same capacity from a network provider, the maximum capacity anyone could have a cell with a capacity of 2Mbit/s is 0.5Mbit/s: this fixed reservation is clearly unsatisfactory and dynamic allocation is required.

of view, because they do business with resource that otherwise may have been unusable.

2.3 Monitoring and Management

The resource agents and negotiation agents of service providers and network providers perform actions dictated by *policies*. Policies will be discussed in more detail below but essentially define how an agent acts in response to particular types of event. All the while the resource and negotiation agents are performing their actions, their activities are being monitored, both internally, by the agents themselves, but also externally by top-level agents representing their owners: the Service Provider Agent (SPA) in the case of a service provider, and the Network Provider Agent (NPA) in the case of a network operator. Agents are monitored to assess how well their activities perform in relation to the SLAs to which they must conform, and the SPA/NPA can tune or change policies used by their resource and negotiation agents. Policies may be changed because of poor performance, or for contingency management, for example in the case of changing business requirements, legislative, environmental or safety-related considerations, or partial network failure. Again, this list is not exhaustive.

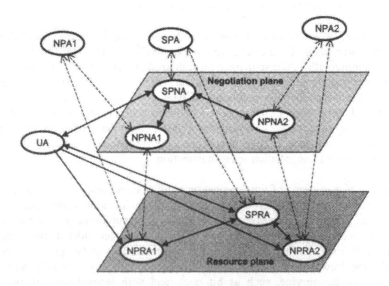

UA – User Agent
SPA – Service Provider Agent
SPNA – Service Provider Negotiation Agent
SPRA – Service Provider Resource Agent

NPA – Network Provider Agent
NPNA – Network Provider Negotiation Agent
NPRA – Network Provider Resource Agent

Figure 2. Functional architecture adopted by SHUFFLE. This example illustrates a scenario with one service provider and two network providers, NP1 and NP2.

Monitoring and policy management interactions are shown in Figure 2 as broken arrows between the NPA and its NPNA and NPRA, and likewise, between the SPA and its SPNA and SPRA.

3. Agent Architecture

Figure 3 shows how the functional architecture maps directly onto the architecture of an individual agent. This is a large system with many agent roles. There are runtime resource management roles, performed by the Service Providers' and Network Providers' Resource Agents (SPRA and NPRA, respectively). There are tactical and strategic roles related to specification of SLA content and Provider management strategies, which are managed by the Service Providers' and Network Providers' overall coordination agents (SPA and NPA, respectively) and negotiation agents (SPNA and NPNA respectively). Every agent has a multi-layered architecture, loosely modelled on, and sharing features of, INTERRAP [9], TouringMachines [10] and the architecture described by Bodanese [8], who used reactive, local planning and cooperative layers. The local planning and cooperative layers are often considered in combination as "the planning component" of an agent.

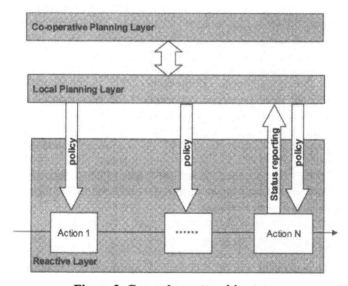

Figure 3. General agent architecture

It is vital in managing individual connections that decisions are made in real time, so the reactive layer is designed for very fast response. It dumbly executes one or more actions, in response to incoming events from the environment, and each of these actions is associated with a policy that specifies it. These policies are formulated by the planning layers of the agents, and may be altered by parameterisation (tuning) or outright substitution of one policy for another. Policies may also be influenced by the SPA or NPA as described above. From one moment to the next, the reactive layer merely acts according to the dictates of its policies, neither knowing nor caring what they are or their results.

The planning component of the agent formulates these policies in an attempt to conform to the QoS requirements specified in the SLAs it has with other actors, and to comply with any other business requirements of its owner. Layering allows the rapid response of the reactive component to be coupled with more complex, longer-term activities in the local planning and cooperative layers. These planning layers can take a slower, more deliberative approach, attempting to predict traffic patterns and adjust policies accordingly.

The local planning layer is so called as its remit is the immediate environment of the agent; in the network provider's resource agent, for example, this could be QoS maintenance in the cell or group of cells controlled by the agent. The cooperative layer exists to coordinate group activities across several agents, for example the alteration of cell coverage patterns to optimise coverage around a hotspot.

There are seven different types of agent in SHUFFLE's multi-agent system. The role of each is summarised below:

- *User Agent* – the UA resides in or near the user's mobile terminal and represents the interests of the user. It is responsible for maintaining SLAs with all service providers with which the user has a subscription, possibly choosing between service providers at the time of connection set-up (unless the user has chosen manually), and relaying connection requests to those service providers' resource agents. There are several other possible roles for a UA, such as user profiling but none of these is core to SHUFFLE's architecture.
- *Service Provider Agent and Network Provider Agent* – both SPA and NPA are top-level agents whose function is to monitor and control their resource and negotiation agents on behalf of their owners, either a service provider in the case of the SPA, or a network provider in the case of the NPA. In addition to the intrinsic policy based mechanisms of these agents, the SPA and NPA may effect changes to policies used in their owner's other agents, for example in the face of changing business considerations.
- *Service Provider Negotiation Agent* – the SPNA has two main roles: (1) negotiation of SLAs with both the UA of a subscribing user, and the NPNA of a network operator from which its owning service provider leases a right to access capacity; (2) negotiation over high bandwidth connections that otherwise could not be served due to lack of capacity, when some service is better than none at all.
- *Service Provider Resource Agent* – the SPRA is considered below.
- *Network Provider Negotiation Agent* – the NPNA negotiates SLAs with service providers wishing to lease the right to access bandwidth over its owner's network, and participates in negotiation over high bandwidth connections as described with the SPNA.
- *Network Provider Resource Agent* – is considered below.

3.1 A Specific Example – the Network Provider Resource Agent

The NPRA is responsible for controlling and managing the radio resource of its network provider, either at the level of individual cells, or a small group of cells controlled by a Radio Network Controller (RNC). This resource is made available for carrying connections (made by users and relayed by service providers) and management attempts to achieve the state where availability matches that specified in the network operator's SLAs with service providers. Figure 4 depicts the internal architecture of the NPRA, and the information it receives when a connection is requested.

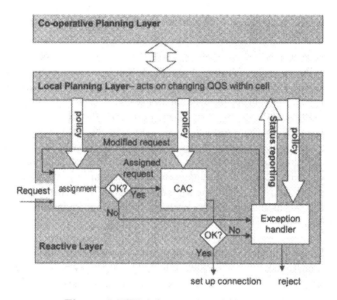

Figure 4. NPRA internal architecture

To handle incoming connection requests, the NPRA must perform at least two actions: assign a cell (radio transceiver, base station) to carry the connection (assignment), and set up the connection at that cell (connection admission control, CAC). In addition, the NPRA may provide a fallback mechanism to permit connection of some services that might otherwise be blocked, probably because the QoS they require (in terms of bit rate) is not deliverable (exception handling).

Each of these actions (assignment, CAC, exception handling) is determined by a separate policy formulated in the planning component of the NPRA. Different strategies for assignment could be used, or the existing strategy could be fine-tuned, for example. Policies are dynamically "passed down" from the higher planning layers, as a result of monitoring the performance of the reactive layer. This permits the planning component to respond to local and more widespread resource issues by changing assignment or CAC policies.

If assignment and CAC are successful, the connection is then set up in the network. In the event of failure, the connection request is passed to the exception handler, which considers whether the request should be rejected, or modified according to its current policy (perhaps reducing the QoS) and resubmitted. This can allow connection requests that would otherwise fail to succeed.

It can be seen that handling of a connection request is very fast at the reactive layer, but that the planning component has a lot of flexibility in changing policies to suit both current and predicted future conditions. Moreover, the planning component can make these decisions as a result of communicating with the NPNA to discover, for example, which service providers should be given preference due to the current state of their SLAs.

3.2 A Specific Example – the Service Provider Resource Agent

The function of the SPRA is to accept connection requests from users (via their UAs) and to choose an appropriate network operator to carry each connection. The SPRA also has a layered architecture. For normal connection requests, that is,. requests that have not been flagged as requiring negotiation, the reactive layer chooses the NPRA with the highest "reputation". At the moment, reputation of an NPRA corresponds to the proportion of requested bit rate allocated to amount requested, though a more general utility function could be substituted. There are two mechanisms for computing reputation. One is a simple modification of "tit for tat" where reputation is incremented or decremented depending on the response of the NPRA. The other method trains a neural network using the same inputs as the tit for tat mechanism, but also includes the demand levels and deviations of performance from the current SLA.

The local planning layer continually monitors the performance of the selections made by the reactive layer and either updates the selection policy using the simple calculations required by the tit for tat mechanism, or by presenting further training samples to the neural network. Future experiments will evaluate the mechanisms.

Selection by reputation, rather than negotiation, is chosen as this gives fast real time response. It is also sensible because it is reasonable to assume that demand for different NPs is correlated, particularly in periods of high demand. (Networks typically have similar busy periods, though this can be controlled to some degree by tariff structures.)

4. Conclusions

This paper has presented the architecture of an overall agent control system for managing resources within a set of 3G mobile networks, subject to competition between service providers and between network operators. The benefits of using agents apply both to the competition between actors and to the detailed management of network resources.

Early work has allowed us to compare novel and traditional assignment and CAC mechanisms for the NPRA and has demonstrated the flexibility of the agent approach. Policies at the reactive layer of can differ in algorithmic structure, and can be parameterised. The local planning layer can select different structural methods and determine "optimal" parameter values for the chosen policy. Future experiments will evaluate the capability of the agent system to control the network under different scenarios. However, it is not appropriate to explain the details, as this requires an understanding of CDMA.

On the architectural side, current work is concentrating on evaluating different approaches to the planning layer in the NPRA and future experiments will evaluate these.

In addition, a powerful approach to radio resource management has been developed at Queen Mary, outside of SHUFFLE, but in parallel[2]. This uses policies formulated in the planning component and enforced by the reactive layer of a network provider's resource agents (NPRAs) to control the radiation patterns of the radio transceivers in its mobile network, and hence the shape and coverage areas of the cells in that network. This provides another action in the NPRA's repertoire for resource management. The use of so-called "smart antennas" is not new in mobile networks, but the use of intelligent agents to cooperatively control radiation patterns is. Preliminary studies show more than 20% increase in capacity using this technique compared with traditional fixed antenna systems.

5. Acknowledgements

The authors would like to gratefully acknowledge financial support from the Commission of the European Union under the Information Society Technologies Programme, as well as contributions from other partners in the SHUFFLE project. The other partners are: Emorphia Ltd (UK), Martel GmbH (CH), Nortel Networks PLC (UK), National Technical University of Athens (GR), Portugal Telecom Inovação SA (PT) and Swisscom AG (CH).

References

1. Kumar G, Venkataram P. Artificial Intelligence approaches to network management: recent advances & a survey. Computer Communications 1997; 20:1313-1322
2. Hayzelden A, Bigham J. Software Agents for Future Communications Systems. Springer-Verlag, Berlin, 1999
3. Hayzelden A, Bigham J. Agent Technology in Communications Systems: An Overview. Knowledge Engineering Review Journal 1999; 14
4. Bigham J, Cuthbert L, Hayzelden A, Luo Z. Flexible Decentralised Control of Connection Admission. In: Proceedings of IMPACT'99, Seattle, WA, USA, 1999
5. Faratin P, Jennings NR, Buckle P, Sierra C. Automated Negotiation for Provisioning Virtual Private Networks using FIPA-Compliant Agents. In: Proceedings of PAAM2000, Manchester, UK, 2000
6. Bodanese E, Cuthbert L. Intelligent Agents for Resource Allocation in Mobile Networks. In: Proceedings of XVII World Telecommunications Congress, Birmingham, UK, 2000

---

[2] This work is the subject of a patent application.

7. Bodanese E, Cuthbert L. Application of Intelligent Agents in Channel Allocation Strategies for Mobile Networks. In: Proceedings of 2000 IEEE International Conference on Communications (ICC2000), New Orleans, LA, USA, 2000

8. Bodanese, E, Cuthbert L. A Multiagent Channel Allocation Scheme for Cellular Mobile Networks. In: Proceedings of 4th International Conference on Multi-Agent Systems (ICMAS2000), Boston, MA, USA, 2000

9. Mueller, J. A cooperation model for autonomous agents. In: Wooldridge M, Jennings NR, Mueller JP (ed) Intelligent Agents III, vol 1193, pp 245-260. Springer-Verlag, Berlin, 1997

10. Ferguson IA. TouringMachines: An Architecture for Dynamic, Rational, Mobile Agents. PhD thesis, Clare Hall, University of Cambridge, Cambridge, UK, 1992

DARBS: A Distributed Blackboard System

L. Nolle[1] K.C.P. Wong[2] A.A. Hopgood[3]

[1]Oxford Research Unit, The Open University
Berkley Road, Oxford, OX1 5HR, UK

[2]Faculty of Technology, The Open University
Walton Hall, Milton Keynes, MK7 6AA, UK

[3]Department of Computing, The Nottingham Trent University
Burton Street, Nottingham, NG1 4BU, UK

Abstract

Prior to this work, an algorithmic and rule-based blackboard system (ARBS) had been developed over a ten-year period. ARBS benefited from a versatile rule structure and the ability to mix computational styles either as separate knowledge-sources or by embedding algorithms within rules. It was a serial system – any knowledge source that was able to contribute had to wait its turn. We report here on a new distributed system, DARBS, in which the knowledge sources are parallel processes. Based around the client/server model, DARBS comprises a centralised database server, i.e. the blackboard, and a number of knowledge source clients. As the clients are separate processes, possibly on separate networked computers, they can contribute to the solution of a problem whenever they have a contribution to make. DARBS therefore achieves the well-established but elusive ideal of opportunism. It behaves as a distributed agent-based system, with the proviso that all communication is via the blackboard. DARBS is currently being applied to automatic interpretation of non-destructive evaluation (NDE) data and control of plasma deposition processes.

1 Introduction

Over the years, ARBS, an in-house rule-based system, developed at the Open University, has been successfully applied to a number of projects for solving engineering problems, ranging from non-destructive evaluation (NDE), controlling plasma deposition processes and controlling telecommunication networks [1-3]. However, ARBS had some limitations. Firstly, it was written in Pop11, which limited its wider acceptability. Secondly, it was originally implemented as a single process, i.e. only one knowledge source could be active at one time. Each knowledge source had a set of preconditions that needed to be fulfilled before a knowledge source could be activated. A separate control module scheduled the knowledge sources using a first-come, first-served strategy. This was clearly a violation of the opportunistic idea of a Blackboard system [4]. In order to overcome this limitation, a distributed architecture has been used. Client/server technology is employed and the communication is through TCP/IP. The new system consists of a Blackboard Server (BS) and a number of modular Knowledge Source Clients. Workloads are distributed to a number of clients which are rule-based modules or other AI systems with specific knowledge in various areas. These clients communicate by adding or removing information to the blackboard. The concept of a blackboard system is analogous to a group of experts discussing a problem by writing and updating information onto the blackboard. The new system is known as the Distributed Algorithmic and Rule-based Blackboard System (DARBS).

2 ARBS

ARBS was originally developed in 1990 with funding from the UK Engineering and Physical Sciences Research Council (EPSRC) and has been refined during several subsequent research projects [1-3,5]. ARBS was written in Pop11 and designed to operate under Unix. It is a blackboard system in which specific tasks are handled by separate knowledge sources that communicate by adding information to an area of the blackboard. Rule-based, procedural, neural networks and genetic algorithm knowledge sources have been successfully integrated into the blackboard system (see Figure 1). The implementation in Pop11 compromised performance. For tackling increasingly complicated engineering problems, it was decided to re-design a new distributed version of the software, DARBS, implemented in standard C++.

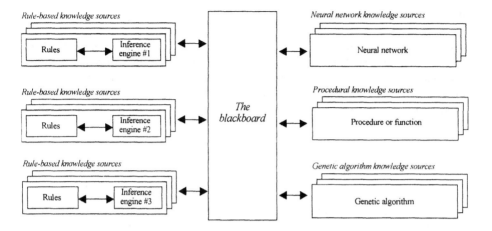

Figure 1 - The Blackboard architecture of ARBS.

3 DARBS

The major improvement of DARBS compared with ARBS is the introduction of parallelism. The knowledge of the problem domain is distributed to a number of client knowledge sources. These knowledge sources can be seen as experts having knowledge in specific areas. The clients are independent and can only communicate through the blackboard. Figure 2 shows the architecture of the blackboard system.

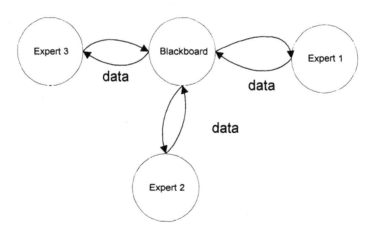

Figure 2 - The architecture of DARBS.

3.1 Blackboard and Knowledge Sources

The blackboard has the appearance of a database. The blackboard can be divided by the knowledge sources during run-time into separate partitions for categorising information. The number of partitions is limited only by the hardware and the operating system used. The knowledge sources can only communicate through the blackboard. All the experts have an equal chance to access the information therein, i.e. on a first-come-first-served basis.

3.2 Parallel Processing

In DARBS, a single blackboard and a number of knowledge sources co-operatively solve a problem. The knowledge sources observe the blackboard constantly and activate themselves when the information interests them. All the knowledge sources run in parallel. Whenever the content of a partition of the blackboard is changed, the blackboard server will broadcast messages to other knowledge sources. The knowledge sources themselves will decide how to react to this change. In other words, the rule-writer should consider how to deal with these broadcast messages when a rule is designed. The requests for reading and writing to the blackboard are atomic, i.e. these requests are non-interruptible. If a new request arrives before the current one has been finished, the new request will be put into a queue for later processing.

3.3 Client/Server Architecture using TCP/IP

DARBS uses client/server technology. The blackboard acts as a server and the knowledge sources act as clients. The communication is through standard TCP/IP (Figure 3). The Internet Protocol (IP) handles the routing from one computer to another, while the Transmission Control Protocol (TCP) handles sequencing, flow control and retransmission to ensure successful delivery [6]. With this approach, the server and clients operate as independent processes. The inter-process communications use the Internet sockets, so that DARBS can be operated over a wide area network (WAN) such as the Internet (Figure 4).

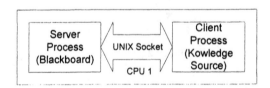

Figure 3 - Client/server communication using UNIX sockets.

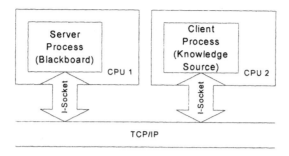

Figure 4 - Client/server communication using INTERNET sockets.

The system is platform-independent. For example, the blackboard server can be run on a Unix machine and knowledge source clients can be run on a number of MS Windows, Mac, Linux and Unix machines. Another advantage of this approach is that the knowledge source client can be written in Java as a web-based applet and thus a knowledge source client can be operated under a web browser and no installation is required.

4 DARBS Knowledge Sources

DARBS integrates various computer techniques into one system. Particular tasks are co-operatively conducted by knowledge sources with specialised expertise. Rule-based and procedural knowledge sources have been integrated into DARBS and neural networks and genetic algorithm knowledge sources will be developed at later stage.

4.1 Knowledge Source Structure

Each knowledge source is encapsulated in a record containing seven fields (Figure 5). The first field specifies the knowledge source name and the second field is the knowledge source type. It can be either rule-based, procedural, neural network or other. For rule-based knowledge sources, there are fields for specifying inference mode (third field) and rules (fourth field). Field 5 is an activation flag that allows individual knowledge sources to be switch on or off. Field 6 is a set of preconditions, which must be satisfied before the knowledge source can be activated. The precondition may comprise sub-conditions joined with Boolean operators AND and OR. Consequently, an additional action field (Field 7) states what actions are to be performed before the knowledge source is deactivated. For procedural, neural network and other non rule-based knowledge sources, the functions and procedures are listed in the action field.

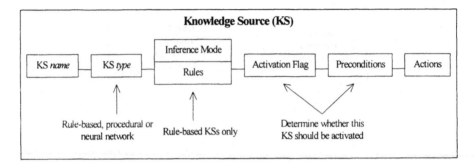

Figure 5 - Knowledge Source Structure.

In DARBS, all knowledge sources run in parallel. They constantly check the blackboard for activation opportunity. Knowledge sources can read data from the blackboard simultaneously. However, to avoid deadlock, only one knowledge source is allowed to write data to the same partition of the blackboard at one time. Whenever the content of the blackboard changes, the blackboard server broadcasts a message to all knowledge sources. The knowledge sources themselves decide how to react to this change, e.g. restart the knowledge source. With this approach, knowledge sources are completely opportunistic, i.e. activating themselves whenever they have some contributions to make to the blackboard.

4.2 Rule Structure

In DARBS, rules can be used for looking up information on the blackboard, making deductions about that information and posting new information on the blackboard. The rule structure is simple, but complex conditions and conclusion can be constructed (Figure 6). Rules consist of four fields. The first field is the rule number. It is followed by a set of conditions and conclusions. Like the precondition field in knowledge sources, the condition may comprise sub-conditions joined with Boolean operators AND and OR. The condition must be satisfied before the conclusion field can be activated. In the conclusion section, information can be added to or deleted from the blackboard and local and external functions can be called. Finally, the last field is for explanation – it is used by the rule-writer to explain why the rule is executed.

4.3 Inference Engines

DARBS offers two types of inference engines, which are based on the principle of multiple and single instantiation of variables [5]. Within a rule, sharing of information can be achieved by employing variables (in contrast to the sharing information between rules, which is carried out via the blackboard). Under multiple instantiation, all possible matches to the variables are found and acted upon with a single firing of a rule. In contrast, only the first match to the variables is found when single instantiation is used. Usually, the multiple instantiation inference mechanism is preferred because it is straightforward and efficient. However, single instantiation might be preferred in circumstances where a time constraint is imposed [2]. An example of a rule is shown in Figure 6.

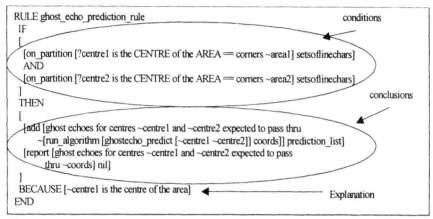

Where:
The match variable, which is prefixed by a "?", will be looked up from the blackboard;
The insert variable, which is prefixed by a "~", will be replaced by the instantiations of that variable.

Figure 6 - A typical DARBS rule.

5 Applications

DARBS is currently employed for automatically interpreting ultrasonic non-destructive evaluation (NDE) data and controlling plasma deposition processes.

5.1 Ultrasonic Non-Destructive Evaluation

Previously, ARBS had been successfully applied to the interpretation of B-scan images from weld defects in flat ferritic steel plates [1]. However, the geometry of the specimen was relatively simple compared with real industrial components. Extensive work is being undertaken for interpreting ultrasonic images of turbine disks and blades, provided by Rolls-Royce. New knowledge sources and rules are under development to cope with the more complex geometric reflections. Artificial neural networks will be developed to classify type of defects.

Figure 7 shows a block diagram of the ultrasonic NDE automatic interpretation system, which is currently under development. Ultrasonic images are loaded to the blackboard for interpretation by rule-based knowledge sources. The stages of interpretation are displayed to the operator through the graphical user interface. The operator can also send commands to the knowledge sources.

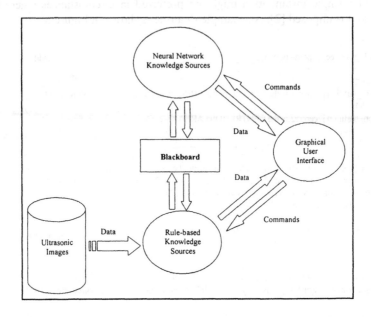

Figure 7 - DARBS-based ultrasonic NDT automatic interpretation system.

5.2 Plasma Process Control

Previous work has involved using artificial intelligence (AI) techniques to control plasma deposition processes from pump-down to switch-off [3]. The AI approach has involved the use of rules and fuzzy logic to mimic the actions of a skilled operator. However, the system is unable to determine for itself the optimum plasma operating conditions. Our current work involves extending the system so that it can explore the parameter space in order to determine the optimum operating conditions. The new system will therefore design the fluxes of species towards surfaces to match the particular process requirements.

Figure 8 shows the control system for low-temperature plasma processes based on DARBS, which is currently under development. It contains a blackboard, which is divided into separate partitions for set-points, measures, commands, and status information. The operator can select process parameters and monitor the process via a graphical user interface. A hardware-driver knowledge source translates the command on the blackboard into suitable signals for the plasma reactor hardware. A timer knowledge source measures the duration of the process and sends a stop command to the blackboard if the maximum process time has been reached. The main control is provided by a rule-based knowledge source. The next step will be to extend the system with a Genetic Algorithm knowledge source.

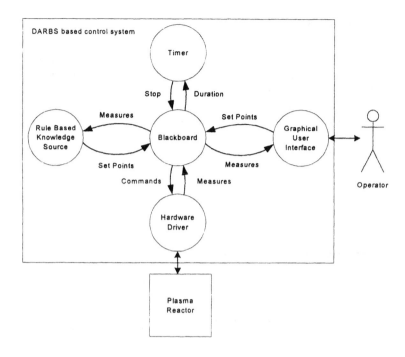

Figure 8 - DARBS-based control system for low-temperature plasma processing.

6 Further Development

DARBS is still in the development phase. The core architecture has been built and tested with simple examples. The results are satisfactory. However, for combating more advanced problems, specialised knowledge sources including neural networks and genetic algorithms need to be built. Initially, DARBS will be run and be tested on a small Intranet. It is anticipated that DARBS will subsequently be operated on the Internet so that knowledge sources developed from different parts of the world can be connected to the central blackboard server.

Currently, the blackboard server and knowledge source clients of DARBS start and terminate manually. It is proposed to develop a DARBS project manager, which will keep track of the project files and the status. It will also launch and terminate the knowledge source clients automatically. A full-featured graphical user interface is also under construction.

7 Conclusion

A blackboard system has been developed with distributed computing features. The project employs client/server technology using TCP/IP, allowing the system to be operated on a LAN, WAN or the Internet. DARBS has been designed to be adaptable so that various kinds of AI approaches can be integrated into the system. Each knowledge source client is equivalent to an agent, with its own specialism. DARBS therefore behaves as a distributed agent-based system, with the proviso that all communication is via the blackboard. The core of DARBS has been built and tested with satisfactory results. To demonstrate the genericity of the system, DARBS is being applied to two different kinds of AI applications, i.e., for automatically interpreting non-destructive evaluation (NDE) data and controlling plasma deposition processes.

8 Acknowledgements

This work was funded by the Open University Strategic Research Initiative and the Engineering and Physical Sciences Research Council (EPSRC) under grant reference GR/M71039/01. The authors are grateful to Mr. Graham Porter of Rolls-Royce for provision of NDT data and advice on its interpretation.

References

1. Hopgood, A.A., Woodcock, N., Hallam, N.J. and Picton, P.D.: Interpreting ultrasonic images using rules, algorithms and neural networks, European Journal of Non-Destructive Testing, 2, (1993), pp 135-149
2. Hopgood, A.A.: Rule-based control of a telecommunications network using the blackboard model, Artificial Intelligence in Engineering, 9, (1994), pp 29-38
3. Hopgood, A.A., Phillips, H.J., Picton, P.D. and Braithwaite, N.S.: Fuzzy logic in a blackboard system for controlling plasma deposition processes, Artificial Intelligence in Engineering, 12 (1997), pp 253-260
4. Engelmore, R.S., Morgan, A.J.: Blackboard Systems, Addison-Wesley, (1998), ISBN 0-201-17431-6
5. Hopgood, A.A.: Intelligent Systems for Engineers and Scientists, 2nd edition, CRC Press, (2000), ISBN 0-8493-0456-3, Boca Raton, FL
6. Matthew N, Stones R.: Beginning Linux Programming, Wrox Press Ltd., (1999), ISBN 1-861002-97-1

A Database Architecture for Reusable CommonKADS Agent Specification Components

Daniel J. Allsopp
Dr. Alan Harrison
Cranfield University
Royal Military College of Science, Shrivenham
Swindon, SN6 8LA, UK
(01793) 785319, (01793) 785648
d.j.allsopp@rmcs.cranfield.ac.uk, ah@rmcs.cranfield.ac.uk

Colin Sheppard
Centre for Defence Analysis
C134 East Court, DERA Portsdown West
Portsdown Hill Road, Fareham, PO17 6AD, UK
(023) 9221 7754
csheppard@dstl.gov.uk

Abstract

Intelligent agent programs and expert systems in certain application domains may share considerable functionality: at an abstract level, specifications of these programs will share some of the knowledge they need to carry out their tasks. If there was a way in which this knowledge could be structured and stored in a repository so that it would be easy to browse, then some of these knowledge components could be reused to specify new intelligent systems in the future. This architecture would also provide an alternative knowledge resource for the developer, shortcutting the knowledge acquisition cycle and speeding up the development process.

This paper describes a prototype database architecture that has been designed to formalize the knowledge repository. The approach taken is founded upon the principles of knowledge specification recommended by the CommonKADS methodology. The repository provides a system of tables, which supports the specification and storage of CommonKADS task, communication, agent and knowledge models. Domain knowledge resides in a 3rd party generic database architecture called the Defence Command and Army Data Model (DCADM) and links (foreign keys) from the knowledge model tables integrate the domain layer into the repository. The repository is built in Oracle 8, and uses a Programming Language SQL (PL/SQL) application layer for standardized data input/output.

1. Introduction

The development of Intelligent Agent programs and Expert Systems is often labour intensive, time consuming and expensive, involving a number of knowledge formatting steps which include knowledge acquisition, knowledge analysis and system design, and system implementation. During knowledge analysis and system design a Knowledge Level specification is produced [1]. The Knowledge Level is an abstract knowledge system or agent specification which allows a knowledge engineer to describe the behaviour of the system under development in terms of its knowledge without making a commitment to its implementation architecture. Once the Knowledge Level representation is transformed into an application, the knowledge encoded within the application becomes more difficult to reuse (unless that same architecture is used for the new implementation), as reverse engineering processes are required to extract the embedded knowledge.

Considerable research has been carried out on formalizing methodologies for deriving Knowledge Level specifications of intelligent systems. In this paper we use the CommonKADS methodology [2] for a number of reasons which we discuss later. During system analysis, specifications and acquired knowledge is often stored in ASCII files or on hand written documents which may be unavailable or unstructured for reuse if a project management scheme is not enforced during development. Alternatively COTS tools for deriving CommonKADS models are used, but data export from these tools is via output files which have a non-standard interface and require bespoke software to import and use effectively with heterogeneous code development applications. A practical knowledge management strategy to format, represent and export these CommonKADS specifications across a wide range of tools using a standard interface would facilitate reusability. This is particularly relevant for supporting the automation of code generation from CommonKADS system specifications [3].

1.1 Research Aims

This research is concerned with the development of a relational database architecture to retain and export CommonKADS specifications of Expert System and agent components to facilitate knowledge reuse across a wide range of applications so that SQL instead of textfiles can be used as a standard medium of data exchange. Our research has shown that there already exist a number of 3rd party database architectures supporting ontological modelling of domain and task data. Rather than implement a database schema for CommonKADS models from scratch, the database architecture upon which our implementation is derived consists of a 3rd party generic schema for object modelling available from the MoD. This database is called the Defence Command and Army Data Model (DCADM). (DCADM is also relevant to us because it comes with instance domain data relevant to our main implementation domain – specifying Computer Generated Force Agent tasks for use in military training simulation). Readers should be aware that the principles underlying the data model of DCADM could be represented in any relational database. We are confident that the database architecture described in this paper could be derived in a relational database without using DCADM, providing that the domain modelling tables are implemented in a similar manner to those described below for the DCADM schema. We are also confident that our database schema is faithful to the CommonKADS methodology and may be used to store a wide range of application specifications.

2. Background

2.1 The CommonKADS Methodology

We acknowledge a number of significant Knowledge Level specification methodologies which include the Generic Tasks approach [4], the Problem Solving Methods approach [5] and the CommonKADS methodology [2]. We have chosen CommonKADS to specify intelligent system components because it has a number of advantageous features. It is well documented, and derived from KADS, a de-facto standard for expert system specification [6]. Knowledge acquisition tools exist to support the specification of CommonKADS models, and these could be used for capturing knowledge for use within the database. In addition, CommonKADS implements many of the best features of the other Knowledge Level specification methodologies listed.

In CommonKADS, a series of models of the knowledge system under development are created. These include a task model of the problem being specified, a communication model specifying interactions between the system and its environment, an agent model describing the agents interacting with the system and a knowledge model that defines how problem solving occurs. The knowledge model is comprised of 3 main knowledge types: domain, inference and task knowledge. Domain knowledge defines real-world entities and concepts represented as class hierarchies. Task knowledge defines procedural, problem solving components such as 'Assess', 'Plan', 'Schedule' and is composed of sub-tasks, inferences and special data input/output tasks called transfer functions. Inferences are atomic tasks, which may be simple algorithms or search mechanisms that act upon and change domain knowledge using rule-sets. CommonKADS defines a library of problem solving task models called Generic Task Models that can be used to build up problem solving knowledge specifications for the system in question.

2.2 Current CommonKADS Tools and Interoperability Issues

There are a limited number of COTS software tools that support the production of CommonKADS models. In addition there are a small number of research tools that support the derivation of parts of these models. The CommonKADS website has a number of links to software available [7].

Currently, the major COTS integrated toolkits for KADS and CommonKADS modelling are PcPACK by Systemics and The CommonKADS WorkBench by Integral Solutions Ltd. [8]. In both applications, persistent data is stored within the application kernel in a 'database' which is not available outside the program. Specification components are output from these applications in the form of textfiles. In PcPACK, knowledge acquired is ultimately processed to derive a knowledge-base containing production rules for the domain. These rules may be exported, but domain ontology entities and lower level CommonKADS model components cannot be exported easily. The CommonKADS WorkBench has more comprehensive data transfer functionality as it supports data exchange between WorkBench software versions using an export facility to produce output textfiles for the various CommonKADS models (note that in version 3.1 of the software, an export file may be produced for the task, agent, communication, and design models only). The format of this file is specific to the WorkBench application, so that the use of these files with other non-WorkBench applications involves producing code to browse these textfiles for import.

The desire to move away from using textfiles to transfer CommonKADS knowledge between applications is a motivation for our approach. We are interested in utilizing the standard features of SQL for data transfer so that the resultant database containing CommonKADS models could be used by as wide a range of applications as possible. Ideally, an application that wishes to use these specifications as a knowledge resource could do so remotely over an Internet connection. As long as the user can access the application layer of the database, then direct data transfer would be supported using SQL: there would be no need to write custom textfile manipulation code simplifying the process of application connectivity.

2.3 Knowledge Storage using Databases – Pros and Cons

Databases offer well understood and well supported storage management and multi-user selection facilities. However, database systems have limited understanding of the meaning of the data stored within them [9]. In contrast, AI research has produced knowledge representation languages such as predicate calculus, semantic nets and production rules to capture the data semantics that cannot be realised in traditional databases. More recently, researchers have found ways of using databases to store data organized in knowledge representation schemes. Wurden has developed a database architecture around a semantic network data model so that the semantics of word and type pairs in the database can be expressed [10]. Other experimental databases for knowledge representation exist organized around frame representation systems such as LOOM [11]. In addition, the CYC knowledge base [12] and the EDR Electronic Dictionary [13] are AI development tools implemented in database architectures.

Our approach to representing the problem solving semantics of domain entities in the database is based on the use of CommonKADS knowledge model rules to define inference strategies. Domain entities form the basis of rules used by problem solving inferences. In the database, the mapping of domain tuples via the domain schema into rules based on First Order Logic (FOL) describes the problem solving knowledge required by inferences to perform their parent tasks.

2.4 The DCADM Database Architecture for CommonKADS Domain Specification

DCADM consists of a generic data model held within an Oracle database. It is primarily a domain representation, although it can be used to store task hierarchies.

DCADM has not been designed to store the semantics of these tasks. The DCADM data model allows for the representation of: items (entities in the universe of discourse), actions (activities, events, tasks), types (generic types of items and actions), classifications, properties (attributes of types), and decompositions (the organization of types and instances into hierarchical structures). DCADM also comes with instance data containing class hierarchies of military domain entities, which although of use to us concerning our main target application [3] is not discussed further [14].

2.5 Fundamentals of DCADM for Modelling Entity and Task Ontology Data

Although DCADM comprises over 40 tables, a subset of the entire schema, comprising 12 tables form the basic domain modelling capability of the database and only this subset is discussed further here (see [14] for the entire schema). In the rest of this paper, database table names are described using capital letters e.g. PCT with their full name in italics. Table column names are given in lower case and are prefixed with the parent table name in uppercase, e.g. the label column of the PCT table is designated PCT.label. Note that a database tuple is equivalent to a database table row incorporating rows of all other tables with which it forms links via foreign keys. Where examples are given in the description below, they are taken from the 'assess-case' knowledge model of the Housing Application Expert System domain. A copy of the knowledge model of this application is available from the CommonKADS website [7] or from [2]. The inference structure for this example domain uses the assessment task template as shown in Figure 1 reproduced from [2].

Figure 1. The Inference Structure for the Housing Application Domain

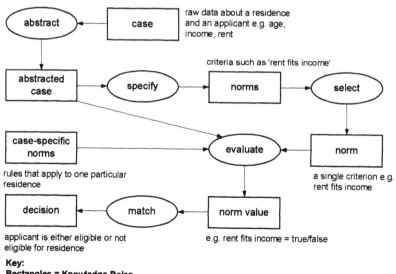

Key:
Rectangles = Knowledge Roles
Ovals = Inferences

2.5.1 Class Instances and Class Types – The Property Concept, Property Concept Type and Classification Tables

Domain and task class types are stored in DCADM using the *Property Concept Type* (PCT) table. A domain or task class name is stored as a string in the PCT.label column. A single character PCT discriminator indicates whether the class is a domain entity (in which case the discriminator is set to 'I' for 'item') or a task (in which case the discriminator is set to 'A' for 'activity'). Instances of PCT types are defined in the *Property Concept* (PC) table. The classification of property concepts as instances of parent concept types involves the *Classification* (CLN) table, which has a foreign key to both the PC and its parent PCT tables.

2.5.2 Hierarchical Classification – Classification Scheme and Cross Classification Tables

For hierarchical classification of class types the *Classification Scheme* (CS) and *Cross Classification* (XCL) tables are used. The CS table contains a foreign key to a PCT tuple and a classification label column (CS.label) that describes the classification relationship being defined for the relevant PCT. For example, a CS tuple used to sub-classify the 'residence' class PCT from the Housing Application domain would contain a foreign key to the 'residence' PCT and might contain the label 'Residence By Type'. A subclass type such as a PCT denoting a 'house' or 'apartment' would then include a pointer to the 'Residence By Type' CS tuple to indicate that this is the classification scheme to which this class belongs. For multiple inheritance relationships, the *Cross Classification* (XCL) table is used. This contains a pair of foreign keys to PCT tuples, allowing one PCT to be linked as a sub-class or refinement of another.

2.5.3 Class Breakdown Structures and Class Ownership – Breakdown Node and Breakdown Type Tables

It is common for class types and instances to be comprised of other classes – for example, a 'residence' might include a 'garage'. In order to model these breakdown structures, DCADM uses the *Breakdown Node* (BN) and *Breakdown Type* (BT) Tables. There are 2 kinds of breakdown node (BN) tuple, a 'root' (parent or owner) node and a 'child' (owned) node. A discriminator character field in the BN table indicates which of these two types is being defined. The BN table contains a foreign key to the PCT table and to the PC table, one or other key may be set. The BN table also contains a mandatory link to the BT table, which contains a label field describing the breakdown type relationship being defined, and a foreign key to a root BN which must be used when defining child BN tuples. Using the 'residence' example, the root BN would contain a link to the 'residence' PCT, and might be classed as a BT 'Residence Object Decomposition'. To associate the 'garage' PCT with its owner PCT, a Child BN tuple would be created with a foreign key to the 'garage' PCT, where the BT for the child node might be 'Residence Component', the ownership cardinality (BN.quantity) might be set to 1, and this tuple would point to its parent 'residence' root BN tuple (see Figure 3).

2.5.4 Class Attributes – Property Type, Property Type Applicability, Property Value, Property Permitted Value and Unit Of Measure Tables

Domain classes have attributes with values, which may be enumerated. The modelling these attributes and values is done using a set of 'Property' tables. A class attribute may be thought of as a *Property Type* (PT), such as the 'address' or 'ZIP code' of a 'residence'. The PT table contains, in addition to the attribute label slot, a foreign key to the *Units Of Measure* (UOM) table, defining the units expected for this attribute. A *Property Type Applicability* (PTAP) tuple is used to associate each PT attribute to its applicable PCT. Thus, a PTAP tuple would link the 'residence' PCT to the 'ZIP code' PT. Values defined using the *Property Value* (PV) table may be set for either PC or PCT tuples. A PV tuple refers via a foreign key to a PT tuple, and contains a value slot, which can contain a number or string. The PV table also contains a foreign key to the *Property Permitted Value* (PPV) table, which may be used to define one of a series of enumerated values allowed for the property value – property type pair.

3. Methodology

Trials indicated that entire CommonKADS specifications could not be stored in DCADM without adding tables to the existing schema. The limitations of the schema were particularly evident when attempting to store components of the knowledge model. The design of the additional database tables required took an iterative approach. Functional groupings of tables were identified and designed in isolation, starting with the 'low level' logic representation tables upward to the 'higher level' task and inference tables that utilize the former structures. When each table group had been created, specification data was input and where semantic deficiencies were identified improvements to table designs were made.

3.1 Software Tools and Architecture

The database described in this paper is built using the Enterprise Edition Release 8.0.4.0.0 of Oracle 8, with SQL*Plus Release 3.3.4.0.0, and incorporates the DCADM schema version 2.4 release 3. Tools used for database programming include 'SQL Programmer Millennium Edition', which was used to write PL/SQL functions, procedures, and triggers and to debug application layer code.

4. The Database Architecture for the Knowledge Model

This section identifies the tables designed to enhance the DCADM schema to allow it to store CommonKADS specifications. Limitations of space do not permit detailed explanation of how CommonKADS task and agent models are defined. This information is essentially hierarchical and can be organized and stored in a similar way to DCADM domain knowledge as previously described. Furthermore, detailed specifications of the structure of tables added to DCADM cannot be included here. Interested readers are referred to [15]. Instead, this section focuses on the representation of the CommonKADS knowledge model, presenting an overview of the tables created to store the semantics of this model. In addition, extensions to the Communication Model to incorporate the 'Communication Primitive' [16] are explained in Section 4.7.

4.1 Domain Knowledge Types, Instances and Breakdown Structures

CommonKADS domain knowledge concepts are represented in the database as PC and PCT tuples. Domain concept attributes are represented by the DCADM Property Tables Group (see Section 2.5.4). For example, a concept 'residence' might have an attribute 'street-address' (defined within the PT table) of type 'string' (defined within the UOM table) as shown in Figure 2. In addition, the representation of domain concept ownership is achieved using the DCADM BN and BT tables (see Section 2.5.3). An example of this is shown in Figure 2. In this example, the 'residence' concept owns the 'garage' concept. The cardinality of this relationship is expressed in the BN.quantity column of the relevant tuple.

Figure 2. Representing Domain Concepts (Classes) in DCADM

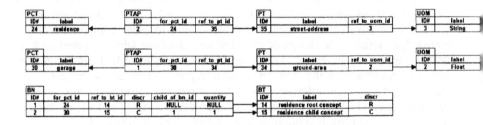

PCT		PTAP			PT			UOM	
ID#	label	ID#	for_pct_id	ref_to_pt_id	ID#	label	ref_to_uom_id	ID#	label
24	residence	2	24	35	35	street-address	3	3	String

PCT		PTAP			PT			UOM	
ID#	label	ID#	for_pct_id	ref_to_pt_id	ID#	label	ref_to_uom_id	ID#	label
30	garage	1	30	34	34	ground-area	2	2	Float

BN						BT		
ID#	for_pct_id	ref_to_bt_id	discr	child_of_bn_id	quantity	ID#	label	discr
1	24	14	R	NULL	NULL	14	residence root concept	R
2	30	15	C	1	1	15	residence child concept	C

4.2 The Domain Schema and Hierarchical Classification

Domain concepts form part of the application domain schema and are classified as such using the CS and XCL tables in the database. In the CommonKADS housing example, the 'residence' concept and the 'applicant' concept are children of the 'housing-application domain schema' as shown in Figure 3.

Figure 3. Hierarchical classification of Domain Concepts (classes) in DCADM

PCT		
ID#	label	within_cs_id
19	generic domain schema	NULL

PCT			CS		
ID#	label	within_cs_id	ID#	label	for_further_desc_of_pct_id
20	housing-application domain schema	1	1	domain schema by type	19

PCT			CS		
ID#	label	within_cs_id	ID#	label	for_further_desc_of_pct_id
24	residence	2	2	housing application schema sub-type	20

PCT		
ID#	label	within_cs_id
25	applicant	2

4.3 Using Domain Schema Concepts in the Knowledge Model

A group of 4 tables are responsible for relating PCT and PC entities to variables or objects used in the knowledge model. These tables include the *Object Variable Term and Knowledge Role* (OVTKR) table, the *OVTKR Membership* (OVTKRMS) table, the *Set and List Definition* (SLD) table and its *SLD Membership* (SLDMS) table. The OVTKR table is responsible for mapping PCT types, PC instances, rule-sets, rule-types, and set and list definitions (defined using the SLD and SLDMS tables) to objects or variables used in logic sentences or in CommonKADS knowledge roles. This table forms the main bridge between the DCADM database layer and all new tables added to store knowledge model data. The *Set and List Definition* table (SLD) and the *Set and List Definition Membership* table (SLDMS) allow objects, variables, knowledge roles, rule sets and rule types to be collected within set or list definitions. This provides additional semantic definition of domain data used within the logic and control groups of tables. The OVTKRMS table allows multiple OVTKR tuples to be linked to other knowledge model tables.

For example, within the Housing Application domain, a variable representing a residence may be defined within OVTKR identified by the string 'Res' which, when output might have the following appearance on the SQL command line (note that 'residence' signifies a PCT type in the DATATYPE_INFO column):

```
LABEL
-------------
DATATYPE_INFO
-------------
Res
Res [Var] [residence]
```

4.4 FOL Sentences of Domain Objects, Variables, Properties and Values

A series of 8 tables are used to specify atomic, logic and quantified logic sentences from the domain objects and variables defined in the OVTKR and OVTKRMS tables described previously. These tables include the *Functional Relational Constant* (FRC) table, the *Functional Expression Term* (FET) table and its *FET Membership* (FETMS) table, the *Atomic Sentence* (ATO) table and its *ATO Membership* (ATOMS) table, the *Logic Sentence* (LG) table and its *LG Membership* (LGMS) table, and the *Quantified Sentence* (QS) table. The grammar rules of FOL are enforced in the design of these tables. Referential integrity constraints between tables and data input triggers ensure that incorrectly formatted data will not break the grammatical rules of the calculus [17]. DCADM property type (PT) tuples may be used to define functional constants in the *Functional Relational Constant* (FRC) table. Functional constants are used to build functional expression terms, which are used to derive atomic sentences. Atomic sentences also incorporate DCADM property value (PV) tuples in association with a relational constant defined within the FRC table. Thus, property value or enumerated property permitted value tuples (PV and PPV tables) may be lifted from the DCADM domain layer to specify the 'right hand side' value of a relation within an atomic sentence. Atomic sentences form the foundation of logic and quantified sentences. For example, the functional expression term 'rent(Res)' may be defined using the FET and FETMS tables, where the functional term tuple 'rent' is related to the 'Res' (residence) variable. This is shown in the following SQL output fragment:

```
     LABEL   DATATYPE_INFO
-----------   -------------------------
  rent(Res)   rent [FRC] [Return Type: Number]
```

This term is used to form the basis of an atomic sentence (ATO), where the Relational Term '>' and numerical value 1007 (defined in the PV table) are also linked to form the sentence: Rent(Res) > 1007. Atomic sentences are joined up within logic sentences to form rules, thus:

```
Gross-yearly-income(App)  >=  70000  AND  Rent(Res)  >  1007
INDICATES rent-fits-income(Res) = TRUE
```

4.5 Rules, Rule-Sets and Knowledge Bases

In CommonKADS, knowledge bases are comprised of rule-sets, which are composed of rules of a certain rule-type and expressed in a 'logic-like' language. In the database, a schema comprising 6 tables stores knowledge base definitions. Thus, *Rule Set* (RS) table data may be composed of one or more *Rule Types* (defined in the RT table) - this link is represented within the *Rule Set Type Membership* (RSTMS) table. Each rule is mapped from the logic table group to its relevant RSTMS table tuple via the *Rule Membership* table (RMS). The *Knowledge Base* (KB) table incorporates multiple rule-sets as defined in the *Knowledge-Base Membership* (KBMS) table: this permits the re-use of rule-sets within various knowledge bases.

Sample output from the database for the 'Measurement-System' knowledge base shown here illustrates how the rule-type string data (bracketed) is output and shows 2 rules as defined in the logic table group:

```
RULE DATA
------------------------------------------
MEASUREMENT-SYSTEM

[RT: RESIDENCE-REQUIREMENT, ANTECEDENT: RESIDENCE-APPLICATION,
CARDINALITY: 1+, CONSEQUENT: RESIDENCE-CRITERION, CARDINALITY:
1, CONNECTION SYMBOL: INDICATES]

subsidy-type(Res) = free-sector INDICATES correct-residence-
category(Res) = TRUE

Gross-yearly-income(App)  >=  70000  AND  Rent(Res)  >  1007
INDICATES rent-fits-income(Res) = TRUE
```

4.6 Control Statements

A group of 7 tables are used to define CommonKADS task, inference and transfer function control statements. A control statement is specified as a control loop defined within the *Control Loop* (CTRL) table, or as a body of pseudo code defined within the *Pseudo-Code* (PSC) table and its *PSC Membership* (PSCMS) table.

Each control loop definition has 2 main components: a control condition or knowledge role status condition, and a block of pseudo code describing the action to take. The *Control Condition* (CCND) and *CCND Membership* (CCNDMS) tables are used to define a control condition within the control loop. Each control condition is comprised of one or more of the following: a function call (a task, inference or transfer function with input and output knowledge roles) as defined in the *Function Call* (FC) and *FC Membership* (RCMS) tables, an atomic sentence, a logic sentence and/or a quantified sentence. The control loop definition can take one of four forms listed below:

Repeat pseudo code (PSC) **until** control condition (CCND) **end repeat**
While control condition (CCND) **do** pseudo code (PSC) **end while**
For-each knowledge role (OVTKR) **in** knowledge role **do** pseudo code **end for-each**
If control condition (CCND) **then** pseudo code (**else** pseudo code) **end if**

The *Pseudo-Code* (PSC) table defines a body of pseudo code that is composed of an algorithm string, or of a sequential list of procedural statements. Each statement may comprise one of the following: a function call (FC & FCMS tables), a control loop (CTRL table), or a role operation (a unary or binary relational operation upon a knowledge role defined within the atomic sentence tables).

For example, the inference 'abstract' (see Figure 1) is linked as a function call tuple (using the FC and FCMS tables) for use within the *Pseudo-Code* and/or *Control Condition* tables, as indicated by this SQL output fragment:

```
LABEL
--------------------------------
DATATYPE_INFO
--------------------------------
abstract(case-description -> abstracted-case)
[IDC Declaration: abstract]  [KNOWLEDGE ROLE DATATYPE INFO:
refer to OVTKR_BUFFER]
```

Here, 'abstract' is an inference declaration (defined within the IDC table described in the next section). The 'case-description' and 'abstracted-case' knowledge roles are defined within the OVTKR table. Further data type information for these knowledge roles is available from the OVTKR output buffer table. These function calls are organized sequentially within the *Pseudo-Code Membership* table thus:

```
SEQ_NO   LABEL
-------  --------------
      1  abstract(case-description -> abstracted-case)
      2  match(abstracted-case + case-specific-requirements ->
decision)
```

4.7 Tasks, Inferences and Transfer Functions

Tasks, inferences and transfer functions are stored in 2 parts: i.e. they have a declaration part and a definition part. A definition describes a specific instance of a declaration. Declarations are stored in the *Task Declaration* (TDC), *Inference Declaration* (IDC) and *Transfer Function Declaration* (TFDC) tables, and definitions are stored in the *Task Definition* (TDF), *Inference Definition* (IDF) and *Transfer Function Definition* (TFDF) tables. Tasks may be comprised of sub-tasks: the *Task Definition Membership* (TDFMS) table is included to link sub-task definitions to relevant super task definitions.

Tasks declarations have input, output and intermediate knowledge roles and a goal pointer to a hierarchical PCT task or a goal string. In the task definition, task pre- and post-conditions are represented by the *Control Condition* table, and a control statement is defined using either the *Control Loop* or *Pseudo-Code* tables.

Inference and transfer function declarations contain a list of input and output knowledge roles and a constraint statement in logic. Transfer function and inference definitions both contain pre-, post- and control condition statements, but are not identical due to the incorporation within the former of the 'Communication Primitive' [16].

The Communication Primitive is essentially an agent communication specification comprising the main body of the message object (or the 'core message'), additional supplementary information ('support message'), together with a message object type flag ('plan', 'goal' ..), the sender agent and recipient agent names, and the transfer function type flag ('send' or 'receive'). The *Transfer Function Definition* table reflects this and includes mandatory slots to define possible courses of action to be taken when the message fails to reach its destination. Although this is not important in the Housing Application domain, in Military domains these additional features are important to define command and control message passing between agents.

There are 2 types of inference definition: procedural inferences and problem-solving inferences. A procedural inference is algorithmic and has a control statement definition. A problem-solving inference uses an axiomatic statement in logic to define its operation as suggested by [18].

When task, inference or transfer function data is output from the database, each declaration and definition part is combined for output as the following example fragment shows for the 'assess-case' task declaration/definition:

```
LABEL
----------------------
assess-case.assess-through-abstract-and-match

PRECONDITION
----------------------
IS-VALID(case-description) = TRUE AND IS-VALID(case-specific-
requirements) = TRUE

CONTROL_STATEMENT
----------------------
abstract(case-description -> abstracted-case);
match(abstracted-case + case-specific-requirements ->
decision);
```

5. Results and Further Work

We are currently attempting to store a range of CommonKADS models to see how expressive the database schema is, and to find limitations so that the schema may be reassessed. Data entry into the database is perhaps the greatest limitation of this approach as this must be done by hand. Tools to automate or support data entry would greatly facilitate usability, but this work would not be trivial and is beyond the funding scope of the current work. We are confident that there is no performance problem in extracting data from the database using complex PL/SQL queries (in our tests, we accessed the Oracle server over a LAN using a Pentium Pro PC client with 130 MB RAM).

The current database schema is a prototype. In terms of the schema, future modifications might include the production of tables or modifications to existing ones to allow robust inference axiomatic statements to be described as in [18]. A robust GUI for the database is also required. The usefulness of our CommonKADS repository needs to be assessed by knowledge engineers to determine where its implementation may be of most value. We believe that a database of this nature is useful to developers of intelligent systems that share considerable domain and task knowledge.

6. Conclusions

Our implementation shows that CommonKADS knowledge models can be stored in a relational database, and furthermore, that the DCADM schema can be used as a basis for the CommonKADS domain model. However, the major drawback to this approach is that data entry to the database is complex and slow. Software tools would greatly facilitate this. However, once data is stored in the database, all of the advantages of SQL, including remote access over the Internet become realized. In our trial domain, i.e. specifying military agent roles for simulation, much domain knowledge is shared by the agents being specified, and so the use of a system like this appears to be an appropriate investment in the time required to input the data into the database.

7. References

1. Newell, A., *The Knowledge Level*. Artificial Intelligence, 1982. **18**: p. 87-127.
2. Schreiber, G., Akkermans, H., Anjewierden, A., de Hoog, R., Shadbolt, N, Van de Velde, W., and Wielinga, B., *Knowledge Engineering and Management, The CommonKADS Methodology*. 1999, Massachusetts: The MIT Press. 447.
3. Allsopp, D.J., Harrison, A., and Sheppard, C. *The Representation and Storage of Military Knowledge to Support the Automated Production of CGF Command Agents*. in *10th Conference on Computer Generated Forces and Behavioural Representation*. 2001. Norfolk, Virginia, USA.
4. Chandrasekaran, B., *Generic tasks in knowledge-based reasoning: High level building blocks for expert system design*. IEEE Expert, 1986. **1**(3 Fall): p. 23-30.
5. Steels, L., *Components of Expertise*. AI Magazine, 1990. **11**(2): p. 28-49.
6. Tansley, D.S.W., and Hayball, C.C., *Knowledge-Based Systems Analysis and Design; A KADS Developer's Handbook*. BCS Practitioner Series, ed. R. Welland. 1993, Hemel Hempstead: Prentice Hall International (UK) Limited.
7. Schreiber, G., *CommonKADS, Engineering and Managing Knowledge (The Common KADS Website)*, . 2001, http://www.commomkads.uva.nl.
8. Integral-Solutions, *CommonKADS WorkBench Installation Guide Version 3.10 Beta*. 1996: Integral Solutions Limited.
9. Date, C.J., *An Introduction to Database Systems*. 6th ed. Addison-Wesley Systems Programming Series, ed. I.E. Board. 1995, Reading, Massachusetts: Addison-Wesley.
10. Wurden, F.L. *Content Is King (If You Can Find It): A New Model for Knowledge Storage and Retrieval*. in *Proceedings of the Thirteenth International Conference on Data Engineering*. 1997. Birmingham, U.K.: IEEE Computer Society.
11. Karp, P.D., Paley, S.M., and Greenberg, I. *A storage system for scalable knowledge representation*. in *Third International Conference on Information and Knowledge Management*. 1994.
12. Lenat, D.B., *CYC: A Large-Scale Investment in Knowledge Infrastructure*. Communications of the ACM, 1995. **Vol 30**(No 11, November): p. 33-38.
13. EDR, *Japan Electronic Dictionary Research Institute Ltd.*, . 1995, http://www.iijnet.or.jp/edr/.
14. ACISA, *DCADM Documentation*, 1999, http://www.cdma.mod.uk/dcadmdoc.htm.
15. Allsopp, D.J., and Harrison, A.H., *STOWSF RCAB Website*, . 2001, http://www.rmcs.cranfield.ac.uk/departments/dois/cismg/rcab/index.html.
16. Haugeneder, H., and Steiner, D., *Co-operating Agents: Concepts and Applications*, in *Agent Technology: Foundations, Applications, and Markets*, N.R. Jennings, and Woolridge, M.J., Editor. 1997, Springer Verlag. p. 175-202.
17. Genesereth, M.R., and Nilsson, N.J., *Logical Foundations of Artificial Intelligence*. 1988, Palo Alto, California: Morgan Kaufmann.
18. Fensel, D., and Groenboom, R., *A software architecture for knowledge-based systems*, in *The Knowledge Engineering Review*. 1999, Cambridge University Press. p. 153-173.

SESSION 4:

KNOWLEDGE REPRESENTATION

UML as an approach to Modelling Knowledge in Rule-based Systems

Anne Håkansson
Department of Information Science, Computer Science
Uppsala University
Uppsala, SWEDEN

Abstract

The Knowledge Acquisition (KA) process within Knowledge Based System (KBS) development has always been a difficult task. Some of the difficulties are connected to the range of different users, from the developers to the end users of a system. These users might be interested in different domain knowledge, which has to be preserved in the KBS. This can be facilitated, e.g. through diagrams from the *Unified Modelling Language* (UML), used for visualising, specifying, constructing and documenting object-oriented systems. UML is a modelling language whose vocabulary and rules focus on a conceptual representation of a system. It is appropriate for modelling systems ranging from enterprise information systems to Web-based applications and real time embedded systems. UML is applicable to a variety of programming languages and it might be quite straightforward applied for developing frame-based systems. Our interest, though, is to apply the UML diagrams to support rule-based KBS development, resulting in modified UML diagrams.

This article suggests an improvement of the KA process from a knowledge representation perspective. The domain knowledge is modelled with modified UML diagrams from both the perspectives of the design user and the end user. These diagrams are used to insert knowledge in the knowledge base as well as generate knowledge about static and dynamic domain knowledge and inform the users about the system's processing etc. The diagrams should be presented by using graphical objects rather than text code, since these objects can support the graphics in UML's diagrams and simplify the understanding of the system.

1. Introduction

One of the steps in Knowledge Based System (KBS) engineering, Knowledge Acquisition (KA), is difficult due to a number of reasons, e.g. problems eliciting the expert's conceptual model, difficulties to create models of the reasoning strategy and elicit the knowledge to support the strategy [19]. Many attempts to facilitate this step have been made but the process still seems difficult and improvements can be suggested.

Different techniques can be used for representing knowledge in a system e.g. rules, frames, semantic networks. They display different representation facilities but we will present our ideas from the perspective of a KBS shell built on top of a rule-based system [12] based on a system giving advice about building dam sites utilised in developing countries [13] in tropical climates. It uses knowledge from a stepwise EIA-method (Environmental Impact Assessment) to advise and educate the end user when assessing the impacts a hydropower development and a river regulation will have on the environment. There is a shortage of expertise and experience and the quantitative background data may be difficult to assess or even be lacking. The same holds for the latest technical information on EIA. Therefore the system is intended to be an intermediate link between the expert and the end user which is more cost-effective than having the expert on the site during the project. After the end user has consulted the system the domain expert follows up the advice offered by the system and meets the end user. EIA employs rule statements because experts seem to find it natural to express their problem solving knowledge in such form. The rule form makes it is easy to expand the system's knowledge which is desirable when applying EIA to other climates [8].

Within Human-Computer Interaction research the *user* is a central concept. The KBS shell area constitutes a good example of when the simple user concept is not strong enough, since the user plays two different roles. The user is both a *system developer* and a *framework user* in the sense that a system developer intends to develop a KBS for an end user. Since the developer in this case uses a KBS shell, i.e. an already developed (framework) system, the developer is also taking the role of a framework user. The developer uses the framework system to develop a final application for another user -- the traditional end user. Since the development of the framework may not include implementing new functions or new interfaces, it may be more appropriate to invent a new term for this type of user, *design developer* or *design user* (the latter term is the one we want to adopt for this paper). The intention of this distinction is to keep the design user separated from the end user in the following discussions.[1]

The end user consults the system and could, in reality, be anyone who needs to use the system and its knowledge. Since the design and the end users will utilise the system for different purposes, they may also have different interests in the system as such and therefore the system should support a range of different users with different views of the internal knowledge. The design user may be interested in the data the system contains and the relationship between data to understand what additional information needs to be inserted in the system to work properly. On the other hand, the end user may want to know what the system is expecting from the user (both domain knowledge and insertion manner) as well as what information is needed to reach conclusions and indicating the different information sets (input, rules and outputs) in the system and the relation between these sets. Moreover, the end user could be interested in understanding the reasoning process behind a certain conclusion.

---

[1] In some cases the developer, as an individual, will use the final application, and under those circumstances he or she will of course be the end user, rather than the design user. It is the task, not the person that is directed by the distinction.

In the article, we use Unified Modelling Language (UML) in the KA-process and modify UML diagrams to suit rule-based systems for supporting different users. The UML's concept is introduced with the notions: things, relationships and diagrams. These notions are close to object-oriented languages and frames but will be modified to suit the insertion and generating of rules in KBS. The result of applying these diagrams is presented and discussed referring to the categories of users (i.e. design user and end user). The graphical diagrams should be implemented in a KBS. Related research indicates the advantages of using UML together with other methods for the entire engineering process.

2. A model of the domain knowledge

The expectations of the users who are developing or using the KBS are often very high. The domain expert needs to be aware of his/her own expertise, extract it and insert it into the system. One problem is to match the domain expert's knowledge into the form of the knowledge base since there can be a mismatch between the expert's expressed knowledge and the computers symbolic representation. The best representation of the domain ought to be the model in the mind of the domain expert, which is also the image that should be presented to the end user. Note, however, that this image may have to be remodelled, to fit the end user's own knowledge set. Thus, the domain expert's knowledge may require remodelling through the KBS to adjust to the end user.

When people use computer systems they form a *mental model* of the system's constitution [18]. This mental model helps them to use the system intelligently and effectively. The structure and behaviour of the underlying objects and the way these are represented in the interface, make the most significant contribution to a product. Some familiar examples of mental models are "schematic maps" (locations) and "analogies and metaphors" (desktop, drag-and-drop).

To simplify the task of knowledge engineering, a conceptual model can be useful. By *conceptual model*, Luger [17] means the knowledge engineer's evolving conception of the domain knowledge. This model could be somewhere between the human expertise and the implemented program [8]. Even if this differs from the domain expert's mental model, this model actually underlies the construction of the knowledge base but is not formal or executable in a computer. The conceptual model is used to evolve conception of the domain and uses, e.g., simple methods to represent the expert's state of reasoning [*ibid*].

2.1 Requirement on the KBS

To use a KBS shell for developing an application with domain knowledge through a suitable user interface, the design user may need expertise from different disciplines. This can be expertise concerning the actual domain that the system will handle, software engineering and cognitive psychology etc. The design user's development of the KBS, by using a shell, requires knowledge about how the system could be implemented to accomplish the desired task. One of the problems is the lack of knowledge about the mechanisms driving the KBS and the type of domain knowledge these systems have to comprise. The design user must also understand how to represent the domain knowledge in the knowledge base, which tends to become rather complex and difficult to comprehend. Furthermore, the design user must understand terms used in the system to be able to utilise them correctly and therefore, some of these terms may need a detailed explanation. Beside the domain knowledge, the system must also have an appealing and comprehensible interface.

The data utilised by the KBS have to be inserted correctly and efficiently by the end user, thus the questions generated must be clear and easy to understand. One parallel is questionnaires in surveys where there are guidelines for how different questions should be asked to get the proper information [9]. Even the conclusion from the system, as presented to the end user, must be easy to understand and useful for an intended task. The intended task is the same as the purpose of the system. Furthermore, the end users have to understand what the system has concluded to be able to use the information in their work etc. For instance, some experts may use terms within a technical language that is not commonly known by others or use terms in another language, e.g. Latin often used within medicine. Such terms must be translated into commonly used words or explained with laymen-oriented explanations.

The design and end users' expectations may not be completely fulfilled but parts of them should be supported. Cognitive psychology describes a large number of theories explaining how humans approach problem solving [8] including the type of knowledge humans use and how humans mentally organise this knowledge, i.e. mental models. Graphical diagrams could support these models.

3. UML

The Unified Modelling language (UML) is a graphical language, offering a standard for writing a system's blueprints, covering "conceptual things" (processes) and "concrete things" (classes in a specific programming language, database schemas and reusable software components) [3]. To deploy good software, modelling is a central part. Models are built to communicate the desired structure and behaviour of the system to the users. Moreover, they let the users visualise and control the system's architecture and support the users' understanding of the system under development offering opportunity for simplifying and reusing software. Moreover, the models can manage risk, guide the construction of a system and document the decisions defined by the users.

A modelling language such as UML can facilitate the KA-process since a model is a simplification of the reality and models are built to give a better understanding the system under development [3]. Modelling can simplify the problem of human's limited ability to understand complex problems by focusing on one aspect at a time. This is an approach to "divide-and-conquer" where a hard problem is attacked by dividing it into smaller, more easily solved, problems.

One single model is not sufficient and every system is best approached through a small set of nearly independent models [3]. "Nearly independent" means that models can be built and studied separately but they are still interrelated. To understand, e.g., the architecture of a system, several complementary and interlocking views can be used. A use case view is exposing the requirements of the system and a design view is capturing the vocabulary of the problem space and the solution space. A process view is modelling the distribution of the system's processes and threads, an implementation view is addressing the physical realisation of the system and the deployment view is focusing on system engineering issues.

3.1 Content of UML

In UML, the conceptual model is illustrated by a set of static structured diagrams [16] and is focusing on the domain concepts, not software entities. The model shows concepts, associations between concepts and attributes of concepts. Informally, a concept is an idea, thing or an object but formally it is a symbol, intention or an extension. Symbols are images or words, intentions are definitions of the concept and extensions are sets of examples to which the concept applies.

UML is a modelling language whose vocabulary and rules focus on conceptual and physical representation of a system [3]. The vocabulary and rules describe how to create and read well-formed models. The vocabulary encompasses three building blocks: things, relationships and diagrams and rules specify the design of well-formed model.

• **Things** are the basic object-oriented building blocks to write models.

Structural represents conceptual or physical elements. There are seven different kinds of structural things. A "Class" represents set of objects and an "Interface" is a collection of operations specifying behaviour of a class. "Collaboration" defines interaction elements that work together. "Use cases" structure behavioural things in a model by describing sets of sequences of the system's actions. "Active class" owns processes or threads and represents elements whose behaviour is concurrent with other elements. "Component" represents physical packaging of logical elements as class, interfaces and collaborations. "Nodes" exist during run time and represent computational resources.

Behavioural is the dynamic part and represents behaviour over time and space. "Interaction" comprises a set of messages exchanged among objects within particular context, including messages, action sequences and links between objects. A "Statechart" specifies the sequences of states an object or interaction goes through, including states, transitions, events and activities.

Grouping is the organisational part in which a model can be decomposed and a package is a mechanism for organising elements into groups. It is purely conceptual.

Annotational is the explanatory part. It describes, illuminates and remarks on the elements in a model. A note is a symbol for rendering constraints and comments attached to elements.

• **Relationships**

Dependency is a semantic relationship between two things. If one thing changes it may affect the semantics of another thing.

Association is a structural relationship that describes a set of links, where a link is a connection among objects.

Generalisation is a specialisation/generalisation relationship in which the specialised element (the child) is substitutable for a generalised element (the parent)

Realisation is a semantic relationship between classifiers where one classifier specifies a contract guaranteed to be carried out by another classifier.

• **Diagrams**

Class contains a set of classes, interfaces and collaborations.

Object presents a set of objects and their relationships. It gives snapshots of a class diagram.

Use case shows a set of possible processes and actors.

Interaction defines a set of objects and their relationships including messages. Interaction diagram includes *Sequence* diagram, which emphasises the time ordering of messages, and *Collaboration* diagram that stresses the structural organisation of the objects that send and receive messages.

State chart shows a state machine consisting of states, transitions, events and activities.

Activity is a special kind of state chart presenting the flow between activities.

Component describes the organisations and dependencies among set of components. Essentially they are class diagrams, focusing on a system's components.

Deployment shows the physical nodes of computers and the mapping of the components of those nodes.

• **Rules**, are semantic rules for names (denoting things, relationships and diagrams), scope (context giving a meaning to a name), visibility (how names can be seen and used by others), integrity (how things properly and consistently relate to one another) and execution (what it means to run or simulate a dynamic model).

Since modelling yields an understanding of a system only one model is not sufficient. Instead, multiple models connected to one another are needed. UML uses a bunch of graphical symbols in the diagrams and behind each symbol there are well-defined semantics. In this manner, different developers can use the same models for different purposes [3].

4. UML for Knowledge Based Systems

In KBS's, UML could be used with frame-based systems since it may be more straightforward to use a representation similar to an object-oriented model and features in frame-based systems are related to object-oriented programming [8]. For instance, the object-oriented system describes objects in terms of appearance and behaviour, as in a frame-based system.

Learning about the world is to learn from experience when using objects in the world. From these experiences, a conceptual understanding of the objects is built and some features used in frame-based systems are related to the issue of cognitive efficiency in humans, i.e. inheritance.

Frame-based systems facilitate the development of knowledge-based systems since the knowledge engineers get support for understanding the relationship among data and enhances the ability of the inference engine to operate on the data and structural relationship [15]. The term class is used to denote knowledge about a set of other classes or objects. Other related knowledge is associated with subordinate frames. In frames a subclass represents a specialisation of the class to which they relate. A subclass represents a narrowing of the concept and is referred to a taxonomy. Taxonomy is a hierarchy where each class represents a generalisation of a subordinate class and the subclass at the lowest level will represent the most specific class. If a class represents multiple objects, instances may be used. Instances would represent a specific case or instantiation of the general concept. This can be compared to UML's things with classes, objects etc.

The frames' internal structure is providing a set of slots in which knowledge, associated with a frame, is stored [15]. Each slot can have procedures or monitors attached to it. Some common monitors are "if needed"(value for empty slot), "when accessed" (value is accessed), "before change" (before value is changed) and "after changed" (after value is changed). The attached procedure can monitor the assignment of information to a slot, ensuring that appropriate action is taken after the value has been changed. This can be compared to UML's semantics and structural relationships.

4.1 UML for Rule-based Knowledge Based Systems

It is possible to use UML, without hard work, for representing the result from the diagrams into frames [11]. But is it possible to use UML as a support in the KA-process for rule-based systems? Since frames are rather similar to UML and rule-based and procedural knowledge representations can operate efficiently in frame-based systems and object-oriented systems, it may be possible to utilise UML on rule-based systems, as well. Many frame-based systems can employ a set of rules that interact with information contained in the frames, so called hybrid systems [8]. Such systems can combine frames and rules for knowledge representation.

UML enables the developers to visualise their work in things (conceptual or physical elements, behaviour, groups and annotations), relationships (between things) and diagrams [14]. These diagrams are used to view the process from different angles [2]. Of course, the notation of UML must be adjusted for this new application area. We suggest that the following ideas from UML can be applied in rule-based system development and we relate them to both the design user and the end user:

• The users interaction with the system.

UML: use-cases show typical interactions the actors have with the system. The idea is to identify the users' goals and not the system's functions. This is accomplished by treating a user's task as a use-case, and asking how the computer system can support it [9]. In UML, use-case diagrams are important in organising and modelling the behaviour of a system [3]. A use case can define the entire

194

sequence of interactions between the user and the system when solving a particular task [1].

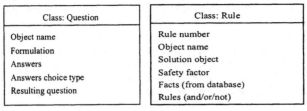

Figure 1 Examples of Use Cases for end users and design users.

KBS: use-cases can be used to describe the tasks the system can perform both from the end user's and the design user's point of views, see figure 1. By designing these models, the requirements of the KBS are modelled. For instance, the end user can consult the system, consult with given answers, fetch old session, save session and list database. Within these alternatives, more detailed tasks are present which also need to be illustrated by use cases. The design user can develop the KBS by adding, deleting or editing rules, questions or conclusions. Moreover, the knowledge bases can be listed (with questions, rules and conclusions) and the rule consistency can be checked.

• The <u>involved objects</u> in the system.

UML: The class diagram describes the types of objects used in the system and the static relationships between them [9]. The object diagram also describes a set of objects and their relationships. These diagrams are used to represent the concepts in the domain under study and the relationships between instances of types. The instance shows the object's structure, attributes and the relationships to other objects [2].

Class: Question	Class: Rule
Object name Formulation Answers Answers choice type Resulting question	Rule number Object name Solution object Safety factor Facts (from database) Rules (and/or/not)

Figure 2 Templates for questions and rules.

KBS: Class diagrams can be used as templates for the parts to be inserted into the system. From the template or the class, objects are created, see figure 2. The classes are questions, rules, conclusions, question definitions etc. These classes have relationships, e.g., rules are related both to questions and conclusions by the relationships, facts (the answers from a consultation) and solution objects (used by the interpreter). The rules can also be related to other rules by comprising them.

The objects, created from classes are stored in different knowledge bases. The end user may not use classes but the objects, e.g. to answer questions correctly by using single or multiple answer alternatives.

• The interactions, including sequences and relations, involved in the consultation and interpretation of the content.

UML: an interaction diagram in UML views the interaction, consisting of objects and relationships [3], including the collaborations and sequences between the objects. These diagrams are used to examine the behaviour of several objects within a single use case [9].

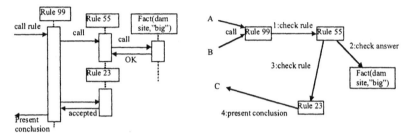

Figure 3 Examples of sequence diagram and collaboration diagram

KBS: The design user must investigate this performance to decide if the system's behaviour is acceptable. The system should behave as a domain expert by drawing the conclusions in the same manner as the design user. This implies, using the same kind of reason strategy as the domain expert, meaning the system uses the same facts and rules to draw the same conclusions. To check this behaviour, the design user may inspect the interaction diagrams.

Sequence: A consultation or an interpretation of the KBS content will involve call sequences, i.e., the sequences different parts (rules) will interact with each other, see figure 3. One of the challenges is to illustrate how different rules are statically related. Usually a single rule is related to several others and becomes dependent of these. The connections or relations are important since the interpretation depends on them. A relation can be: Rule99 if Rule55 and Rule23, Rule55 if Fact (question "dam site", answer "big"). The input from the end user becomes the fact, when a specific question has been answered. Of course, the fact can previously be included in the knowledge base.

Collaboration: It is difficult to control and overview relations between different parts: input, output and rules. The collaboration between these parts shows how different parts are linked together, see figure 3. This would be a stepwise exposition of the parts that are involved in an interpretation for a specific conclusion. For example, to reach the conclusion C, one input, A or B, may be used together with the rules, Rule99, Rule55, Rule23 and the fact Dam site. Since, the collaboration is dynamic, it is possible to check the result based on other data.

By using collaboration diagrams, it may be easier to get an overview of the entities in the sets.

The interaction diagrams can be used to visualise Why and How-questions. Through Why explanations, the end user can check the answers' role in the consultation. Furthermore, the explanation may be used to simplify the end user's comprehension of the system's reasoning process. The reasoning process may also be viewed by using How explanations. This may be interesting if the end user is not satisfied with the conclusion. The end user can check the kind of data the system utilised and change it in the next consultation.

• The <u>activities</u> taking place in the system and the <u>states</u> different parts have.

UML: the activity diagram focuses on activities and shows the flow from one activity to another [2] and results in some action. Activity diagrams are useful when the user wants to describe a behaviour, which is parallel, or show behaviours in several interacting use-cases. Statechart diagrams give an explicit, even a formal definition of the objects' behaviour. These diagrams are ideal for describing and modelling the behaviour of an interface, class, collaboration and event-ordered behaviour of an object.

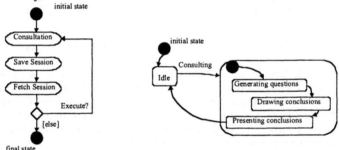

Figure 4 Examples of activity diagram and state chart diagram.

KBS Activity: the activity can show a procedural behaviour of a declarative representation, giving an understanding of how use cases are working in the system, see figure 4. On a detailed level it is possible to view the consultation and it is even possible to follow the interpretation. Compared to the interaction diagrams, see figure 2, this diagram displays the reasoning on a higher abstraction level. The design user can follow the process, stepwise, and judge if it is acceptable. Even the end user can follow this reasoning process, hence, the why and how explanations are generated on another level. Notice, the more explicit the representation of the knowledge underlying the system's design, the better explanations can be generated [5].

KBS Statechart: all states and their content should have a description of how they behave, what constraints there are, the dependency between others etc. For instance, the chart can present the objects' or interpreter's states and the information flow between them. A state diagram can view, for example, the performance: generating questions, drawing conclusions and presenting conclusions and the flow between them, see figure 4. At a detailed level, state diagrams can be utilised to insert production rules with facts and other rules. When several rules have been inserted it is possible to produce meta-rules, as well.

During the consultation, a kind of Statechart may be generated, where each part involved should be presented to the end user. A specific part, a question, can be studied to get information about when and in what context it is used. This may also clarify the systems reasoning process. For instance, the design user must be aware of the resulting questions and whether a question is more specific than another. Besides, the end user can be aware that there is a follow-up question (resulting question), which means there is a dependency between different questions.

• The comprehending of the content in large systems.

UML: large systems are special challenges and often problematic to comprehend. A technique to handle models for large systems in UML is grouping or packages, where each class is corresponding to a single package. Each package contains, of course, several depending objects. The overall picture of the system is the picture of packages and their dependencies, the aim is to keep these dependencies to a minimum.

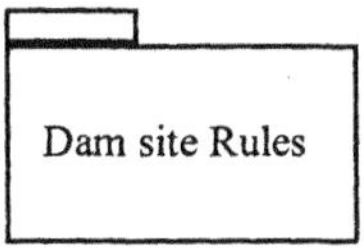

Figure 5 Package of rules that handle dam sites.

KBS: To comprehend large systems, a package can encapsulate data to decrease the complexity of the system's content. Hence, the design user does not have to deal with all the information simultaneously and can easier comprehend the whole content. For example, the rules that are connected with other rules can all be packed into one package, see figure 5. The problem with the package is the rules shared by several other rules have to be denoted to inform the design user about the sharing. By unfolding this package, all rules can be presented in a sequence or in a collaboration diagram. This will support the design user when a rule is edited since it can be rather easy to notice the depending rules.

The package can present the knowledge in a hierarchy structure and on the highest level the most abstract knowledge is found. By using packages, the end user only has to deal with one piece of knowledge at a time and at different level of details. This can be a benefit to end users with different expertise since they may need various kinds of knowledge.

Component and Deployment diagrams are not discussed here but can be useful for viewing the system's file structure (making the system's content more transparent) and for putting notes in the diagrams (producing and viewing explaining text), respectively. Neither is the UML's additional conceptual model used for showing concepts in the domain with associations and attributes [17] discussed. These are similar to DFD and can be used to describe the real-world concepts in the domain.

Beside structure and behaviour, the design user should be able to handle and develop the interface of the system, as well. To develop a useable interface is difficult but very significant for the success of the final system since the end user will judge the interface from a usability perspective, not supported by UML.

5. Further work

Since different user categories will develop or execute the KBS, they may need different interfaces. The interface has to support both the design users and the end users by displaying the necessary knowledge. It should, of course, be highly supportive, intuitive and convenient for the user to use, which is the definition of usability [18].

There are possible solutions, which can solve design user's and end user's needs. It may be feasible to present knowledge on different levels of details and to use multiple representations of the same task [10]. Some systems are linked to a set of standard data models (relational, hierarchical, object-oriented etc), where the designer chooses the model to use [19]. Instead of using only one representation, the design user should be able to choose among several representations and to perceive the state of the computation easier, the knowledge should be expressed graphically in the interface.

The models used in object-oriented systems and UML can graphically be displayed by using boxes, lines and figures, etc. The concept of user monitoring a "view" of an object is central to interface design [18]. A view is a visual presentation of an object and there may be many views of a single object.

In our case, the information gathered by UML diagrams is presented in a rule-based KBS interface. The best solution for this would be to implement the diagrams directly in the system, graphically. The design user would not have to transform the data in the diagrams into the knowledge system. If this is not possible, other suitable data representations must be found and used to represent the UML diagrams.

6. Related work

To the best of our knowledge, there is no work where UML has been used with rule-based KBS. However, relating or using UML with other systems has been discussed. CommonKads is a methodology to support structured knowledge engineering and is a standard for knowledge analysis and knowledge-intensive information systems [20]. It provides a link to object-oriented development and uses notations compatible with UML wherever possible, in particular class diagrams, activity diagrams and state diagrams.

RDF-schemas have been discussed with UML[6]. A RDF-Schema is specified by a declarative language, which uses knowledge representation ideas as semantic nets, frames and database schema representation models and graph data models. The RDF-schemas specify information about classes, including properties (attributes) and relationships between classes.

A three-dimensional spiral model has been used with UML for an iterative and incremental solution for developing expert systems. It is used as a software life cycle model [1] to develop an application for isokinetics interpretation. In this model, use cases can be employed as a means of modelling system requirements and outputting appropriate specifications. The use cases illustrate the actors using the system, which are represented in actor interaction diagram and activities flow diagram. The knowledge is represented as rules in the system.

An example where a methodology is based on UML is MWOOD [7]. It is more specific than UML and the purpose is to provide a practical, implementation based framework for rapid development of applications supporting organisational frameworks. The class and object concepts have been re-implemented in a frame based functional object-oriented language to represent decision of analysis, specification, design and implementation.

7. Conclusions

We have illustrated how the design user can be supported during insertion of knowledge and also keeping track of the inserted knowledge. It is important that the design user has a mental model of the content of the system. The users' perception of persistent characteristic structure in different images, the frame effect [4], must be explicitly considered in order to avoid disorientation. Furthermore, it is important to know how the system processes this content. The method we use to support the developer in software design is UML applied to suit rule-based systems.

We have given several examples of how the content of a KBS can be displayed through different presentations by showing how various diagrams can support the design user, a very important user of KBS's. By providing these presentations we believe it will be easier to design knowledge bases, avoiding logically and physically errors, and from the perspective of the domain instead of the system's characteristics. The end user will also be supported by some of these presentations. However, one important issue is to let both the design user and the end user share at least one diagram to simplify the communication between users and the comprehension of the domain. This sharing of diagrams and the explicitness of the knowledge in diagrams makes it possible for the design user to have expectations on the knowledge inserted by the end user.

References

1. Alonso, F. Fuertes, J.L. L. Martinez, L. & Montes, C. An incremental solution for developing knowledge-based software: its application to an expert system for isokinetics interpretation. Expert Systems with Applications 2000 Vol 18: 165-184
2 .Apicella, M. UML simplifies Project notation. http://www.infoworld.com/articles/ec/xml/00/03/27/000327ecuml.xml, 2000
3. Booch, G. Rumbaugh, J. Jacobson, I. The Unified Modeling Language User Guide. Addison Wesley Longman, Inc, 1999

200

4. Bottoni, P. Chang, S-K. Costabile, M.F. Levialdi, S. and Mussio, P. Dimensions of Visual Interaction Design IEEE, 1999

5. Chandrasekaran B., Swartout W. Explanations in Knowledge Systems, the Role of Explicit Representation of Design Knowledge, IEEE expert, June 1991, pp 47-49 1991

6. Chang, W. A Discussion of the Relationship Between RDF-Schema and UML, 1998. http://www.w3.org/TR/NOTE-rdf-uml/

7. Demmer, C. Unified Modeling Language vs. MWOOD-I, 1997 http://stud4.tuwien.ac.at/~e8726711/ummw2.html

8. Durkin, J. Expert Systems Design and Development. Macmillian Publishing Company, USA, 1994

9. Fowler, M. Architecture and Design: Unified Modeling Language (UML), 1996. http://www.cetus-links.org/oo_uml.html

10. Galitz, W. User-Interface Screen Design. Jown Wiley & Sons, Inc. USA, 1993

11. Helenius E. UML och systemutveckling av framebaserade kunskapssystem (UML and Knowledge Engineering of Frame Based Knowledge Systems). Master Thesis, Department of information science, Computer Science Division, Uppsala University, Fourthcoming

12. Håkansson, A. Widmark, A. & Edman, A. The KANAL-system, an intelligent rule editor supporting the knowledge acquisition process. Swedish Artificial Intelligence Society Annual Workshop 2000 (SAIS 2000), 2000

13. Håkansson, A. & Öijer C. Utveckling av expertsystem för miljökonsekvensanalys (A Development of an Expert System for Analyse of Environmental Consequences). Bachelor Thesis, Computing Science Department, Uppsala University, Sweden, 1993

14. Jacobson, I. Booch, G. & Rumbaugh, J. The Unified Software Develo;.ment Process. Addision Wesley, USA, 1999

15. Kwok, L-F. Hung, S-L. & Pun, C-C. J. Knowledge-based cabin crew pattern generator. Knowledge-Based Systems, 1995, Vol 8(1)

16. Larman C. Applying UML and Patterns. An Introduction to Object-Oriented Analysis and Design. Prentice-Hall Inc, USA, 1998

17. Luger, G. F. & Stubblefield, W. A. Artificial intelligence - structures and strategies for complex problem solving. USA: The Benjamin/Cummings publishing Company, Inc, 1993

18. Redmond-Pyle, D. & Moore, A. Graphical User Interface Design and Evaluation, (GUIDE). Prentice Hall Inc. UK, 1995

19. Sandahl, K. Developing Knowledge Management System with an Active Expert Methodology. Dissertation No. 277, Linköping University, Sweden, 1992

20. Schreiber G., Akkermans H., Aanjewierden A., de Hoog R., Shadbolt N., Van de Velde W., Wielinga B., Knowledge Engineering and Management - The CommonKADS Methodology. ISBN 0-262-19300-0, December 1999

Modeling Knowledge and Reasoning using Locally Active Elements in Semantic Networks

Jürgen Klenk
Definiens AG
Munich, Germany
klenkj@member.ams.org

Gerd Binnig
IBM Research
Zurich, Switzerland
gbi@zurich.ibm.com

Elias Bergan
Spring Consulting AS
Kolbotn, Norway
elias@spring.no

Abstract

A model for knowledge and reasoning based on self–organizing semantic networks is presented. The self–organization is driven by locally active elements in the network, which allows to model the cognitive process of understanding as an iteration of classification and segmentation, both of which are particular locally active elements. Applications to Natural Language Understanding are indicated.

1 Introduction

In our increasingly complex world there is a growing need for systems that intelligently assist people by taking over some of their tasks. Current research and state–of–the–art tools for handling such tasks — which can be extremely complex — are concentrated around topics such as searching and indexing, data mining, classification and clustering, summarization and information extraction, and case–based reasoning, among others. The underlying mathematical models come from disciplines such as statistics, logic, and optimization theory. Depending on the complexity of the problem these methods achieve their tasks with varying degree of success. By contrast, humans, using their talent of knowledge and reasoning, perform much better when confronted with the same tasks. Consequently, we need to concentrate our studies on how the human talent of knowledge and reasoning can be best modeled if we want to fundamentally improve today's intelligent systems.

Research on network–based approaches such as neural networks [19] and semantic networks [17] does concentrate on this aspect. Neural networks which simulate the brain functions on a micro–scale represent an extremely basic approach, and it probably takes simulating the entire evolution of our mind before such systems can deal with the complexity of our world. We believe that semantic networks are more efficient for this task, as they jump into this evolution on a higher semantic level. In other words, semantic networks don't have to re–invent human knowledge and reasoning because these *inventions of nature* can be built right into the network.

Another important aspect of knowledge and reasoning comes from considering complexity theory as originally developed in the biological sciences as a means of understanding how organic entities or communities form when modeled as self–organizing network–like structures. The important insight is that certain cognitive processes require an evolutionary mechanism, which is why we included a self–organizing principle in the underlying semantic network of our model. It is important to note that the self–organization of networks can be an extremely complex process because the number of causal factors and the degree of interdependence between them is too great to permit the use of mechanistic prescriptive models to solve it. Instead, self–organization of a complex system is driven on a small (local) scale by a collection of (typically) relatively simple processes, the causal factors. In this paper we call these causal factors *locally active elements*. The global outcome very much depends on these local processes and the initial state of the system. Despite the fact that everything is deterministic the outcome usually cannot be predicted because the system exhibits chaotic behavior due to its non–linearity caused by the interdependence of its local processes.

A third important aspect when dealing with knowledge and reasoning comes from the fact that there are internal and external factors that influence a human's knowledge and reasoning. Both the internal and external factors can be modeled as self–organizing semantic networks, but since the human itself is part of the external network, his internal network automatically becomes part of the external network, and we are really dealing with one large network which consists of two self–organizing semantic networks on different levels of hierarchy. If we extend this idea to more than two levels of hierarchy, we end up with a self–organizing semantic network that in turn consists of a multitude of self–organizing semantic networks distributed across different scales. In fact, many semantic networks that have been used in practice have such a multi–hierarchical structure [31].

As mentioned above, the self–organization of a network should be driven by locally active elements. If the network has a multi–hierarchical structure, these locally active elements should be similar on all scales, which is only possible if the network looks the same at every level of hierarchy. In other words, the self–organizing semantic network must be self–similar across all scales by being constructed out of a few fundamental generators. Mathematical objects that are self–similar across hierarchical scales are called fractals, which is why we call our model a self–organizing fractal semantic network.

For the reasons given above we believe that our model of a self–organizing fractal semantic network captures the principles of human knowledge and reasoning. In this paper we will lay the theoretical foundations of our model and show how it can be applied it to the complex problem of Natural Language Understanding.

2 Self–Organizing Fractal Semantic Networks — Structures for Knowledge and Reasoning

In this section we introduce the theoretical framework for our model. We provide a set of definitions including comments which relate all definitions to well–known concepts. Finally we define the global structure of our model, a self–organizing fractal semantic network, within the given framework.

In our model knowledge is represented as associative semantic networks [22, 21]. In accordance with Minsky's ideas [16], knowledge elements obtain their meaning through a multitude of relations with other knowledge elements, which implies that meaning cannot be defined (and is not definable) in an absolute way, but only in a relative way. Furthermore, our model employs the standard hierarchies and inheritance principles of semantic networks. The key point of this section and of our model is that we equip the semantic network with a set of locally active elements which can operate locally and in parallel on the network. It is precisely these active elements which will allow us to model particular cognitive processes.

Definition 1: A semantic network is a directed or non–directed graph with the additional property that its nodes and links carry semantic information. All graph elements of a semantic network, i.e. all nodes and links, are called semantic objects. The semantic information carried by a semantic object is given in the form of a symbolic name.

It is often convenient to associate certain rules with a symbol representation of a semantic information. For instance, the symbol *is–a* on a directed link not only establishes a particular hierarchical relationship between the two semantic objects it connects, but also activates particular inheritance rules across this link.

Definition 2: A hierarchical network is a directed or non–directed graph with the additional property that some of its links carry hierarchical information. Such links are called hierarchical links. The hierarchical information specifies which of the network elements connected to a hierarchical link is at a higher level of hierarchy than the other network element.

It should be noted that this definition does not yield an absolute value for the level of hierarchy, i.e. it does not assign to every node an integer that corresponds to its level of hierarchy. Instead it gives a relative definition for the level of hierarchy. While this approach is more general, it can cause conflicts because one can have cycles (loops) of hierarchical links. This conflict exists only on a global scale and can be resolved if one considers only local neighborhoods of the whole network at any one time. Local neighborhoods are introduced by the notion of a topology.

Definition 3: A topological network is a directed or non–directed graph with the additional property that for every node and every link one or several local neighborhoods are defined. The local neighborhoods of a node or a link are sets consisting of this node or link and other nodes or links of the network.

In many cases topological networks are obtained by assigning a weight between 0 and 1 to every link of the network. The negative logarithm of this weight then yields a metric or distance function on the network. The local neighborhoods are defined with the help of some thresholding mechanism applied to this metric. Every metric determines a topology, but the converse is not true; therefore, the above definition is more general than the method of assigning weights.

In the special case of semantic networks it is often required that a semantic object be used both as a node and as a link. For example, a semantic object labeled *friendship* can be viewed both as a node (*friendship is-a relation*, here it is a node connected hierarchically to the node *relation*) and as a link (*friendship between two people*, here it is a link between the two nodes representing the two *people*). This gives rise to the following definition.

Definition 4: A higher–order network is a directed or non–directed graph in which links can at the same time be nodes. This means that a link can connect two nodes, one node and one link, or two links.

In the next definition we capture what we mean by a fractal network. We will not give an exact mathematical definition (for ideas on how to do this see [14, 8]) but rather a working definition, which will suffice for the scope of this paper. This definition will not allow us to explore in more detail the fractal structure of semantic networks used in our model. In particular, we will not be able to give a definition for the fractal dimension, which, according to our current studies, seems to be related to the more subjective quantity of complexity.

Definition 5: A fractal network is a hierarchical network with the additional property that all of its nodes and links on all levels of hierarchy are derived from a small set of basic building blocks called generators. In this sense a fractal network exhibits a self–similar structure because it looks the same everywhere on all levels of hierarchy.

The following definition introduces the important active elements into the semantic network, which can perform transformations of the network through their local operations and thus drive an evolution of the network. Since they are considered parts of the network, we also say that the network performs a self–organizing task.

Definition 6: A locally self–organizing network is a directed or non–directed graph with the additional property that at least some of its nodes and links are connected to one or several locally active elements out of a set of locally active elements. A locally active element contains an algorithm which can perform a transformation of the network in the local neighborhood of the node or link the locally active element is connected to. The locally active elements are event–triggered and operate in parallel on the network.

A particular event that triggers a locally active element is a change in the state of the node or link it is connected to. For most practical purposes the state of a node or link is a function of its local neighborhood in the network. For example, when dealing with semantic networks a semantic object is often connected to attributes, and the values of these attributes determine the state of the semantic object.

After making all of the above definitions we are now in the position to define

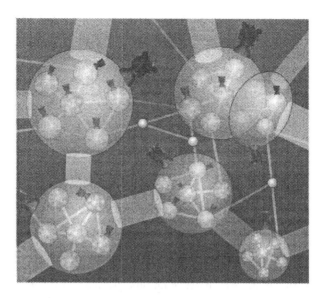

Figure 1: A sample self–organizing fractal semantic network

our model, a self–organizing fractal semantic network.

Definition 7: A self–organizing fractal semantic network is a hierarchical, topological, higher–order, fractal, locally self–organizing semantic network.

Figure 1 illustrates a self–organizing fractal semantic network. Nodes are depicted as spheres, links as cylinders, and locally active elements as Janus heads (more details later). The hierarchical structure is clearly visible from the fact that nodes contain internal networks.

3 Semantic Objects — Generators of Self–Organizing Fractal Semantic Networks

In this section we define the local structure of our model, that is, the generators or basic building blocks out of which we construct self–organizing fractal semantic networks.

As specified in Definition 1, nodes and links of the network are called semantic objects. All semantic objects are subdivided into concepts and instances as is usual [5]. We further subdivide nodes into information objects, attribute objects, and locally active elements or Janus objects. In our model we use the metaphor of a Janus [12] for a locally active element. Information objects are general elements that can represent concepts or instances, and they are identified by specific symbols. Attribute objects are identified by specific symbols, types, and values, which can be set, retrieved, or computed.

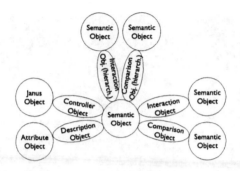

Figure 2: The generators

All links of the network are either hierarchical or non–hierarchical. Standard inheritance principles [5] are defined across all hierarchical links, making use of the network's topology. Links are further subdivided into comparison objects, interaction objects, description objects, and controller objects. Non–hierarchical comparison objects allow us to describe the degree of similarity or dissimilarity of two semantic objects, while hierarchical comparison objects allow us to describe how close one semantic object comes to being an instance of another semantic object, or how close one semantic object comes to being a special case of another semantic object. Non–hierarchical interaction objects allow us to describe the type of interaction of two semantic objects, while hierarchical interaction objects allow us to describe the role one semantic object plays as part of another semantic object. Description objects connect semantic objects to their attribute objects, which describe the semantic objects in more detail. Finally, controller objects connect semantic objects to their Janus objects, which in turn control and act upon the semantic objects' local neighborhoods.

Figure 2 shows how the generators are used to construct a self–organizing fractal semantic network. Note that each generator labeled *Semantic Object* can be substituted by any other generator. Information objects do not appear in this diagram, as there is no restriction on their use. In practice most of the building blocks labeled *Semantic Object* are information objects.

The state of a semantic object is a (possibly complex) function of all semantic objects of its local neighborhood. A simple example for the state of a semantic object is the state of *usefulness* of the information object representing a *soccer ball*. The *soccer ball*'s local neighborhood with respect to the state of its *usefulness* may consist of the attribute object *size* and the attribute object *pressure*, together with their respective values. The state of the *soccer ball*'s *usefulness* can then be computed from the current values of its two attribute objects, preferably in terms of fuzzy set theory [20].

A more complex example is the *mood* state of a *human being*. Here clearly the attribute objects describing the *human being*, such as *height* and *weight*, among others, are not sufficient to describe his *mood* state. Psychologists tell us that the whole context within which the *human being* lives affects his *mood* state. There are many theories about what factors should and should not be taken into account when determining this context, and what kind of influence each of these factors has on the *mood* state. In our model it is precisely this context that makes up a *human being*'s local neighborhood with respect to his *mood* state, and it is precisely the kind of influence each of these factors has that determines the *mood* state function.

4 Janus Objects — Locally Active Elements in Self–Organizing Fractal Semantic Networks

In this section we define the dynamic aspect of our model, that is, the locally active elements or Janus objects which drive the self–organization or evolution of a fractal semantic networks. It is important to note that in our model each Janus object is considered a particular semantic object and thus also part of the network it evolves.

To motivate the choices for the particular Janus objects used in our model, we continue with our examples from the last section. There are Janus objects that influence the *usefulness* of the *soccer ball*, or the *mood* state of the *human being*. Semantic objects that are in the local neighborhood of the *soccer ball* or the *human being* typically control and trigger these Janus objects. If the *soccer ball* becomes *useless* because it goes flat (caused by a Janus object), it may get thrown away (caused by another Janus object) and thus removed from the network, and a new *soccer ball* may be purchased (caused by yet another Janus object) and thus a new information object representing the new *soccer ball* is created. As for the *human being*, he may identify himself as the typical representative of a certain group, and may consequently join this group to improve his *mood* state, or he may found a new interest group and invite others to join it. To this extent he may even acquire new skills or knowledge.

These examples illustrate which basic locally active elements are required in our model. We have Janus objects that are able to create new semantic objects, to modify or destroy existing semantic objects (and even themselves), to create links between semantic objects, to classify or identify semantic objects as other semantic objects, and to create new groups or segments in the network. Other Janus objects must be able to set, retrieve, or compute values of attribute objects and to determine the states of semantic objects. Finally, there must be Janus objects that can perform more complex tasks which are composed of the above basic locally active elements.

As can be seen from the above examples, the processes carried out by Janus objects can range from generic to specific, meaning that they use generic properties of the set of generators that make up the self–similar structure of the network, or very specific properties of the local neighborhood of a certain semantic object, respectively. Therefore, some Janus objects can be connected to any semantic object, while others require the presence of particular semantic objects in their local neighborhood.

Clearly the Janus objects that simply create, modify, or destroy semantic objects (including the ones that create links, as this is a special case of creating semantic objects) perform very generic tasks. The Janus objects that perform the evaluation of attribute objects' values have a set of mathematical tools at hand from areas such as fuzzy set theory, statistics, geometry, topology, and algebra, among others. Therefore, these Janus objects are more specific as they can be applied only to attribute objects whose values satisfy certain type constraints. Finally, the Janus objects that determine the states of semantic objects are even more specific, as their processes might only be applicable to one or a small group of semantic objects.

5 Classification and Segmentation — Basic Components of Cognitive Processes

In this section we will discuss the processes of classification and segmentation. They are the key drivers in the self–organization of the fractal semantic network and make up the fundamental components of complex cognitive processes such as understanding and reacting/responding.

Complex tasks like Natural Language Understanding or Image Recognition are typical examples of problems that can be solved using our model. In these cases one uses a world knowledge, constructed as a self–organizing fractal semantic network, to perform the processes of understanding and reacting when presented with an input (a text or an image). During a pre–processing step such as grammatical parsing or pixel analysis the input itself is transformed into an initial input network. Then this initial input network is restructured and enriched by comparing it to the world knowledge to eventually be able to understand the input and react to it appropriately. It is exactly these steps that transform the initial input network to a final input network which are carried out by the classification and segmentation processes.

The process of classification stands for the common task of comparing one semantic object of a fractal semantic network to others of a (possibly different) fractal semantic network. Since every semantic object obtains its meaning from its embedding into its local neighborhood, the goal of the classification process is to find comparable local neighborhoods of the semantic object in the sense that they are alike, can perform similar tasks, contain similar semantic objects, are more general or more specific, are constituents or groups, or are in similar states, among other things. In our model the process of classification is performed through such extensive local neighborhood analyses. This means that the degree of similarity of two semantic objects is determined by the degree of similarity of their local neighborhoods with respect to the above comparison factors.

As with determining the status of a semantic object, when comparing a semantic object to others it is not enough to simply take into account the values of the attribute objects of the semantic object. Instead, the topology of the network, i.e. the entire local neighborhood of the semantic object, must be considered. Therefore, the process of classification deals with the more general task of finding similar structures or subgraphs in addition to finding similar values of attribute units.

The particular match–making strategy applied during the classification process is determined by the local neighborhood of the semantic object to be classified. In other words, the classification process varies from semantic object to semantic object and is governed by the neighborhood structure or local context of the semantic object. This allows the system to deal with complex situations which require locally different and adaptive strategies to achieve optimal classification results. This idea is adopted from cell biology — each cell in a host contains the entire genetic code of the host, but only the portion which fits to the cell's context or environment is used. This allows each cell to adaptively carry out its tasks.

Because of the self–similar structure of the network, this classification process can be implemented in a generic way, thus allowing the Janus object representing the classification process to be re–used throughout the entire network.

Classification focuses on finding similar structures among semantic objects. It does not alter the network structure around the semantic objects. This is done by the second process called segmentation, which focuses on adapting the local structures or neighborhoods around semantic units which have been matched by the classification process.

As mentioned at the beginning of this section, one usually has one fixed structure, the network comprising the world knowledge, and one variable structure, the network comprising the input. The classification process matches semantic objects of the two networks. At the end of each classification process a likelihood measure is computed for the match that has been established. In a typical situation of a classification process an input semantic object is matched to a multitude of world knowledge semantic objects with varying likelihood measures which correspond to different conjectures about the meaning of the input semantic object and their certainty.

During the segmentation process, the input semantic network is re–structured and enriched around the matched semantic object according to the structure found in the world knowledge network. For this purpose the classification results are selected according to their likelihood measure. This is done for all input semantic objects which could be classified. Because this may result in competing structures to be formed around neighboring semantic objects in the input network, the segmentation process also performs a local optimization procedure and creates structures by using classification results which — despite a possibly lower likelihood measure — have the best mutual fit.

This process enriches the input network in two ways. First, it adds new semantic objects from the world knowledge network to the input network at the same level of hierarchy as the classified semantic objects of the input network, including new connections between the input semantic objects. Second, it adds new semantic objects from the world knowledge network to the input network at higher levels of hierarchy. This means that the input is enriched with more general and abstract context information.

It is now possible to perform a new classification step which — due to both enrichment processes described above — can classify previously unclassified input semantic objects and find even more abstract context information about the input. The processes of classification and segmentation are carried out iteratively until as many input semantic objects as possible are classified and as much context information as possible is generated.

Because the classification and segmentation processes are carried out in parallel and at all levels of hierarchy and employ the feedback mechanism described above, the resulting final input network represents the most consistent structure that can be created from the initial input network given the world knowledge network.

It is obvious that the successful completion of the entire process does not depend on the successful completion of every classification and segmentation process involved. In fact, the system still succeeds in creating a resulting final input network even if just a few of the classification and segmentation processes succeed. Because the entire process is driven on a local scale with relatively simple locally active elements, no handling of exceptions is necessary. The degree of understanding as represented by the final input network is dependent only on the degree of overlap between the world knowledge and the content of the input.

6 Natural Language Understanding as an Application

Now that we have introduced the theoretical framework of our model in detail, in this section we illustrate how we can apply it to tackle the concrete problem of Natural Language Understanding. It should be noted that the problem of Natural Language Understanding is an extremely complex one which has kept researchers busy for many decades (and probably will for many decades to come). Our aim is not to show that with our model all other approaches become obsolete. Rather, we would like to give a proof of concept by showing that in principle the problem of Natural Language Understanding can be solved within the framework of our model. It should also be noted that there are many other complex problems that our model can be applied to, ranging from relatively similar problems like image recognition to areas such as complexity theory of dynamical systems.

In Natural Language Understanding, a system is presented with a particular input in spoken or written form. The system has to understand the input to be able to react appropriately. Appropriate reactions depend very much on the goal of the system and can range from categorizing the input to summarizing it to responding to it in the form of a dialog.

Our system first generates an initial input network from the given input, and then uses a world knowledge network to understand the input by transforming it into a final input network. The result of this transformation then allows our system to choose an appropriate, goal dependent reaction. For the generation of the input network we use a standard grammatical parser, the Slot Grammar System [15], to translate written text into parse trees, and a particular set of transformation rules which generate from these parse results the initial input network. If the input is presented in spoken form, it can be converted into written text beforehand with the help of a standard speech–to–text system. The overall architecture of our system is comparable to SynDiKATe system [13] which also uses an initial grammatical parser and then a world knowledge based on KL–ONE [3] to perform its understanding task.

This initial input network is then linked to the world knowledge network by an initial classification process, carried out locally by corresponding Janus objects that have been attached to the elements of the input network. Afterwards an iteration of segmentation and classification processes is carried out as described in the last section, during which the input network self–organizes with respect to the world knowledge network. This process typically results in the creation of a hierarchical structure in the input network. The multitude of linkages on all scales which the locally active elements dynamically form between the input network and the world knowledge network represent the understanding of the input.

This means that our system does not conduct a step–by–step analysis of the input (syntactic, semantic, pragmatic analysis with lots of additional detailed analyses such as anaphora resolution, word sense disambiguation, object matching, etc.). Instead, we prepare an initial input network from the input and then try to understand the whole input network (and thus the whole input at once) within a world knowledge network. However, our model allows the implementation of any of the above–mentioned individual analyses to any desired level of detail into the world knowledge network as particular Janus objects. In this sense our model can also be seen as a framework (or language) in which the above theories can be expressed.

Based on the result of the above understanding process, our system then employs reaction processes to generate a meaningful response. These reaction processes are again performed by particular locally active elements in the world knowledge network, which evaluate the result of the understanding process. These locally active elements get triggered by network activities in their neighborhoods during the understanding process, and then determine one or several network elements which will be used in assembling the response. The strategy they follow when determining these network elements depends on the system's overall goal.

It is conceivable to have a very generic reaction process that only triggers network elements in the neighborhood of the highest network activity during the understanding process. This corresponds to a relatively open system that has a rather generic goal of coming up with just some appropriate response to any given input. On the other hand, as we demonstrated in one particular implementation of our system which represents an intelligent phone book assistant, one may have a particular goal (in this example the goal is to find a list of appropriate phone numbers), in which case the reaction process follows a more specific strategy and determines only network elements which represent phone numbers.

The intelligent phone book assistant currently comprises a world knowledge network of about 400 semantic objects which capture certain aspects of the knowledge of an average member in our research group. It can be demonstrated by using either its voice phone interface (based on VoiceXML, see [27]) or text interface (based on WAP, see [28]).

7 Related Work and Limitations

There is a lot of related work on semantic networks, knowledge modeling, and reasoning. Semantic networks as defined in Section 2, Definitions 1 and 2, first received a thorough attention in the 70s by the pioneering articles of Woods [29] and Brachman [1, 2]. This work resulted in many research programs and families of representations, such as conceptual dependency pioneered by Schank [23], conceptual graphs by Sowa [26], connectionist models by Derthick [7] and others, CYC by Guha and Lenat [11], KL–ONE by Brachman and Schmolze [3] and its derivatives LOOM, CLASSIC, K–REP, KRYPTON, L–LILOG, and NIKL, NETL by Fahlman [10], and SNePS by Shapiro [25], to name just a few. FABEL, a project which was started in 1992, was an attempt to integrate model–based and case–based approaches to the development of knowledge–based systems [9]. More recently, the Semantic Web [24] is an effort to set a standard on the Internet for representing knowledge and reasoning. It is mainly based on semantic networks and frame languages as currently specified in the DAML+OIL [6] standard.

Some aspects of our locally active elements are discussed in works on procedural attachments. It has long been known that procedural knowledge should be included in semantic networks. Early works in this area are from Woods [30], and more recently neural networks have been used to represent procedural knowledge [18]. Finally, activation and marker passing, important mechanisms of our locally active elements, are discussed in the PhD thesis of Brown [4].

Obviously the model we present in this paper relies heavily on the size and quality of the semantic network and the locally active elements. While the number of knowledge sources for semantic networks increases quickly, most of the domain–specific knowledge still needs to be entered manually. Machine Learning methods are now being investigated which would allow to automatically build semantic networks, and a lot of progress has been made in this area over the past years. However, it is still open whether these methods can be extended to automatically create locally active elements.

Another important issue — as with all knowledge–based systems — is scalability. It is still unclear if it will be possible to implement the proposed model so that for example in the natural language understanding domain large amounts of text can be processed and understood efficiently when using a large network with many locally active elements. However, because of the local character of the locally active elements it can be shown that the processing time has a less than linear dependency on the network size, which is a necessary prerequisite for scalability.

8 Conclusion

In this paper we presented a theoretical framework for knowledge and reasoning, based on semantic networks which self–organize by locally active elements. We explained how cognitive processes can be modeled as particular locally active elements. As illustrated in the section on Natural Language Understanding, the advantage of our model lies in the massively parallel application of different strategies to performing the understanding task, which gives systems built on our model a certain degree of robustness.

References

[1] R.J. Brachman. What's in a concept: Structural foundations for semantic networks. International Journal of Man–Machine Studies 9, 127–152 (1977).

[2] R.J. Brachman. On the epistemological status of semantic networks. Reprinted in *Readings in Knowledge Representation*, ed. R.J. Brachman, H.J. Levesque.

[3] R.J. Brachman, J.G. Schmolze. An overview of the KL–ONE knowledge representation system. *Cognitive Science*, 9(2):171–216, April–June 1985.

[4] M. Brown. A Memory Model for Case Retrieval by Activation Passing. PhD Thesis, Department of Computer Science, University of Manchester, Technical Report Series 94–2–1.

[5] G. Cohen. *Memory in the Real World*. Erlbaum, Hove, 1989.

[6] DAML+OIL. http://www.daml.org/2001/03/daml+oil-index.html

[7] M. Derthick. A connectionist architecture for representing and reasoning about structured knowledge. In *Proceedings of the Ninth Annual Conference of the Cognitive Science Society*, pages 131–142. Lawrence Erlbaum, 1987.

[8] G.A. Edgar. *Measure, Topology, and Fractal Geometry*. Springer, 1990.

[9] A. Voß et. al. Survey of FABEL. FABEL–Report No. 2, 1993

[10] S.E. Fahlman. NETL: A system for representing and using real–world knowledge. The MIT Press, 1979.

[11] R. Guha, D. Lenat. CYC: A midterm report. AI magazine *11(3)*, 32–59 (1990).

[12] The Encyclopedia Mythica. *An Encyclopedia on Mythology, Folklore, and Legend.* http://www.pantheon.org/mythica/articles/j/janus.html.

[13] U. Hahn, M. Romacker SynDiKATe — Gemerating Text Knowledge Bases from Natural Language Texts. In *Proceedings of the 1999 IEEE Conference on Systems, Man, and Cybernetics* Vol. 5, pages V-918 – V-923, Tokyo, Japan, 1999. Computer Society Press of the IEEE.

[14] B.B. Mandelbrot. *The Fractal Geometry of Nature*. Freeman, 1982.

[15] M.C. McCord. Slot Grammars. *Computational Linguistics*, 6:31–42, 1980.

[16] M. Minsky. *The Society of Mind*. Simon & Schuster, 1986.

[17] M. Minsky. *Semantic Information Processing*. MIT Press, 1988.

[18] R. Moratz et. al. Representing procedural knowledge for semantic networks using neural nets. Proceedings of the 9th Scandinavian Conference on Image Analysis, Uppsala, pp. 819–828 (1995).

[19] B. Müller, J. Reinhart, M. T. Strickland. *Neural Networks: An Introduction*. Springer, 1995.

[20] T. Munakata. *Fundamentals of the New Artificial Intelligence: Beyond Traditional Paradigms*. Springer, 1998.

[21] N.J. Nilsson. *Artificial Intelligence: A New Synthesis*. Morgan Kaufmann Publishers, 1998.

[22] E. Rich, K. Knight. *Artificial Intelligence*. McGraw–Hill, 1991.

[23] R. Schank. Conceptual dependency: A theory of natural language understanding. Cognitive Psychology *3*, 552–631 (1972).

[24] SemanticWeb.org. http://www.semanticweb.org/.

[25] S. Shapiro. The SNePS semantic network processing system. In *Associative Networks: The Representation and Use of Knowledge by a Machine*, ed. N. Findler, Academic Press, 1979.

[26] J.F. Sowa. Conceptual graphs as a universal knowledge representation. In *Semantic Networks in Artificial Intelligence*, ed. F. Lehmann.

[27] The VoiceXML Forum. http://www.voicexml.org/.

[28] The WAP Forum. http://www.wapforum.org/.

[29] W.A. Woods. What's in a link: foundations for semantic networks. Reprinted in *Readings in Knowledge Representation*, ed. R.J. Brachman, H.J. Levesque.

[30] W.A. Woods. Procedural semantics for a question–answering machine. Proceedings of the Fall Joint Computer Conference. AFIPS Conference Proceedings *33*, 457–471 (1968).

[31] WordNet — A Lexical Database for English. Cognitive Science Lab, Princeton University, http://www.cogsci.princeton.edu/~wn.

Using Meta-level Knowledge to Improve Solutions in Coordination Problems

Tristan Pannérec
Laboratoire d'Informatique de Paris VI
Tristan.Pannerec@lip6.fr
www-poleia.lip6.fr/~pannerec

Abstract

For most decision-coordinating problems, it is impossible to find specific knowledge which allows a general system to construct always the best solution. This is why such a system has to search among the good solutions it can generate. As for the construction process, it is then very useful to use specific knowledge for the improvement process. This possibility has been implemented in the MARECHAL system and applied to a game with interesting results.

1. Introduction

Decisions coordination covers a large amount of interesting problems, which include resource assignment, scheduling problems, coordination of agents' actions, object placement and so on. These problems, like coordinating the action of an individual processor in distributed computing or automatically placing electronic components on a circuit, can be of great importance in industry.

The MARECHAL system is a general coordination problem solver currently in development. It is based on the use of knowledge to allow efficiency in spite of its generality. To solve such problems, an artificial system cannot explore the whole search space, because of the number of potential solutions. Specific domain knowledge allows then constructing solutions by taking a sequence of decisions. This knowledge gives a priori advice to the system for each decision. But, as for other expert systems, it is in practice very hard and often impossible to find perfect heuristics to construct always the best solution, because these heuristics work a priori and the associated decision can be proved bad a posteriori.

That is why the MARECHAL system is able to improve the constructed solutions to achieve better results. For this purpose, it uses a mechanism based on specific *meta-knowledge* to find improvement possibilities. The remainder of this paper intends to present this mechanism. It is organized in four main sections. The first section introduces a concrete example of coordination problem that will be used to illustrate the description and discusses the methods that are usually used in such coordination problems. The second section gives a brief description of the MARECHAL's architecture to globally replace the mechanism in the system. The third section then presents the improvement process with the use of specific meta-knowledge. Finally, the last section provides the results we have achieved.

2. Coordination Problems

For this paper, a simple problem has been extracted from a game which is used as test application for the MARECHAL system. This problem is described in the first part of this section. The second part discuses the methods usually employed to solve coordination problems and explains why we have developed another way.

2.1 The "StrateGE" Example

For its development, the MARECHAL system is applied to a game of strategy. In Artificial Intelligence, such test beds are very interesting because the evaluation is easy and it is a simplification of reality. They are not toy problems, like blocks world, because they are complex and challenging. At the moment, programs are well below the level of human players, except for some games where complexity is small enough to use brutal combinatory (e.g. chess).

"StrateGE" is a two-player game, played on a draughtboard, like chess. Each player has a set of pieces of one colour (black or white) at his disposal. Unlike chess, players program movements for all their pieces at each turn. The pieces of a player are then moved simultaneously and a catch rule applies after each turn, depending on the position of the pieces. This catch rule is the following: if a piece has an enemy piece adjacent to it with a current rank two points or more higher, the piece is caught. Each piece has a basic rank of one, two or three points. The current rank of a piece is its basic rank minus the number of adjacent enemy pieces. Some types of piece gain a bonus rank under certain conditions. An example of catch is shown on Figure 1. Pieces 4, 14 and 13 are actually used to catch pieces 20 and 24. Pieces 3, 12 and 7 move to occupy bonus squares and piece 16 moves back to offer a better defence line.

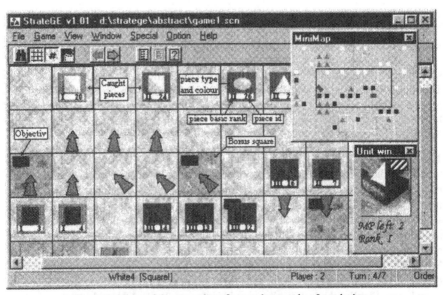

Figure 1: View of the game interface and example of a solution.

Playing to "StrateGE" presupposes you're not only able to coordinate tactical movements of pieces, but you can also manage the characteristics of your pieces, as well as analyse globally the situation (power ratio, terrain occupation) and conduct strategic level reasoning. As the description of the complete application of MARECHAL to "StrateGE" is out of the scope of this paper, we will focus on a simplified problem extracted from the tactical part of the game. This problem is *the maximisation of the number of caught enemy pieces at the end of the turn*. We will suppose that both players have only one type of piece with no special characteristic and which can move two squares. The catch of a piece gives (2 + basic rank of the piece) points. This simplified problem represents the heart of the tactical questions which lie within "StrateGE".

Like for decision coordinating problems in the real world (such as scheduling, resource assignment...), the system has also to anticipate the consequences of its choices and to build the best choice combination which satisfies a set of constraints and optimize a given criterion.

2.2 Classical Methods Used in Coordination Problems

Three main approaches are classically used to deal with coordination problems. The first one is the *VCSP[1] framework*, where backtrack methods allow to explore the search space. This framework is the adaptation of the CSP framework to the optimisation problem. Unfortunately, these methods fail for problems like the "StrateGE" game because of the large number of variables (from 40 to 120 variables are required to implement a problem) and of the low importance of the constraints (most solutions are coherent).

The second possible approach is proposed by the Operational Research with the local search methods like Genetic Algorithm ([4]), Tabu search ([3]) and so on. The principle is to construct one solution or maintain a set of solutions and to improve them by applying a sequence of modifications. At each cycle, the best modification is chosen among a neighbourhood set. The philosophy is to have a simple and fast evaluation heuristic to do many tests. Once again, these methods are not well suited for problems where there is no good simple heuristic and the complete evaluation of a solution is time consuming. In the "StrateGE" game, the evaluation of the number of caught enemy pieces obliges to anticipate the position of all pieces at the end of the turn and also takes a lot of time. Only about five tests per second can be made and the system has to answer in a few seconds. But the most important obstacle is the form of the fitness function. It is a very discontinued function with very narrow peaks and many local optimums. In these conditions, the methods of the Operational Research cannot find a good solution within a short time period.

As with the VCSP framework, methods of the Operational Research are relatively blind and brutal search methods. In an Artificial Intelligence perspective, they clearly do not represent the complexity of the reasoning process of a human mind, which solves the same problem without testing many different solutions. The

---

[1] Valued Constraint Satisfaction Problem. See [12] for an introduction to VCSP..

common answer of Artificial Intelligence is the Multi Agent paradigm ([1 & 5]). Our first attempt to solve the "StrateGE" game problem was centred on a Multi Agent System, but this experiment was unsuccessful. It was very difficult and unnatural for the expert to give decentralized knowledge in order to get a decentralized resolving process. Thus, the coordination of the agents (there was mainly one agent for each piece to control) was not efficient. Constructing a solution was feasible, but the achievement of a good solution was not possible without a centralized reasoning.

We have also developed a method based on the local search principle (construction and sequence of improvements) but with an extended use of domain specific knowledge and an opposite philosophy: the idea was to accept large time consuming heuristic functions to select the improvement in order to minimize the number of tests. This idea has been made possible by the use of meta-level rules ([7 & 9]) that analyse the own reasoning of the system ([11]). These rules are domain-specific and this kind of knowledge has already been used in some systems such as SOAR ([6]), but never to improve, a posteriori, heuristic solutions in the decisions coordinating problem framework.

3. The MARECHAL System

The MARECHAL system is also designed to solve complex coordination problems. Its functioning can be divided in two main functionalities: the *construction* and the *improvement* functionalities. As the second one is the subject of this paper, it will be described in details in the next section. But this description cannot be done without presenting briefly the construction functionality in the second part of this section. Prior to this, the first part gives a global view of the currently implemented architecture.

3.1 General Architecture

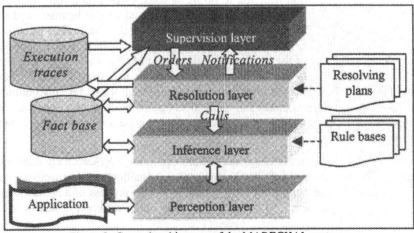

Figure 2: General architecture of the MARECHAL system.

The architecture of the MARECHAL system is classically divided into four layers as shown in Figure 2. The lower layer is the interface with the application, which asks a solution to a problem (e.g. the "StrateGE" game). The second layer uses rule bases to produce facts by inference. The third layer is the heart of the system and is responsible for the resolution of the problem at a basic level. This layer implements the construction functionality described in the next part of this section. The highest layer is a meta-level layer that supervises and manages the resolution layer. The improvement mechanism belongs widely to the supervision layer.

3.2   Construction Functionality

In the MARECHAL system, the construction of a solution for a given problem is based on two main principles: the *decomposition of the problem* and the use of *declarative resolving plans* for each sub-problem.

As a coordination problem is often difficult to solve directly, it has to be decomposed in pseudo-independent sub-problems. For instance, the main problem of maximizing the number of caught enemy pieces can be decomposed in a sequence of single catch tests for each enemy piece. The system starts also at the main problem level and searches for weak adversary pieces to catch. For each piece, it opens a new sub-problem consisting in catching the given piece. It resolves each sub-problem independently but these ones are not fully independent because of the limited number of friendly pieces (two enemy pieces which can be separately caught could not be together). Although we only use here two problems[2], the whole "StrateGE" application involves more than ten different sub-problems.

For each problem defined for the application, declarative resolving plans are given to control the construction of a solution for this problem. These plans describe the different steps of the construction, the calls to the inference layer, the sub-problems to resolve, the decisions to take and the criterion to choose a priori the best decisions. Above all the resolution layer is also a plan execution module. During the executions of the plans, it generates an execution trace of its activity. The resolving plans and the called inference rule-bases form the construction knowledge of the system for a given application.

4.   Improvement Process

After having constructed a solution for a sub-problem or for the main problem, the system tries to improve it. The first issue is of course to find good improving possibilities. To achieve this, the system uses knowledge that analyses the resolution process, at meta-level. General remarks on this knowledge are given in the first part of this section.

---

[2] In the remainder of the paper, the term "problem" will refer to the main problem or a sub-problem without distinction.

The improvement cycle is then normally composed of ~~the~~ three main steps occurring at different moments:

1. *Meta-information generation*
2. *Improvement possibilities analysis*
3. *Improvement possibilities selection and execution*

These steps are described in details in this section. The second problem in the improvement mechanism is to *monitor* the sequence of improvements. We will touch on this aspect in the last part of the section.

4.1   The Improvement Knowledge

In order to find good improving possibilities, the system uses meta-knowledge that analyses resolution processes. As this knowledge is linked to problem dependent processes, it is essential that it should itself be *problem dependent*. The improvement knowledge is also *declaratively* given for each sub-problem to the system in the same languages that are used for the construction knowledge (see [8] for a description of these languages). An example of an improvement meta-level rule is given in Figure 3. $e, $m and $o are parameters defined in the call of the expertise which is used when the catch of the piece $e has failed. $m and $o give the internal reasoning segment numbers for the sub-problem which failed and its last resolving session. The rule indicates that when a usable piece $u cannot find a path to attack $e due to the movement of a piece $v, an improvement possibility lies in changing the path of $v.

```
// First rule of the first improvement expertise.
(   IF SUPERIOR[NbPotDestinations 0]
    FOR_EACH_FACT[MetaInfo(SR($r) SR($t)
            DisturbedByFriendlyMove(piece($u) piece($v)
            point($i $j)point($x $y)))]
        IF EXIST_FACT[Locked(piece($v))]
        IF NOT EQUAL[side($v) side($e)]
        IF EXIST_FACT[SubPbSon(SR($r) SR($o))]
        IF EQUAL[Engaged(piece($u)) 0]
        IF EQUAL[PieceInCase(point($x $y)) 0]
        LET[$a RSRespAdd(NbMvOrder(piece($v)))]
        IF EQUAL[BelongToSubPb(PR($a) SR($o)) 1]
)
GOOD <80> TO_DO ADD[ImprovementPossibility(RSeg($m) RSt($a)
    List(Execution(RSeg($a) ForbiddenChoice(GoingThrough (
    piece($v) point($i $j))) val(1))))].
```

Figure 3: Example of a simplified improvement meta-level rule. Letters preceded by a "$" represent variables and words in uppercase are domain-independent keywords.

New specific instructions have also been added to these languages to allow the analysis of resolution processes. Some of these instructions call internal services that return a resolution segment/step number representing a decision or a sub-problem that is in charge of a given consequence. Instructions equally exist to get the current construction session number or the current sub-problem resolution process number. Some facts are automatically added to the fact base to describe the relationship between the problems. Finally, some new sections have been defined in the fact base to group meta-information or improvement possibilities.

4.2   Meta-information Generation

During the construction process, the system *generates meta-information* on this process. The goal is for the system to remember why the resolution happened that way, how decisions were made and so on. For a single piece catch problem, for instance, the system generates information about the pieces that could be used to solve the problem but which have not been used because they were already used to catch another piece[3] or because they had no possible destination to attack the piece to catch. It also generates information about pieces that prevent use of another piece due to movement incompatibility[4]. This information will be fundamental to find improvement possibilities if the resolution of the current problem failed or if a criterion has to be optimised. To generate such meta-information, the system uses declarative rules inserted in the construction knowledge of the problem. The meta-information is retained as facts in the meta-information section of the fact base and is also easily accessible to the improvement knowledge.

4.3   After Construction Session Analysis

After a construction session, if the solution is not correct or if a criterion has to be optimised, the system *searches local improvement possibilities* for the current problem. This time, the rules used are part of the improvement knowledge of the problem. Of course these rules analyse the meta-information produced during the construction process, but the generated improvement possibilities are restricted to decisions taken during this process. For instance, for the single piece catch problem which failed, the program can find that a friendly piece p1 could attack at position s1 instead of position s2 and that an unused friendly piece f2 could then attack at position s2. That is what happens on Figure 4, where piece 7 has not been used. During the construction, the system has also applied the following heuristics: selecting the most powerful friendly piece and affecting it to the closest adjacent square of the enemy piece. The modification of the destination of piece 13 allows the use of piece 7 and therefore the catch of piece 25.

If the catch is already a success, the program searches if the involved friendly pieces can attack other pieces by changing their destination without changing the catch result. Such a case occurs on Figure 5, where the modification of the destination of piece 3 allows to attack piece 19 with the conservation of the catch of piece 20.

---

[3] The system uses a resource locking method for this purpose. When a move is defined for a piece, this one is immediately locked, because a piece cannot have two different moves.

[4] Two pieces cannot go to the same square at the same moment.

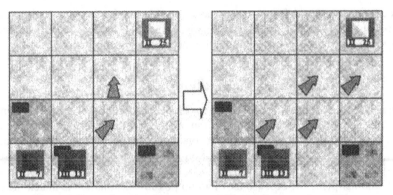

Figure 4: Example of local improvement for the single catch problem.

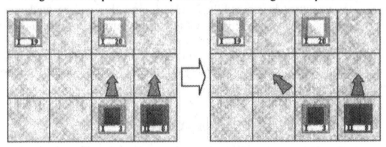

Figure 5: Example of local improvement for the single catch problem.

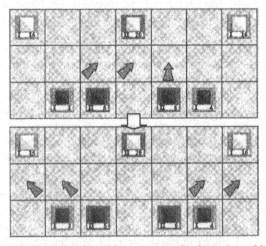

Figure 6: Example of local improvement for the main problem.

At the end of a construction session for the main problem, the system equally analyses the possibilities of improvement but at a higher level, because decisions for this problem deal with catch possibilities. The analysis rules search for instance if a successful catch can be abandoned to allow other catches with a higher value. This is the case in Figure 6, where the catch of two pieces (15 and 16) of basic rank one is more interesting than a catch of a single piece (20) of basic rank two.

Each improvement possibility is retained as a fact in the improvement possibilities section of the fact base. They are always defined by three components:
1. *The relative session* to which the possibility is associated.
2. *The cancel command* that describes what part of the solution has to be cancelled. In practice, it is often only a single decision (affectation or path of a piece).
3. *The execution command* that describes what part of the construction process has to be redone to complete the solution. It is a list of segments (to fully redo the resolution of a sub-problem) and steps (to only redo an instruction such as a path search). With each segment and step can be associated a set of constraints that allows to manage the new execution in a precise way.

The following fact is an example of a simple improvement possibility *generated by the system*:

ImprovementPossibility(RSeg(217) RSt(58) List(Execution(RSeg(47) Lock(Piece(7)))))

This improvement possibility, which is associated to the session 217, specifies that the reasoning step 58 has to be cancelled and the reasoning segment 47 have to be redone with the constraint of locking piece 7. With this form, the system can generate complex and precise improvement commands that will be interpreted in the next step of the improvement cycle (cf. following paragraph). As a result, the improvement mechanism is more flexible and efficient than a classical backtrack method. With backtrack, it is impossible to cancel a decision without cancelling all the following decisions and this generates many useless executions.

4.4 Improvement Possibility Selection and Execution

If no improvement possibility is found for the session during the previous step, the resolution of the current problem end with an END_SUCCES or END_FAILURE signal, depending on the resolution status. If at least one improvement possibility exists, the system then selects one of them and applies a reconstruction phase in a new construction session. This reconstruction phase consists of deciphering and interpreting the cancel and execution commands of the selected improvement possibility.

With the cancel command, the system has to cancel the consequence of a previously executed resolution segment. To achieve this, it studies the execution trace for the given segment. It cancels each instruction by applying the inverse instruction in order to cancel every consequence of a decision. These modifications are added to the end of the execution trace, like a normal instruction. As a result, the system never needs to backtrack at this level[5].

With the execution command, the system calls the construction functionality for each resolving segment to redo. It automatically manages the needed variables and

---

[5] Backtrack can only occur at a higher level of reasoning, to cancel improvement sessions, see 4.6.

fact restorations. It can interrupt the process under certain conditions. For instance, if it tries to improve a sub-problem which had failed, the non-improvement of this sub-problem (in term of distance to success) causes the process to be abandoned before the end. The system then searches for another improvement possibility to select.

4.5 After Sub-problem Resolution Analysis

After the resolution of a sub-problem ended with a END_FAILURE signal, the system analyses the global improvement possibilities, that is, the possibilities that imply the modification of the solution belonging to another sub-problem. During this step, the possibilities are only listed. They are evaluated and selected at the end of the construction session of the "father" problem. For instance, if a piece f1 is used to catch a piece e1 (previous sub-problem), and is needed to catch a piece e2 (current sub-problem), the possibilities are saved in the fact base and the resolution of the main problem goes on with catch tests of other enemy pieces. At the end of this resolution, the system evaluates the possibility of affecting f1 to e2 instead of e1. It studies in particular the possibility to solve the catch of e1 without f1. Such an example is given on Figure 7. The piece 13 is replaced by 7 for the catch of 23 and can then participate in the catch of 25.

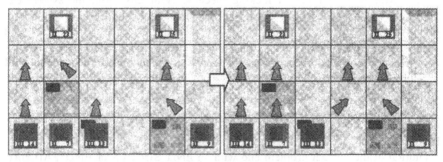

Figure 7: Example of global improvement.

4.6 Improvement Process Monitoring

Once the problem of finding, selecting and applying improvement possibilities have been solved, the main difficulty is to control the improvement sequences that arise. Currently, each selected improvement possibility is going to a new construction session which can generate new improvement possibilities and so on. To avoid infinite loop or recurrent tests, the system deletes irrelevant improvement possibilities.

Often, an improvement possibility can prove bad after its execution and construction sessions will have to be cancelled. In order to do all this, the system uses a backtrack method which is both simpler than the reconstruction algorithm and not inefficient. But sometimes, an improvement can temporarily degrade a solution till another improvement reaches the optimal solution on this basis. It is the well-known local optimum problem. That is why the system tries going on applying improvements before cancelling a bad improvement.

For the moment these control rules are written directly in C++ because they are not domain dependent. But it would be perhaps better to implement them in a declarative way like the remainder of the improvement expertise.

5. Results

5.1 Experimentation

To evaluate the improvement efficiency of the method described in this paper, we have randomly engendered over 90 game situations for the problem of maximizing the number of caught enemy (white) pieces. The situations have been generated in a way favouring catch possibilities. White pieces are set up first and black pieces are set up so that they are not adjacent to a white piece (they would not be able to move if they were) and have at least one white piece in a three squares radius. We have made three series of 30 situations, each for a given size of the problem (see Figure 8). Thus, the search space goes from about 10^{24} to 10^{70} possible solutions.

	Series 1	Series 2	Series 3
Number of white pieces of basic rank one	6	12	18
Number of white pieces of basic rank two	4	8	12
Number of black pieces of basic rank one	4	8	12
Number of black pieces of basic rank two	8	16	24
Draughtboard size	10*15	15*20	15*30

Figure 8: Characteristics of the situations for each test series.

5.2 Results

For each situation, we have first established the value of an optimal solution. The average optimal values for each series are 15.3/30.3/48.3, that is to say about 5/10/15 successful catches. We have then run the MARECHAL system with and without the improvement mechanism. The results are given in percentage of the optimal value on Figure 9.

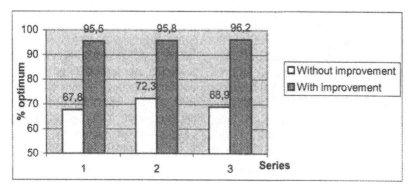

Figure 9: Results of the experimentations.

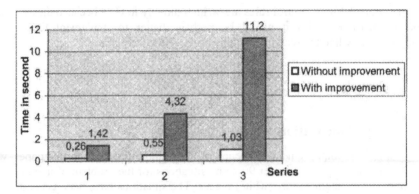

Figure 10: Average computation times.

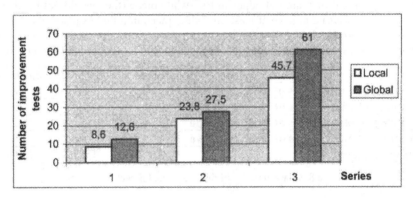

Figure 11: Average numbers of local and global improvement tests.

5.3   Discussion

We can first remark that the results we got without improvement are not bad, which points out the good value of the construction knowledge. Several attempts have been made to further improve this knowledge but without real success. The results indicate that the level of the system without improvement is well above a beginner human player, but is below an experienced player.

With the improvement mechanism, the system clearly gains a broad qualitative jump. It is near the optimal value and fits to the level of an expert human player reasoning in a limited time. Of course, the system answers more quickly than a human player. As the latter has to search for several minutes, the former needs only a few seconds to reach the same value. With this improvement mechanism applied to the complete "StrateGE" game, the system is currently a challenging player for an experienced human player but suffers still some limitations in its strategic knowledge, which should be soon resolved. To our knowledge, MARECHAL is the first system to achieve this level of play in a game of thought where brutal combinatory cannot be used[6].

But for the simplified problem studied in this paper, an expert human is able to reach the optimal solution if the searching time increases, when the MARECHAL system cannot for the moment use extra time to get better results. In the context of the complete game, it is not an important limitation because it is often sufficient to find a good (non optimal) solution in a short time to this kind of tactical problem. But it is not satisfactory for the simplified problem. To avoid this, the system has to enlarge its search by accepting a priori poor improvement possibilities which are currently rejected. This will of course increase the computing time. To preserve the capacity of finding quickly good (non optimal) solutions, it will then be necessary to introduce strong time management functions. According to the foreseen resolution time, the system will accept or reject poor improvement possibilities. Resolution time management is another feature of the monitoring activity ([10]).

6.   Conclusion

In this paper, we have described a mechanism implemented in the MARECHAL system that allows to improve solutions for coordination problems. The efficiency of this mechanism has been demonstrated on a simplified problem of optimisation. Thanks to the improvement method and without using any combinatorial technique, the system becomes an experienced-level player for "StrateGE", a complex game of thought. Without the mechanism, the level was near to a beginner player.

As for the remainder of the system, this mechanism needs specific knowledge to be applied to a new domain but is otherwise general. To demonstrate its generality, we have started to apply it to a new application concerning the full automated positioning of electronic components on a printed board from the logical schema, with the routing of the tracks.

References

1.   Barbuceanu, M. & Fox, M.S. Capturing And Modeling Coordination Knowledge For Multi-Agent Systems. International Journal of Cooperative Information Systems, 1996.
2.   Bouzy, B. & Cazenave, T. Computer Go: An AI-Oriented Survey. To appear in Artificial Intelligence 2001/2002.
3.   Glover, F. Tabu search - Part 1. ORSA journal on computing, 1989; (1-3): 190-206.

---

[6] For instance, the best computer programs for the game of Go have a beginner level, but this game is more difficult because of the long experience (over 1000 years) of humans in this domain (see [2] for the Go problem in Artificial Intelligence).

4. Goldberg, D. Genetic algorithms in search, optimisation and machine learning. Addison Wesley, 1989.

5. Jennings N.R. Toward a Cooperation Knowledge Level for Collaborative Problem Solving. In Proceedings 10-th European Conference on AI, Vienna, Austria, 1992; 224-228.

6. Laird, J.E., Newell, A. & Rosenbloom, P.S. SOAR: An architecture for general intelligence. Artificial Intelligence 33, 1987; 1-64.

7. Maes, P. & Nardi, D. Meta-level Architectures and Reflection. Elsevier Science Publishers B. V., 1988.

8. Pannérec, T. Gestion implicite de la concurrence dans un système à base de tableau noir. Actes du colloque Intelligence Artificielle de Berder, rapport interne LIP6 n°2000/002, 2000; 42-53.

9. Pitrat, J. Métaconnaissance, futur de l'intelligence artificielle. Hermès, 1990.

10. Pitrat, J. Monitorer la recherche d'une solution. Actes du colloque Intelligence Artificielle de Berder, rapport interne LIP6 n°2000/002, 2000; 3-15.

11. Pitrat, J. An intelligent system must and can observe his own behavior. Cognitiva 90, Elsevier Science Publishers, 1991; 119-128.

12. Schiex, T., Fargier, H. & Verfaillie, G. Valued Constraint Satisfaction Problems : Hard and Easy Problems. In Proc. of the 14th International Joint Conference on Artificial Intelligence (IJCAI-95), Montreal, Canada, 1995; 631-637.

A Case Study in Ontologies for Probabilistic Networks

Eveline M. Helsper and Linda C. van der Gaag

Institute of Information and Computing Sciences, Utrecht University,
P.O. Box 80.089, 3508 TB Utrecht, The Netherlands
{eveline,linda}@cs.uu.nl

Abstract. Building a probabilistic network for a real-life domain of application is a hard and time-consuming process, which is generally performed with the help of domain experts. As the scope and, hence, the size and complexity of networks are increasing, the need for proper documentation of the elicited domain knowledge becomes apparent. To study the usefulness of ontologies for this purpose, we have constructed an ontology for the domain of oesophageal cancer, based upon a real-life probabilistic network for the staging of cancer of the oesophagus and the knowledge elicited for its construction. In this paper, we describe the various components of our ontology and outline the benefits of using ontologies in engineering probabilistic networks in general.

1 Introduction

More and more knowledge-based systems build on the formalism of *probabilistic networks* for their knowledge representation, as is demonstrated by an increasing number of successful applications in such domains as medical diagnosis and prognosis, information retrieval, and weather forecasting. A probabilistic network consists of a graphical structure, encoding the important variables from the domain of application along with the influential relationships between them, and an associated numerical part, encoding a joint probability distribution over the represented variables [1].

Building a probabilistic network for a real-life domain of application is generally considered a hard and time-consuming process. The process involves three basic tasks [2]. The first of these is to identify the variables that are of importance in the domain, along with their possible values. Once the important variables have been identified, the second task is to identify the relationships between them and to express these in a graphical structure. The last task is to obtain the probabilities that are required for the network's numerical part. The various tasks are typically performed with the help of domain experts from whom the knowledge required is elicited in a series of interviews.

In building a probabilistic network, numerous design decisions are taken. Many of these decisions originate from the trade-off between the desire for a large and rich model on the one hand and the costs of construction and maintenance on the other hand. Other decisions are enforced by the formalism itself, for example because it requires modelling domain concepts into (single-valued) statistical variables. As a result of these design decisions, the knowledge from the domain experts may not always be recognizable from the resulting probabilistic network. For a small-scaled network that is developed in a laboratory setting by a single knowledge engineer, the elicited domain knowledge is readily shared between the experts and engineer, and the various design decisions can easily be reconstructed. We have experienced, however, that for larger probabilistic networks that are being developed over various years involving different engineers, construction and maintenance are seriously hampered if the elicited domain knowledge is not made explicit by proper documentation.

While the scope and, hence, the complexity and size of real-life probabilistic networks have increased over the last decade, the literature on engineering network-based systems is still quite scarce. Recently, however, an overall systems engineering approach has been advocated for building probabilistic networks [3]. We feel that in this approach explicit documentation of elicited domain knowledge should and can be accommodated. In this paper, we investigate the use of ontologies for this purpose.

In the field of engineering knowledge-based systems, the term *ontology* is used to denote an explicit specification of the domain knowledge that is shared, for example by the experts and knowledge engineers involved [4]. An ontology specifies not just the knowledge that is explicitly captured in a system, but also the more implicit background knowledge of the domain and the meta-level knowledge of its regularities. To this end, an ontology typically consists of various components specifying domain knowledge at different levels of abstraction and from different perspectives.

To study the usefulness of ontologies in engineering probabilistic networks, we have created an ontology for the domain of oesophageal cancer, through reverse engineering of a real-life network for the staging of cancer of the oesophagus and building upon the knowledge that has been elicited for its construction. In doing so, we have noticed that a considerable amount of background knowledge underlies the network, which renders it practically inaccessible to anyone other than the domain experts and the knowledge engineer involved. We have found that our ontology serves to make this background knowledge explicit. Since the pathological processes involved in a tumour's growth play a crucial role in the domain of oesophageal cancer and, hence, in the oesophagus network, we have further found our ontology to have a strong emphasis on the dynamic perspective of the domain under study.

In this paper, we describe the oesophagus ontology and its construction. It is not our intention to introduce a new methodology for developing ontologies or for specifying their components. Our main goal is to propose the use of ontologies in engineering probabilistic networks. The paper is organised as follows. Section 2 briefly introduces the oesophagus network. In Section 3, we use ontologies for making the knowledge in our domain of application explicit, both at different levels of abstraction and from different perspectives. In Section 4, we elaborate on the benefits to be expected from constructing and maintaining ontologies to support engineering of probabilistic networks in general. The paper ends with our concluding observations and directions for further research in Section 5.

2 The oesophagus network

Every year some eighty patients receive treatment for *oesophageal cancer* at the Antoni van Leeuwenhoekhuis of the Netherlands Cancer Institute. These patients are assigned to a therapy by means of a standard protocol that includes a small number of prognostic factors. Based upon this protocol, 75% of the patients show a favourable response to the therapy provided; one out of every four patients, however, develops more or less serious complications as a result of the therapy. To arrive at a more fine-grained protocol with a more favourable response rate, a knowledge-based system is being developed for patient-specific therapy selection. The kernel of our system is a probabilistic network that captures state-of-the-art knowledge about cancer of the oesophagus. In this paper, we focus on the part of the network that pertains to the staging of a patient's oesophageal cancer.

A primary tumour of the oesophagus has various characteristics that influence its prospective growth. These characteristics include the tumour's location in the oesophagus, its length and its macroscopic shape. The tumour typically invades the oesophageal wall and upon further growth may affect such neighbouring organs as the trachea and bronchi or the diaphragm, dependent upon its location in the oesophagus. In time, the tumour may result in secondary tumours, or metastases, in lymph nodes and in other organs, such as the liver and the lungs. A distinction is made between lymphatic metastases and haematogenous metastases that result from transference of cancer cells via the lymph vessels and via the blood vessels, respectively. The depth of invasion and the extent of metastasis, summarised in the cancer's stage, largely influence a patient's life expectancy and are indicative of the effects and complications to be expected from the different available therapeutic alternatives.

The oesophagus network has been constructed and refined with the help of two experts in gastrointestinal oncology from the Netherlands Cancer Institute. In a sequence of eleven interviews of two to four hours each over a period of two years, the experts have identified the relevant diagnostic and prognostic factors to be captured as statistical variables in the network and the relationships between them. For the graphical structure, almost 1000 probabilities have been specified. The elicitation of these probabilities has taken five interviews of approximately two hours each over a period of fifteen months [5]. The graphical structure of the oesophagus network is depicted in Figure 1; the figure also shows the prior probability distributions for the various variables.

3 An ontology for oesophageal cancer

To study the usefulness of ontologies in engineering probabilistic networks, we have constructed an ontology for the domain of oesophageal cancer. We have based our ontology on the network described in the previous section and on the

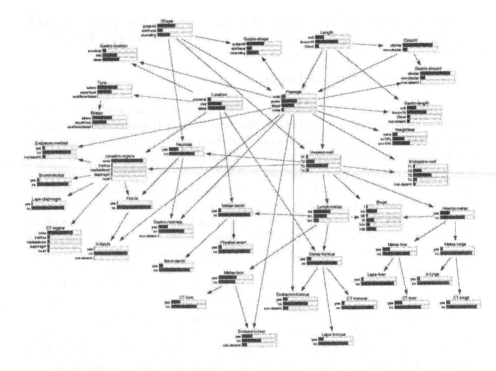

Fig. 1. The oesophagus network

knowledge that had been elicited from the domain experts during the network's construction. We would like to note that one of the authors of the present paper has engineered the network. The ontology has been constructed mainly by the other author, who initially had no experience with the domain. In the construction of the ontology, it has become apparent that a considerable amount of background knowledge underlies the oesophagus network. The background knowledge being implicit, in fact, forestalls a thorough comprehension of the network by anyone who has not been involved in its construction. Other difficulties in interpreting the network arise from the design decisions that have been taken, for example, in the translation of domain concepts into statistical variables. For the construction of the oesophagus ontology, this additional knowledge had to be shared between the two authors.

The construction of the oesophagus ontology has been far from straightforward, even given the available knowledge in the domain of application. Although we could build upon a wealth of literature on ontologies, we still had to resolve numerous methodological issues. In this section, we describe the oesophagus ontology and some of the issues we have been confronted with during its construction. In Section 3.1, we give an overview of our ontology; the Sections 3.2 through 3.4 describe its different components.

3.1 An overview of the ontology

As described in the introduction, an ontology is an explicit specification of the domain knowledge that is shared by the experts and knowledge engineers involved in the construction of a knowledge-based system. The domain knowledge is typically composed of concepts and relations between concepts, and comprises both declarative and procedural knowledge. In this paper, we focus on the declarative knowledge of the domain of oesophageal cancer.

The main purpose of developing an ontology for a knowledge-based system under construction, is to make the elicited domain knowledge explicit. The ontology serves to help the knowledge engineers in understanding the intricacies of the domain and to facilitate communication between the knowledge engineers and the domain experts, thereby supporting the development and maintenance of the system. To this end, an ontology should meet a number of criteria. Th.R. Gruber identifies five criteria for ontologies that have knowledge sharing for their main purpose [6]. We adopt these criteria and describe their implications for the oesophagus ontology.

- *Clarity*: the meanings of the concepts and relations that are specified in the ontology must be clear to both knowledge engineers and domain experts.
- *Coherence*: the ontology should be internally coherent.
- *Extendibility*: the ontology should be easy to extend and maintain, without inducing the need to change major parts of the ontology.
- *Minimal encoding bias*: the representation language used for expressing the domain knowledge should introduce as little bias as possible.
- *Minimal ontological commitment*: the ontology should be based on as few assumptions as possible about how the ontology, and the knowledge it contains, will be used.

To meet the *clarity* criterion, the oesophagus ontology contains a *glossary*, listing the names of the relevant concepts in the domain of application along with their meaning. The glossary serves to avoid confusion and ambiguity of terms. For example, the experts in the domain of oesophageal cancer use the term *metastasis* to refer to the process of transference of cancer cells via the blood or lymph vessels, but also to indicate a secondary tumour resulting from this process. We have chosen an unambiguous name for each meaning and have included these names and their associated meanings in the glossary.

To ensure that no internal inconsistencies will arise in the ontology, for example upon maintenance, it includes various *validity axioms*. These axioms specify requirements that the represented knowledge should adhere to, and thus are instrumental in meeting the *coherence* criterion.

To provide for *extendibility*, the oesophagus ontology is decomposed into separate components specifying different types of knowledge from different perspectives. We distinguish between two perspectives. The *static perspective* on the domain knowledge mainly addresses the organisation of concepts in hierarchies. The *dynamic perspective* focuses on the causal relations between the concepts.

The decomposition of the ontology provides for a knowledge engineer to concentrate on a particular component and to modify it independently of other components.

The criterion of *minimal encoding bias* states that the language used in the ontology for representing the domain knowledge should introduce as little bias as possible in the contents and structure of the knowledge. If the criterion is not met, the ontology may not properly reflect the intricacies of the domain. The language of probabilistic networks, for example, fails to meet the criterion. Using this language may cause loss of information because it does not allow for explicitly capturing the different natures of the relations that exist between the various concepts. Also, important information may be lost in the translation of domain concepts into statistical variables. We feel moreover, that an ontology that is expressed as a probabilistic network cannot serve as a communication medium between our domain experts and knowledge engineers, mainly because the conceptual distance between the ontology and the way the experts think and talk about their domain would be too large. A more suitable representation language should therefore be selected for expressing the knowledge from our domain of application. Some authors suggest that domain knowledge may be represented by a language that is highly informal, semi-informal, semi-formal or rigorously formal [4]; others argue that ontologies should be formal and machine readable [7]. For the oesophagus ontology, we have chosen a semi-informal representation language, including tables, graphs and natural language, that is flexible and easy to read for both domain experts and knowledge engineers. We feel that a more formal representation language would be less suitable for our goals, because the use of formal languages is uncommon in our domain of application.

Commitments to the projected use of an ontology and its contents may also introduce biases in the represented knowledge. For example, any commitment to the problem-solving method that will be applied to the domain knowledge will influence the way the knowledge is captured in the ontology [8]. Commitments may thus hamper extendibility and reuse of an ontology, yet should not always be avoided, for reasons of clarity and of ensuring coherence. For our oesophagus ontology, for example, we have decided to commit to our application in the sense that the background knowledge that facilitates understanding of the domain is included, but knowledge about other diseases of the oesophagus and about tumours at other sites is not captured.

3.2 The glossary

The *glossary* of the oesophagus ontology specifies the names of the relevant concepts in the domain of application along with a description of their meaning. A domain concept can in essence refer to any type of item, such as a concrete entity, a set, a process, or a more abstract item. The purpose of the glossary is to list the terms used in the domain of application in such a way that their meaning is unambiguous and agreed upon by the domain experts and knowledge engineers. Table 1 shows a part of the glossary of our oesophagus ontology.

Term	Meaning
lamina propria	the first inner layer of the oesophageal wall
lymphatic metastasis	a metastatic tumour in a lymph node
metastasis	the transference of cancer cells from the primary tumour via blood or lymph vessels, giving rise to metastatic tumours
metastatic tumour	a secondary tumour at another site than the primary tumour
site	location in the human body

Table 1. Part of the glossary of the oesophagus ontology

3.3 The static perspective

The oesophagus ontology explicitly captures the static relations between the various concepts in the domain. We say that a relation is *static* if time does not play a role in it. We distinguish between three types of static relation: *structural* and *definitional* relations, and *validity* relations or *axioms*.

Structural relations. The concepts in a domain typically play different roles with respect to one another. A concept may, for example, be a generalisation or a superset of another concept. It may also be a property of another concept. This type of knowledge is captured by *structural relations*, which are often represented as standard *is-a, part-of* and *object-attribute-value* relations.

Studying the structural relations in the domain of oesophageal cancer has resulted in a number of *hierarchies*. Figures 2 and 3 show the hierarchies of pathological processes and pathological entities, respectively; the hierarchies are simplified for ease of presentation. Pathological processes and entities, where the term pathological indicates that a process or entity deviates from what is considered normal, play a central role in the domain of oesophageal cancer. They often relate to specific parts of the human body. This (background) anatomical knowledge is also represented in our oesophagus ontology, as is knowledge about manifestations and tests. The hierarchies capturing these types of knowledge are

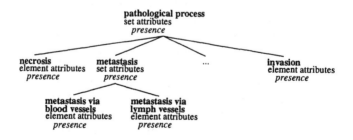

Fig. 2. The hierarchy of pathological processes

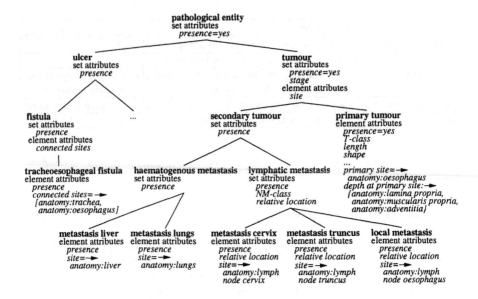

Fig. 3. The hierarchy of pathological entities

not shown here. We would like to note that several different ways of organising concepts in hierarchies are possible [9].

We briefly discuss the hierarchy of pathological entities. In the hierarchy, each node represents a set of individuals. The links capture set inclusion. The set of *secondary tumours*, for example, is a subset of the set of *tumours*. Two types of attribute are associated with the various nodes. An *element attribute* describes a property of each individual in the associated set. For example, all individuals in the set of *tumours* have a *site*. Element attributes are inherited in the hierarchy. *Set attributes*, on the other hand, specify properties of a set as a whole; they are not inherited by subsets. For example, the set attribute *presence* of the node *tumour* represents the presence of at least one tumour in a patient. An attribute, whether an element or a set attribute, can specify a reference to another node. For example, the attribute *site* of the node *metastasis liver* specifies a reference to the node *liver* in the hierarchy of anatomical knowledge. The hierarchies may further contain domain declarations for attributes. For example, the depth of invasion of a primary tumour into the oesophageal wall is specified to be one of the layers *lamina propria*, *muscularis propria* and *adventitia*.

We feel that the hierarchies that we have constructed to describe the structural relations in the domain of oesophageal cancer are close to the experts' view on the domain. In the hierarchies, we have made little commitment to the ontology's projected use. An example of a commitment that we have made is the value *yes* for the element attribute *presence* that is associated with the node *primary tumour*. This value reflects the assumption that a patient is known to have oesophageal cancer. As the Netherlands Cancer Institute is a specialised centre for cancer treatment, this assumption seems reasonable; in fact, it also underlies the oesophagus network. We have made no commitment with respect to the problem-solving method used. However, we have decided to keep the hierarchies restricted in scope, which is in essence a commitment to the application aimed for. For extending the ontology, for example to include knowledge about tumours at other sites, the necessary modifications will be limited in scope.

Definitional relations. A *definitional relation* is a relation between values of attributes: it basically defines the value of an attribute in terms of the values of some other attributes. As an example, Table 2 shows how the value of the *stage* of an oesophageal cancer is defined in terms of the presence of haematogenous metastases, the extent of the lymphatic metastases, and the T-class of the primary tumour. Another example pertains to the attribute *presence* of the set of *haematogenous metastases*. This attribute has the value *yes* only if the attribute *presence* of at least one of its subsets has the value *yes*.

haematogenous metastasis *presence*	lymphatic metastasis *NM-class*	primary tumour *T-class*	tumour *stage*
no	N0	T1	I
no	N0	T2 or T3	IIA
no	N1	T1 or T2	IIB
...	...	...	...
yes	-	-	IVB

Table 2. The definitional relation for the stage of an oesophageal cancer

Validity axioms. To meet the coherence criterion, we have specified various validity axioms that knowledge represented in the structural and definitional relations of our ontology should adhere to. An example of such a validity axiom pertains to the domain declaration of the attribute *depth at primary site* of the *primary tumour*. The domain of this attribute is the set of nodes that are linked by *part-of* relations to the node that serves as the value of the *site* of the *primary tumour*.

3.4 The dynamic perspective

A domain of application may involve processes that have important effects over time. In the domain of oesophageal cancer, for example, the pathological process of metastasis via the blood vessels may result in a secondary tumour in the liver. The process of metastasis precedes, in time, the presence of metastatic cancer in the liver. We use the term *dynamic relation* to refer to such time-involving relations between concepts.

Studying the dynamic relations in the domain of oesophageal cancer has revealed several high-level regularities. These regularities are not easily recognised, however, as they are implicitly present. We have made them explicit by using different *description levels* in our ontology: the dynamic relations are represented at the level of attribute values, at the level of the attributes, and at the level of the nodes in the hierarchies. We note that the idea of representing domain knowledge at different levels of abstraction has been described before [7, 9]. The properties that the dynamic relations should adhere to, again are specified in various *validity axioms*.

Dynamic relations. At the lowest description level, dynamic relations among attribute *values* are captured, along with their nature. An example is the dynamic relation that expresses that the attribute *presence* of the process of *metastasis via blood vessels* having the value *yes* may result in the attribute *presence* of *metastasis liver* adopting the value *yes*. This relation is an example of a *resulting* relation. We would like to note that the relation involves uncertainty. Dynamic relations can in essence be deterministic or uncertain, but are almost always uncertain in the domain of oesophageal cancer. To incorporate the uncertainties involved in our ontology is a subject of further research.

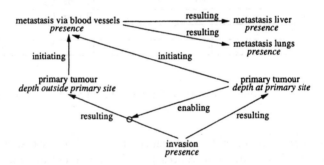

Fig. 4. Part of the attribute-level graph of dynamic relations

At the next description level, dynamic relations among *attributes* are represented. These relations capture whether or not two or more attributes are related at the value level. They thus abstract from specific values. Figure 4 is a graphical representation of some of the dynamic relations at the attribute level of the oesophagus ontology. It shows, for example, that the pathological process of invasion may affect the depth of invasion of the primary tumour into the oesophageal wall. The primary tumour may also invade organs outside the oesophagus, *provided* it has grown through the entire oesophageal wall. We say that the depth of invasion of the tumour at the primary site *enables* the invasion outside the oesophagus. Furthermore, a tumour that has invaded the oesophageal wall may initiate a process of metastasis via the blood vessels, which in turn may result in metastases in the liver or lungs.

The graphical representation of the dynamic relations at the attribute level captures various regularities in the domain knowledge, albeit implicitly. Abstraction of the knowledge in this attribute-level graph, using the *is-a* relations from the hierarchies, results in a high-level graph that explicitly represents these regularities. Figure 5 depicts the high-level graph. In constructing the graph, *metastasis via blood vessels* and *metastasis liver*, for example, have been generalised to *pathological process* and *pathological entity*, respectively. The graph shows that pathological processes may result in pathological entities. It further reveals a causal relation from manifestation to manifestation. For example, a patient's difficulties with swallowing food may cause weight loss. The graph also reflects that a pathological entity may in essence be observed, but only if an appropriate test is performed to this end. For example, a gastroscopic examination, that is, letting a camera into the oesophagus, may reveal the length of the primary tumour. The test basically *enables* the observation. If the oesophagus is obstructed by the primary tumour, however, the camera cannot pass the obstruction upon a gastroscopic examination and may not give the results aimed for: the observation then is disabled, or negatively enabled.

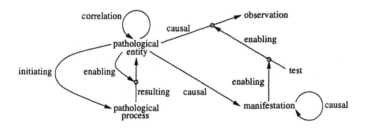

Fig. 5. The high-level graph of dynamic relations

We would like to note that the knowledge that a pathological entity may initiate a pathological process, which in turn may result in a pathological entity, could also have been modelled as a causal relation between pathological entities, leaving the pathological process underlying this dynamic relation implicit. We have decided, however, to represent explicitly the pathological processes that play an important role in the domain of oesophageal cancer and in the communication with the domain experts. To meet the clarity criterion, however, not all processes underlying dynamic relations have been specified in our ontology.

Validity axioms. To meet the coherence criterion, the dynamic perspective of our ontology once again specifies various axioms that the represented knowledge should adhere to. An example of a validity axiom that pertains to the collection of dynamic relations is the axiom that states that a tumour can only invade organs that are adjacent to previously affected organs.

We would like to note that the validity axioms could have been modelled explicitly in a collection of dynamic relations, using static anatomical knowledge. There is an important conceptual difference between the axioms and relations, however. While the high-level graph describes the occurrence of dynamic relations in the knowledge that has been acquired so far and may be extended after additional knowledge has been elicited, the validity axioms describe relations that are not allowed. We feel that the dynamic perspective in which we have distinguished between the two is closer to the language of the domain experts.

4 Benefits of ontologies for probabilistic networks

The common practice of engineering probabilistic networks is to model knowledge directly into a network. In our experience, however, domain knowledge often cannot be represented straightforwardly into a probabilistic network. For example, a multi-valued domain concept has to be decomposed into a number of single-valued statistical variables; the nature of the relations between these variables is then hidden in the probabilities of the network. A similar observation applies to the knowledge that a specific dynamic relation is enabled. Furthermore, the oesophagus network represents, by means of its arcs, probabilistic dependences between the nodes *haema-metas* and *metas-liver*, and between the nodes *passage* and *weightloss*. It does not show, however, that the former dependence captures a static *is-a* relation, whereas the latter represents a dynamic *causal* relation. Moreover, background knowledge is often not explicitly represented in a probabilistic network. For example, for pragmatical reasons, the processes of *metastasis via blood vessels* and *metastasis via lymph vessels* have not been included in the oesophagus network. These issues can hamper the communication between the experts and knowledge engineers involved, and may impede further development and maintenance of the network. To forestall these problems, we feel that constructing an ontology should be integrated in a systems engineering approach to developing probabilistic networks.

One of the concrete benefits of representing domain knowledge in an ontology is that it renders background knowledge explicitly available. Moreover, the ontology enables explicit representation of all elicited concepts and relations from the domain of application, as opposed to the language of probabilistic networks. Since we have used a rather informal language for specifying our ontology, we feel that the knowledge contained is readily recognizable for both experts and knowledge engineers.

As an additional benefit, we observe that, since an ontology explicitly represents the elicited domain knowledge, it can be used to guide further acquisition efforts [10]. Also, the represented knowledge can be validated more easily against completeness and consistency. For example, if a new test is to be represented in our ontology, then the knowledge engineer should establish whether or not this test will always yield results, irrespective of the presence of certain manifestations. Moreover, if a dynamic relation is to be added to an initial collection of relations, the knowledge engineer should verify that it meets the regularities in the domain. An irregularity, for example an indication that a test affects a pathological entity, then serves as a warning to further investigate the newly acquired relation. If it appears to be correct, the high-level graph should be adjusted accordingly. We note that the validity axioms on the other hand represent requirements that have to be met by newly added knowledge.

5 Conclusions and future research

Building a probabilistic network for a real-life domain of application is a hard and time-consuming process. In this process, numerous design decisions are taken. We have further noticed that background knowledge often is not represented explicitly in a probabilistic network. Construction and maintenance of a network are seriously hampered if the elicited domain knowledge is not made explicit by proper documentation. In this paper, we have studied the usefulness of ontologies for this purpose by constructing an ontology for the domain of oesophageal cancer, based upon our probabilistic network for the staging of cancer of the oesophagus and the knowledge elicited for its construction.

The oesophagus ontology is composed of various components that represent different types of knowledge from different perspectives at different levels of abstraction. Although the ontology has not been validated as yet against the domain experts involved in the construction of the oesophagus network, we feel that it represents a rich, well-organised body of knowledge for further reference. So far, the documentation of the oesophagus network captures knowledge of the domain only. We are now in the process of studying the design decisions that have been taken in the network's construction, for example pertaining to the translation of domain concepts into statistical variables. These decisions basically constitute the link between the oesophagus ontology and the network. As the design decisions should be shared among all knowledge engineers involved, we feel that the documentation should be extended to include an explicit specification of these decisions.

Based upon our experience with constructing the oesophagus ontology, we see many benefits from the use of ontologies for explicitly documenting domain knowledge in engineering probabilistic networks. We plan to further study these benefits in the domain of oesophageal cancer and in other domains of application of probabilistic networks.

Acknowledgements. This research has been (partly) supported by the Netherlands Computer Science Research Foundation with financial support from the Netherlands Organisation for Scientific Research. We are grateful to Babs Taal and Berthe Aleman from the Netherlands Cancer Institute, Antoni van Leeuwenhoekhuis, who provided the domain knowledge for the construction of the oesophagus network.

References

1. F.V. Jensen (1996). *An Introduction to Bayesian Networks*. UCL Press, London.
2. M.J. Druzdzel, L.C. van der Gaag (2000). Building probabilistic networks: "Where do the numbers come from?" Guest editors' introduction. *IEEE Transactions on Knowledge and Data Engineering*, vol. 12, pp. 481 – 486.
3. K. Blackmond Laskey, S.M. Mahoney (2000). Network engineering for agile belief network models. *IEEE Transactions on Knowledge and Data Engineering*, vol. 12, pp. 487 – 498.
4. M. Uschold, M. Gruninger (1996). Ontologies: principles, methods and applications. *Knowledge Engineering Review*, vol. 11(2), pp. 93 – 136.
5. L.C. van der Gaag, S. Renooij, C.L.M. Witteman, B.M.P. Aleman, B.G. Taal (1999). How to elicit many probabilities. In: K.B. Laskey, H. Prade (eds). *Proceedings of the Fifteenth Conference on Uncertainty in Artificial Intelligence*, Morgan Kaufmann, San Francisco, pp. 647 – 654.
6. Th.R. Gruber (1995). Towards principles for the design of ontologies used for knowledge sharing. *International Journal of Human-Computer Studies*, vol. 43, pp. 907 – 928.
7. R. Studer, V.R. Benjamins, D. Fensel (1998). Knowledge engineering: principles and methods. *Data & Knowledge Engineering*, vol. 25, pp. 161 – 197.
8. T. Bylander, B. Chandrasekaran (1988). Generic tasks for knowledge-based reasoning: the "right" level of abstraction for knowledge acquisition. In: B.R. Gaines, J.H. Boose (eds). *Knowledge Acquisition for Knowledge-Based Systems*, vol. 1, Academic Press, London, pp. 65 – 77.
9. B. Chandrasekaran, J.R. Josephson, V.R. Benjamins (1999). What are ontologies, and why do we need them? *IEEE Intelligent Systems & Their Applications*, vol. 14(1), pp. 20 – 26.
10. G. van Heijst, A.Th. Schreiber, B.J. Wielinga (1997). Using explicit ontologies in KBS development. *International Journal of Human-Computer Studies*, vol. 46(2/3), pp. 183 – 292.

SESSION 5:

KNOWLEDGE ENGINEERING

WebShell: The development of web based expert systems

Andrew Stranieri
Donald Berman Laboratory for Information Technology and Law
La Trobe University, Bundoora Australia
stranier@cs.latrobe.edu.au

John Zeleznikow
Centre for Forensic Statistics and Legal Reasoning,
Faculty of Law, University of Edinburgh, Scotland,UK
john.zeleznikow@ed.ac.uk

Abstract

It is rare to find knowledge based appearing on the World Wide Web. This is, in part, due to difficulties associated with porting expert system shell environments to the world wide web. For instance, many real world applications require shell environments that do more than make mere inferences with rules. However, integrating rule based reasoning with other approaches exacerbate the difficulties in placing hybrid systems on the World Wide Web. In this paper, we present a knowledge based system shell, WebShell that enables knowledge based systems to be developed and executed on the World Wide Web. WebShell models knowledge using two distinct techniques; decision trees for procedural type tasks and argument trees for tasks that are more complex, ambiguous or uncertain. Rather than translate decision tree knowledge into rules, we map the decision trees into sets we call sequenced transition networks. These sets can readily be stored in a relational database format in a way that simplifies the inference engine design. The inference engines for both the argument tree and the decision tree models execute on the server side and have been implemented using a very small (30K) PHP program.

1.   Introduction

The majority of knowledge based systems in commercial use have not been designed to execute on the World Wide Web. There are a number of reasons for this. First of all, few expert systems shells have been developed for web environments. Those developed are typically very expensive and beyond the reach of most user groups. Furthermore, traditional rule based system architectures are not particularly well suited for web-based shells. For example, the traditional separation of domain knowledge from control knowledge [11] requires that the inference engine scans large segments of the knowledge base in order to find candidate rules to fire. If both inference engine and knowledge bases reside and execute on the server then the time required for this in a web based knowledge based system, in addition to transmission delays from the client to the server and time required for the resolution of rule conflicts is prohibitive. Furthermore, the opportunity for potentially any number of simultaneous users to access a web-based knowledge based system places real constraints on concurrency control mechanisms.

According to Huntington, difficulties with the introduction of web based expert systems diminish if shells are designed to execute largely on the client's machine as opposed to the server [7]. Java applets are promoted for this. However the appeal of this approach is diminished because client side shells are difficult to realise in practice. The knowledge base and inference engine components of a knowledge-based system are typically large programs that require substantial resources and time to download. Furthermore, execution on the client side is likely to be limited to users with powerful computers restricting the universality of the approach.

JESS, the Java Expert System Shell encodes CLIPS rules [http://herzberg.ca.sandia.gov/jess/]. A server side architecture using Jess has been described by [6]. This architecture supports client side knowledge based development. The disadvantages of client side systems include the additional overhead in the transmission of knowledge bases and inference engine programs, security concerns and the restrictions on universality due to the resource demands placed on the client.

Although server side applications such as Jnana [www.jnana.com] have been developed for web environments they are typically too expensive to enable small to medium size enterprises to use them. In this paper we describe a server side web based shell that is both small and simple. The separation of domain knowledge from control knowledge that was the hallmark of traditional expert systems has been relaxed. This allows the shell to be compact, fast and inexpensive to build. Knowledge is stored in a relational databases and modelled using two representations; a variant of a standard decision tree and an argument tree. This facilitates on-going maintenance.

The decision tree representation is particularly well suited to parts of domains that are procedural. This captures knowledge where decision-makers have little discretion or room for interpretation. The argument tree representation involves knowledge where an expert has more discretion. A knowledge based system for a rule based, procedural domain can be built in WebShell using only decision trees. On the other hand, a knowledge based system for a discretionary domain can be built using only argument trees. However, the two representations are tightly integrated for domains that involve a mix of procedural and non-procedural knowledge. The distinction between procedural and non-procedural knowledge is discussed in [14]

Procedural knowledge is modelled using decision trees. A decision tree is a directed graph in which nodes are domain concepts and arcs are values for concepts. Typically, decision trees, are converted to rules for use with an expert system shell. In the next section of this paper, a variation on the conventional decision tree will be introduced. This results in a labelling of nodes and arcs in a pre-specified manner for conversion into sets called sequenced transition networks (STN). The sets are stored as tuples in a relational database.

Discretionary knowledge is modelled using argument trees. We have used an argument structure based on the work of the philosopher, Stephen Toulmin [13]. A survey by [12] reveals that the majority of researchers that have adopted the Toulmin Structure have not used the original structure but variations of Toulmin's original concept. An analysis of those variations has motivated the structure we used for the argument trees in WebShell. The argument tree component of WebShell is described in section 3 of this paper.

WebShell has been evaluated by developing knowledge-based systems for Victoria Legal Aid (VLA). VLA is a government-funded provider of legal services for disadvantaged clients, based in Victoria, Australia. When an applicant approaches VLA, his/her application is assessed to determine whether he/she should receive legal aid. This task chews up more than 50% of VLA's operating budget, yet provides no services to its clients. The provision of a web-based expert system which advises potential clients as to their likelihood of being granted legal aid has great financial benefits for VLA. It will allow them to use their meagre resources on giving legal advice and support.

After passing a financial test, applicants for legal aid must pass a merits tests. The merits test involves a prediction about the likely outcome of the case if it were to be decided by a Court. The merits test is assessed by VLA grants officers who have extensive experience in the practices of Victorian Courts. This assessment involves the integration of procedural knowledge found in regulatory guidelines with expert lawyer knowledge that involves a considerable degree of discretion.

2. Decision trees for representing procedural knowledge

A decision tree is a directed graph in which the nodes represent domain concepts and possible values for each concept are captured in arcs emerging from each nodes. Leaf nodes represent conclusions. Figure 1 depicts a decision tree that represents reasoning used by lawyers VLA, to determine whether an applicant for legal aid, who is scheduled to appear in a minor (Magistrates) court, has met statutory guidelines.

The decision trees used for representing procedural knowledge in WebShell differ cosmetically from the conventional decision tree depicted in Figure 1. The variation, illustrated in Figure 2, enables user prompts and explanations to be more easily generated directly from information in the tree and also facilitates the maintenance of the system. The labels for concepts, arcs and conclusions are replaced with sentence fragments that can be directly converted to user prompts in a web page. Text in each node in conjunction with text on arcs emanating from a node form alternate sentences that conform to the syntax; <Text before choices>, <choices>, <text after choices>. The sentences are used as user prompts (and for explanations) without modification. The precise form of words for user prompts is elicited directly from experts.

Koers et al found that when determining user acceptability of a knowledge-based system, the sequence of questions an expert asks is more important than the logical structure of the reasoning [8]. We believe that it is far less demanding to elicit the sequence of questions from an expert than it is to model the logical structure of the expert's reasoning.

When using a conventional expert system, the decision tree is converted into rules. During a consultation, the expert system shell's inference engine generates user prompts from the rules and, based on user responses, fire rules until a conclusion is reached. Our approach differs in that the decision tree is not converted into rules. Instead, the information in the tree is entered into a relational database in a way that facilitates the retrieval of a sequence of user prompts leading to a conclusion.

The conversion of a decision tree into a relational model is performed by labelling the nodes in a graph as follows:

1. Label the first node '0'

2. Consecutively (and arbitrarily) number the arcs emergent from each node 1 to n where n is the number of arcs leaving the node

3. Label each node with the path taken to reach the node

For example, the conclusion node (rounded rectangular) 0121 corresponds to the path taken by selecting arc 1 from the initial node, 0, then arc 2 to reach node 012 then arc 1 to reach node 0121. The set of all paths through a graph is called a sequenced transition network set (STN) and is stored in a relational database. The three rows in Figure 3 correspond to three paths through the graph in Figure 2.

The inference engine commences forward chaining by executing a database query that retrieves all information associated with an STNID of '0'. The engine generates the form depicted in Figure 6. Once the user makes a selection and presses the next, ($\rightarrow$) button, the inference engine appends the selection number (say 2) to the current (0) and calls itself by retrieving all information associated with node 02.

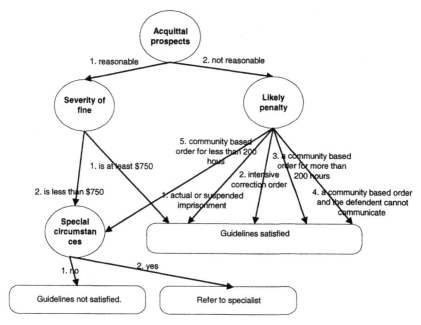

Figure 1 Decision tree for eligibility for legal aid.

The current implementation is a small recursive program (14K) written in PHP that reads data stored in a mySQL database. The STN for the graph in Figure 2 is:

{{0}, {01}, {011}, {012}, {0121}, {0122}, {02}, {021}, {0211}, {022}, {023}, {024}, {025), {0251}, {0252} }

Inference and explanation requirements of a web-based expert system shell are performed by operators defined on the set. These are informally described as follows:

- Forward chaining involves the retrieval of the next node from the STN set. The next node is defined as the current choice number appended to the current node path.

- A 'How' (rule trace) explanation is generated from the path for a conclusion by retracing the user prompts along the path's subsets. Thus, the rule trace for conclusion {012} is generated by appending the user prompts for subset nodes {0}and {01}.

- 'Why' explanations inform a user about the reasons for the user prompt. In traditional expert system shells, Why explanations need to be hard-coded into the shell. Using our approach a form of this type of explanation is possible by making reference to conclusions that will not be reachable if a particular choice is made. For example, a Why explanation at node {02} will indicate to the user that if they selected choice 1 (*an actual or suspended term of imprisonment*) then the conclusions, *Guidelines not satisfied* {0125, 0251} and *Refer to specialist* {0122, 0252} cannot be reached. This operation is achieved with the use of two sets defined on an STN set; a reachable conclusion set and an unreachable conclusion set.

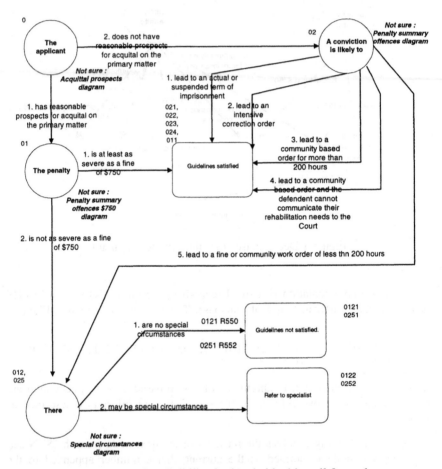

Figure 2 Decision tree for eligibility for legal aid with well formed sentences.

The STN reachable and unreachable sets can be defined more formally as follows:

We define an STN graph, S as a directed acyclic graph comprising n vertices and e edges which has the following properties: There is one vertex labelled, I, the initial vertex. I has an indegree = 0 and outdegree > 1.

Edges from a vertex, v_i are labelled 1,2,..n where n = outdegree of the vertex . We define a conclusion vertex, L_i as a vertex with outdegree = 0.

We define an STN ID as a path, P through a STN graph, S from X to any other vertex. P is a finite sequence P = $\{a_1, a_2, ..a_m)$ a_i is taken from the alphabet set $V = \{0, 1, ..n\}$ where n is the largest outdegree in the graph and 0 represents I.

We define a sequenced transition network, N as the set of all STN ID's, P_i through the STN graph, S. N = $\{P_1, P_2, .. P_r\}$

We define a conclusion path, P = $\{a_1, a_2, ..a_m\}$ as a path within a sequenced transition network from which there are no arcs from P. This is a path that leads to a conclusion vertex.

We define a conclusion set, C for a vertex of an sequenced transition network, N as the set of all conclusion paths in N that lead to the same conclusion vertex.

We define a reachable conclusion set from a sub graph, SG of the STN graph, S as a conclusion set, where there exists a path in SG from a given path, P to a conclusion set.

We define U to be an unreachable conclusion set of a sub graph, SG of the STN graph, S as a conclusion set, where there is no path in S from a given path P to any conclusion set.

We define a difference segment, D between two sets of distinct paths, P_1 = $\{a_1, a_2, ..a_m\}$, and $P_2 = \{x_1, x_2, ..x_n\}$ as

(1) $\{a_1, x_1\}$ if a_1 does not equal x_1

(2) $\{(a_1, a_2, ..a_r, a_{r+1}), (x_1, x_2, ..x_r, x_{r+1})\}$ if $a_i = x_i$ for $i <= r$ and a_{r+1} not equal x_{r+1}

Each node in a decision tree is not necessarily uniquely labelled because a node has as many STN ID's as there are paths to reach the node. If every path is stored in the database then many records would unnecessarily duplicated. To avoid this we arbitrarily define one STN ID as the actual identifier for a node and define all other labels for that node as virtual identifiers. The mapping between virtual and actual identifiers is stored in an additional table illustrated in Figure 5.

In the STN approach, there is no requirement to convert graphs to rules because graphs are converted into sets that corresponds to paths through the graph. All paths through a directed graph are currently transferred to a relational database manually but development is in progress to automate this so that an expert need only draw a graph in order to produce a system that represents procedural knowledge.

The STN based approach facilitates the development of knowledge based systems for knowledge that can readily be captured as a decision tree. However, as illustrated in the introduction not all knowledge is procedural. For example, the node in Figure 2 relates to the prospects an applicant for legal aid has to be acquitted of a charge. Determining the possibility of a successful defence to a charge requires legal expertise, especially since judges and juries are granted considerable discretion. Such knowledge cannot readily be modelled using decision trees. The next section describes the use of argumentation structures to represent discretionary reasoning. The two approaches; procedural knowledge represented by the use of decision trees and discretionary knowledge represented by the use of argument trees are integrated through the decision tree *Not sure* option.

STN ID	Graph ID	Before Text	After text	notSureID
0	CS	The applicant	have reasonable prospects for acquittal on the primary matter	acquittalProspects
01	CS	The penalty	at least as severe as a fine of $750	penalty750
012	CS	There	special circumstances	specialCircum

Figure 3 Sample entries in the Node/Path table.

STN ID	Graph ID	Choice ID	Choice Text
0	CS	1	does
0	CS	2	does not
01	CS	1	is
01	CS	2	is not
012	CS	1	are
012	CS	2	are not

Figure 4 Sample entries in the Choice table

virtual STNID	graph ID	actual STNID
01	CS	01
02	CS	02
021	CS	021
022	CS	021
023	CS	021
024	CS	021
012	CS	012
025	CS	012

Figure 5 Sample entries in the Virtual path table

Each node in the variant of decision tree we use has a NOT SURE option. This is conceptually equivalent to an additional arc emanating from a node. The NOT SURE arc is followed if a user is unsure about the path to select. The NOT SURE option can lead to another decision tree, or as is the case for the first node in Figure 2, to a system that represents knowledge as arguments.

Figure 6 Screen of the first user prompt generated by the inference engine.

3. Argumentation for representing discretionary knowledge

A number of researchers have assumed that knowledge is often used in arguing for or against an assertion and have therefore used argumentation theories to model reasoning. The use of argumentation in this way draws heavily on insights from philosophy. Over two thousand years ago, Aristotle presented two types of syllogisms that he called analytic and dialectic syllogisms. Dialectic syllogisms concern opinions that are adhered to with variable intensity. The objective of an exponent of this type of reasoning is to convince or persuade an audience to accept the claims advocated. In contrast, analytic syllogisms do not involve opinions and differ from dialectic syllogisms in that conclusions are reached by the application of sound inference rules to axioms. Argumentation can be seen to be have been used by researchers in two distinct ways; to model discourse and to structure knowledge.

Applications of argumentation to model discourse automate the construction of an argument and its counter argument typically with the use of a non-monotonic logic. In the majority of dialectical approaches, knowledge is represented using predicate clauses and operators are defined to implement discursive elements such as *attack, rebut,* or *accept.* Mechanisms are typically required to identify implausible arguments and to evaluate the better argument of two or more plausible ones. For example, Fox and Parsons [5] analyse and extend the non standard logic LA reported in [9]. In that formalisation, an argument is a tuple with three components: (Sentence : Grounds : Sign) where the sentence is the Toulmin claim though this may be a simple claim or a rule and the Sign is a number or symbol that indicates the confidence warranted in the claim. The Grounds are the sentences involved in asserting the claim and can be seen as the reasoning steps used to ultimately reach the conclusion.

In contrast, applications of argumentation that aim to structure knowledge include Dick [3][4], Marshall [10], Ball [1] and Clark [2]. These approaches involve the use of the argument structure advanced by Toulmin [13].

Toulmin advanced a structure for arguments that was constant regardless of the content of the argument. Figure 7 illustrates the structure of a TAS with an example similar to one he uses. He concluded that all arguments, regardless of the domain, have a structure which consists of six basic invariants: claim, data, modality, rebuttal, warrant and backing. Every argument makes an assertion based on some data. The assertion of an argument stands as the claim of the argument. Knowing the data and the claim does not necessarily convince us that the claim follows from the data. A mechanism is required to act as a justification for the claim. This justification is known as the warrant. The backing supports the warrant and in a legal argument is typically a reference to a statute or a precedent case. The rebuttal component specifies an exception or condition that obviates the claim.

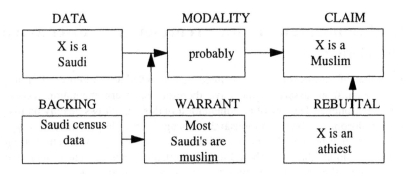

Figure 7 Toulmin argument structure

The TAS has often been adapted to structure knowledge yet most studies that apply the Toulmin structure do not use the original structure but vary one or more components. The variation we employ in WebShell draws a distinction between a generic argument and an actual argument and is described fully in [12]. The variations pertinent to the use of the argument structure in WebShell are:

- Variable-value representation for data and claim values. We adopt a variable/value representation for claim and data items in order to structure linguistic variables more tightly than suggested by Toulmin and enable the user prompts to be generated more easily.

- Inference mechanism. We replace the Toulmin warrant component with inference mechanisms and a reason for relevance. The statement "Most Saudis are Muslim" in Toulmin's famous example, is a warrant that communicates two distinct meanings. On the one hand the warrant indicates a reason for the relevance of the fact "X is a Saudi". On the hand the warrant can be interpreted as a rule which, when applied to the fact that "X is a Saudi" leads us to infer that "X is a Muslim". Clearly identifying an inference mechanism variable enables us to represent different mechanisms such as rules, inferential statistics, neural networks or other techniques.

Knowledge about an applicant's prospects for acquittal could not readily be represented by experts as a decision tree as was the case for knowledge regarding statutory guidelines. This motivated us to model the decision as a tree of Toulmin arguments. The first of these is illustrated in Figure 8. In this figure only claim variables/values and data variable/values are included. During knowledge acquisition, the expert is prompted to articulate factors (i.e data items) that may be relevant in determining a prospect for acquittal claim without any concern about how the factors may combine to actually infer a claim value. For every factor (data item) articulated, a reason for the items relevance must be able to be articulated. The next step in the knowledge acquisition exercise using the generic argument is to expand each data item. For example, the expert is asked to articulate relevant factors for determining the strength of the crown case.

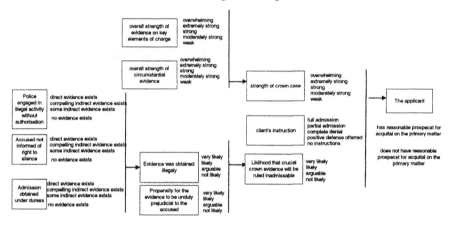

Figure 8 Argument tree for acquittal prospects

Once the tree is developed as far back as the expert regards appropriate for the task at hand, attention is then focussed on identifying one or more inference mechanisms that may be used to infer a claim value from data item values. For the ultimate argument (i.e on the extreme right of Figure 8) this proved difficult for the principal expert to articulate. She could not express her heuristic as rules because the way in which the factors combine is rarely made explicit. Her expertise was primarily a result of the experience she had gained in the domain. Although it is feasible to attempt to derive heuristics, the approach we used was to present a panel of experts with an exhaustive list of all combinations of data items as hypothetical cases and prompt the panel for a decision on acquittal prospects. Six experts and the knowledge engineer were able to record their decision in all of the exhaustive hypothetical cases (for that argument) in approximately 40 minutes. The decisions from each rater were merged to form a dataset of 600 records that were used to train neural networks.

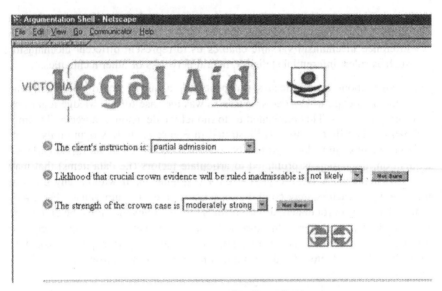

Figure 9. WebShell based on Argument tree

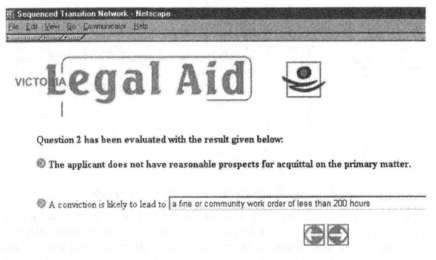

Figure 10. WebShell based on Argument tree

The inference mechanism in WebShell consists of two components; a lookup table for exceptions and a weighted sum formula. Once the user has supplied values for data items, the WebShell inference engine attempts to looks up a claim value in the lookup table of exceptions. This table stores values that are exceptions to the weighted sum formula that are detected during the evaluation phase of knowledge based system development. If no entry is found in the lookup table, the inference engine applies a weighted sum formula according to weights associated with each data item. Using a lookup table to store the mapping between data values and claim values also enables the use of inference methods other than neural networks.

Neural network inferences can be implemented by storing all possible data item inputs and corresponding claim value outputs in the lookup table. A real time, web based implementation cannot rebuild a neural network for each inference without causing consultation delays so storing all inputs/outputs as a lookup table enables fast inferences even when the source was a neural network.

A user engages with the GetAid system via the web pages that are generated from the decision tree described above. If a user follows the 'Not-Sure' link on the web page depicted, for example in Figure 6, he/she is taken to a page that presents three user prompts that derive directly from the argument depicted in Figure 8; *strength of the crown case*, *client's instruction* and *likelihood that crown evidence is ruled inadmissible*. This page is illustrated in Figure 9. Values are selected there then inferences are drawn as illustrated in Figure 10. The user is presented with a consistent user interface throughout and is generally unaware that some pages are generated from the argument tree and others from the decision tree.

The PHP program that implements the argument based inferences is somewhat more complex than the STN but it is still a small and relatively simple program that executes on the server side very quickly and is not memory intensive. The GetAid system is currently being tested by VLA experts and is being developed in conjunction with web based lodgement of applications for legal aid.

We are also using WebShell to represent legal knowledge about family law property division, computer copyright and sentencing.

4. Conclusion

It is our goal to make legal decision making accessible to a large number of people, consistent and transparent. By placing enable legal knowledge based systems on the World Wide Web, we believe we can help meet these objectives.

One obstacle to this goal is the enormous cost associated with expert system tools for web based KBS development. We present a methodology called sequenced transition networks that models knowledge as decision trees that experts can maintain themselves with little effort. The graphs are converted to database files that a simple PHP program uses to generate web pages. No rules are written and all information for user prompts and explanations are contained in the graph. Inferences and explanations are generated by set operators defined on the database.

Most real-world applications require techniques to model knowledge that cannot readily be represented as decision trees. We modelled these elements using a knowledge representation structure based on the Toulmin argument structure. The integration of the decision and argument tree models leads to a shell environment that enables web based knowledge based systems to be built easily. The inference engine is small, fast and executes easily on the server side.

References

1. Ball, W. J. 1994. Using Virgil to analyse public policy arguments: a system based on Toulmin's informal logic. *Social Science Computer Review.* Volume 12 Issue 1 pp. 26-37. Spring

2. Clark, P . 1991. *A Model of Argumentation and Its Application in a Cooperative Expert System.* PhD thesis. Turing Institute. Department of Computer Science. University of Strathclyde. Glasgow.

3. Dick, J. P. 1991. *A conceptual, case-relation representation of text for intelligent retrieval.* Ph.D Thesis. University of Toronto. 1991. Canada.

4. Dick, J. P. 1987. Conceptual retrieval and case law. *Proceedings of the First International Conference on Artificial Intelligence and Law.* Boston. May 27-29. ACM Press. p106-115.

5. Fox, J., and Parsons, S., 1998. Arguing about Beliefs and Actions. In Hunter, A., and Parsons, S., (Eds). 1998. *Applications of Uncertainty Formalisms.* Springer. Berlin. Pp 266-302.

6. Grove, R, F., and Hulse, A, C., 1999. An Internet based expert system for reptile identification. *PAJava99. Proceedings of the First International Conference on the Practical Application of Jave.* Practical Application Company Ltd. pp 165-73.

7. Huntington, D. 2000. Web-based expert system are on the way: Java bsed Web delivery. *PCAI Intelligent Solutions for Desktop Computers* vol 14, no 6. Nov-Dec, pp34-36

8. Koers, A. W., Kracht, D., Smith, M., Smits, J. M. and Weusten, M. C. M. 1989. *Knowledge Based Systems in Law.* Computer/Law Series. Kluwer. The Netherlands.

9. Krause, P., Ambler, S., Elvang-Goransson., and Fox, J., 1995. A Logic of Argumentation for Reasoning under Uncertainty. *Computational Intelligence.* Volume 11, Number 1. pp113-131

10. Marshall, C. C, 1989. Representing the structure of legal argument. *Proceedings of Second International Conference on Artificial Intelligence and Law.* ACM Press, USA. pp121-127

11. Shortliffe, E. H. 1976. *Computer based medical consultations: MYCIN.* New York: Elsevier.

12. Stranieri, A., Zeleznikow, J., Yearwood, J., 2002. Argumentation structures that integrate dialectical and monoletical reasoning. *To appear in Knowledge Engineering Review*

13. Toulmin, S. 1958. *The Uses of Argument.* Cambridge University Press. Cambridge

14. Zeleznikow, J. and Stranieri, A. 1998. Split—Up: An intelligent decision support system which provides advice upon property division following divorce. *Journal of Law and Information Technology*: 6(2): 190-213. Oxford University Press.

Logical Approach in Knowledge-Based Control*

S. Vassilyev

Institute of System Dynamics and Control Theory

of Siberian Branch of Russian Academy of Sciences (ISDCT),

Irkutsk, Russia

snv@icc.ru

Abstract

This paper presents a survey of some results which have been obtained in ISDCT in the field of development of some new methods for logical control of dynamical systems. This scientific direction originates from 60th, but some fundamental difficulties of deduction problem were a barrier to the wide development and application of automated deduction in the loop of control.

The main point of this paper is to show that automatic theorem proving technique can and should be used in intelligent control. There are two basic reasons for that. The 1st reason is that the modern intelligent control systems lack the required intelligence yet. The 2nd one is determined by the merits of new logical tools which allow to overcome the obstacles of extensive application of the 1st and higher order logics in specific classes of on-line problems like control. Such 1st order logical instrument is described and discussed here. We present the basic logical tools with some examples of application in intelligent control.

1 Introduction

The common fundamental goals of intelligent control are: to fully utilize available knowledge of a controlled object, to control in an "intelligent manner", to improve the capability of controlling the object over time through accumulation of experiential knowledge, etc. [21].

Among the tools of intelligent control which have gained rather high recognition in control community are knowledge-based systems, neural networks, and genetic algorithms. These and some other tools of artificial intelligence suitable for intelligent control were considered during last 40 years. However a fundamental problem associated with this technological development is that these intelligent control systems lack the required intelligence at present yet. Among the knowledge-based systems the following techniques are popular: rule-based reasoning, automatic theorem proving (ATP), automatic hypothesizing, analogical reasoning, object-oriented intelligent systems.

Here logical approach is very important (in ATP, especially). Automated reasoning programs with logic as the basic have been achieved dramatically

---

*The research was supported by the RFBR (grant N 0001-00922), FPS LSS (grant N 00-15-96037) and FGP "Integration" (grant N 2.1-186).

more than any program based on an approach taken by people. Of such logic-based programs, those based on what has come to be known as the clause language paradigm have recieved the most recognition [22, 23]. Resolution method [13] (along with its many refinements) is the best known and most widely used in comparison with other logic-based methods and calculi (Frege-Hilbert calculi, Gentzen natural deduction and sequent calculi, Beth-Smullyan tableau calculi, connection and connection structure calculi by Bibel-Eder, and so forth).

We consider the required intelligence organization as a hierarchical control system which couples a reflex behavior ("thoughtless" reaction), rule-driven behavior, and general reasoning. The 1st level is based on artificial neural networks with fast computations. The 2nd level realizes the "if-then" reasoning ("if-then" control synthesis). The 3rd level as the highest one has to use some powerful logics for deduction and hypothesizing (induction, abduction, etc.). All the levels process not only a priori ("theoretical") knowledge, but also experiential knowledge accumulated over time. It is purposeful to have procedures of transforming over time the higher level's knowledge into knowledge of the lower one for more efficient using.

We will consider here the using automated deduction (the 3rd level) only. The modern systems of intelligent control lack the required intelligence because they do not have the powerful 3rd level. E.g., today the most powerful tools of automated deduction are automatic theorem proving techniques in mathematical domains [22, 23], and in contrast to that, real-world problems of control have not experienced a similar success of using such well developed automatic reasoning capabilities. The existing knowledge based systems of intelligent control, especially very popular rule-based systems, are created mostly for rather restricted classes of real-world problems. The main reason is that there is some contradiction between expressiveness of traditional formal languages and decidability of deduction problem. The propositional logical language has low expressiveness, but the classical propositional theory is theoretically decidable. The 1st and higher order logics have essentially more expressive languages, but are only semi-decidable: there exists an algorithm which proves all theorems, but for any such algorithm there exist some formulas which are not theorems and cannot be recognized by the algorithm as unprovable ones (A. Church, A. Turing). Besides it is not possible to estimate uniformly by finite number of steps the length of derivation (refutation) of theorems (their negations). Moreover, even theoretically decidable fragments of theories can be practically undecidable due to complexity of computations.

That is why, it is important to provide a practical decidability [9] when we try to build a logical machine which has not to be a general problem solver (A. Newell, H. Simon), but has to have a "creative" power comparable with the power of human intelligence in special fields of activity.

There exists the opinion that with the belief in resolution in the early 1960s it was wrong not the uniform mechanism as such but the naive strategy applied to it [1]. We do not share these views, although we agree to the crucial role of such additional strategies, domain specific knowledge and heuristic guidance. Moreover, the above mentioned observation about increasing of complexity of deduction problem with the extension of language is not absolute. Recently heuristics and knowledge became fashionable, but we do believe that the efficiency of their applying can be increased and the needs of them as such can be reduced if we will replace the basic deduction mechanism (with the clause language paradigm). The clause language destroys substantially a'priori given structure of knowledge and after that the deduction is not well compatible with heuristics. We propose new logical language of positively constructed formulas and a deduction twchnique which have a lot of merits in comparison with the clause language paradigm. We describe also possibilities of pure logical control of dynamical systems (of course, with incorporated procedure of dealing with "non-logical" predicates, if it is necessary). Transition to the more expressive and powerful logical instrument allows to extend the class of solvable control problems and to improve, in particular, the performance criteria of control system. The approach we offer allows us, at least for important wide classes of tasks, to overcome the scourge of non-monotonicity and recursiveness, and at the same time to remain in some "neoclassical" framework.

Unfortunately, indisputable and undeniable comparison of our technique with the clause language paradigm (and its remarkable implementation OT-TER) is difficult to do, because our technique (and its implementation QUANT/1 [3]) has applied more to intelligent control in real-world problems yet and has shorter experience as a whole. More experimentation is required including mathematical problems for which OTTER has experienced a great success.

2 LANGUAGE AND CALCULUS OF POSITIVELY CONSTRUCTED FORMULAS (PCFs)

2.1 SYNTAX AND SEMANTICS OF PCFs

The syntax of our basic language is defined by the following way [17]. For simplicity we do not consider here functional symbols (the general case has been developed too [15]).

We use: *variables:* $x, x_1, x_2, \ldots, y, y_1, y_2, \ldots$; *predicate symbols:* $P, Q, \ldots$; *atoms:* $P(x_{i_1}, \ldots, x_{i_n}), \ldots$; the set *Con* of *conjuncts* which are finite sets of atoms or **T** (true) or **F** (false), where by definition a) **T** is the empty set of atoms, and b) any conjunct A is the subset of **F** ($A \subseteq \mathbf{F}$, i.e. **F** is infinite set of atoms).

We introduce the expressions which are said to be *positive quantifiers* and represent the particular case of type quantifiers [2]:

$$\forall X : A \stackrel{\mathrm{df}}{=} \forall X(A \to \sqcup), \quad \exists X : A \stackrel{\mathrm{df}}{=} \exists X(A \& \sqcup),$$

where $A \in Con$, and X is a set of variables (may be, empty); (it is possible that a set of variables from A and X do not intersect).

The positive quantifiers $>| : \mathbf{T}$, $>|\mathbf{F}$, $>| \in \{\forall, \exists\}$, are lumped together as *auxiliary* quantifiers.

Positively constructed formulas (PCFs) are defined as follows:

i) if $A \in Con$, X is a set of variables, then ($\forall X : A$) is $\forall$-formula, and ($\exists X : A$) is $\exists$-formula;

ii) let $B \in Con$, Y be a set of variables; if $\mathcal{F}_1, \ldots, \mathcal{F}_n$ are $\exists$-formulas, then $(\forall Y : B)\{\mathcal{F}_1, \ldots, \mathcal{F}_n\}$ is $\forall$-formula, and if $\mathcal{F}_1, \ldots, \mathcal{F}_n$ are $\forall$-formulas, then $(\exists Y : B)\{\mathcal{F}_1, \ldots, \mathcal{F}_n\}$ is $\exists$-formula;

iii) there are no other ∀- and ∃-formulas; any PCF is either ∀- or ∃-formula.

We do not call these formulas simply positive formulas since in the literature positive formulas usually mean 1st order formulas without negations and implications [12].

A *semantics* of PCF $\mathcal{F}$ is defined by a common semantics of a corresponding formula in the 1st order predicate calculus $(\mathcal{F})^*$:

1) if $A \in Con, A \notin \{\mathbf{F}, \mathbf{T}\}$, then $A^\& = \&\{\alpha : \alpha \in A\}, \mathbf{F}^\& = False, \mathbf{T}^\& = True$;

2) $(\exists X : A\ \Phi)^* = \exists x_1 \ldots \exists x_m (A^\& \& (\Phi)^*), (\forall X : A\ \Psi)^* = \forall x_1 \ldots \forall x_m (A^\& \to (\Psi)^*)$, where $\{x_1 \ldots x_m\} = X$, $(\Phi)^* = \&\{(\alpha)^* : \alpha \in \Phi\}, (\Psi)^* = \vee\{(\alpha)^* : \alpha \in \Psi\}$.

The common concepts of logical satisfiability, validity, inconsistency, equivalence, free and bound occurrences of variables and so on for PCF $\mathcal{F}$ are understood as for $(\mathcal{F})^*$.

Proposition 1 [19]. The language L of PCFs is complete w.r.t. expressibility in the 1st order predicate calculus.

Example 1. The formula $H = (\exists x\ (A^\& \& \forall y\ (B^\& \to (\exists z\ C^\& \vee \exists u\ D^\&))))$ of the 1st order language, where $A, B, C, D \in Con$, is written in L as follows $\mathcal{F} = \exists x : A\ \forall y : B\ \{\exists z : C, \exists u : D\}$ (for simplicity we write x instead of $\{x\}$, etc.). It is easy to check that $(\mathcal{F})^* = H$.

It is apparent that the negation of PCF is obtained merely by inverting all symbols ∀, ∃ only. We will use instead of proving PCF G the refuting its negation $\mathcal{F} = (\neg(G)^*)^L$, where $\neg(G)^*$ is the negation of the image $(G)^*$ of the PCF G in the predicate calculus, and $(\cdot)^L$ means a result of PCF-representation of the 1st order formula $(\cdot)$ in L.

Thus, we can consider any PCF as a tree structure (a graph), where a branching in ∀-node (∃-node) means disjunction (conjunction). Without loss of generality we will assume that

a) any PCF $\mathcal{F}$ is a finite set of trees, the roots and leaves of those are existential (positive) quantifiers,

b) in any root with empty conjunct the set of variables is nonempty.

The formulas corresponding to these trees of the $\mathcal{F}$ are called as *basic subformulas* of $\mathcal{F}$. If the set of trees for $\mathcal{F}$ is not a singleton, then image $(\mathcal{F})^*$ of $\mathcal{F}$ is the disjunction of images of formulas, corresponding those trees, otherwise the image $(\mathcal{F})^*$ is described as above in the definition of semantics. This representation will be denoted the *canonical* form. Each PCF is taken to be in that form. Instead of $\rightarrowtail X : A\ \Phi$ where $\Phi = \{\mathcal{F}_1, \ldots, \mathcal{F}_n\}$, $n \geq 0$, we write also $\rightarrowtail X : A\ \{\Phi$. In accordance to that the formula

$$\mathcal{F} = \left\{ \begin{array}{l} \exists X : A\ \{\Phi \\ \Psi, \end{array} \right. \tag{2.1}$$

where $\Psi \neq 0$ means the formula $(\exists X : A\ \Phi)^* \vee (\Psi)^*$ and the 2nd bracket in (2.1) means conjunctive branching (if the number of branches more than 1).

2.2 CALCULUS OF PCFs

The root $\exists X : A$ of any tree from the set of trees of $\mathcal{F}$ is referred to as the *base* of the tree. It includes the conjunct A which is spoken of as *data base*. Any immediate successor $\forall Y : B$ of the root is designated the *inquiry* to the data base A (or the *question* to the base $\exists X : A$). Any substitution $\Theta : Y \to X$ such that the result of simultaneous substitutions of all variables y from Y by variables $x = \Theta(y) \in X$ in any atom from B belongs to A, i.e. $B\Theta \subseteq A$, is said to be the *answer* for the question $\forall Y : B$ to the base $\exists X : A$.

If one has found some answer Θ, then in a way the data base A can be supplemented by a conjunct $C\Theta$, where C is a conjunct from an immediate $\exists$-successor $\exists Z : C$ of the question $\forall Y : B$ (see below).

In order to refute the PCF $\mathcal{F}$ it is sufficient to obtain in any of its bases the atom $\mathbf{F}$ by the above mentioned *question-answering procedure* of supplementing the data bases by new atoms. The rigorous definition of this procedure is determined by an inference rule ω defined below.

Let in (2.1) (with arbitrary subformulas Ψ, Φ) Φ includes a subformula

$$\forall Y : B \left\{ \begin{array}{l} \exists Z_1 : C_1 \{\Phi_1 \\ \ldots \\ \exists Z_k : C_k \{\Phi_k . \end{array} \right.$$

Then the result $\omega\mathcal{F}$ of application of the *inference rule* ω to the question $\forall Y : B$ with the answer $\Theta : X \to Y$ is the formula

$$\omega\mathcal{F} = \left\{ \begin{array}{l} \exists X \cup Z_1 : A \cup C_1\Theta \left\{ \begin{array}{l} \Phi \\ \Phi_1\Theta \end{array} \right. \\ \ldots \\ \exists X \cup Z_k : A \cup C_k\Theta \left\{ \begin{array}{l} \Phi \\ \Phi_k\Theta \end{array} \right. \\ \Psi. \end{array} \right.$$

Theorem 1 [19]. For any PCF $\mathcal{F} \vdash (\mathcal{F})^* \leftrightarrow (\omega\mathcal{F})^*$.

Here the symbol $\vdash$ ($\underset{J}{\vdash}$) means the deducibility in the classical predicate calculus (in J resp.). Theorem 1 means that the formulas $(\mathcal{F})^*$ and $(\omega\mathcal{F})^*$ are logically equivalent, i.e. soundness of the calculus $J = \langle \exists : \mathbf{F}, \omega \rangle$. We assume that each application of ω is completed by simplification of the result on the basis of the substitutions

$$\exists : \mathbf{F}/\exists X : A \cup \mathbf{F} \quad \Phi, \quad \Psi / \left\{ \begin{array}{l} \exists : \mathbf{F} \\ \Psi \end{array} \right. , \text{ if } \Psi \neq \emptyset.$$

Any finite sequence of PCFs $\mathcal{F}, \omega\mathcal{F}, \omega^2\mathcal{F}, \ldots, \omega^n\mathcal{F}$, where $\omega^s\mathcal{F} = \omega(\omega^{s-1}\mathcal{F})$, $\omega^1 = \omega, \omega^n\mathcal{F} = \exists : \mathbf{F}$, is called *a derivation* of $\mathcal{F}$ in J. The calculus J has one unary inference rule ω and one axiom scheme being contradiction. Accordingly to Theorem 1 the calculus J has the soundness property: if $\underset{J}{\vdash} \mathcal{F}$, then $\vdash \neg(\mathcal{F})^*$.

Example 2. Consider the 1st order formula

$$\exists x P(x) \ \& \ \forall y (P(y) \to Q(y)) \to \exists z (P(z) \& Q(z)).$$

The image of its negation in the L can have the form

$$\mathcal{F} = \exists : \mathbf{T} \quad \Phi = \exists : \mathbf{T} \left\{ \begin{array}{l} \forall : \mathbf{T} \ \exists x : P(x) \\ \forall y : P(y) \ \exists : Q(y) \\ \forall z : P(z), Q(z) \ \exists : \mathbf{F}. \end{array} \right.$$

The following sequence of PCFs is the J-derivation of $\mathcal{F}$: $\mathcal{F}$, $\exists x' : P(x')$ Φ, $\exists x' : P(x'), Q(x')$ Φ, $\exists : \mathbf{F}$.

Some examples of problems which have been complicated for many provers known in the literature, has been solved by our software program system QUANT/1 [3, 19] which implements the calculus J. Among them there is the known Shubert's steamroller problem [20]. It should be noted that in the clause language paradigm only by debelopment a many-sorted version of resolution this problem has been solved [20].

Theorem 2 [19]. The calculus J is complete, i.e. for any PCF $\mathcal{F}$ if $\vdash \neg(\mathcal{F})^*$, then $\vdash_J \mathcal{F}$.

We will assume that a basic search strategy tests the questions in consecutive order without omissions (with repeating only after the whole cycle of bypass) and does not use reapplication of ω to a question with the same Θ.

Example 3. Let us consider the problem of action planning for a mobile robot when the goal is to grab some object which is located in a certain place and after that to release it in a container. The world is changeable and accordingly to the known robot's actions is absolutely predictable. Let it be the discrete time scale with instants $t_0, t_1, \ldots$ The formula for the generating the instants has the form

$$\forall t : T(t) \; \exists t' : T(t'), N(t, t'), \tag{2.2}$$

where $T(t)$ iff "t is an instant", $N(t, t')$ iff "t' is immediate successor of t".

An initial state of our closed world is described by the formula

$$\exists : P(obj, a, t_0), P(cont, b, t_0), P(arm, c, t_0), A^-(t_0), T(t_0), \tag{2.3}$$

i.e. in the initial instant t_0 the object, the container and the "hand" of the robot are situated in the positions a, b, c respectively, and the hand is in non-working state, i.e. the robot is empty-handed ($A^-(t_0)$).

The goal of planning is given by the formula

$$\exists tx : P(obj, x, t), P(cont, x, t)),$$

and the actions are described as follows:

i) "to grab":

$$\forall xytt' : P(arm, x, t), P(obj, x, t), P(cont, y, t), A^-(t), N(t, t')$$

$$\exists : P(arm, x, t'), P(obj, x, t'), P(cont, y, t'), A^+(t'), \tag{2.4}$$

i.e. if the hand and the object are located in the same position, then the object can be grabbed ($A^+(t')$);

ii) "to move to the object":

$$\forall xyztt' : P(arm, x, t), P(obj, y, t), P(cont, z, t), A^-(t), N(t, t') \tag{2.5}$$

$$\exists : P(arm, y, t'), P(obj, y, t'), P(cont, z, t'), A^-(t');$$

iii) "to move to the container and to release the object in it":

$$\forall xytt' : P(arm, x, t), P(obj, x, t), P(cont, y, t), A^+(t), N(t, t') \tag{2.6}$$

$$\exists : P(arm, y, t'), P(obj, y, t'), P(cont, y, t'), A^-(t').$$

The whole PCF for the planning has the form

$$(2.3)\ \{(2.2), (2.4), (2.5), (2.6),\ \forall tx : P(obj, x, t), P(cont, x, t)\ \exists : \mathbf{F}\}. \qquad (2.7)$$

For brevity, the derivation which uses the basic strategy is described by Table 1. Any line of this table contains in the 1st column the indicator of question, which is used with some answer Θ, in the 2nd column – the corresponding answer Θ, and in the 3rd column – new knowledge derived and supplemented to the base of the PCF (2.7).

It is easy to check that the derivation is correct, i.e. all the substitutions from the 2nd column are answers and all the new facts from the 3rd column are derived really too. Actually this derivation is minimal (time-optimal), and the following programmed control (i.e. the sequence of robot's actions) is constructed as the result of the intelligent planning: ii), i), iii).

Table 1

2.2	t	$\to t_0$	$T(t_1), N(t_0, t_1)$
2.5	x, y, z, t, t'	$\to c, a, b, t_0, t_1$	$P(arm, a, t_1), P(obj, a, t_1),$ $P(cont, b, t_1), A^-(t_1)$
2.2	t	$\to t_1$	$T(t_2), N(t_1, t_2)$
2.4	x, y, t, t'	$\to a, b, t_1, t_2$	$P(arm, a, t_2), P(obj, a, t_2),$ $P(cont, b, t_2), A^+(t_2)$
2.2	t	$\to t_2$	$T(t_3), N(t_2, t_3)$
2.6	x, y, t, t'	$\to a, b, t_2, t_3$	$P(arm, b, t_3), P(obj, b, t_3),$ $P(cont, b, t_3), A^-(t_3)$
	t, x	$\to t_3, b$	$\mathbf{F}$

Thus, the peculiarities of this style of formalization are as follows. Each action is described by a PCF

$$\forall \overline{x} tt' : A(\overline{x}, t), N(t, t')\ \exists : A'(\overline{x}, t'),$$

where $A(\overline{x}, t)$, $A'(\overline{x}, t')$ are the complete descriptions of the world in the instant t and the immediately next instant t'. If some precondition $A(\overline{x}, t)$ is the same for some different actions (it is not the case of Example 3), then for the corresponding time interval more than one action can be planned. If the actions are inconsistent in one instant, then we need to supplement the strategy by the heuristics which forbids the derivation of more than one action for one time interval. For that it is sufficient after each single answering a question from (2.4)-(2.6) to use the next answer in turn for the question from (2.2).

The merit of this style of formalization is its pure logical modeling the time scale and dynamics of the world (see also [8]). The known system STRIPS [6] couples logic with algorithmic deletion of obsolete facts, resulting in a failure to some extent of the main goal of artificial intelligence and logic programming (to reach pure descriptive style of programming).

Yet another style of formalization which does not use the extra-variable of time and fills an intermediate place between our and STRIPS's approaches is described in [19].

Example 4. Consider the world without any reliable prediction. We model the alternative futures assuming that the future has not happened yet. We use two time scale of reasoning: real-time scale and abstract (more fast) time scale.

We model the properties of multiple futures in abstract time scale under actions of different admissible controls. This modeling allows to predict to some extent the evolving world (its reaction on the controls), and to estimate logically as well as to select logically the "best" control. In the real-time scale a fixed length of time interval of one step of the decision-making is limited by a priori time sampling in control system. In the abstract time scale the total duration of fast multi-step predicting immediate futures with selecting the most preferable one cannot exceed the length of the aforementioned decision-making interval of real-time scale and depends on throughput of computer. Instead of proving a given theorem we derive a priori unknown theorems as some immediate logical consequences of the past and present state of controlled object under alternative controls. By the initial instant of next interval of real-time scale some information on real world changes is entered into the control system by special sensors and is accounted as updated set of facts (atoms).

In the abstract time scale we are looking at the future from the imperative point of view: create a future in which the specific control is used. In the case when this specific control has been selected as the best one, the results of actual operating of control system in real world (world dynamics under selected control) is registered by the sensors; in so doing the actual state of the world reached under the control which in fact due to either model errors or uncontrolled perturbations can not be the best is used for the next step of control derivation.

This approach has been proposed in [18] and is discussed there with application to control of group of passenger elevator cabins when there are floor calls as external perturbations.

The main point of real-time application of J consists of the outstripping modeling trajectories for different admissible controls (on the time interval between two corrections of control) with eliminating nonrational (bad) trajectories. This approach means the continuous synthesis of theorems on trajectory properties in the calculus J for estimating and selecting the most preferable controls. We use only the axiom of the next instant existence (2.2) and a relevant inference strategy compatible with heuristics. We *do not prove a priori given theorem*; we *only derive consequences* of our knowledge such as trajectory properties.

The 1st part of the complete logical model of real-time system must directly describe the operating of the system and be used to construct a tree of possible variants of system's operation in global and inexact terms. Each of the variants may possibly be a solution of our problem. Simultaneously, by using a knowledge in the language L we must maximally reduce the number of acceptable variants under consideration. We can describe heuristic control principles (2nd part) intended to reduce the number of admissible variants of control generated in the 1st part. The final selection from the reduced set of solutions (i.e. irrefuted disjunctive branches of the formula describing the state of a controlled object a few cycles in advance) may be realized with the help of special logical axioms (3rd part).

The well-known call assignment method of numerical multicriteria optimization widely implemented in practice of elevators' control can be successfully replaced by our approach which is more flexible for accounting many peculiarities of specific maintenance of buildings.

3   ON CONSTRUCTIVE SEMANTICS AND HYPOTHESIZING

In many cases the classical derivation is not suitable for solving control problems. E.g., classical derivation of the formula $A \vee \neg A$, where A means "control u_0 is optimal", is trivial and gives nothing for the question on optimality of u_0; the derivation has to be constructive, when it is possible to extract from the derivation the constructive procedure of answering what is valid specifically: either A or $\neg A$?

Without description of a constructive version J_c [19] of J, we only formulate the following theorem which points a constructive part of J.

Theorem 3. The constructive task $F \Rightarrow G$, where G has the form $\forall \bar{x}(A \to \vee \{\exists \bar{y}_i : B_i, i = \overline{1,n}\})$, may be replaced by solving the classical task $\exists : \mathbf{T} \{\forall : \mathbf{T} F, \overline{G}\} \Rightarrow \exists : \mathbf{F}$ in the calculus J, i.e. by the J-refutation of the formula $\exists : \mathbf{T}\{\forall : \mathbf{T} F, \overline{G}\}$.

Example 5. Consider the simple (propositional) example of formalization of a task of structural reconfiguration of attitude control system after detecting the failure, say, of yaw angle sensor (f_3). Let the other 2 angle sensors (f_1, f_2) and 3 angle velocity sensors (g_1, g_2, g_3) are trouble free, and there are a digital P-controller (h) and on-board algorithm (H) of computing the yaw angle $\tilde{\theta}$ on the basis of 2 others and 3 angle velocities. This example presents the constructive task $F \Rightarrow G$, where $G = \forall \varphi, \psi, \theta, \varphi', \psi', \theta' \; \exists u$, and

$$F = \exists : \mathbf{T} \{\forall \tilde{\varphi}, \tilde{\psi}, \tilde{\theta} \; \exists u, \qquad (h)$$
$$\forall \varphi \; \exists \tilde{\varphi}, \; \forall \psi \; \exists \tilde{\psi}, \qquad (f_1, f_2)$$
$$\forall \varphi' \exists \tilde{\varphi}', \; \forall \psi' \exists \tilde{\psi}', \; \forall \theta' \exists \tilde{\theta}', \qquad (g_1, g_2, g_3)$$
$$\forall \tilde{\psi}, \tilde{\theta}, \tilde{\varphi}', \tilde{\psi}', \tilde{\theta}' \; \exists \tilde{\theta} \}. \qquad (H)$$

Since G belongs to the class of formulas pointed in Theorem 4, we do not need the calculus J_c : it is sufficient to derive in J the formula $\exists : \mathbf{T} \{\forall : \mathbf{T} F, \overline{G}\} \Rightarrow \exists : \mathbf{F}$. One of the possible derivation has 10 steps and is attended with the following evolution of the content of the base of PCF F: $A_0 = A_1 = \mathbf{T}, \; A_2 = \{\varphi, \psi, \theta, \varphi', \psi', \theta'\}, A_3 = A_2 \cup \{\tilde{\varphi}\}, A_4 = A_3 \cup \{\tilde{\psi}\}, A_5 = A_4 \cup \{\tilde{\varphi}'\}, A_6 = A_5 \cup \{\tilde{\psi}'\}, A_7 = A_6 \cup \{\tilde{\theta}'\}, A_8 = A_7 \cup \{\tilde{\theta}\}, A_9 = A_8 \cup \{u\}, A_{10} = \mathbf{F}$. The desirable structure extracted from the derivation has the form of the composition $h(f_1, f_2, H(f_1, f_2, g_1, g_2, g_3))$ (instead of $h(f_1, f_2, f_3)$ for the normal mode of operation) and eliminates the uncertainty of yaw angle θ.

Theorem 3 extends the known (Horn) part of 1st order logic which has the procedural semantics [11]. A 1st order example of applying the constructive part of the calculus J in on-board telescope guidance system with automated diagnostics and reconfiguration of measurement system and with sliding mode of control synthesis has been described in [16].

Since high-order logics are often only semi-decidable and moreover many applications are characterized by restricted resources of time, memory, information, etc., we have developed also a flexible combination of deduction and hypothesizing [15]. This method can supplement similar methods in mathematics, computer science and cognitive psychology such as methods of induction, generalizing, abduction, explanation of examples, knowledge discovery (R. Aubin, J. Cheng, G.I.Davydov, P.A. Flach, B. Hummel, D.B. Lenat, S. Muggleton, A. Stevens, Ch. Walther, and others), as well as method of 1st order logical equation solving (with application to automated synthesis of nontrivial theorems in system dynamics and control theory) [14]. The main idea is in alternating deduction and hypothesizing which is controlled logically by accounting for some features of either unprovability or exhaustion of resources.

This method is based on solving 1st order logical equations (LEs). A PCF is said to be *Horn PCF* if any $\forall$-node has not branching. We introduce a class of so-called *quasi-Horn equations* as incompletely given PCF

$$G = \{\exists X_i : A_i \ \Phi_i \cup \{V_i\}\}_{i=\overline{1,k}}, \tag{3.1}$$

where $k \geq 1$, Φ_i are the Horn PCFs, and V_i are some pairwise different, propositional variables as unknown subformulas, $i = \overline{1,k}$. To solve this 1st order LE means to construct some PCFs $W_1, \ldots, W_k$ completely known and such that the result of their substitutions in (3.1), i.e. $G(W_1/V_1, \ldots, W_k/V_k)$, will be a PCF derivable in the J (see [15] for details).

Thus, if during ATP some difficulties arise, then this LE approach is capable to generate some set of hypotheses, under which the original problem is solvable, and this set of hypotheses from viewpoint of some possibilities to satisfy them can be estimated, e.g., in human-machine mode.

This approach can be used in other logical systems too (e.g., in inductive programming [7]). Some analogous elements of our LE approach can be found in Prolog III like systems [4]. There is an example [19] of application of this LE approach to recognition of flying objects under incomplete information in intelligent assistant of pilot (in a fighter).

4 ADVANTAGES OF PCF-FORMALISM

Consider the peculiarities of the language L. Although the elements of PCFs belong mostly to the classical predicate calculus syntax, PCFs have as a whole rather unconventional and ingenious form.

1. Any formula of L has *large-block structure* and *positive quantifiers only*.

2. Any PCF has *simple* and *regular structure*, i.e. the formula has to some degree a predictability of the structure, determined by the order of $\exists$- and $\forall$-nodes which alternate in each branch.

3. The *negation* of PCF is obtained *merely by inverting* the symbols $\exists, \forall$ (followed by canonization).

4. The PCF-representation is *more compact* than the representation in the clause language [5] and more compact than representations in standard disjunctive or conjunctive normal forms.

5. It is not necessary to preprocess the formulas by the elimination of all existential quantifiers. Known Scolemization procedure for this elimination leads to increasing the complexity of terms [5].

6. With the L, the natural structure of the knowledge is *preserved* better. We mean here that in the original form the description of knowledge does not use "theoretical" quantifiers $\forall x$, $\exists x$, and instead of them does use the type quantifiers $\forall x(A \to \sqcup)$, $\exists x(A \& \sqcup)$ with simple and natural forms of conditions A (e.g., without symbols $\forall, \exists$ inside of A). The PCF structure most closely resembles the original structure of the knowledge if the latter is written as an expression formulated from atoms and/or their negations by positive quantifiers and logical connectives $\&, \vee$, because in this case the PCF structure can differ from the original structure merely by appending auxiliary quantifiers $>| : \mathbf{T}$ (instead of some connectives $\&, \vee$ mentioned above) and/or replacing the negations of atoms $\neg A$ by the structures $\forall : A \ \exists : \mathbf{F}$.

Let us consider the features 5, 6 in some detail. To illustrate them consider the following example.

Example 6. The formula

$$\forall x(A^\& \to (\exists y_1 \ B_1^\& \vee \ldots \vee \exists y_k \ B_k^\&)), \tag{4.1}$$

where $B_i^\& = C_1^i \& \ldots \& C_n^i$, $A^\& = A_1 \& \ldots \& A_l$, $i = \overline{1, k}$, in the PCF-representation has $l + n \cdot k$ atoms. In the clause language it will have the form

$$\&_{(i_1, \ldots, i_k) \in (\overline{1, n})^k} (\neg A_1 \vee \ldots \vee \neg A_l \vee C_{i_1}^1 \vee \ldots \vee C_{i_k}^k), \tag{4.2}$$

i.e. contains $(l + k)n^k$ atoms (n^k clauses)!

It is obvious also that not counting the auxiliary quantifiers, the number of atoms in PCF-representation is no more than in any classical disjunctive (conjunctive) normal form. Moreover, the following theorem is valid.

Theorem 4 [24]. For all $k > 0$ there exists a sequence $f_1, \ldots, f_n, \ldots$ of Boolean functions such that the complexity of PCF-representation of f_n is $k^{k^{n-1/2}}$ times less than the complexity of representation of f_n in disjunctive (conjunctive) normal form.

It is apparent that the representation (4.2) of (4.1) not only more complicated, but also destroys substantially the original structure, although in L it preserves the original structure: $\forall x : A \ \{\exists y_1 : B_1, \ldots, \exists y_k : B_k\}$.

The clause language has been used in the resolution method due to homogeneity of representation (4.2) in comparison with the formulas of the classical predicate calculus. That has allowed to J.Robinson to create on the basis of Herbrand's results [10] the most popular method of automated deduction with the single, binary inference rule (resolution rule).

7. The calculus J has only *single, unary* and *large-block inference rule* (ω), leaving no room for much redundancy in a search space. Such a rule decreases the complexity of the search space to a greater extent than the resolution rule which is also the single rule, but it is binary and small-sized. We was able also to develop the calculus with the single rule ω, but is has been done for the PCF-representation which is essentially more attractive due to the features 1-6 than the clause language.

8. The deduction (refutation) technique described has centered on application of ω to the questions only, i.e. to the successors of the PCF roots.

This is based on the features 1, 2 and allows *to focus "the attention* of the technique" on the *local* fragments of PCF without loss of completeness of the technique and avoiding stupid processing many irrelevent parts of the formula under refutation.

9. The deduction technique can be described in meaningful terms of question-answering procedure instead of technical terms of formal deducibility (i.e. in terms of logical connectives, atoms, etc.). This technique is easy to combine with procedures like solving 1st order logical equations for operating under *incomplete* information (see the section 3).

10. Owing to the features 1, 2, 6, 8-9 the deduction technique is *well compatible with heuristics* of specific applications as well as with general heuristics of control of derivation. Owing to the feature 7 the derivation process consists of *large-block steps* and is *well observable* and *controllable*. Thus, all these features allow to incorporate domain specific knowledge and heuristic guidance.

11. The deduction technique offers *natural OR-parallelism*, because the refutations of basic subformulas are performed independently of one another.

12. The derivations obtained are well *interpretable by human* through the features 9, 10. This is important in man-machine applications. Thus, conceptually, the language L and the calculus J are not only machine-oriented, but also human-oriented: to a greater or lesser degree an implementation for specific application can use these both possibilities. E.g., Example 3 illustrated the machine-oriented deduction technique.

13. Due to the peculiarities of the language L and the calculus J there is very important merit of the logic: her semantics can be modified without any changes of the axiom $\exists : \mathbf{F}$ and the inference rule ω. Such modifications are realized merely by some restrictions of applying the ω and allow us to transform the classical semantics of the calculus J in non-monotonous semantics, constructive (intuitionistic) semantics (see the section 3), etc. A theoretical basis of such modifications with applications to control of dynamical systems is given in [19].

5 CONCLUSIONS

We agree with many researchers who emphasizes the crucial role of diverse strategies, domain specific knowledge and heuristic guidance of derivations. We share also the view that the integration of numerous ideas and results available in regard to calculi and strategies is one of the major challenges in the field of automated deduction. However, we call reader's attention to the necessity of the utmost caution in selection of basic logical mechanism. Resolution is no longer the only candidate for such a mechanism.

In this paper we have considered the new logical instrument with applications in intelligent control problems. We have described the logical language and calculus which have many important merits in comparison with traditional logical basic systems for knowledge representation and processing. We have described some examples of using the language and calculus which confirm the efficiency of the presented logical means.

6 ACKNOWLEDGEMENTS

The author would like to thank his colleagues Dr. A.K. Zherlov and Dr. E.A. Cherkashin, in co-authorship with them some results used in this survey have been obtained. I greatly appreciate also referees for their comments on preliminary version of this paper.

References

[1] W. Bibel, E. Eder, Methods and Calculi for deduction, **Handbook of Logic in Artificial Intelligence and Logic Programming**, pp. 67-181, Gabbay D.M, Hogger C.J, Robinson J.A. (eds), vol. 1, Clarendon Press, Oxford, 1994.

[2] N. Bourbaki, **Set Theory**, MIR, Moscow, 1965.

[3] E.A. Cherkashin, Software System QUANT/1 for Automatic Theorem Proving. **Cand. of Sci. Thesis**, ISDCT SB RAS, Irkutsk, 1999.

[4] A. Colmerauer, An Introduction to Prolog III, **Communications of the ACM**, vol. 33(7), 1990.

[5] M. Davis, H. Putnam, A Computing Procedure for Quantification Theory, **J. ACM**, vol. 7, pp. 201-215, 1960.

[6] R.E. Fikes, N.J. Nilsson, STRIPS, a Retrospective, **Artificial Intelligence**, vol. 59(1-2), pp. 227-232, 1993.

[7] P.A. Flach, Towards the Inductive Logic Programming, **Proc. BENELEARN-91**, Depart. of Social Science Informatics, Univ. of Amsterdam, pp. 88-96, 1991.

[8] D.M. Gabbay, M. Reynolds, Towards a Computational Treatment of Time, **Handbook of Logic in Artificial Intelligence and Logic Programming**, vol. 4, Epistemic and Temporal Reasoning. Clarendon Press, Oxford, pp. 351-437, 1995.

[9] V.M. Glushkov, **Computer is Proving**, vol. 2, pp. 850-855, ZNANIE, Moscow, 1979.

[10] J. Herbrand, **Recherches sur la théorie de la demonstration**, Travaux de la Soc. des Sci. et des Lettres de Varsovie, III, vol. 33, pp. 33-160, 1930.

[11] R. Kowalski, Predicate Logic as a Programming Language, **Proc. IFIP-74**, North Holland, pp. 569-574, 1974.

[12] A.I. Mal'tsev, **Algebraic Systems**, Moscow, Nauka (Science),1970.

[13] J.A. Robinson, Machine-Oriented Logic Based on the Resolution Principle, **J.ACM**, vol. 12, pp. 23-41, 1965.

[14] S.N. Vassilyev Machine Synthesis of Mathematical Theorems, **J. of Logic Programming**, vol. 9 (2 & 3), pp. 235-266, 1990.

[15] S.N. Vassilyev, Method of Synthesis of Derivability Conditions for Horn and Some Other Formulas, **Siberian Math. Journal**, vol. 38(5), pp. 896-906, 1997.

[16] S.N. Vassilyev, E.A. Cherkashin, Intelligent Control of Telescope, **Siberian J. of Industrial Mathematics**, vol. 1 (2), pp. 81-98, 1998.

[17] S.N. Vassilyev, A.K. Zherlov, On calculus of formulas with type-quantifiers, **Dokl. Akad. Nauk**, vol. 343(5), pp. 583-585, 1995.

[18] S. Vassilyev, A. Zherlov, Logical Approach to Intelligent Control, **Proc. of CESA'98**, Vol. 2, pp. 111-116, 1998.

[19] S.N. Vassilyev, A.K. Zherlov, E.A. Fedosov, B.E. Fedunov, **Intelligent Control of Dynamical Systems**, FIZMATLIT, Moscow, 2000.

[20] C. Walther, A Mechanical Solution of Schubert's Steamroller by Many-Sorted Resolution, **Proc. of 4th National Conference on Artificial Intelligence**, pp. 330-334, 1984.

[21] D.A. White, D.A. Sofge, Editors' Preface, **Handbook of Intelligent Control. Neural, Fuzzy, and Adaptive Approaches**, pp. XVII-XVIII, Van Nostrand Reinhold, New York, 1992.

[22] L. Wos, Solving Open Questions with an Automated Theorem Proving Program, **Lecture Notes in Computer Science**, vol. 138, pp. 1-31, 1982.

[23] L. Wos, R. Veroff, Logical Basis for the Automation of Reasoning: Case Studies, **Handbook of Logic in Artificial Intelligence and Logic Programming**, pp. 1-40, Gabbay D.M., Hogger C.J., Robinson J.A. (eds), vol. 2, Clarendon Press, Oxford, 1994.

[24] A.K. Zherlov, On the Propositional pg-formulas and the Realization of Boolean functions, **Optimization, Control, Intelligence**, vol. 2, pp. 151-155, 1997.

An Advanced Stemming Algorithm for Creating Concept Signatures of Medical Terms

Thorsten Kurz[1,2] and Kilian Stoffel[1]

[1] University of Neuchâtel, IIUN
Pierre-à-Mazel 7, 2001 Neuchâtel, Switzerland

[2] University of Lausanne, HEC-INFORGE,
Dorigny, 1015 Lausanne, Switzerland

Thorsten.Kurz@unil.ch

Kilian.Stoffel@unine.ch

Abstract. We present a stemming algorithm that does not only remove the endings of words, but also separates prefixes and suffixes from the remaining stem. The output of this algorithm creates more precise concept signatures for indexing and classifying documents. The algorithm has been successfully tested with prefix and suffix lists for medical terms.

1 Introduction

Stemming is a well-known technique in information retrieval (IR) systems to reduce variant word forms to common roots in order to improve the systems ability to match query and document vocabulary. Basically, it consists in removing the plural, verb or attribute endings of words for example, the words hopeful, hopefulness, hopes, and hoping, are reduced to their stem hope.

The standard application of stemming in IR is in document retrieval, i.e. increase the recall when retrieving documents that contain the words that of a query without loosing too much precision. We apply stemming in the context of a medical code retrieval system, in which medical concepts have codes and corresponding descriptions, like for example:

A39.8X-002: Arthrite postméningococcique

The goal is to make a match between a query term and the concept descriptions and then to return the correct code for the query. Therefore we create concept signatures the from concept descriptions, i.e. the typical key words by which a concept can be recognized.

The examples we use in the article are based on the French language, but the reader will easily recognize that the underlying concept can be applied as well to medical terms in English, German, Spanish or Italian.

The rest of the paper has the following structure: In the following Section 2 we will present the problem and the motivation that is underlying to this work. In Section 3 we give an overview over conventional approaches to stemming and in Section 4 we introduce our advanced stemming algorithm. Our experiences and the evolution of this algorithm after its implementation are discussed in Section 5 and the results that we obtained with the final version of our algorithm are presented in Section 6.

2 Motivation

Medical terms differ from current language words in such as that they are often combinations of several latin or greek words. Each of these words carries meaning and contributes to the meaning of the term. An example for a complex medical term is the word:

```
acrocéphalopolysyndactylie:
ACRO-CEPHALO-POLY-SYN-DACTYLIE
```

Sometimes such word parts can also stand alone or as an attribute for another term. This way, many medical concepts can be expressed in one term or with several words. For example the following lines are synonymous:

```
A: Kératoconjonctivite
B: Kérato-conjonctivite
C: Kératite superficielle avec conjonctivite
```

If we remove stopwords like avec, conventional stemming algorithms produce the following concept signatures for these lines:

```
A: KERATOCONJONCT
B: KER CONJUNCT
C: KER SUPER CONJUNCT
```

A simple matching algorithm that calculates the quota of corresponding and total words in both signatures delivers the following results:

```
A with B: 0/3 =   0%
A with C: 0/4 =   0%
B with C: 4/5 = 80%
```

This means that only one out of three synonym pairs produces a partial match at all. However, if we would cut a medical term into its components, we would receive concept signatures like in the following:

```
A: KER CONJONCT ITE
B: KER ITE SUPER CONJONCT ITE
C: KER CONJONCT ITE
```

In this case the same matching algorithm performs considerably better:

```
A with B: 7/8 =  88%
A with C: 6/6 = 100%
B with C: 7/8 =  88%
```

For this reason we aim for a stemming algorithm that reduces a medical term into the smallest possible meaningful pieces and cuts off meaningless pieces.

3 Overview on Stemming Algorithms

Elementary methods

The simplest form of term conflation is case-folding, thus allowing case-insensitive match. Case-folding is likely to be helpful in most cases, but it is worth noting that this elementary approach can cause errors, for example when the title Major is conflated with major, or the acronym AIDS with the term aids. That is, for even the simplest stemming technique there is potential for degrading precision for some queries.

Another simple method for English words is the S stemmer [1], in which only a few common word endings are removed: ies, es, and s (with exceptions). Some practical systems use the S stemmer as, although it does not discover many conflations, it is conservative and rarely produces conflations that surprise the user.

Porter's method

One of the best-known stemmers used in experimental IR systems is the Porter stemmer [5] that removes about 60 endings in a multi-step approach, successively removing short endings without exceptions. Each step results in the removal of a ending or the transformation of the root.

Lovins's method

The Lovins stemmer [3] uses a longest match algorithm and exception list to remove over 260 different endings. It is the most aggressive of the three algorithmic approaches to stemming.

Other techniques

In addition to testing Porter and a Porter variant, Krovetz introduced a new diction-ary-moderated inflectional stemmer and a new dictionary-moderated derivational stemmer (now known as KSTEM) [2]. The latter technique stemmed by removing derivational endings, with the requirement that resultant terms must themselves be present in the dictionary. Their experiments showed that this technique, which in principle is similar to Porter with restrictions, yielded small but significant im-provements in retrieval effectiveness.

Xu and Croft introduced a novel technique that combines the use of an aggressive initial stemmer (using trigram conflation or Porter) with term co-occurence data to create corpus-specific equivalence classes; they reported similar or improved re-trieval performance compared with that when using KSTEM or Porter stemming [6].

Our Contribution

We developed a stemming algorithm for French words that works similar to the Porter algorithm [5] with the difference that its structure is more modular in order to allow easier modifications and adaptations during its evolution. Then we added a prefix and suffix recognition module to this algorithm that refined it through extensive tests with medical term lists.

4 Advanced Stem Processing

Stems, Prefixes and Suffixes

In Stemming, often the term *Suffix* is used for plural, verb and attribute endings. However especially in medical terms there are suffixes that carry some further meaning, like the suffix −ITE stands for an inflammation or the suffix −OSE stands for a degenerative process. On one hand these suffixes need to be cut off to get to the real stem, on the other hand their meaning needs to be preserved. Prefixes always carry meaning and thus have to be preserved. Examples for prefixes are INTRA-, SUB-, HEMI-, ANTI-, but also radicals like CARDIO- or GASTRO-.

Prefixes, stems and suffixes are distinguished by the following definitions (cf. Fig. 1):

- A *Prefix* appears in front of other prefixes, stems, or suffixes. A word can contain several sequential prefixes.

- A *Suffix* is at the end of the word and is followed only by a plural, verb or attribute ending. There is only one suffix in a word and this can be preceded either by a stem or by a prefix.

- A *Stem* can be preceded by prefixes or followed by suffixes and endings. The main difference between a stem and a prefix is that a stem does not appear in front of other stems, on the other hand a prefix has to appear by definition in front of different other prefixes and stems.

Prefix 1	Prefix n	Stem	Suffix	Ending

Fig. 1. Compositional Model for Medical Terms

Link-Letters

When prefixes and stems are joined together in medical terms, most times they are connected with Link Letters like -e-, -i-, -o-, -eo-, -io-, -ico-, or -ato- in between them as shown in the following example:

```
cardialgie:    CARD-i-ALGIE
cardiopathie:  CARD-io-PATHIE
cardiaque:     CARD-ia-que
```

These letters don't carry any meaning and thus can be discarded. Nevertheless it is necessary to be careful, for there are some prefixes that have these letters as ending and for which these letters are the only way to distinguish them from other prefixes, as for example HEMI- and HEMO- or ANTI- and ANTE-.

The Advanced Stemming Process

In order to identify prefixes, suffixes and link letters correctly in medical terms, we established lists for each of these groups. These lists contain the normalized form of prefixes and suffixes without their usual link letters or endings, e.g. this means:

```
leuco-     becomes  LEUC-,
cardio-    becomes  CARD-,
radiculo-  becomes  RADIC-, and
anti-      remains  ANTI-
```

Then in first step, a standard stemming algorithm removes the plural, verb or attribute endings. The next step is to use the suffix list to determine the presence of a known suffix. Since this step is done after the removing of the endings, also the endings of the members of the suffix list have to be removed. The advantage of this procedure is that there is no need to keep the noun and the attribute form like -PATHIE and -PATHIQUE, but only the reduced suffix form -PATH. In the third and last step is to separate the prefixes and link letters from the stem. Fig. 2 illustrates these three steps in the stemming process.

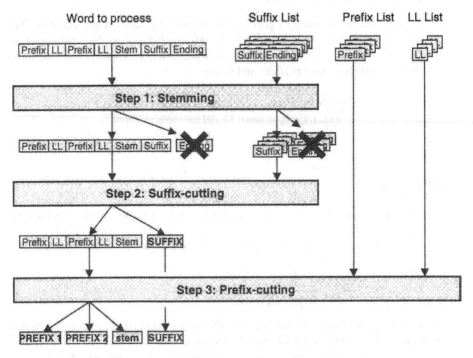

Fig. 2. The stemming process goes through three steps

5 Implementation and Observations

The algorithm has been implemented in JAVA. For the core we have developed a stemming algorithm for French words that works similar to the Porter algoritm [5] with the difference that the structure itself is more modular, so that it can be easier modified and adapted to our needs. For testing the system we used a list with more than 15,000 medical terms that we have extracted from the ICD 10 coding system [4]. The results show a good performance of our algorithm, its effectiveness in separating prefixes and suffixes depends naturally strongly on the completeness of the prefix and suffix lists. During the test phase, two important enhancements were made to the algorithm and the lists:

Rule for Short Prefixes

Short pre- and suffixes are often falsely recognized, e.g. the prefix AC- that is present in the word **ac**commodation is falsely found in the words

acalculie   leading to AC-ALCUL   instead of A-CALCUL
achlorhydrie leading to AC-HLORHYDR instead of A-CHLOR-HYDR

This error prevents either further prefixes in the term from being found or in the worst case leads to a chaotic decomposition of the remaining stem into other falsely recognized short prefixes. This problem was found to be significant for prefixes with less than 3 letters, prefixes with 3 or more letters are most times recognized correctly. To avoid this problem without ignoring prefixes with less than 3 letters completely, the following rule has been established:

A prefix with less than 3 letters is only separated from the stem, if it is followed by a known prefix with more than 3 letters.

This introduction of this rule lead to a considerable improvement of the results for short prefixes.

Prefixes in the Suffix Lists

Our algorithm works basically by trying to strip of the stem one suffix and as many prefixes as it can find in a sequence. If however a term contains a prefix, which is not in the list, the algorithm will ignore this and all the following prefixes. To compensate this limitation, we started to include into our suffix list more and more elements from the prefix list. For example ENCEPHAL is a normally a prefix, like in

encéphalomyélopathie,

but since it appears also at the position of the suffix or stem, like in the words

dys**encéphal**ie,
encéphalite.

we added it to the suffix list too. The performance of the algorithm for words which contain partially unknown prefixes, increased as expected, so we developed the general policy to transfer such elements of the prefix list that are not pure prefixes like PRE-, DIS-, or INTER- but radicals like GASTR(o)- or CEPHAL(o)- also to the suffix list.

6 Resulting Concept Signatures

With this enhanced lists and refinements our algorithm is now able to create for medical terms the kind of concept signatures that we have called for in Section 2. In the following, there is a commented list of examples. Known prefixes or suffixes that are in the lists are printed in **bold**.

The algorithm handles complex terms with several prefixes and a suffix correctly:

    agammaglobulinémie: **A-GAMMA-GLOBUL-EMIE**

The stemmer creates useful and differentiated concept signatures even in the case that a prefix is unknown, i.e. not in the prefix list:

    tympanosclérose: TYMPANO-**SCLER-OSE**
    artériolosclérose: ARTERIOLO-**SCLER-OSE**

Noun and attribute forms are conflated to the same signature:

    érythrocytes: **ERYTHR-CYT**
    érythrocytaire: **ERYTHR-CYT**

    achondroplasie: ACHONDRO-**PLAS**
    achondroplasique: ACHONDRO-**PLAS**

A difference of the functional endings leads to the corresponding differences in the concept signature:

    spondylarthrite: **SPONDYL-ARTHR-ITE**
    spondylarthrose: **SPONDYL-ARTHR-OSE**

The concept signatures reflect the fine functional and etymological differences, but create signatures that reflect also the similarity of the concepts:

    staphylococcus: **STAPHYL-COC**
    staphylocoques: **STAPHYL-COC**
    gonococcie: **GON-COC**
    pneumococcique: **PNEUM-COC**
    échinococcose: **ECHINO-COC-OSE**

7 Conclusion and Future Work

We have designed and implemented an advanced stemming algorithm and we have shown that it is able to generate more detailed concept signatures than conventional stemming algorithms. In general the results we obtained are encouraging, but one of the weak points is the need for exhaustive lists that need to be manually edited from dictionaries, and which are prone to errors. Therefore the consequent next step in our future research will be an algorithm for automatic learning or recognition of prefixes and suffixes from the statistical analysis of large quantities of clinical documents.

The work presented in this article is the basis for a system for automatic code retrieval and classification. The performance of such a system depends critically on the ability to generate precise concept signatures, and our work on advanced stemming will continually evolve together with the rest of the system.

Acknowledgements

We would like to thank J.-C. Vergriete for his advice on medical terms and his extensive work on establishing lists of medical prefixes and suffixes.

References

1. Harman, D., How effective is suffixing?, Journal of the American Society for Information Science, Volume 42, Number 1, pp 7-15, 1991.

2. Krovetz, R., Viewing morphology as an inference process, In Robert Korfhage, Edie Rasmussen and Peter Willett (editors), Proceedings of the 16th Annual International ACM-SIGIR Conference on Research and Development in Information Retrieval, pp 191-202, Pittsburg, U.S.A., 1993. ACM.

3. Lovins, J.B., Development of a stemming algorithm, Mechanical Translation and Computational Linguistics, Volume 11, Number 1-2, pp 22-31, 1968.

4. Organisation mondial de la santé, Classification statistique Internationale des maladies et des problèmes de santé connexes, Genève, 1995.

5. Porter, M., An algorithm for suffix stripping, Program, Volume 14, Number 3, pp 130-137, 1980.

6. Xu, J., and Croft, W.B., Corpus-based stemming using co-occurence of word variants, ACM Transactions on Information Systems, Volume 16, Number 1, pp 61--81, January 1998.

Developing an Information System for Framework Reuse *

Mercedes Gómez-Albarrán and Pedro A. González-Calero

Dep. Sistemas Informáticos y Programación
Universidad Complutense de Madrid, Spain
email: {albarran, pedro}@sip.ucm.es

Abstract

This paper presents the development process and the contents of an information system that assists framework users during the framework learning and understanding process. The development of the system is faced by means of a domain analysis process. The contents of the information system consist of framework domain, code and design knowledge. The paper shows the cognitive gaps that these pieces of information let framework users fill.

This information system forms a part of a more comprehensive project that tackles framework usage and understanding problems.

1   Introduction

Object-oriented frameworks are collections of interdependent classes that define extensible architectural designs for developing software applications in a specific domain. The framework-based application development follows a top-down approach in which the new software application is built by understanding, and customizing and/or extending, the extensible design provided.

A framework, like any extensible system, is sophisticated and complex. Its users do not initially know the basic usage modes (basic customisation and extension modes) neither the underlying concepts, commitments and decisions involved. The solution to this ignorance comes from complete and efficient framework documentation. Unfortunately, the vast majority of the frameworks lacks good documentation [2]. Besides, frameworks lack traceability, so that a domain entity is not modelled by one specific class but by a group of classes that collaborate.

Our work faces the problems of usage and understanding related with frameworks, and proposes an architecture for tools that help in framework reuse. Framework-based application developers need prescriptive information that guides in framework customisation and extension, along with descriptive information that helps in framework understanding. Taking into account these needs, we propose tools that consist of an information system and a Case-Based Reasoning (CBR) system.

---

*Supported by the Spanish Committee of Science & Technology (CICYT TIC98-0733)

The information system contains descriptive information. Several works in the literature focus on the development of information systems to solve the problems caused by the inefficient documentation associated to large software systems. Under the influence of these works, we propose to develop an information system where knowledge about the framework domain, code and design is represented. By means of the access mechanisms included in the information system, the user can obtain useful information about the framework:

- The code of a framework class (i.e., variables defined, methods implemented, inheritance relations among the classes, etc.) or the code of a method implemented by a framework class (i.e., the messages sent in the method code).

- The commitments that must be respected when extending a framework class (i.e., identifying the class elements that are replaceable and the conditions that the replacement should satisfy).

- The correspondences between the domain and the framework (i.e., identifying the classes that model a concrete domain entity).

The CBR system contains prescriptive information. When developing an application from a framework, the experience in solving specific framework usage problems is a valuable resort. Thus, framework usage experiences are an essential piece of information and we propose to develop a CBR system on them. We have developed:

- A mechanism to retrieve the framework usage experiences (cases) most similar to a new problem. This mechanism is made up of a sequence of query formulation and location tasks.

- An interactive mechanism that guides in the adaptation of the usage experiences when they do not exactly fit the new problem.

- A learning mechanism that lets the tool user incorporate new useful usage experiences (i.e., the experiences resulting from adaptation processes) into the case base.

Each system covers a specific type of the framework user needs. Besides, part of the information represented in the information system is used in the development of the case base and the case-based mechanisms of the CBR system. The framework domain terminology represented in the information system is used to build the case indexes and, during the case retrieval, the user queries. The restrictions included in the framework domain model help to maintain the consistency of the case base when new cases are included and to assist in the query construction process. Besides, the framework domain model, which as we will show in Section 3.1 is taxonomically organised, implicitly includes similarity knowledge among the domain terms. This similarity knowledge is used in the location step in case retrieval, when comparing descriptions built from the domain terminology (the case index and the query).

This paper focuses on the understanding problems of framework-based developers and, particularly, on the development of the information system in the tools built following our approach. Details about the construction of the CBR system (case base and case-based mechanisms) can be found in [7]. These works also describe OoFRA, a prototype tool developed following our approach in order to help in the reuse of a framework in the Graphical User Interface (GUI) domain, and exemplify the interaction with the tool.

The development of an information system raises two issues. The first one is the identification, extraction, representation and organisation of a huge amount of knowledge in a certain area. The second one is the selection of a knowledge representation technology that eases the representation and organisation of the knowledge, at the same time that it provides mechanisms to reason with the knowledge represented. The first issue is faced following the method of Domain Analysis (DA) presented in [1]. As far as the knowledge representation technology is concerned, we use one with high expressiveness and several inference and incoherence detection mechanisms: Description Logics (DLs).

This paper is organized as follows. Section 2 sketches the domain analysis process. Section 3 describes the characteristics of the knowledge representation technology used and presents the different kinds of knowledge represented. Section 4 concludes the paper and presents related and future work.

2 Domain Analysis

In the software reuse field, DA is an essential task that allows to identify, gather and represent the knowledge about the specification and implementation of potentially reusable software artefacts within a given domain.

Several methods for DA have been defined and used. In [1] some of them are briefly described and compared, and the processes common to them are gathered in a DA method. This method consists of the following steps:

- Domain characterization. This phase evaluates the suitability of the domain in terms of cost-benefit relation, limits the domain, and identifies the knowledge sources and their accessibility.

- Information collection. This step gets the information that will be later processed.

- Information analysis and classification. The identification of the relevant information within the collected one is made in this phase. Elements (entities, actions and relations) in the domain are modelled. From the descriptions of the domain elements their common characteristics are extracted, defining abstractions and organising them in a generalisation-specialisation hierarchy. Besides, a domain vocabulary is defined and the term meaning is formalised by means of the descriptions that compound the domain hierarchy obtained previously.

- Evaluation. This phase assesses the results obtained.

These high level guides can be followed in order to analyze a framework and its domain and identify and structure the information included in the information system. Next, let us show how these steps are then particularized in the development of the information system in OoFRA:

- Domain characterization. First, the domain and its limits are determined. Three different domains are studied: an abstract knowledge area which is Object-Oriented Programming (OOP); a concrete software entity, the framework; and the abstract area of the GUIs. The resulting domain is the intersection of the three mentioned and the most concrete domain (the framework considered) determines their limits.

  As far as the suitability in terms of the cost-benefit relation is concerned, it is justified by the wide use of the frameworks in order to develop applications, in general, and the wide use of frameworks for developing applications with GUI, in particular.

  The information sources considered are the own framework and its documentation, experts in the GUI domain and in the framework use, and, when possible, the own framework developers.

- Information collection. Code information can be frequently extracted from the own framework environment. Design information is provided by framework experts (and developers) and/or found disseminated in the framework documentation. Domain experts provide domain terminology.

  When available, documents generated by framework developers during the framework development process can be scanned to extract domain terminology from them. We have developed text analysis tools that make use of lexical analysis to extract terms from the files containing the documents. In the line of Information Retrieval systems, these text analysis tools use *stoplists* to remove terms with high occurrence and low significance (i.e., articles, prepositions, conjunctions) and apply stemming techniques in order to convert terms into their canonic forms.

  In order to obtain a seed domain terminology, when possible, the information collection step can also profit from the efforts of the ontological engineering community [8]. The Ontology Server (http://www-ksl-svc.stanford.edu:5915/) is a set of tools and services to support the building of ontologies shared by geographically distributed groups and manage a library of ontologies. For instance, the Device-Ontology and the Component-Assemblies-Ontology can provide domain terminology for frameworks in the manufacturing domain. Unfortunately, the maturity level of the Interface-Ontology is nowadays low, but, when completed, will be of great help due to the high number of frameworks in the GUI domain.

- Information analysis and classification. The elements of the domain that results from the intersection of the three mentioned are identified, together with the relations among them. The descriptions of elements and relations are formalized and, when convenient, taxonomically organized. The results of this step are widely described in the next section.

- Evaluation. This task is made on applying the result of the analysis in developing systems that use it. In OoFRA, the framework domain knowledge represented in the information system has been successfully used in order to build the indexes of the cases in the CBR system. It has also been used during the query formulation and location tasks that compound the case-based retrieval process. As far as the framework implementation and design knowledge is concerned, OoFRA users have intensively inspected it. A global evaluation of the effectiveness of our approach, which implicitly includes the assessment of the domain analysis results, is presented in [6].

3 Knowledge Representation

An important feature of our approach is the use of Loom, a knowledge representation system based on DL and descendant of the KL-ONE system [3]. DLs are knowledge representation formalisms that unify and give a logical basis to the well-known traditions of Frame-based systems, Semantic Networks and KL-ONE-like languages, Object-Oriented representations, Semantic data models, and Type systems.

In DL there are three types of formal objects: *concepts, relations* and *individuals. Concepts* and *relations* are descriptions with a potentially complex structure formed by composing a limited set of description-forming operators. *Individuals* are simple formal constructs intended to represent objects in the domain of interest, which may be recognized as concept instances and related to other individuals through relation instances.

DL reasoning mechanisms are based on *subsumption*, to determine whether a description –concept or relation– is more general than another, and *instance recognition*, to determine the concepts that an individual satisfies and the relations that a tuple of individuals satisfies. Subsumption supports classification, i.e., the ability of automatically classifying a new description within a (semi)lattice of previously classified descriptions; and instance recognition supports completion, i.e., the ability of drawing logical consequences of assertions about individuals, based on those descriptions they are recognized as instances of. Contradiction detection, both for descriptions and assertions about individuals, completes the basic set of reasoning mechanisms provided by DL systems.

We have chosen DLs in order to build the information system because of their richness and expressiveness. Besides, the classification and the contradiction detection mechanisms allow reduce the effort to organize the information: each new concept/relation/individual is automatically classified in the existing (semi)lattice and the restrictions that have been already defined are used to automatically detect contradictions in the new descriptions. The completion mechanism helps in the individual construction by automatically inferring values for certain relations from the restrictions that the concepts contain.

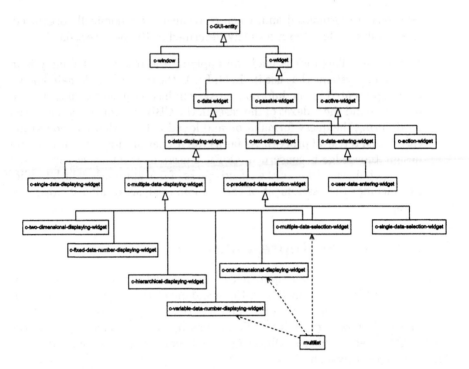

Figure 1: A partial view of the OoFRA domain taxonomy.

Next subsections sketch the different kinds of knowledge represented: (a) a formal categorisation of the framework domain (the GUI domain in the case of OoFRA) and the use of it in describing the domain terminology; (b) a structured representation of the framework code (classes and methods); and, (c) a representation of the framework design decisions and commitments.

3.1 Domain knowledge

We adopt a domain knowledge organization around two types of domain elements: entities and actions. The domain knowledge is organized in a taxonomy implemented in Loom as a network where concepts represent a conceptual model of the domain (describe categories of entities and actions) and individuals represent the domain terminology (the actual elements in the domain).

Let's first describe the knowledge represented about the GUI entities. We have initially distinguished between windows and widgets. A part of the OoFRA domain taxonomy that results from analysing the widgets is shown in Figure 1: concepts represent categories of widgets; the individual shown represents the domain entity multilist.

Two characteristics have been used to classify widgets: activity and functionality. Regarding activity, we distinguish between active and passive widgets, depending on whether the user can interact through the keyboard/mouse with the widget or not, respectively. Regarding functionality, we distinguish between action and data widgets. Action widgets produce application operations, while data widgets communicate data. Data widget functionality can be specialized in data display, data input, data edition, etc. In its turn, data display widgets can be subdivided into different categories. For instance, according to the number of data shown, data display widgets can be classified into single data display widgets or multiple data display widgets, respectively. And two characteristics can be considered for multiple data display widgets: data layout (one-dimensional, two-dimensional or hierarchical) and the number of data shown (fixed or variable).

Once these characteristics are identified, the concepts representing different categories of widgets are defined. For instance, the concept C-ONE-DIMENSIONAL-
-DISPLAYING-WIDGET (Figure 1) corresponds to the category of the widgets that display data in a one-dimensional layout. The concepts are used as vocabulary to define the actual GUI entities. Actual entities are represented by means of individuals that are instances of the concepts. For instance, a multilist, a widget that displays a variable number of data in a one-dimensional layout and lets us select multiple data, is represented by an individual that is instance of the concepts C-VARIABLE-DATA-NUMBER-DISPLAYING-WIDGET, C-
-ONE-DIMENSIONAL-DISPLAYING-WIDGET and C-MULTIPLE-DATA-SELECTION-
WIDGET (Figure 1).

Domain action definitions result from analysing the operations performed by/on the GUI entities. A domain action is defined as a generic action (i.e., update, access) plus a number of attributes –DL relations– that modify it. These attributes can be specific to a generic action or shared by different ones. Attributes common to the two sample generic actions are:

- The entity which is the object of the action. The type of the value for this attribute is C-GUI-ENTITY. The concrete value can be any individual that is an instance of any of the subconcepts of C-GUI-ENTITY.

- The entity feature affected by the action. Some possible values for this attribute are:

  - The activity setting of the GUI entity, i.e., the accessibility of the entity in a specific moment in the application running (a menu option can not be accessible in a specific moment); the ability of an entity that lets introduce data to turn into a read-only entity; etc.

  - The appearance setting of the GUI entity, i.e., the visibility of the entity in a specific moment in the application running; the size of the entity; the color of the entity; etc.

In order to obtain a complete enough representation and ease the representation task, when several generic actions are synonymous, one of them is completely described and the rest are represented as synonymous of it. Access, obtain and get are an example of synonymous generic actions.

3.2 Knowledge about Framework Implementation

Implementation knowledge consists of a structured representation of some common aspects in the OOP code, in general, and in the framework code, in particular. This representation reflects the typical OOP entities (classes, methods) and the relations that exist among them ("structural" relations –i.e., the inheritance relations and information about which classes implement the methods– and "behavior" relations –i.e., the messages sent in the code of the methods). Next we describe the structure of the code representation, identifying the kinds of entities being represented and the attributes of these entities.

Two basic kinds of entities are considered: classes and methods. The attributes of a class are the following: its superclass(es); its comment; its name; the methods implemented; and the variables defined. The attributes of a method are: its name; the class that implements it; its code and comment; and the messages sent in its code.

Each kind of entity is represented by a Loom concept and each entity attribute is represented by a Loom relation. For example, the Loom concept C-CODE-CLASS, defined as follows,

```
(defconcept c-code-class
  :is-primitive (:and c-code
                      (:all r-superclass c-code-class)
                      (:the r-comment string)
                      (:all r-implements c-code-method)
                      (:all r-defines string)))
```

represents the kind of entity "class". The concept C-CODE includes a restriction corresponding to the attribute "name", which is inherited by its specialisations (C-CODE-CLASS and C-CODE-METHOD, the second one is the concept that represents the kind of entity "method").

Once the concepts and the relations are defined, the implementation information about a specific framework code entity is represented by means of an instance of the corresponding concept. Thus, the implementation information about a specific class is represented by an instance of the concept C-CODE-CLASS, with the appropriate values for every relation. For instance, the values of the relation R-IMPLEMENTS will be instances of the concept C-CODE-METHOD; the value of the relation R-SUPERCLASS will be an instance of C-CODE-CLASS representing the superclass of the class; and the values of the relations R-COMMENT and R-DEFINES will be strings.

As it was previously indicated, the information about the code of the framework can frequently be extracted from the environment[1], as it happens in our case. From a file containing the code of a class, obtaining the information requires: first, identifying the variables defined, the methods implemented, the inheritance relations and the comment of the class, and identifying the code

---

[1] We are aware that some organizations may be reluctant to provide some parts of this information. So, the implementation information finally represented in the tool depends on the organization's policy.

and the comment of the methods; and, second, identifying the messages sent in the code of the methods. Both tasks require building parsers for specific parts of the language grammar.

The reader could argue about the necessity of creating a structured representation for the code, instead of using simple text documents containing the code. This structured representation lets us develop code browsing tools to obtain some pieces of information implicit in the code, for instance: the methods that a class inherits; the classes that implement a method; the methods in whose code a concrete message is sent; the messages sent in the code of a method; the classes where a method is redefined. In order to retrieve this information, we use the Loom query language. For instance, when retrieving the name of the classes that implement a method X, the query formulated is:

```
(retrieve ?classNamed
          (:and  (r-name ?class ?classNamed)
                 (c-code-class ?class)
                 (:for-some ?method
                   (:and (r-implements ?class ?method)
                         (r-name ?method X)))))
```

The reader could also argue about the necessity of representing the framework code information if this information is available in the own programming environment. However, representing this information is necessary in order to build self-sufficient tools for helping in framework reuse.

3.3 Knowledge about Framework Design

The third kind of knowledge represented in the information system consists of the design decisions and commitments about the framework development: aspects about the internal interface of the classes, along with the correspondences between the entities of the domain and the classes in the framework.

3.3.1 Internal Interface

Object-oriented class libraries and frameworks are extensible. Abstractly, the extensions can be made in any direction: any class can be specialized and any method can be redefined. However, in practice, certain extensions can destroy the integrity of the class library or framework.

In order to guide the reuse of the framework in such a way that its integrity is not destroyed, the user should know which framework pieces are extensible and which restrictions should satisfy the extensions. Thus, when needed, we represent some of the following pieces of information for a class:

- Its deferred methods. They do not have an effective implementation. Their implementation is a responsibility of the subclasses of the class.

- The inherited methods that are invalidated. In theory, all the methods of a class are valid for its subclasses. In practice, as a consequence of non well-conceived designs, some inherited methods have to be invalidated.

- The methods that should not be redefined by its subclasses.

Let's see how these pieces of information, together with the code information described in the previous subsection, help during framework extension. The operations available on the objects of a class (the messages that can be sent to them) is a useful information. Due to inheritance, the messages that can be sent to an instance of a class (its effective protocol) are not those ones corresponding only with (all) the methods implemented in the class. Initially, one may conjecture that the effective protocol of a class consists of those messages corresponding to the methods implemented in the class, along with those corresponding to the inherited methods. However, on the one hand, a class can inherit or implement a deferred method or can invalidate an inherited method. One way or the other, the message corresponding to this method can not be included in the effective protocol of the class because the method does not have an effective implementation. On the other hand, a class can inherit or implement a method in whose code a message M corresponding to a method without effective implementation is sent. Thus, the message M does not form a part of the effective protocol either. Ultimately, then, the effective protocol of a class consists of the messages corresponding to all the methods implemented or inherited by the class except those without an effective implementation.

In the sample framework, let's consider the classes VISUALCOMPONENT, VISUALPART and DEPENDENT-PART (VISUALCOMPONENT is the superclass of VISUALPART and VISUALPART is the superclass of DEPENDENT-PART). The internal interface of these classes includes the deferred methods, the invalidated methods, and the methods that should not be redefined by their subclasses, together with the conditions that the redefinitions of some methods should comply with. For instance, the method DISPLAYON: in the class VISUALCOMPONENT is a deferred method; the method INVALIDATE in the class VISUALCOMPONENT should not be redefined by its subclasses; and when the method MODEL: of the class DEPENDENTPART is redefined in its subclasses, the new method should include a certain fragment of code.

The previous information, along with the code information corresponding to the methods implemented by each class and the messages sent in the method code, lets the information system provide information such as the following:

- The message corresponding to the method DISPLAYON:AT:, inherited by VISUALPART from the class VISUALCOMPONENT, is not part of VISUALPART's effective protocol because VISUALPART does not implements the deferred method DISPLAYON: and the message corresponding to DISPLAYON: is sent in the DISPLAYON:AT:'s code.

- A restriction that the definition of a new class, subclass of DEPENDENT-PART, should satisfy is that the method INVALIDATE should not be redefined. The information system also informs about the code to be included in a redefinition of the method MODEL:.

Once the code and the internal interface of a class are defined, all the information about the class is gathered by an instance of the concept C-CLASS:

```
(defconcept c-class
  :is-primitive (:and (:all r-has-method c-method)
                      (:the r-has-code c-code-class)
                      (:all r-has-deferred-methods c-method)
                      (:all r-has-invalidated-methods c-method)
                      (:all r-has-shouldNotImplement c-method))
```

where:

- The values of the relation R-HAS-METHOD are instances of the concept C-METHOD gathering all the information relevant for the methods implemented in the class.

- The values of the relations R-HAS-DEFERRED-METHODS, R-HAS-INVALIDATED-METHODS and R-HAS-SHOULDNOTIMPLEMENT are the internal interface of the class. These values are the instances of the concept C-METHOD that act as values for the relation R-HAS-METHOD and, at the same time, are the methods deferred, the methods inherited that are invalidated and the methods that should not be redefined in the subclasses, respectively.

3.3.2 Correspondence between Domain Entities and Framework Classes

The most direct correspondence between a framework and its domain is that a framework class models a domain entity. However, one framework class does not model a domain entity, but several classes of the framework collaborate in order to model a domain entity. The methods that can be used to implement the actions on this entity are not implemented in one class and its superclasses. They are dispersed among the group of classes that collaborate to model the entity (and their corresponding superclasses). This situation is known as a lack of *traceability*.

We represent a collaboration among several classes by means of a *contract*, a unit of information that links the knowledge represented individually for each class in the group of classes that collaborate with the entity modelled. Each collaboration is represented by an instance of the concept C-CONTRACT:

```
(defconcept c-contract
  :is-primitive (:and (:the r-has-target c-GUI-entity)
                      (:all r-has-contract-comp c-class)))
```

The information about the correspondences between the domain entities and the framework classes represented by the contracts helps to understand and extend the design of the framework. For instance, when modelling a new domain entity, contracts let us know which are the classes that model the entity most similar to the new one, which are the most appropriate to be specialised in order to define the classes that model the new entity.

In order to find the classes that collaborate to model a domain entity, the user has to describe the entity modelled. (S)He can make direct use of the

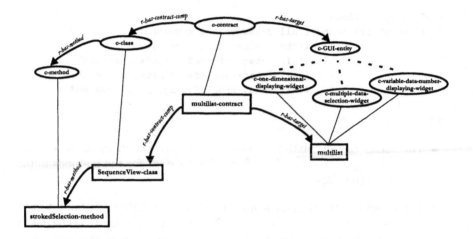

Figure 2: Organisation of the contents in the information system.

domain terminology represented. But, if the user does not find a domain term that exactly describes the domain entity (s)he is interested in, (s)he can build a description of the entity selecting one or several categories of entities (concepts) and giving value to some/all the characteristics (relations) included in the descriptions of these categories. Using this partial/complete description and the inference mechanisms of Loom, the most similar term among the ones defined can be found. This term is used to look for the best matching collaboration.

Figure 2 sketches the organisation of the contents in the information system. The contents are organised around the contracts. In the right upper corner of the figure, part of the domain concept taxonomy appears. The left upper corner of the figure shows the concepts gathering the information about classes and methods (C-CLASS and C-METHOD). In the middle appears the concept used to link domain knowledge and framework knowledge (C-CONTRACT). MULTILIST-CONTRACT, an instance of C-CONTRACT, represents the correspondence between a group of classes of the framework and the domain entity they model. The domain entity is a multilist and it is represented by an individual that is an instance of the corresponding domain concepts. The individuals representing the classes are instances of the concept C-CLASS. In the figure, only the individual representing the class SEQUENCEVIEW, one of the four classes that collaborate to model a multilist, appears. An individual that is an instance of C-METHOD gathers the information about STROKEDSELECTION, a method of the class SEQUENCEVIEW.

3.4 The Reusability of the Representation

The conceptualisation of the framework domain acts as a vocabulary that is used to describe specific elements of the GUI domain. This vocabulary can be reused when developing other information systems that, following the architecture proposed for the help tool, help in understanding other frameworks in the same domain.

The structure of the code information is the result of identifying kinds of entities usual in OOP, along with their attributes and relationships. This knowledge is useful when representing the code information in information systems developed for frameworks or class libraries.

The structure of the internal interface knowledge and the correspondence between classes and domain entities can also be reused when developing an information system in the same domain or a different domain.

4 Conclusions and Related and Future Work

The work presented in this paper tackles and helps to reduce the understanding problems that framework-based application developers should overcome in order to increase their productivity. An information system gathering framework domain, code and design knowledge assists framework users during the framework learning and understanding process. This information system forms a part of a more comprehensive project that tackles framework usage and understanding problems. The feasibility of this project has been proved developing a tool that helps in the reuse of a framework in the GUI domain.

The identification, extraction and organisation of the knowledge included in the information system are faced as a DA process. As knowledge representation technology we use Description Logics due to their high expressiveness and powerful inference and incoherence detection mechanisms.

Other works in the literature have also required a previous DA process in order to ease the (re)use of different types of software entities. The work in [10] faced the problem of classifying, locating and retrieving software components from a large collection. After analysing the collection of software components, a faceted classification scheme based on the library science was built. Since software components usually have orthogonal aspects describing their properties, they were classified according to more than one specific aspect (facet). LaSSIE [5], an information system that helps to learn, use and maintain a large and complex software system in the telephony domain, also results from analysing the telephony domain and the software system. The knowledge base of LaSSIE was built using Kandor, a knowledge representation system that, like Loom, is based on DLs. More close to our work, there are others that focus on supporting the reuse of software architectures. The KASE system [4] provides an automated support when designing software systems at the architectural level. Our knowledge base contains information about the framework; KASE's knowledge base contains information about a software architecture. The knowledge base of KASE also contains information about the domain model that can be used to interpret the design problem specifications and heuristics (customisation knowledge) describing how the architecture can be customised. The major drawback of this approach is that they identify useful classes of software systems and abstract their designs as a generic architecture. That is, this work requires an extra analysis effort in order to obtain first the software architecture. Other work closely related to KASE is the LEAP project [9]. LEAP also uses architectures as a basis to synthesising systems. Unlike KASE, LEAP does not explicitly represent the domain model for applications and the design customisation rules are acquired interactively form the end-user.

As far as the future work is concerned, we are working on the process of framework knowledge acquisition, by applying reverse-engineering and program understanding techniques that would semi-automatically identify framework relevant information and would facilitate the process of connecting domain and framework knowledge.

References

[1] G. Arango, "Domain Analysis", in *Software Reusability*, eds. W. Schäfer, R. Prieto-Díaz and M. Matsumoto, (Ellis Horwood Workshop Series, 1994).

[2] J. Bosch, P. Molin, M. Mattsson, P. Bengtsson, and M. Fayad, "Framework Problems and Experiences", in *Building Application Frameworks, Object-Oriented Foundations of Framework Design*, eds. M. Fayad, D. Schmidt and R. Johnson (John Wiley and Sons, 1999).

[3] R.J. Brachman, and J.G. Schmolze, "An overview of the KL-ONE knowledge representation system", *Cognitive Science*, 9, 2, (1985), 171-216.

[4] S. Bhansali, "Software Synthesis using Generic Architectures", *Automated Software Engineering*, 1, (1994), 239-279.

[5] P. Devanbu, B.W. Ballard, R.J. Brachman, and P.G. Selfridge, "LaSSIE: A Knowledge-Based Software Information System", in *Automating Software Design*, eds. M.R. Lowry and R.D. McCartney, (AAAI Press, 1991).

[6] M. Gómez-Albarrán, and P. González-Calero, "Applying Case-Based Reasoning to Support Dynamic Framework Documentation", *International Journal of Software Engineering and Knowledge Engineering* (in press).

[7] M. Gómez-Albarrán, P. González-Calero, B. Díaz-Agudo, and C. Fernández-Conde, "Modelling the CBR Life Cycle Using Description Logics", in *Case-Based Reasoning Research and Development*, Lecture Notes in Artificial Intelligence, vol. 1650, Procs. Int. Conf. on CBR, eds. K.-D. Althoff, R. Bergmann and L.K. Branting, (Springer Verlag, 1999).

[8] A. Gómez-Pérez, "Knowledge sharing and Reuse", in *The handbook on Applied Expert Systems*, ed. J. Liebowitz, (ED CRC Press, 1998).

[9] H. Graves, "Lockheed Environment for Automatic Programming", *Procs. Sixth Annual Knowledge-Based Software Engineering Conference*, (1991), 78-89.

[10] R. Prieto-Díaz, "Implementing Faceted Classification for Software Reuse", *Communications of the ACM*, 34, 5, (1991), 88-97.

SESSION 6 :

INTELLIGENT SYSTEMS

Let's see What Happen if we Integrate AI Planning with Workflow Management System

MD R-Moreno[1], Paul Kearney[2]

[1]Departamento de Automática. Universidad de Alcalá. (Madrid). Spain
mdolores@aut.alcala.es

[2]BTexact Technologies, Adastral Park, Martlesham Heath, Ipswich,. UK.
paul.3.kearney@bt.com

Abstract

There is a variety of applications that can benefit from the ability to find optimal or good solutions to a proposed problem automatically. The Artificial Intelligent (AI) community has been actively involved in efficient problem-solving in complex domains such as military or spacecraft problems with successful results. In this paper we describe the integration of AI planning techniques with an existing Workflow Management System. We show how these techniques can improve overall system functionality and can help to automate the definition of business processes. The work is based on a short study carried out at BT Research Laboratories as part of a larger programme that aims to provide technologies for a new generation of business support systems.

STREAM TYPE: Technical.

1. Introduction

Every organisation tries to shape its processes to optimally suit the market and offer the best service to the customer. When an organisation is analysed with the purpose of identifying possibilities for optimising its routines and procedures, three basic facets are outlined:

- A task or activity describes what should be done.
- An organisation model describes who should do something.
- An information model describes which information is needed to perform an activity.

From an historical perspective, the first issue that companies focused on was the design of organisational units. In the years to come, control logic (when should something be done) is set to play a central role in connection with optimisation of business processes.

Numerous issues need to be considered when designing business processes [6,18] and implementing them in IT systems. These include: reusability of past processes, accessibility from the different agents, consistency of usage, and selection of the right model.

In recent years, a new class of software infrastructure product to support business processes has emerged: Workflow Management Systems (WfMS) [4,17,25]. A WfMS can provide active support to a business process by controlling the routing of work around the organisation automatically. This is done based on input describing the flow, the decisions, the exceptions, the resource to be used, etc. It co-ordinates user and system participants, together with the appropriate data resources, which may be accessible directly by the system or off-line to achieve defined goals by set deadlines. The co-ordination involves passing tasks to participants' agents in correct sequence, and ensuring that all complete their tasks successfully. In case of exceptions, actions to resolve the problem can be triggered, or human operators alerted.

Prior to WfMS, many enterprises created special-purpose bespoke applications to support their processes. The advantage of WfMS-based solutions is that the workflow representation is explicit, and separated from the application code. This means that a WfMS can be customised quickly to support a new business or process, and that workflows are relatively easy to modify should a process change. Current WfMS do not address all aspects of the problem, however. Specifically, they do not deal with scheduling or resource management/allocation. Similarly, while they provide means of generating exception events when things go wrong they do not have a built-in re-planning function. They do, however provide interfaces so that application-specific modules performing these functions can be integrated.

Recently, there has been considerable interest in the application of Artificial Intelligence techniques to Workflow Management systems. The lack of maturity that the area of Workflow Management presents due to its short history can be addressed by introducing techniques from other fields. Some researchers have seen the advantages of the integration of this approach, as shown by the existence of a Technical Co-ordination Unit of the European research network on planning and scheduling, PLANET [28], on applications of planning and scheduling to workflow. This has lead to some exploratory work reflected in a roadmap and some published papers [16,21,23,26]. Although the MILOS project [7] of the Artificial Intelligence Group at the University of Kaiserslautern and the Software Process Support Group at the University of Calgary or the AI group at Edinburgh University in the TBPM project [15,31] have addressed the problem, to date very few tools have been developed using these ideas [24].

In this paper we highlight the improvements that a legacy system can gain by incorporating AI planning techniques into its day-to-day operation. We first introduce the phases that both systems have in common. After this, COSMOSS, a purpose-built legacy workflow application in use at BT is described. Then we review contingent planners, an AI technology that addresses issues found in the COSMOSS application. After this, the similarities between both workflow management and planning are presented. We conclude with an example, based on a COSMOSS scenario that illustrates how ideas from the two fields may be merged.

2. Phases

To provide a frame of reference, we identify four stages in Workflow Systems as in [26], although some authors only identify three since the Monitoring phase is included in the Enactment phase [14,30]:

- Process Modelling: is the stage where the user designs, models, optimises, simulates the organisation's processes. We include in this stage design of the process templates that can be instantiated and enacted by a workflow system.
- Process Planning: is the stage where the activities required to achieve a user goals are instantiated in a determined order, resources assigned, and preliminary scheduling performed.
- Enactment/Execution: in this stage the agents (software and humans) carry out the activities, with the workflow system co-ordinating execution .
- Monitoring: this is conducted concurrently with Enactment/Execution. The system enacting the workflow is monitored, with status information being made available to human operators. Exceptions, such as deviation from the plan, and subsidiary processes initiated to rectify problems.

In AI Planning systems the following phases can be identified:

- Domain modelling: in this phase the user introduce the knowledge to the system, that is, the operators, the initial conditions and goals. Each planner has its own syntax although lately it is been an effort to unify the syntax in a unique language: the Planning Domain Definition Language (PDDL) [22].
- Process Planning: the plan is outlined as a set of instantiated actions in a determined order. Commonly, plans do not contain information about resources, so in some problems planning and scheduling can be separated. In other cases, this idea has to be abandoned and mechanisms to treat resources through constraining equations must be integrated to solve the problem as in O-Plan [8].
- Execution: this stage is concern with the actions' execution.
- Monitoring: the results of the actions execution can differ from the actions expected results so monitoring must take place to anticipate events or re-plan if the initial plan can not be achieved.

3. A Legacy Workflow System

COSMOSS (Customer Orientated System for the Management Of Special Services) [5] provides support for progressing orders concerning provision of private lines. It was built at the beginning of 90's and it handles about a dozen main product families divided into digital and analogue categories.

The business processes start with a customer contacting a call centre to place an order. The representative in the call centre gathers information from the caller about the customer and the service required in the form of a Service Order. This is passed automatically to COSMOSS for completion where it becomes a job. The job is decomposed into activities by matching against a set of job templates. Target times are then derived for these activities based on information stored in the job and activity templates and the customer requirements. These activities, with target start and completion dates, are passed to other OSSs[1] where they are allocated and enacted. Progress is reported back to COSMOSS.

The main COSMOSS modules are:

- Order taking module.
- Product Register. This interface to the portfolio database - PDB – which holds information on 90% of BT's product range. This is also used by other systems.
- Customer and site database. This holds information on customers and their premises, and is basically specific to the COSMOSS system.
- An engineering database.
- Job Management module.

All the information that COSMOSS can handle is organised in templates. Each time new products are introduced, new templates are created. The *Process Modelling* stage corresponds to design and creation of the Job and Activity Templates. In AI Planning systems, each activity template corresponds to an operator.

A service order (with its parameters) is used to create a job, which is decomposed into activities linked by dependencies.

Activity templates may have conditions to be met for them to complete. Activities also have 'input criteria': these are similar to pre-conditions. They can be used to prune branches of the process tree that are no longer potentially relevant. When a process is initially instantiated, it generally is under-specified, including alternative branches, only, some of which will be used.

Conditional processing controls which activities actually become part of the job by prompting the users with questions that they must answer. Different answers will cause different activities to be created in the job. Sometimes the same question may be repeated in some activities; the reason to repeat the questions is to avoid redoing all the design if the user answers the question incorrectly by an oversight. However, the system allows an Automatic conditional response, that is, the system will assume that the question is correct and will jump it.

This corresponds to the *Process Planning* phase, that is, the appropriate template is identified, instantiated, and the instance is elaborated in sufficient detail to be executed. For Process Planning in the AI sense, we obtain an instantiated plan without having in mind temporal/resources constraints, just activities linked by dependencies. As we describe below, the resource assignment is done separately.

After template selection, the software constructs a schedule for a job by trying to meet either the Customer Requirement by Date (CRD) or the Target Completion Date (TCD), whichever is the later. COSMOSS uses a common algorithm – critical path analysis to apply date rules to a template to adjust the overall dates of the order and the window lengths of the activities within the template, to ensure the Job is completed by the CRD. It is worth noting that when the job is created it will be scheduled according to the content of the whole template. Once the job and the corresponding activities have being selected, they are assigned to 'owners' (or

---

[1] Operational Support Systems

rather queues) for its completion. Usually an owner is an organisational unit, but it could be a queue for another system.

At this point, the activities are assigned to agents (bearing in mind the computer programs and the human and material resources available in the system as well as the roles they can hold), and the *Execution phase* begins. During execution, completion of activities, and delays and other problems must be detected and reported; this is the *Monitoring phase*. In COSMOSS this information is sent to a human manager in the customer service centre. This manager can take the appropriate measures to rectify the situation, or at least to try to ensure that the situation does not recur: in some cases, the problem can be resolved adding some templates. In other more drastic cases, a new job template must be required (that is, a new plan).

Readers knowledgeable about AI planning will recognise many of the issues addressed here, though the terminology may be unfamiliar. The designers of COSMOSS developed an *ad hoc* and domain specific solution without knowledge of the great body of planning research that might have enabled a more elegant and manageable solution. As an example of the improvements that could have been achieved, we consider how AI planners can help to avoid the 'oversight' problems in the template answers and speed up all the design templates.

4. Contingent Planners

To automate COSMOSS job template design we need a planner that could have different outputs depending on the action that is required to complete the service.

Most classical planners use the assumption that there is no uncertainty in the world: every action has a predictable output. A contingent plan is a plan that contains actions that may or may not actually be executed, depending on the circumstances that hold at the time. A contingent planner must be able to produce plans even if the initial conditions and the outcomes of some of the actions are not known. Several contingent planners can be used to automate Activity Template selection in a Job Template: Cassandra [29] is a partial-order, contingency, domain-independent problem solver architecture based on UCPOP [13]. SGP[32] is an extension of the Planning Graph Analysis algorithm Graphplan [2] to support uncertainty in initials conditions and actions. CNLP [27] uses the basic SNLP algorithm to construct contingents plans, PLINTH [12] is a total order plan very similar to CNLP in its treatment of contingency plans. SENSp [10] like Cassandra is based on UCPOP but differs in the way it represents uncertainty. All have in common the way they represent operators, based on STRIPS representation. An operator consists of preconditions (the conditions that have to be true to apply the operator) and the post-conditions, with add-list (the new conditions after applying the operator) and delete-list (the conditions that are not any more true). These conditions are represented by a set of logical formulae, the conjunction of which is intended to describe the given state. Another type of planner that we considered was the probabilistic contingency planner exemplified by C-BURIDAN [9]. However, the fact that those planners are based on a probabilistic model make them unsuitable for use with COSMOSS.

For the purpose of this study we have used the planner Cassandra, but any of the others mentioned could be used. To construct plans in Cassandra, all the possible uncertainty outcomes of actions must be known *a priori*, that is, the planner must be able to enumerate these contingencies. Each single operator may introduce any number of sources of uncertainty with mutually exclusive outcomes. Every source of uncertainty is a decision to make. Figure 1 shows an example of a syntax operator of the Cassandra planner [29] corresponding to the example introduced in the last section.

```
Action        (InstallingL ?line)
Preconds: (:and   (required-service ?client)
                  (not-occupied    ?worker))
Effects:   (:when (:unknown  ?spare-available Yes)
                                        ;uncertain effect
                  :effect (connect   ?line))
           (:when (:unknown  ?spare-available No)
                                        ;uncertain effect
                  :effect (built     ?line))
```

Figure 1. Representing the action of installing a line

As explained in the last section, each Activity in COSMOSS may have conditions that define possible user answers. All the possible answers are known at design time. These answers will cause different Activity templates to become part of a job at execution time. This is also how Cassandra works: if a decision cannot be made in advance due to lack of information, the agent will choose which branch to follow when the information becomes available during execution of the plan.

In addition to the domain theory, one has to provide the problem description in terms of initial states and goals. Those states are represented by a logical formula that specifies a situation for which one is looking for a solution. The initial state specifies the starting situation of the posed problem. Goals are often viewed as specifications for a plan. They describe the result that successful execution of the plan should produce: what one would like to be true at the end of the solution of the problem. Figure 2 shows an example of some initial and goal conditions in Cassandra.

```
Initial:(and (required-service Mary-Thompson)
             (installed-telephone Mary-Thompson No)
             (spare-available Yes)
             (card-available No)
             (not-occupied Smith))
Goals:   (and (agree Mary-Thompson Yes)
             (installed-telephone Mary-Thompson Yes))
```

Figure 2. Initials and goals of installing a line

5. Points of Correspondence

To can understand how a contingent planner could be integrated with COSMOSS, let us introduce the following relationships: (for a high level description of merging AI planning techniques and Workflow, go to [24]).

Inputs of the planner:

- **Domain theory**: actions are represented by so-called operators. Each operator will be used to represent each Activity in COSMOSS. The pre-conditions of the operator are the pre-conditions of the Activity, and the post-conditions or effects are the expected results after completion of the Activity. If the Activity has conditions (that will be used to prompt to the user at execution time), each of the possible answers will be used to represent each source of uncertainty in the operator.
- **Problem**: in COSMOSS the problem is to determine a process that will result in a service that will satisfy the customer's requirements. These requirements will be used to specify the initial state and goals. Actually in COSMOSS, the design of the process is done manually by a user who chooses which Activity template must be part of the Job in order to complete the service.
- **Initial state**: is determined by the information in the customer order, that is, the user location, the existence of a line that can be reused, the urgency of the work, etc.
- **Goals**: The service the user requires and that is offered by COSMOSS, e.g. the on-time installation of the telephone line.

Outputs of the planner:

The planner generates a sequence of instantiated Activity Templates that will be part of the Job. As Cassandra is derived from UCPOP, it also allows actions that can be executed in parallel.

In the next section, we present a simple example that illustrates all the concepts introduced in the preceding sections.

6. A Simple Example

A customer contacts BT customer service (over the phone, in a BT shop or via the Internet). Let us say Mary Thompson contacts BT to ask for a new telephone line. At this point the business process starts (if the user agrees to the terms and conditions). The customer details are needed to see if she is an existing customer and already has a line with BT (in that case, a discount will be applied to the second line). If the customer is asking a line for the first time, a spare pair of wires must be available from the house to make a connection from the Distribution Point (DP, e.g.: telegraph pole). If no pair is available then a new cable must be built (and the customer must be notified that the delivery date will be delayed).

Afterwards, it is necessary to check that there is a spare line card available in the exchange (in that case it is reserved/allocated). If none is available installation must be arranged. Installation involves making the connection at the DP (connecting a drop wire to the pair of wires that lead back to the exchange).

Then, someone must:

- contact the customer to arrange a visit to the house to fit new NTE (network terminating equipment, that is, the box on the wall that the phone is plugged into);
- arrange for an engineer to turn up on the right day/time to test the line end to end and install the NTE;
- allocate a telephone number to the new line and configure the exchange;
- update the exchange, line plant and customer records;
- and of course, check with customer that he/she is happy with the service.

Figure 3 shows the plan that Cassandra builds for this particular example. The decision-steps in the plan and all possible outcomes of uncertainty are represented in same way that the authors of Cassandra use in [29]. This particular plan has three sources of uncertainty: the existence of a line, the existence of spare pair and the availability of a card spare. The operator/activities are underlined.

We start with an incomplete portion of the plan with two uncertain effects: the availability of the line or of the availability of the spare. If the line is not available, we arrive at another incomplete portion of the plan with two possible situations: the availability or non-availability of the spare. If the spare is not available we just need to build the cable. Once the cable has been built (in the case is needed) or checked the availability of the line or spare, the third incomplete portion of the plan depends on the card availability. If it is not available, the card must be installed. After this, the rest of the plan does not present any uncertain effect and the control follows a linear flow.

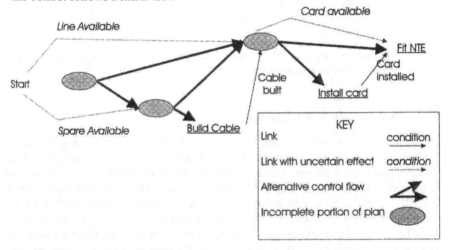

Figure 3. A partial plan showing the sources of uncertainty for providing a new line.

Each of the possible actions/operators in Cassandra will be matched to a particular Activity Template in COSMOSS. Figure 4[2] shows the Job template with its activities for the example of Figure 3. The code represents each possible situation (activity templates) and the arrows show the different paths depending on the user answers in each activity template. So LIAV01 represent the template for the AVailable LIne with two possible paths (arrows) for the two user answers: Yes or No. Each answer will add different activity templates to the job template. If the answer is Yes, the AVailable CArd template will be added or AVailable SPare template in the other case.

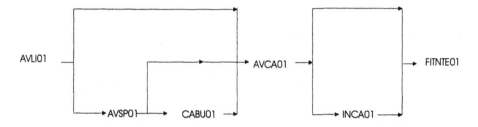

Figure 4. Partial Job Template corresponding to the partial plan of Figure 3.

If we consider the problem of Figure 2 Cassandra would generate the following plan:

```
InstallingL line501 - InstallingC card327 - FitNTE
Mary-Thompson - Test&Install line501 - AllocateNumber
line501 - UpdateL line501 - UpdateC Mary-Thompson -
CheckCustomerOrder Mary-Thompson.
```

7.   Related Work

Several research groups have integrated AI techniques with Workflow Management Systems (support the modelling and the enactment phase of the software engineering process). Some have applied planning tools in the enactment phase and very few have integrated planning techniques with BPR tools during the modelling phase.

The SWIM system [3] integrates process instantiation, task allocation, execution, monitoring and optimisation for improvement in the schedule. There is a Process Library that provides the correct process definition to the Dynamic Process Manager. New processes can also be added to this library.

The MILOS project [30] is a process modelling and enactment approach that provides project planning and management support like resource allocation and time scheduling for tasks in the project. The MILOS workflow engine allows the model and plan to be changed during project enactment and provides support for process restarts whenever necessary. The library of process models contains

---

[2] The template shown in the Figure has been created for this particular example, and does not exist as such in COSMOSS

descriptions of best practices in software development for a given company. The project manager selects processes and methods from the library creating an initial project plan. The plan is uploaded to standard project management tools as MS-Project.

The TBPM project is based on work carried out in the Enterprise project [31] and centres around an intelligent workflow engine that includes an interactive process planner. The planner uses AI techniques based on O-Plan [8] to assist in task planning, while permitting the user to participate in planning decisions. An agent-based architecture supports the execution and co-ordination of the planned process among multiple participants and distributes processes across computer networks. The user is able to plan a task by assembling fragments and then to refine it, generating a hierarchical model of the process to be performed. For more flexibility, the user is able to edit the process model before and during its enactment, in order to specialise it.

In all these systems the modelling phase is based on a process library but there is no automatic generation as we have outlined in this integration of COSMOSS and Cassandra. Each time new products/templates are created, there is no need to create a library; the planner will generate the correct model.

8.   Conclusions

We have shown the potential of applying AI planning techniques within workflow management systems. This benefit will be realised as much by introducing workflow specialists and software engineers to planning concepts and representations as by direct application of planning software.

We also want to outline the issues that AI planners can gain with this approach. Generally, to specify the domain theory, a deep understanding of the way AI planners work and its terminology is needed. However, if we use an existing system, the description language is closer to the user (at least quite familiar for the COSMOSS user). Therefore, we try here to solve the planning domain modelling task by using BPR representation models and technology. In fact, it is really a symbiosis in the sense that, once we have defined the domain using a WfMS, AI planning and scheduling technology can help in the automatic generation of process models.

In this paper we have focussed on how the contingent planner, Cassandra, can help to automate the design of appropriate templates in a legacy system used to support the business processes at BT.

9.   Future Research

Particular areas worthy of attention that can take advantage of AI techniques are: scheduling and resource allocation, monitoring [19] for (and anticipation of) deviations from plans, and re-planning in the event of such exceptions. Learning techniques [20] could also be applied, allowing e.g. optimisation of processes over time.

10. Acknowledgements

The first author wants to thanks all the Intelligent Business Systems Research Group for their help and collaboration shown during the period of time at BT Adastral Park, specially Paul O'Brien, Jamie Stark and Simon Thomson. Also to Simon Martin the comments on this paper and Nigel Irons for all the support that he has given us with COSMOSS. We also want to thank Daniel Borrajo.

References

1. Austin Tate, James Hendler, Mark Drummond. *A Review of AI Planning Techniques*. Knowledge Engineering Review Volume 1, Number 2, pages 4-17, June 1985.
2. Blum and M. Furst, *Fast Planning Through Planning Graph Analysis*. Artificial Intelligence, 90:281--300 (1997).
3. Berry P.M., Drabble B. *SWIM: An AI-based System for Workflow Enabled Reactive Control*. In the 16th IJCAI99 Workshop on Intelligent Workflow and Process Management: The New Frontier for AI in Business. Mamdouth Ibrahim, Brian Drabble and Peter Jarvis editors
4. C. Mohan. *Recent Trends in Workflow Management Products, Standards and Research*. In Proc. NATO Advanced Study Institute (ASI) on Workflow Management Systems and Interoperability, Istanbul, August 1997, Springer Verlag, 1998. http://www.almaden.ibm.com/cs/exotica/exotica_papers.html
5. Chandler J. *Management of special services: designing for a changing world*. BT Technological Journal, Vol 15, No 1, January 1997.
6. Davenport, T. and Short, J. *The New Industrial Engineering: Information Technology and Business Process Redesign*. Sloan Management Review, pp 11-27. 1990.
7. Dellen, B. Maurer, F. and Pews, G. *Knowledge Based Techniques to Increase the Flexibility of Workflow Management*. Data and Knowledge Engineering, North-Holland. 1997. http://wwwagr.informatik.uni-kl.de/~comokit
8. Drabble, B., Tate A. *The use of optimistic and pessimistic resource profiles to inform search in an activity based planner*. In Proceedings of 2nd Int. Conf. AI Planning Systems, 1994.
9. Drapper D., Hanks S., & Weld D. *A probabilistic model of action for least-commitment planning with information gathering*. In Proceedings of the Tenth Conference on Uncertainty in Artificial Intelligence, pp 178-186 Seattle, WA, Morgan Kaufmann.
10. Etzioni O., Hanks S., Weld D., Draper D., Lesh N. and Williamson M. *An approach to planning with incomplete information*. In Proc 3rd International Conference on Knowledge Representation and Reasoning, pp 115-125. Boston, MA. Morgan Kaufmann.
11. Fikes R. E, Nilsson N. J. *STRIPS: a new approach to the application of theorem proving to problem solving* . In Artificial Intelligence, 2:189-208.
12. Goldman R.P. and Boddy M.S. *Conditional Linear Planning*. In Proc. 2nd International Conference AI Planning Systems, pp 80-85. Chicago, IL. AAAI Press.

13. J.S.Penberthy and D. Weld. UCPOP: *A sound, complete, partial order planner for ADL*. In Proc. 3rd Int. Conf. On Principles of Knowledge Representation and Reasoning, pages 103-114, Oct 1992.

14. Jarvis P, Stader J, Macintosh A, Moore J, & Chung P. *A Framework for Equipping Workflow Systems with Knowledge about Organisational Structure and Authority* .In Proceedings of the Workshop on Systems Modeling for Business Process Improvement (SMBPI-99), University of Ulster, County Antrim, Northern Ireland, UK, pp 205 - 219.

15. Jarvis P. et al. *What right do you have to do that?*. In ICEIS – 1st International Conference on Enterprise Information Systems. Portugal,1999. http://www.aiai.ed.ac.uk/project/tbpm/

16. Karen L. Myers and Pauline M. Berry. *At the Boundary of Workflow and AI*. In AAAI-99 Workshop on agent-Based Systems in The Business Context. Brian Drabble and Peter Jarvis Cochairs.

17. Leymann. F., and Roller. D. *Business Process Management with FlowMark*. Proceedings of IEEE Compcon, March 1994.

18. M.Hammer and J. Champy. *Reengineering the Corporation*. Harper Business Press, New York, 1993.

19. Manuela Veloso, M. E. Pollack, and M. T. Cox. *Rationale-based monitoring for planning in dynamic environments*. In Proceedings of the Fourth International Conference on AI Planning Systems, 1998.

20. Manuela Veloso. *Learning by Analogical Reasoning in General problem solving*. PhD thesis, Carnegie Mellon University, Pittsburgh, PA, 1992.

21. Markus Hannebaeur. *From formal Workflow models to Intelligent Agents*. In AAAI-99 Workshop on agent-Based Systems in The Business Context. Brian Drabble and Peter Jarvis Cochairs.

22. McDermott, D.*PDDL the planning domain definition language*. Technical report, Yale University 1998. http://www.cs.yale.edu/users/mcdermott.html.

23. MD R-Moreno, P. Kearney and D. Meziat *A case study: using Workflow and AI planners*. Proc. of the 19th Workshop of the UK Planning & Scheduling Special Interest Group. PLANSIG2000. The open University, UK

24. MD R-Moreno, D. Borrajo, D. Meziat. *Process modelling and AI planning techniques: A new approach*. 2nd International Workshop on Information Integration and Web-based Applications & Services. IIWAS2000. Yogyakarta.

25. Medina-Mora, R. Winograd, T. and Flores P. *Action Workflow as the Enterprise Integration Technology*. Bulletin of the Technical Committee on Data Engineering, 6(2), 1993. IEEE Computer Society.

26. Paul Kearney and Daniel Borrajo. *An {R\&D} Agenda for AI Planning applied to Workflow. Management* Proceedings of the eBusiness and eWork Conference 2000.

27. Peot M.A and Smith D.E. *Conditional Nonlinear Planning*. In Proc. 1st International Conference AI Planning Systems, pp189-197. College Park, Maryland. Morgan Kaufmann.

28. PLANET: European Network of Excellence in AI Planning. http://planet.dfki.de/

29. Pryor L, Collins G. *Planning for Contingencies: A Decision-based Approach*. Journal of Artificial Intelligence Research 4 (1996) 287-339.

30. Sigrid Goldmann, Jürgen Munich, Harald Holz. *Distributed process planning support with MILOS*. To appear in Int. Journal of Software Engineering and Knowledge Engineering, October 2000.

31. Stader J. *Results of the Enterprise Project*. Proc. 16th Int. Conference of the British Computer Society Specialist Group on Expert Systems. Cambridge, UK, 1996.

32. Weld D., Anderson C, Smith D.E. Extending *Graphplan to Handle Uncertainty and Sensing Actions* . AAAI98. 1998.

A Non-binary Constraint Satisfaction Solver: The One-Face Hyperpolyhedron Heuristic.

Miguel A. Salido, Adriana Giret, Federico Barber

Dpto. Sistemas Informáticos y Computación
Universidad Politécnica de Valencia, Camino de Vera s/n 46071
Valencia, Spain
{msalido,agiret,fbarber}@dsic.upv.es

Abstract. Constraint satisfaction is gaining a great deal of attention because many combinatorial problems especially in areas of Artificial Intelligence can be expressed in a natural way as a Constraint Satisfaction Problem (CSP). It is well known that a non-binary CSP can be transformed into an equivalent binary CSP using some of the actual techniques. However, when the CSP is not discrete or the number of constraints is high relative to the number of variables, these techniques become impractical. In this paper, we propose an heuristic called "*One-face Hyperpolyhedron Heuristic*" as an incremental and non-binary CSP solver. This non-binary CSP solver does not increase its temporal complexity with the variable domain size. It carries out the search through a hyperpolyhedron that maintains those solutions that satisfy all metric non-binary temporal constraints. Thus, we can manage more complex and expressive problems with high number of constraints and very large domains.

1 Introduction

Nowadays, many researches are working on non-binary constraints, mainly influenced by the growing number of real-life applications. Modelling a problem with non-binary constraints has several advantages. It facilitates the expression of the problem, enables more powerful constraint propagation as more global information is available, etc. Problems of these kind can either be solved directly by means of non-binary CSPs by a search method or transformed into a binary one [7] and then solved by using binary CSP techniques. However, this transformation may not be practical in problems with some particular properties [1][3], for example when the number of constraints is high relative to the number of variables, when the constraints are not tight or when the CSP is non-discrete [2].

In this paper, we propose an algorithm called "*One-face Hyperpolyhedron Heuristic* " (OFHH) that manages non-binary CSPs with very large domains, and many variables. OFHH maintains only one vertex in each hyperpolyhedron face. Thus the temporal cost of the hyperpolyhedron algorithm is reduced to $O(n)$, while the complete hyperpolyhedron maintains 2^{n-1} vertices in each face.

This proposal overcomes some of the weaknesses of other techniques. Moreover, we can manage temporal constraints that can be inserted incrementally into the problem without needing to solve the whole problem again.

We extend the framework of simple temporal problems studied originally by Dechter, Meiri and Pearl [4] to consider non-binary temporal constraints of the form:

$$\sum_{i=1}^{n} p_i x_i \leq b$$

(1)

where x_i are variables ranging over continuous intervals $x_i \in [l_i, u_i]$, b is a real constant, and $n \geq 1$. This represents a wide class of temporal constraints that can be used to model a great variety of problems.

The consistency of these problem types may be solved by means of techniques based on constraint satisfaction problems (CSPs) and techniques based on closure processes. These two techniques have a similar graphic representation, (a directed graph), but they have different goals.

- CSP has been widely studied in the Artificial Intelligence community for many years. It has been recognised that CSPs have practical significance because many problems arising in scheduling, in operational research and other real problems, can be represented as CSPs. The main goal of a CSP is to find one or several solutions in a previously consistent system.

- We can also solve these problems by means of the closure processes. The main aim of closure techniques is to guarantee the consistency of the existing constraints, which may be included and/or excluded by means of a dynamic behaviour. There exist several levels of consistence depending on the solution exigency, from the lowest levels (path consistency [6]) to the most demanding ones (global consistency [5]).

Both techniques may have a common graphic representation by means of a temporal constraint network, where nodes represent temporal points and arcs represent binary temporal constraints between two temporal points. Arc and node consistency work well for pruning the domains in networks of this kind. However, they do not work well if the problem contains primitive constraints that involve more than two variables (non-binary) since such primitive constraints are ignored when performing consistency checks.

2 Specification of the One-face Hyperpolyhedron Heuristic

Briefly, a constraint satisfaction problem (CSP) consists of:
- a set of *variables* $X = \{x_1, ..., x_n\}$;
- each variable $x_i \in X$ has got a finite set D_i of possible values (its *domain*);
- and a finite collection of *constraints* $C = \{c_1, ..., c_p\}$ restricting the values that the variables can simultaneously take.

A solution to a CSP is an assignment of a value from its domain to every variable, in such a way that every constraint is satisfied.
The objective may be:
- get only one solution, with no preference as to which one;
- get all solutions;
- get an optimal, or a good solution by means of an objective function defined in terms of some variables.

In this paper we assume a non-binary temporal CSP where *variables* x_i are time points which are bounded in continuous domains (for example: $x_i \in [l_i, u_i]$) and a collection of non-binary temporal *constraints* of the form (1). Time is considered dense. Thus, a finite interval (i.e. [10, 20]) can be viewed as an infinite temporal interval due to the fine granularity with which time is considered.
This assumption represents a great variety of real problems.

The specification of the *One-face Hyperpolyhedron Heuristic* (OFHH) is presented in (Fig.1). Initially, OFHH has a static behaviour such a classic CSP solver. The hyperpolyhedron vertices are created by means of the Cartesian product of the variable domains ($D_1 \times D_2 \times \cdots \times D_n$) (step 1) This Cartesian product is carried out only among several variables in order to guarantee that each hyperpolyhedron face contains only n vertices.
For each constraint, OFHH carries out the consistency check (step 2). If the constraint is not consistent, OFHH returns *not consistent problem*; else, OFHH determines if the constraint is not redundant, updating the hyperpolyhedron (step 3).
We must take into account that the heuristic might fail due to the hyperpolyhedron does not maintain all the vertices of the hyperpolyhedron.
Finally, OFHH can obtain some important results such as:
- the problem consistency;
- one or many problem solutions;
- the new variable domains;
- the vertex of the hyperpolyhedron that minimises or maximises some objective function.

Furthermore, when OFHH finishes its static behaviour (classic CSP solver), new constraints can be incrementally inserted into the problem, and OFHH studies the consistency check such as an incremental CSP solver.

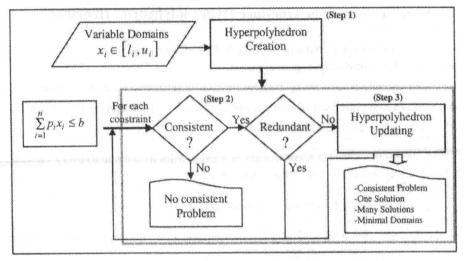

Fig. 1. General Scheme of the One-face Hyperpolyhedron Heuristic.

2.1 The Hyperpolyhedron Search Algorithm

The main goal of the OFHH is to solve a problem as an incremental and non-binary CSP solver. The OFHH is defined in Fig. 4. We include three procedures:

- *Hyperpolyhedron_creation (Dimension, Domain))* (Fig. 2) is a module that generates the hyperpolyhedron vertices by means of the Cartesian product of the variable domains obtaining some of the hyperpolyhedron vertices. *domain[0][j]* represents the lower bound of the variable *j* and *domain[1][j]* represents the upper bound of the variable *j*.

```
Hyperpolyhedron_creation (Dimension=DIM, Domain)
{
For i=0 to 2*DIM-1 do:        // for each face do
        {
        Make(NewVertex);  // New empty vertex is generated
        If i< DIM then
        div ← DIM * i;                // Formula to distribute the vertices
        div ← (DIM*(-DIM +1+ i))-1;  // Formula to distribute the vertices
        For j=DIM-1+(i*DIM) to j=(i*DIM) do:  // Assign the values
                {
                NewVertex[j] ← domain[div % 2][j −i * DIM] ;
                div = div/2;
                }
        }
Return ListV ;   // the module returns a list with 2*DIM vertices.
}
```

Fig. 2. Hyperpolyhedron_creation.

- *Satisfy(C_i, v_i)* is a module that determines if the vertex v_i satisfies the constraint C_i. Thus, this function only returns true if the result is $\leq b$ when the variables ($x_1, x_2, \cdots, x_n$) are fixed to values ($v_1, v_2, \cdots, v_n$).

- *Hyperpolyhedron_updating* ($\bar{v}, L_{yes}, L_{no}$) (Fig. 3) is a module that updates the hyperpolyhedron eliminating all inconsistent vertices (L_{no} are the vertices that do not satisfy the constraint) and that includes the new vertices generated by the intersection between arcs that contain a consistent extreme (vertex) and the other $\bar{v}$.

Hyperpolyhedron_updating ($\bar{v}$, L_{yes}, L_{no})

{

For each arc $\bar{a} = (\bar{v}, v)$ do:

        OFHH obtains the straight line $\bar{l}$ that unites both $\bar{v}$ and v points.

        OFHH intersects $\bar{l}$ with the hyperpolyhedron obtaining the new point $\bar{\bar{v}}$

        $L_{yes} \leftarrow L_{yes} \cup \bar{\bar{v}}$

return L_{yes} ;

}

Fig. 3. Hyperpolyhedron_updating.

Hyperpolyhedron Algorithm (Constraints, Dimension, Domain)

{

Step 1 *ListV* $\leftarrow$ *Hyperpolyhedron_creation (Dimension, Domain)*;

$L_{yes} \leftarrow \phi$; $L_{no} \leftarrow \phi$;

Step 2..For each $C_i \in$ *Constraints do:*

  {

  $\forall v_i \in ListV$ do:

      {

      If *Satisfy(C_i, v_i)* $\leftarrow$ true then:

           $L_{yes} \leftarrow L_{yes} \cup \{v_i\}$; // C_i *is consistent with the system*

      else $L_{no} \leftarrow L_{no} \cup \{v_i\}$;

      }

  If $L_{yes} = \phi \Rightarrow STOP$;   // C_i *is not consistent with the system*

  If $L_{no} = \phi \Rightarrow$ " C_i *is consistent and redundant* ";

    else

Step 3 $\forall \bar{v} \in L_{no}$ *Update_hyperpolyhedron* ($\bar{v}$, L_{yes}, L_{no})

  }

return output; // OFHH returns the consistency check, and some extreme solutions

}

Fig. 4. One-face Hyperpolyhedron Heuristic.

Example

Let's see an example in $\Re^3$ in which we can observe the evolution of the OFHH.

Let x_1, x_2, x_3 be three variables ranged in the domains $x_i \in [0,1]$. The complete hyperpolyhedron generated by HSA [8] is shown in Fig 5a. However OFHH only chose one vertex in each hyperpolyhedron face that has not been chosen in other adjacent face previously (see Fig 5b).

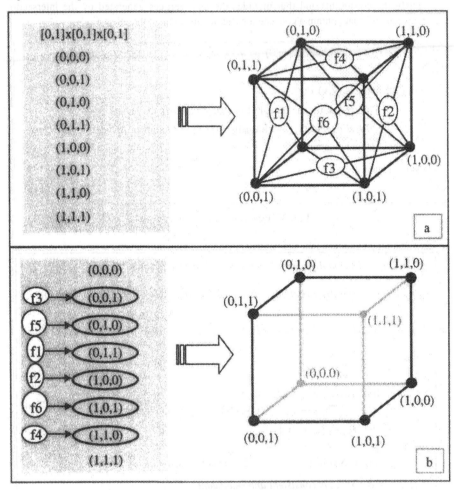

Fig.5. Hyperpolyhedron generated by HSA and OFHH.

2.2 Graphical Interface

OHFF allows the user to introduce the needed parameters to execute random or manually problems. In Fig. 6 the graphical interface is presented. In the upper part of the screen it is showed the parameters that the user must configure: number of variables, number of constraints, domain length, number of desired solution if the problem is consistent, and finally number of problem if the user wants to generate several random problems. Then, when the parameters are fixed, the user pushes the button 'OFHH' and the number of selected problems are randomly generated and solved by OFHH.

If the user wants to generate manually a problem, selects the radio button 'Generate a problem' with the parameters selected and new screens appear to introduce the variable domains and the constraints selected in the corresponding parameters.

In the lower window the generated and solved problems are showed. This screen shows the selected parameters, the random or manually generated variable domains and the constraints. Also, this screen displays some information about the execution, showing a partial solution and the CPU time for checking each constraint. Finally this screen displays the consistency problem and the total CPU time. If the problem is consistent the desired solutions are showed.

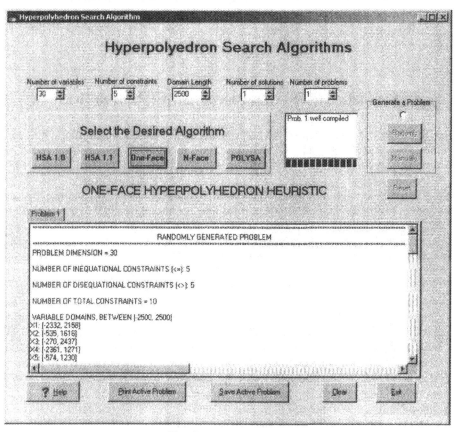

Fig. 6. Graphical Interface.

3 Analysis of the One-Face Hyperpolyhedron Heuristic

The OFHH spatial cost is determined by the number of vertices generated. Initially, the OFHH generates $2n$ vertices, where n is the number of problem variables. For each constraint (step 2), OFHH might generate n new vertices and eliminate only one. Thus, the number of hyperpolyhedron vertices is $2n+c(n-1)$ where c is the number of constraints. Therefore, the spatial cost is $O(n)$. However the spatial cost would increase to $O(2^n)$ if the algorithm generate all the hyperpolyhedron vertices HSA [8], and it would be impractical in problems with many variables.

The temporal cost is divided in three steps: initialisation, consistency check and actualisation. The initialisation cost (step 1) is $O(n)$ because the algorithm only generates $2n$ vertices. For each constraint (step 2), the consistency check cost depends linearly on the number of hyperpolyhedron vertices, but not on the variable domains, so the temporal cost is $O(n)$. Finally, the actualisation cost (step 3) depends on the number of variables $O(n)$. Thus, the temporal cost is: $O(n) + c * (O(n) + O(n)) \Rightarrow O(n)$.

4 Evaluation of the One-Face Hyperpolyhedron Heuristic

In this section, we compare the performance of Forward-checking (FC), Real Full Look-ahead (RFLA)[1] and OFHH. In order to evaluate this performance, the computer used for the tests was a PC with 68 Mb. of memory and Windows NT operating system.

The problems were randomly generated by modifying the parameters $<v,c,d>$, where v was the number of variables, c the number of constraints, and d the length of the variable domains. Thus, we generated three type of problems, fixing two parameters and varying the other parameter. We tested 100 problems for each value of the variable parameter, and we present the mean CPU time for these problems.

Following, three sets of graphics are shown (Fig. 7, Fig. 8, Fig. 9). Each set summarises the algorithm behaviour in three graphics. The left upper one shows the temporal cost of the solved problems. The right upper one shows the number of unsolved problems. Finally the lower graphic shows the mean time behaviour. This last graphic contains a horizontal asymptote in time=100 because we assigned a 100-second run time and aborted, those problems whose run time exceeded 100 seconds. Also the problems that did not obtain the expected solution were assigned a 100-second run time in order to penalise its wrong behaviour.

In Fig.7 the number of constraints and domain length were fixed $<v,2,2500>$, and the number of variables was increased from 10 to 26.

---

[1] Forward-checking and Real Full Look-ahead were obtained from CON'FLEX, that is a C++ solver that can handle constraint problems with interval variables.
It can be found in: http://www-bia.inra.fr/T/conflex/Logiciels/adressesConflex.html.

The mean CPU time in FC and RFLA increased exponentially with the number of variables. OFHH did not increase its temporal complexity due to its linear cost.

The number of unsolved problems fluctuated in FC and OFHH. RFLA increased linearly with the number of variables. However OFHH decreased the number of unsolved problems when the number of variables increased.

Finally the lower graphic shows a global view of the behaviour of the algorithms. When the unsolved problems were fixed to time=100, and the others maintained their real time cost, we could observe that FC was worse than RFLA. However, as the number of variables increased, OFHH had a better behaviour.

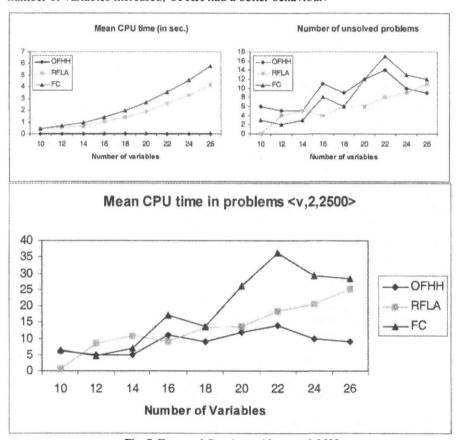

Fig. 7. Temporal Cost in problems <v,2,2500>.

In Fig.8 the random domains and the number of variable were fixed <30,c,2500>, and the number of random constraints ranged from 1 to 5.

It can be observed that both FC and RFLA increased exponentially their mean CPU time with the number of constraints while OFHH practically did not increase its temporal cost.

The number of unsolved problems also increased exponentially in FC and RFLA. OFHH increased linearly with the number of constraints, because when the number of constraints increased, also increased the probability that not selected vertices (by OFHH) could be the only solutions.

The main graphic shows that FC and RFLA had similar performance. OFHH maintained its linear behaviours.

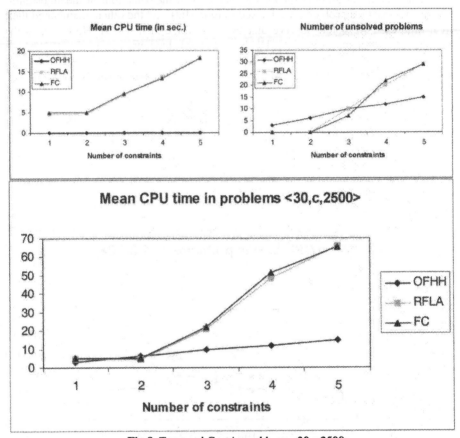

Fig.8. Temporal Cost in problems <30,c,2500>.

In Fig.9 the number of variables and the number of random constraints were fixed <5,7,d>, and the domain length were increased from 20 to 20000.

It can be observed that FC, RFLA and OFHH maintained a constant performance when the domain length enlarged. This is because the test problems only varied in domain length. So, when a solution was found in the first domain length (500) then this solution was found also in greater domains at equal time.

The number of unsolved problems fluctuated in FC and OFHH. However OFHH did not increased with the domain length. While RFLA and FC increased exponentially with the number of variables.

Finally, the main graphic summarises the performance of the algorithms. It can be observed that OFHH had a uniform behaviour.

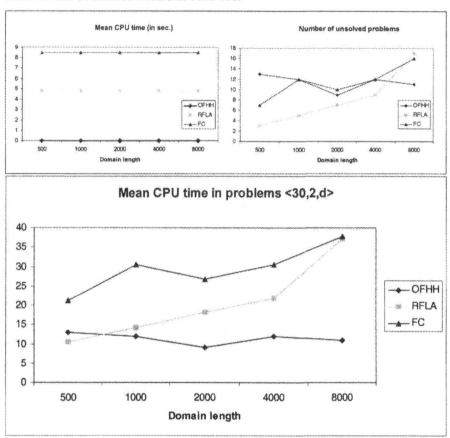

Fig. 9. Temporal Cost in problems <30,2,d>.

5 Conclusion and Future Works

In this paper, we have proposed an algorithm called OFHH as an incremental and non-binary TCSP solver. This proposal carries out the consistency study through a hyperpolyhedron that maintains in its vertices, those values that satisfy all metric temporal constraints. Thus, solutions to CSP are all vertices and all convex combination between any two vertices: (x_i and $x_j \Rightarrow \alpha x_i + (1-\alpha)x_j$, $\alpha \in [0,1]$).

The computational cost depends linearly on the number of variables, while other approaches depend exponentially on the number of variables, constraints and the domain size.

In order to improve the behaviour of OFHH and due to the low temporal cost, we can run an unsolved problem several times in order to reduce the probability that the OFHH fails. This technique is carried out varying the selected vertices that compose the hyperpolyhedron.

In future work, we will apply this technique to more complete heuristics in order to decrease the probability of unsolved problems. Currently, we are working on *mix-face hyperpolyhedron heuristics*. This heuristic works on a hyperpolyhedron that mixes some heuristics like OFHH, NFHH [9] and POLYSA [10] in order to obtain a more suitable heuristic depending on the problem topology.

References

1. Bacchus F., van Beek P.: On the conversion between non-binary and binary constraint satisfaction problems. In proceeding of AAAI-98, (1998) 311-318
2. Bessière C., Meseguer P., Freuder E.C., Larrosa J.: On Forward Checking for Non-binary Constraint Satisfaction. In Proc. Principles and Practice of Constraint Programming (CP-99), (1999) 88-102
3. Bessiere C.: Non-Binary Constraints. In Proc. Principles and Practice of Constraint Programming (CP-99), (1999) 24-27
4. Dechter, R., Meiri, I., Pearl, J.: Temporal Constraint Network, Artificial Intelligence 49, (1991) 61-95
5. Dechter R.: From Local to Global Consistency, Artificial Intelligence 55, (1992) 87-107
6. Montanari U.: Networks of constraints: fundamental properties and applications to picture processing. Information Sciences 7. (1974) 95-132
7. Rossi F., Petrie C., Dhar V.: On the equivalence of constraint satisfaction problems. In proceeding of European Conference of Artificial Intelligence, ECAI-90, (1990) 550-556
8. Salido M.A., Barber F.: An Incremental and Non-binary CSP Solver: The Hyperpolyhedron Search Algorithm. In Proceedings of Seventh International Conference on Principles and Practice of Constraint Programming (CP2001),(2001)
9. Salido, M.A., Giret, A., Barber, F.: Realizing a Global Hyperpolyhedron Constraint via LP Techniques. In Proceedings of Joint German/Austrian Conference on Artificial Intelligence (KI-2001). Workshop on New Results in Planning, Scheduling and Design (PUK2001), (2001)
10. Salido, M.A., Barber, F.: POLYSA: A Polynomial Algorithm for Non-binary Constraint Satisfaction Problems with <= and <>. Technical Report (DSIC-UPV), (2001)

AUTHOR INDEX